Napoleon's Integration of Europe

Napoleon's Integration of Europe

Stuart Woolf

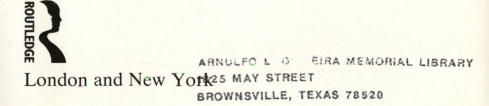

London and New York

First published 1991
by Routledge
11 New Fetter Lane, London EC4P 4EE

Simultaneously published in the USA and Canada
by Routledge
a division of Routledge, Chapman and Hall, Inc.
29 West 35th Street, New York, NY 10001

Typeset in 10/12 Times Linotronic 300
by Florencetype Ltd, Avon
Printed and bound in England
by T.J. Press, Padstow, Cornwall

British Library Cataloguing in Publication Data

Woolf, S. J. (Stuart Joseph)
  Napoleon's integration of Europe.
  1. Europe, 1715–1815
  I. Title
  940.253

Library of Congress Cataloging in Publication Data

Woolf, S. J. (Stuart Joseph)
  Napoleon's integration of Europe / Stuart Woolf.
    p.   cm.
  Includes bibliographical references and index.
    1. Europe—History—1789–1815.   2. Napoleon I, Emperor of the
French, 1769–1821—Influence.   3. Europe—Relations—France.
4. France—Relations—Europe.   I. Title.
D308.W66   1991
940.2′7—dc   90-24135

ISBN 0-415-04961-X

Contents

List of maps

Preface

Napoleon as man and military leader has always attracted writers and readers. Such has been the fascination of his meteoric career that historians have been hard put to defend their hegemony against the incursions of more creative novelists, artists and film-makers. The fascination is easy to understand, the closer one approaches this most private of public personages. There is an unknown Napoleon (perhaps many unknown Napoleons) of whom glimpses are caught unexpectedly in the vast literature. Who would expect the Emperor to be a discerning connoisseur of Paisiello's music (as Berlioz recalled)? Or that this eternal military hero's 'keen sense of smell ill tolerated the stench that accompanied a pillage', in the words of his aide-de-camp, Ségur? The personal sobriety of this corrupter of men is well established; but where did the reality blur into a consciously constructed myth? As Denon, his official fine arts adviser, instructed Gérard: 'Take care to emphasise the full splendour of the uniforms of the officers surrounding the Emperor, as this contrasts with the simplicity he displays and so immediately marks him out in their midst.' To quote the great poet Giovanni Pascoli, writing three quarters of a century later: 'my silent room is filled with the echo of Napoleon dictating'.[1]

But history does not just consist of great men, nor are the years of Napoleonic domination explicable in terms of his battlefields.

My concern has been to understand what I believe to be the central problem of the Napoleonic period: the attempt by the political class that had emerged from the Revolution to extend their ideals of progress and civilisation to every region of Europe touched by French armies. The military victories were the necessary premiss and condition of the French presence; but it is simplistic to regard the wars as either the causal factor or indeed an adequate explanation of the Napoleonic years. For contemporaries, the political changes and imposition of a new and uniform model of administrative modernisation constituted a continuous and uninterrupted experience of a dramatically radical nature. It is necessary to follow this experience as it evolved, from the years of the Directory to the collapse of the Empire, in terms of the interaction between the attempt of the French conquerors to create a new and integrated Europe in their own image and the responses of the conquered to this unprecedented experiment. Without French arms, the experiment could never even have been initiated. But in all other respects, to write of conquerors and conquered risks misunderstanding. The aim of the Napoleonic administrators was to convince the peoples who came under their control of the benefits of integration or imitative association by demonstration of the superiority and applicability of the French model of government; it was essentially peaceful and dependent on active collaboration rather than enforced submission. The fundamental problem was the resistance posed by the heterogeneity of the societies over whom the French established control, the multiplicity of cultural identities that have always characterised Europe.

To study this remarkable experience, which was to influence the course of European history through the nineteenth century, has meant reversing the conventional historiographical approach in which what happened outside the frontiers of present-day France is regarded almost as an appendage to the internal history of Napoleonic France or – seen from the other side – as (a usually undesirable) interruption in a teleologically oriented history of individual nation-states. I have attempted to bring together in an explicitly comparative manner the experiences of French rule across the entire Continent. This has meant, on the one hand, a constant attention to the relationship between internal developments in France during the Directory, Consulate and Empire and the evolution of the French administrative presence outside her frontiers; and, on the other hand, a concern to highlight the similarities and dissimilarities between different European societies, as they responded to the French presence. Hence, geographically, I have not limited myself to the regions progressively annexed by France, but have sought to bring into my discussion states which were directly controlled by France, whether they were satellites (like Westphalia or Naples) or formally more independent allies (like Bavaria).

Inevitably there are limitations to so vast and challenging an enterprise. The first is linguistic. My inability to read the historiography in Dutch, Flemish, Polish or Russian has necessarily impeded me from acquiring that depth of knowledge that provides the historian with confidence; I hope my discussions of the relevant regions are not too superficial. In one case – the Russian response to Napoleon's invasion – I have preferred, out of ignorance, not even to attempt any remarks.

The second limitation is that a work of synthesis and interpretation of this sort cannot be based on original research on all aspects. I began my research in the archives many years ago on Italy under French rule and then extended this, in the Archives Nationales of Paris, to prolonged study of the mechanisms and social implications of the administration of the Empire, and in particular of the significance attributed to statistics and of the problems of poverty. But necessarily I have been dependent on the research of generations of scholars across Europe in order to understand the overall dimensions of the task I had set myself. The hypotheses which lay at the origins of this book emerged out of a combination of my own research and the cumulative results of such historiography. My knowledge remains deeper of some parts of Europe than of others, although I hope this has not affected my overall interpretation.

I owe a debt of gratitude to more people than I can name here. I would like to thank Louis Audibert for offering me the challenge of writing this book. It could not have been written without the exhilarating experience of my years in the Department of History and Civilization of the European University Institute, where the juxtaposition of national intellectual approaches and academic traditions necessitates an unending reflection on the meaning of Europe and its cultural identities; I am deeply grateful to my colleagues and research students from whom I have learnt so much in formal seminars, innovative theses and informal discussions. I wish to thank Paola Querci, Anna Debenedetti and Bonnie Bonis for their eagle eyes in spotting obscurities of expression. Daniel Roche and Heinz-Gerhard Haupt have been patient and understanding friends, as well as professional colleagues, always ready to read and suggest improvements. Naturally the responsibility for the opinions and conclusions expressed in this book remains wholly mine.

May 1990

1   The Revolutionary-Napoleonic ideals of conquest

Not everything that the wisdom of the legislator decrees for the good of one of the various nations under his dominion can be applied equally to all the others, as the natural differences among peoples in terms of climate, character, genius and customs play too great a role.

(Kaunitz to the Empress Maria Theresa, 14 December 1769)[1]

A political State is a very difficult machine to direct, as general laws must often yield to circumstantial needs; if everything is to be subjected to a single regulation, it is impossible to maintain the form of policing and protection appropriate to the inhabitants of each part of an empire.

(Jacques Peuchet, *Statistique générale et particulière de la France et de ses colonies . . .*, Paris, an XII (1803–4), vol. 1, p. vi)

THE FRENCH AND EUROPE

What did French men and women know about Europe at the end of the ancien regime? The question offers a convenient starting-point for a discussion of the quarter of a century in which French arms and Napoleon's political ingenuity constructed and imposed on the greater part of the Continent their particular model of the modern nation-state.

A wealth of indications can provide us with at least an impressionistic response to so apparently simple a query. For the overwhelming majority of this profoundly rural society the 'foreigner' was any 'stranger' from distant parts. Frequently he was the product of the massive, ubiquitous machine of military conscription, which recruited some 2.5 million men (both French and others) between 1700 and

1789 and itself stimulated the flow of emigration. He was not necessarily unknown – for pedlars and migratory rural artisans regularly followed the same routes – but unattached to the standard networks of identification, kin and village, and frequently speaking a different native tongue. Few of the 1 million French men and women who took to the roads every spring and summer of the later eighteenth century ventured as far as Italy, Spain, Germany or the Low Countries; nor indeed were 'national' frontier posts so different in kind from the multiplicity of customs and toll barriers within France. For the other 20-odd million peasants, whose daily life was firmly rooted within the physical limits of walking distances, the elements of information about other peoples and states, on which they constructed their mental world, must have come essentially through the channels of such migrants, the lurid fireside fantasies of the soldiers, or the tales of pedlars' chapbooks.

A mere generation later, as a result of Napoleonic conscription, every French peasant family must have acquired knowledge of one or more of the countries of Europe directly or indirectly, through the military experiences of relatives or neighbours. One can hypothesise that, in the early years, this immediate contact with other peoples and places must have juxtaposed uneasily with the traditional knowledge and practices, based on maps, memoirs and hearsay, of the pre-Revolutionary professional soldiers. How such experiences filtered into and modified the popular representation of the outside world is an interesting but ultimately probably unanswerable question.

Not only the peasantry, but also (as Daniel Roche has shown) the great majority of the local elites who provided the public of the enlightenment had rarely travelled afar, and then usually only to Paris. Their knowledge of foreign parts was based on the written 'voyages' of travellers and that more or less intense correspondence so characteristic of the 'republic of letters', occasionally enriched by meetings at their local academy or masonic lodge with the wealthy, cultured foreigner on his grand tour or the officer returning from foreign parts. Undoubtedly the numbers of educated and curious travellers increased continuously and rapidly in the latter decades of the century, possibly even more than the printed voyages and descriptions. Within this corpus of publications, Europe – and finally France as well – occupied an increasing space. The geographer Langlet-Dufresnoy could assert in 1742, following the publication of the great Jesuit *Geographical, historical, chronological, political and physical description of the Empire of China and of Chinese Tartary* (1735), that China – a recurrent ideal of western political thought –

was known 'with as much detail and precision as France or the states of Europe'.[2] The attraction of these distant lands remained strong – as can be seen in the *chinoiseries* and Turkish motifs of the decorative arts – and was accompanied by the newer scientific and anthropological explorations and descriptions of the Australasian Pacific and extra-European worlds. But with the prolonged peace following the end of the Seven Years' War (1763), this traditional cult of the unusual and the exotic, an extension of the 'cabinet of marvels', ceded prime of place to nearer and more easily accessible regions. In Boucher de la Richarderie's vast listing of travel-books published as the *Bibliothèque universelle des voyages* in 1808, accounts of European countries constituted 35 per cent of the total of seventeenth-century publications, but 53 per cent of eighteenth-century ones.[3] Europe was 'discovered' by travellers and readers alike, assisted in their voyages by increasingly stereotyped descriptions and practical guides: no travellers of today, nurtured on their *Blue Guides*, would be surprised (except by the length of title) at L. Dutens' *Itinerary of the most popular routes, or Journal of a tour of the main cities of Europe, including . . . the time needed to go from one place to another, the distances in English miles . . . the most remarkable things to see . . . To which is added the exchange rate of moneys and a table of travel and linear distances.*[4]

Europe was visited in its remotest parts, from Iceland and Scandinavia to Russia and Turkey. Geography and history went hand in hand, for – as Voltaire preached and practised – it was essential to describe to the reader the unfamiliar. Voltaire was well placed to do so, with 137 volumes of voyages as well as geographical dictionaries in his library of nearly 4,000 works. But, in general, the remoteness of the country was in inverse proportion to the informative detail authors of voyages provided about it. The countries of the grand tour continued to attract most attention. For the French reader and traveller, cultural and historical traditions ensured the continuing primacy of Italy, while Britain attracted ever greater attention, based on that intimacy resulting from a secular rivalry that now related to political structures as well as to economic activities. By the 1780s the major novelty was the massive increase in publications, travel and contacts with the German states, where commercial opportunities, administrative models and reforming princes aroused growing interest.

The dimensions of this fashionable boom in travel and travelogues of the late eighteenth century can be gauged by comparing Voltaire's collection of voyages to the 700 books of geography and history in the

2,000-volume library of Adrien Duquesnoy, a little-known but influential administrator of the Consular years.[5] But if travel was fashionable, its purposes had changed: it was pedagogic and utilitarian, philosophic and scientific. Rousseau had exalted the benefits that would result for mankind from a voyage round the world by *philosophes*; Duquesnoy, more mundanely, argued that through knowledge of foreign examples, 'one can compare facts and theories, establish a body of principles and adopt a plan which will be practicable at home'.[6]

It was this particular interest for the classification of useful information that explains the rapid development of statistical topographies. Of German origin, a direct offshoot of the *Kameralwissenschaft*, these numerical descriptions of the physical environment, history, political structure, economic activities and social organisation of administratively delimited areas encapsulated at one and the same time the educated public's thirst for easily acquired knowledge, the trader's need for practical information and the scientifically oriented administrator's search for classified and hence comparable empirical data. The statistical topography, the favoured mode of diffusing information about the departments in Directorial-Consular France, can be regarded as the logical culmination of the vast growth of interest in travel, in the double sense that it selected and moulded the information to meet the requirements of 'social utility', and turned attention from foreign parts to the 'discovery' of the homeland itself. In so doing, it combined the acquisition of useful knowledge as the basis for policy with the illustration of the progress of the different regions of France since the Revolution.[7]

It is obvious that Frenchmen's knowledge of Europe was not limited to travel and travel books. The very propaganda of the *philosophes*, like the international expansion of economic activity in the later decades of the eighteenth century, thickened the intimate, complex, never interrupted web of personal contacts and interchange on which the European economy and culture had always depended. Observation of practices and methods employed in other societies and states stimulated a widely shared search for improvement, whether in the private or the public domain. It was precisely with this intent, for example, that Duquesnoy translated into French the major treatises on institutional means to deal with poverty published in Britain, the United Provinces, Philadelphia, Switzerland, Germany, Scandinavia and Italy.[8] What to do with the poor was an issue to which late-eighteenth-century elites were particularly sensitive. But it formed part of a far larger problem of effective government, or 'social utility', which was in the forefront of the attention of French, as of other European savants and administrators, following on the wide-ranging and contradictory criticisms and preaching of the *philosophes*. The interest among the leading French intellectuals, both before and after 1789, in Scottish political economists and the late *aufklärische* Göttingen school of public administration derived directly from the apparent success of the analytical methods, and (at least in part) the solutions they proposed. What was needed, wrote Volney, was 'a sufficiently large number of facts that can be compared with due reflection in order to extract from them other new truths or the confirmation of established ones, or even the disproof of accepted errors'.[9]

Direct observation and experience abroad was a precious asset (possibly because it remained so unusual), which came to be particularly valued by the Revolutionary political class and assisted administrative careers. Highly illustrative is the early career of C. E. Coquebert de Montbret, future head of the Napoleonic bureau of statistics and secretary-general of the ministry of manufactures and commerce: before the Revolution he had spent nine years at Hamburg as French commissioner of the merchant marine and consul, then to be employed by the Directory and Consulate as commercial and shipping representative at Dublin, Amsterdam and, after the peace of Amiens, at London.[10] As significant was the request made by the thermidorian ministry of foreign affairs to the geographer and *idéologue*, C.-F. Volney, to prepare a list of *Statistical questions for the use of travellers*, so that the ministry's diplomatic agents abroad could collect useful facts in a systematic manner.

It is evident that knowledge of Europe was acquired through many channels and functioned at different levels. In terms of private contacts, unquestionably the most diffuse and continuous level, networks of correspondents and relationships ignoring national frontiers had always existed, deriving from kin and patterns of sociability. The cosmopolitan veneer of aristocratic pretensions was based on the reality of a model of marriage in which status counted for far more than nation and encouraged matrimonial alliances that ignored national frontiers. Social modes (in which the French Court played the leading role) transcended the boundaries of the individual state and circulated across Europe in the persons of preceptors (such as Gilbert Romme), chefs, clothes designers or Casanova's actresses. At the less mundane level of the 'republic of letters', authors – of whom Voltaire and Rousseau were only the most publicised and best known – and learned societies, especially the medical profession, transmitted cultural knowledge and models of comportment. At yet another level, economic exchange explained the wide-ranging information about Europe possessed by French commercial families.

The group of Frenchmen probably best informed about, and most sensitive to changes in European affairs, alongside, or even more than, official representatives, were the manufacturers and traders. Despite the loss of much of her empire in 1763, France had participated actively in the expansion of the international economy in the latter half of the century. The rapid growth in colonial trade, in which France divided the lion's share with Britain, not only benefited the great ports of Bordeaux, Nantes and Marseille, but also had a multiplier effect on the general level of economic activity and urban demand. By the eve of the Revolution, re-exports to other European countries of colonial goods – sugar, coffee, tea, spices, rum, tobacco – amounted to about one-third of total French exports, while colonial demand in the Antilles and Spanish colonies – for silks and other luxury products, as well as slaves – absorbed perhaps a quarter of French industrial production. By the eve of the Revolution, British technological superiority in textile production and ironworks was impinging on traditional French export markets in the Levant and Mediterranean. But if the entrepôt trade was unquestionably the most rapidly growing sector of the French economy, some manufactures – especially silk and fashionable goods – and agricultural products such as wine benefited from the growth of both domestic and European markets. In a world of poor and seasonably impossible communications, the development of a national market in France was facilitated by an inland transport system admired by foreign travellers, even the British. The great centres were developing their trade contemporaneously within France and across Europe. Marseille was expanding its activities from its traditional Levant woollen exports to re-export of North American colonial goods; Bordeaux developed contacts with Hamburg, at the expense of Amsterdam; Paris and Lyon imposed their needs on the ports and sold their silks and fashion products throughout the interior. The Rhineland areas, Alsace, the Bishoprics and Lorraine, were drawn into the national network; exchanges with the Italian states and Spain developed primarily with Lyons and the Midi; above all, northern and eastern Europe – the German states, Poland and Russia – provided important markets via the Baltic and the fairs at Frankfurt and Leipzig, for French wines, silks and luxury goods.

Much attention has been paid, understandably, to the activities and merchants of the maritime ports. But the traders, merchants and merchant-manufacturers throughout the kingdom formed the infantry (or at best the non-commissioned officers) of this army of international trade. In an economy which remained overwhelmingly agricultural, the numbers and geographical range of activities of these manufacturers and traders should not be exaggerated. The market, for most producers and merchants, was an extremely local one, although indirectly through the exchange of goods, the links with the great ports and metropolises of Paris and Lyons, via river traffic and inland trading towns, were increasing rapidly. In the absence of a banking system, credit was in short supply at all levels, from the pedlars who stocked up at Lyons to the Alsatian calico print manufacturers reliant on the sleeping partnership of Basel bankers. Throughout France, along the frontiers and coasts, elaborate and sophisticated systems of smuggling involved entire villages and towns, from carters and bargees to respectable businessmen and Customs officers. Smuggling (except of domestic salt, a state monopoly) implied a considerable knowledge and network of supply routes and markets, at least across the neighbouring frontiers. Far more general were the regular and routine exchanges of manufacturers and merchants at their warehouses, or with clients on their order-books, either directly or on commission.

The eighteenth century witnessed a growing concern in the technical education of manufacturers and merchants, in France as elsewhere, with proposals of professional courses and publication of technical instructions and guides. The *Encyclopédie* had already popularised the technology of production, with articles by educated skilled artisans. Jacques Peuchet, former secretary of Morellet, saw the market for a *Universal dictionary of trading geography*, published in six volumes in the Years VII–VIII. But most manufacturers and merchants undoubtedly learnt their trade on the job. A small minority acquired their apprenticeship (and languages) abroad. The political vagaries of the Revolution increased their number, through the forced apprenticeship in foreign trading houses of many children of the wealthy bourgeoisie, such as the future prefect H. C. F. Barthélemy at Mainz, or the *idéologue* and civil servant J. M. de Gérando at Naples. The larger merchant houses, such as Briansiaux of Lille, were engaged in intense commercial correspondence with expeditioners and commissioners across all western Europe. Whether through direct experience or business correspondence, these manufacturers and merchants were acutely conscious of their reliance on the established trading routes around which they had so carefully cultivated their networks. Natural or man-made interruptions, such as through a poor olive crop in Apulia or threat of war in Poland, were registered immediately with the sensitivity of a thermometer. Whatever the geographical range – from the pre-Revolutionary small tobacco processor of Strasbourg trading across the Rhine to the Restoration Swiss merchant and liberal G. P. Vieusseux, who wrote accounts of the European-wide commerce in Scandinavian salted cod and Black Sea grain – knowledge of Europe was an essential pre-requisite for the businessman.

THE POLITICAL MODEL OF THE REVOLUTION

By 1789 the leading role of France in the forward march of civilisation was accepted by educated elites throughout Europe – even by the British. Although the reforms advocated by the *philosophes* seemed to have made far greater progress in other states, such as Tuscany, Austria, even the Russia of Catherine II, and although the economic success of Britain was undeniable, France – which usually meant Paris – remained the intellectual powerhouse of enlightenment ideas about how to improve the present and construct the future. Such a role was based on France's remarkably high and intense level of philosophic and scientific enquiry. But it was also a consciously constructed reputation, based on a self-confidence in the superiority and leadership of French civilisation, that dated back to the cultural affirmations of the Court of Louis XIV and appeared continuously confirmed by the generalised acceptance of French as the language of international discourse. The cosmopolitan diffusion of the French model of aristocratic sociability, which imbued the practices and comportment of the European nobilities, underpinned such self-confidence and para-doxically was reinforced by the abrupt and massive emigration of nobles with the Revolution.

Civilisation, a new word that entered the French language only in the mid-eighteenth century to describe the level of perfection of a society, was identified with the progress of reason. In the hands of so influential a writer as Voltaire, it was demonstrable through the evidence of history, from the millennial 'barbarism' and 'superstitions' that followed the fall of ancient Rome to the early manifestations of the new spirit of reason of the Renaissance, culminating in the current age of enlightenment. Each progressive age was characterised by the achievements of a particular people: in classical times the Greeks and Romans, in recent centuries the Italians, then the British and now the French.

This identification of the most advanced stage of civilisation with the French nation was consolidated by the Revolution, not only among the French themselves, but also initially among all who believed in progress. It was an identification based on optimism, faith in the possibility and reality of peaceful change, to which the first euphoric year of radical reforms seemed to bear witness. It is a truism – and misleading, at least in the short term – to explain the fundamental influence of the Revolution in the future development of western civilisation in terms of the universality of its political values. For some of its key ideas – such as 'fraternity' – rapidly degenerated, at best into slogans, at worst into mockery, whether on the French political scene or in the territories 'liberated' by French armies; while others – such as liberty, equality or popular sovereignty – were to undergo deep and anguished redefinitions through the often fratricidal political struggle up to and beyond Brumaire, from which they emerged almost unrecognisably transformed.

Nevertheless, there are few indications that the French political and military class ever doubted its mission as vector of the most advanced form of civilisation, to be carried to, or imposed upon, less fortunate peoples. Already in October 1789 Mirabeau argued that:

> The example of the French Revolution will only produce a greater respect for the law, a greater rigidity in discipline and social hierarchy in England. But there will be incalculable tremors in the Batavian provinces, where the revolutionary fever was cut short; in the Belgian provinces, where habits and opinions are restless and seditious; in the Helvetic cantons, unless the aristocrats double up in good sense and firmness . . . in the splendid provinces of Germany along the Rhine, unless their federal ties are rapidly strengthened.[11]

By August 1797, Bonaparte's Italian army broadsheet could proclaim, with that irritating self-congratulatory complacency that never abandoned the French military presence: 'Every step of the Great Nation is marked by blessings! Happy is the citizen who is part of it! Happy is he who can say about our great men: these are my friends, my brothers!'[12] In May 1799, as the Austro-Russian armies seemed on the point of victory, General Masséna announced publicly that: 'Only the efforts of France impede Europe from falling into the barbarism into which her enemies are hurling her'.[13] In later years, in ever more cynical tone, Napoleon would justify French actions, however self-serving, in terms of the benefits resulting from French arms. As he wrote to his stepson Eugene de Beauharnais on 23

August 1810 about the kingdom of Italy (but the same sentiment applied to every country where French armies had passed): 'It would be shortsighted not to recognise that Italy is independent only because of France; that this independence is the price of France's blood and victories, and that Italy must not misuse it'.[14]

Rhetoric, the stock-in-trade of political figures of all times, too easily rings false in later ages, because (like style of clothing) it is so integrally disciplined by the conventions of its period. But, when the rhetoric is put aside, the evidence remains that the French political model, in its successive Revolutionary and Napoleonic incarnations, was perceived by its representatives as not only superior to, but also to be emulated by, existing states and societies. There is no doubt that French elites of both the Revolutionary and the Napoleonic years felt themselves to be participants in an experience of unique historical significance. And precisely because France was Europe's mentor, it seemed appropriate to many that Paris, the new Rome, the capital and heart of civilisation, should be enriched with the most significant artefacts of the arts and sciences to be found elsewhere in Europe. 'The time has come when the kingdom [of fine arts] must pass over to France as confirmation and embellishment of that of liberty', asserted the Directors in May 1796, authorising the pillaging of Italian museums.[15] At the height of the Empire, Montalivet, minister of the interior, proposed transferring from Italian, Dutch, Belgian, German and other conquered repositories to the new national archives at Paris all documentation relating to the earlier political history of their states.[16]

A missionary zeal, as vectors of civilisation, resulted from this sense of historic novelty, of personal embodiment of the values of a new age. Robespierre, virtually alone, had warned at the outset that liberty was not bestowed at bayonet-point; but his message was ignored, long after liberty had ceased to be a popular word. His compatriots remained persuaded that the values of the Revolution were universal and hence exportable. Precisely because French elites were convinced that they had created a new political model, it is important to identify what they understood by such a model, as it changed in content. For it incorporated the underlying ideals which the French and their most dedicated followers strove to apply, amidst the ever harsher buffeting of economic and military demands, in the countries over which they assumed responsibility.

In the first instance, the Revolution offered a model of a new relationship between the state and society, or more precisely a rapidly changing succession of constitutional devices which endeavoured to regulate the degree of political participation of the new citizens. The intense debates and bitter political struggle over equality and liberty that characterised the early years of the Revolution were never directly experienced in the neighbouring countries: at most, they echoed in the discussions, debates and propaganda of the Italian and Dutch democratic patriots, or in the shadowy conspiratorial aspirations of a handful of 'neo-Jacobins' or 'anarchists' (to use the contemporary terms) associated in some form with the Babeuf conspiracy (1796). Of the thirteen constitutions promulgated in the 'sister republics', eleven were modelled on the thermidorian constitution of the Year III, with its elaborate, rigid and ultimately unworkable separation of powers and graduated system of election. Hence in the countries subject to the control of the Directorial armies, and even more in those invaded after Brumaire, the terms of the political debate had shifted decisively away from the sovereignty of the people, in the direction of a definition of representation restricted to the appropriately qualified (whatever the criteria employed to define them).

Secondly, a new concept of political nation had provided the early revolutionaries with their political strength and had become increasingly sharply defined with the patriotism engendered by the wars. It was a concept initially based on the Revolutionary unity of the patriots, aspiring towards the utopian vision of a unified fraternal society which, particularly in the sections and among the sansculotte volunteers of the armies of 1792–3, was expressed in the form of direct popular sovereignty. There was growing uneasy awareness of the fragility of this new construct, evidenced internally by popular reluctance or resistance to so many of the Revolutionary practices and beyond the frontiers by incomprehension among the conquered peoples of the appeal to fraternise. This did not destroy the belief itself in the identification of 'people' and 'nation', only in the optimism of Revolutionary spontaneity as an adequate method to achieve it. Alternative but complementary means were elaborated. On the one hand, it was seen as necessary to eliminate, albeit carefully and gradually, the historical, traditional and customary legacies of a superstitious past, whose survival in popular practices was regarded as a fundamental obstacle to the existence of an ultimately uniform nation. On the other hand, the suppression of elective procedures within the army already in 1794–5 and the return to traditional methods of advancement heralded a different form of combative patriotism, embodied in the superiority of the *Grande Nation* and expressed in the disciplined élan of the Grande Armée.

Thirdly, the new social and economic order was defined most clearly in negative form, by contrast to the highly elaborate juridical and institutional orders and ties identified with the society and economy of the ancien regime. At the simplest level, the abolition of 'intermediary bodies', the feudal regime and internal customs tolls exemplified the initial optimistic expectation that the new individualism and economic liberalism would generate social harmony and economic productivity. Once again, the painful experiences of the Revolutionary decade did not modify the basic faith in either individualism or the 'hidden hand' of the free market, but focused attention on those best equipped, by resources, education and capacity, to turn the opportunities to good use, and to provide the social homogeneity and solidity on which the social fabric was believed to depend.

Finally, the prerequisite for the achievement of all other aims was the provision of appropriate institutional, administrative, financial and juridical structures, based on the application of enlightened reason to the body politic. In a sense, it is hardly surprising – given the lengthy preparation of an enlightenment increasingly oriented towards the end of 'social utility' – that, to accomplish these ends, reliance should have been placed on the state, almost uninterruptedly even in the Revolutionary years. Particularly after the failure of the Directory to fulfil this role, the state acquired the right to intervene, protect and direct civil society in order to 'liberate' both individual and productive forces. What was novel in this relationship was the increasing centrality and legitimising of the executive bureaucracy, the extension of whose role was indirectly stimulated by the *idéologues*' utilitarian conviction that systematic classification of empirical facts provided the basis for the identification and demonstration of the social interest to potentially irrational individuals.

It was on this bureaucracy that the direct responsibility was to fall for the extension of the French political model to the rest of Europe. For reasons of climate, levels of civilisation, forms of social organisation and human egoism, in so vast a geographical area as the Empire and its satellite states, genuine (and ultimately desirable) uniformity could not be expected. But there was an increasingly explicit belief in the Napoleonic years that the new nation-states could and were to be remoulded from above, through the application of an administrative blueprint. The evidence of progress and benefits that would result from such institutional remodelling of state structures and social relations would attract the support of educated and hence rational elites and local notables. But the anonymous mass of the people were slow to reject the prejudices and practices of the past. Precisely because the greater number of individuals who constituted society were lethargic in their acceptance of the advantages of modernity, an administrative grid, elaborated according to rational and enlightened criteria, was expected to force the pace and orient society in the appropriate direction.

THE REVOLUTIONARY EXPERIENCES OF EXPANSION

The administrative project for modernity was to be developed only after Brumaire and to reach its fullest elaboration at the height of the Empire, in the very years when its fulfilment was rendered ever less plausible by the competing military and economic ambitions of Napoleon. But already before Brumaire, the experience of territorial expansion had revealed contradictions and conflict, particularly in the years of the Directory, when the diffusion of power permitted, indeed encouraged, the contemporaneous pursuit of incompatible policies.

As is well known, at the outset of the Revolution the members of the Constituent Assembly, wholly engaged in the regeneration of France and imbued with the pacific ideals of the enlightenment, had formally renounced any aggressive intent: 'The French nation renounces any intention of engaging in a war of conquest and will never employ its forces against the liberty of any people' (22 May 1790). Within two years, on 20 April 1792, the Legislative Assembly, almost unanimously, had declared war on the 'king of Bohemia and Hungary', and within ten months found itself at war with Prussia, Sardinia, Britain, the Low Countries and Spain. (See Appendix for a chronology.) How the revolutionaries reached this position has been recounted innumerable times and requires little recapitulation. The right of peoples to determine their nationality and allegiance, initially formulated by the populations of Avignon and Alsace (subject respectively to papal sovereignty and the feudal lordship of German princes) raised an issue of far wider import than the specific cases, as it challenged the validity of international law and encouraged the populations of other states to follow suit, particularly in francophone regions economically or socially close to France, such as Savoy, Nice, areas of romand Switzerland or Belgium. As fears of counter-revolution and international conspiracy grew, cause and consequence of the deepening divisions between Court and Assembly and among the revolutionaries, the appeals of foreign exiles, especially the Dutch and Liégeois, who acted as organised pressure groups, fell on increasingly responsive ears. War was urged and finally declared by Brissot and the Girondins, with almost casual nonchalance (to our contemporary ears), in rhetoric redolent with references to the ancient Greek city-states and the recent victory of the Americans, to the tempering effects of war on the character of peoples and the innate strength of free peoples against despots. How this came about can most easily be understood in the context of what was then unprecedented and has become too sadly familiar in the twentieth century – the search for a solution to domestic problems by an appeal to the ideology of patriotism.

The experience of war (as historically is usually the case) assumed forms and dimensions wholly unforeseen by its initiators. As all historians agree, it conditioned the internal development of the Revolution, from the overthrow of the monarchy and the Jacobin dictatorship to the anti-Jacobin reaction of Thermidor and Directory until the coup of Brumaire. In terms of France's relations with Europe, it requires discussion from three different perspectives – political, military and economic – as in each case they contained important elements of Napoleon's future policies.

There can be no doubt about the deliberately subversive ideological fervour of the revolutionaries in the earliest stages of the war, a response in kind to the counter-revolutionary declaration of Brunswick (25 July 1792) and immediate consequence of the victories of Valmy (20 September) and Jemappes (6 November). Between 19 November 1792 and 8 January 1793 the republican Convention declared its will to accord 'fraternity and aid to all peoples who want to recover their liberty' and instructed its generals, on occupation of enemy territory, to encourage the local populations to 'enfranchise themselves . . . to give themselves a free government, through the exercise of their legitimate sovereignty . . . to regenerate themselves by a universal change in accordance with the principles of equality and liberty'.[17] Words were followed by actions, with the Convention's confirmation of a vote by the peoples of Savoy and Nice to become part of the French republic (27 November 1792, 31 January 1793).

The Convention accepted the will of the people in this instance. But the conflict between a disinterested policy of liberation and one of national power emerged at once over the explicit request of the democrats in occupied Belgium that their independence be recognised by France, and the obvious hostility of the populations of other occupied areas to annexation. By the end of March 1793, inebriated by success, the Convention had decreed that the French and

Flemish-speaking Belgians, the French and German-speaking populations of substantial areas of the left bank of the Rhine, form part of the 'Great Nation'. In the following years (1793–9), at successive upturns of the wars, 'liberation', 'reunion' and 'sister republics' became the code words to describe the occupation, annexation or restructuring as satellite states of the entire left bank of the Rhine, the Low Countries, Switzerland, and all mainland Italy. Even the Muslims of Egypt were 'liberated' by Napoleon (1798–1801).

Certain aspects of the political expansionism initiated by the Girondins merit comment. In the first instance, throughout these years, the form and direction taken by the expansionist policy remained unclear, because they were internally contested. The basic conflict was between France's 'natural frontiers' – by which the Alsatian Director Reubell meant the Rhine – and expansion elsewhere. There seem to have been few hesitations about the annexation of Belgium, only about how to ensure that Austria (its legitimate sovereign) and Britain would accept this in a future peace treaty. The main bone of contention was the deployment of French victories in other areas – primarily the Dutch Low Countries, western Germany, Switzerland and northern Italy – and the character of the institutional arrangements to be established in these areas, in the light of a future settlement. 'Natural frontiers' conflicted fundamentally with the policy of 'sister republics', in that it implied a territorial expansion of France, even at the expense of like-minded revolutionaries from such areas. The 'sister republics' – for their supporters – served at one and the same time ideological, political and military purposes: to hold faith to the ideals of the Revolution by creating states in the image of republican France; to requite the expectations of the native patriots, the most loyal supporters of the French; and to strengthen French defences through a semi-circle of cushion states. But even the supporters of sister republics were careful not to allow them to become political or economic threats to France. If, after much hesitation, the Dutch patriots were allowed to create a state with a far more unified political structure than the previous federation of jealously independent provinces, Dutch merchants were crippled economically and financially by loss of territory, a heavy indemnity and a costly alliance with France. The Italian Jacobins' aspirations for a large unitarian republic were consistently rejected by the Directors, as by Bonaparte.

In theory, total victory could have reconciled the two policies. But even in 1795, when French successes induced Tuscany, Prussia, the new Batavian (Dutch) republic and Spain to sign peace treaties

(February–July), a general European settlement remained implausible, given the irreducible hostility of Britain and Austria.

In subsequent years, the pursuit of such a peace became ever more a mirage, essentially for two reasons. On the one hand, the Directory proved increasingly incapable of controlling its generals and army commissaires. Kléber rejected a policy of conquest, Hoche urged the creation of a 'Cisrhenian' republic, the commissaires Saliceti and Garrau encouraged the Italian patriots in their hopes of an independent republic, Championnet set up the Parthenopean republic against the explicit orders of the Directory. Above all, Bonaparte pursued his private policy, creating the Cisalpine republic, negotiating its recognition by Austria at Leoben and Campoformio (1797), and obtaining the expedition to Egypt. This lack of authority of the Directors derived not only from their need to make the war pay for itself, but also increasingly from their dependence on successful war to enable them to overcome their financial and political problems at home. But the consequence of the very multiplicity of initiatives, at different levels and locations, was to negate the capacity and credibility of the Directors to follow a coherent policy, and frustrated Reubell's efforts – even after he had gained a majority within the Directory – to obtain the Rhine frontier by concessions in Italy and elsewhere. On the other hand, by pursuing simultaneously different and contradictory policies, the wars of the Directors spread to an ever wider geographic area, hence confirming the mistrust of existing enemies and inciting new ones. The extension of military activities and political changes from the Low Countries and Rhineland to Switzerland and Italy, with the annexation of the Rhineland and Geneva and the creation of the Roman and Helvetic republics (1798), effectively nullified the Campoformio agreement. The further extension of strategy to the entire Mediterranean, with the annexation of the Ionian islands and Malta and the invasion of Egypt and Syria, added Russia and Turkey to France's enemies.

At the same time, the very policies of occupation and creation of new states destroyed the sympathy enjoyed earlier by the French revolutionaries, even among the patriots. Wherever French armies passed, pillaging, billeting, requisitions and war contributions followed. After the victory of Fleurus (26 June 1794), official policy was to consider all occupied countries initially as enemy territory, in which the army was expected to live off the land. Local proposals for a change in status – 'reunion' with France or the creation of a republic – dressed up with the fiction of popular support, owed not a little to hopes that the army presence would be removed or at least regulated.

The inadequacy of logistic arrangements for mass armies before the state of emergency declared by the Jacobins, and the subsequent inflation and chronic financial collapse of the thermidorian and early Directorial government, offered justification and opportunity for private initiatives. Generals, like Masséna and Macdonald, and army suppliers, like Flachat and Haller, engaged in looting and exactions, which were protected by the corruption of politicians and Directors, such as Barras and Talleyrand. The 'sister republics', like the other occupied territories, were forced to pay extraordinary taxes as well as maintain their 'protector' armies. Whatever the overall amount of such exactions (estimated by Godechot as at least 360 million francs between 1792 and 1799), they constituted an essential part of the Directory's revenues, perhaps a quarter by the Years VI and VII.

The undisciplined behaviour of French troops and heavy exploitation of the occupied territories aroused popular peasant resistance in Belgium, Switzerland, Spain and – most spectacularly – in Italy during the retreat of 1799. Unquestionably, the novelty and scale of the military problem of creating a national army was partly responsible. The restructured army, following the breakdown of authority, mass desertions and the withdrawal from service of 60 per cent of the officer corps (1791–3), was dependent initially on a major influx of volunteers, which must have presented problems of discipline, in times of victory as much as of defeat. At the peak of Year II, when the 'nation in arms' had developed a formidable instrument of war, there were 750,000 soldiers (compared to an army of about 165,000 in 1789), creating logistic problems on an unprecedented scale.

The continuing war on multiple fronts required many sizeable armies, which the Directory proved incapable of paying and equipping. The consequences were dramatic and of importance in two particular respects, which were to mark Napoleonic policies in subsequent years. On the one hand, desertion began again on a massive scale: by the beginning of Year VII, the armies had dropped to 325,000. The introduction of conscription in 1798 marked the Directory's recognition that Revolutionary patriotism was no longer able to arouse a voluntary response. On the other hand, the very ambiguities of the policies of expansion confused and ultimately submerged the patriotism of the early Revolutionary years: the quality of altruistic idealism was lost, the rhetoric of France's mission remained. Despite the official powers of the civil representatives, the army commissaires, the Directory's delegation to the generals was in reality unlimited, since the latter had to provide for the needs of their armies. Effectively this forged a bond between each army unit and its general, in which military success and the daily problems of pay and food explained the degree of identification between soldier and commanding officer. This fundamental shift in mentality is demonstrated by the sharp contrast between the fiasco of General Dumouriez's attempted coup of March 1793, when his troops turned against him, and the constant suspicion and occasional employment of generals by the Directors to bolster their own authority. The much-quoted promise of Bonaparte to his ragged penniless troops in April 1796 that they would find 'happiness, glory and riches' in the mythically wealthy Italian plain was perhaps less important in gaining the loyalty of the Army of Italy than the triumph of actual victory and the part-payment of their wages in hard cash.

If military comportment and the internal logic of maintaining large armies explained popular resentment, the economic policies of the successive revolutionary governments in the occupied territories disillusioned and alienated the urban elites. To write of economic policies in this decade of revolution is probably excessive, as it consisted of economic hopes and ambitions, constantly overtaken and confused with immediate contingencies. The realities of economic policy in the short term, in relation to the occupied territories, fell into two, overlapping phases, the first characterised by the 'extraction agencies', set up in the Belgian and German lands in 1794, the second by the return to private initiative in the supply of the armies. The ransacking of the occupied territories by the extraction agency and related requisitioning agencies in Belgium was so uncontrolled and inefficient that it was a major cause of the annexation and reorganisation of the country in departments, on the French model (1795). The power and abuses of the speculators and bankers who formed companies to supply the armies was legendary, as they tried to protect themselves against paper money and a defaulting state by requisitions and contributions in the occupied lands: the neutral Tuscan port of Leghorn was occupied by Bonaparte in 1796 under pressure from the Flachat-Laporte company, who demanded compensation for its credits in the form of the English merchandise stocked in this entrepôt.

But if day-to-day problems dominated and effectively created the economic policy of the Directory, projects and plans about the future of the Great Nation were not lacking and are of interest because of their similarity to aspects of later policies introduced under Napoleon. The main author of these proposals was Charles Delacroix, one of the foreign ministers of the Directory, but he expressed ideas that were circulating in the thermidorian Year III among such leaders as

Sieyès, Merlin de Douai and Pelet de la Lozère. The continuity with pre-Revolutionary preoccupations is as marked as the total abandonment of the initial Revolutionary respect for the rights and interests of other peoples. By 1789 there was considerable worry among textile producers – documented in the *cahiers de doléances*—about the moderate liberalisation of trade with Britain resulting from the Eden treaty (1786), and a more generalised concern for technological modernisation. The outbreak of war rapidly led to confirmation of British naval superiority, not least through the haemorrhage of officers from the French navy. Colonial trade, the most dynamic sector of the French economy, was wholly disrupted, despite attempts to substitute supply routes through Spanish and Dutch ports.

Economic nationalism was the French response. The extraction agencies in Belgium and the Rhineland in 1794, the commissaires and generals who crossed the Rhine in 1796, were instructed to send back to Paris potentially useful mechanised machinery, and even to destroy machinery in direct rivalry to national textile production. With the conquest of Belgium, the river Scheldt (closed in the sixteenth century by the Dutch during their war of independence) was reopened to international traffic, possibly to please the Belgian patriots, certainly in order to embarrass the British and Dutch, while developing French trade routes to northern and eastern Europe. Plans were drawn up to negotiate trade treaties with other continental states which would favour French exports and prohibit imports of British goods. The Cisalpine republic was forced to grant France exclusive navigation rights and customs reductions for trade between the two states. Although Delacroix's project for negotiating favoured market outlets for French products in the neighbouring states was never realised, it continued to circulate in government milieux after Brumaire.

Before Bonaparte's coup of 18 Brumaire Year VIII (9 November 1799), revolutionary France's relationships with Europe had already been set. Political frontiers had been drastically modified to France's benefit and, primarily, Austria's loss. If France proved unable to achieve peace because of her continuously expanding ambitions, her enemies were equally incapable of defeating her decisively. Masséna's victory over the Russians at Zürich (25–7 September 1799) was the latest example of France's apparently unlimited military resources and superior fighting skills. With the extension of her frontiers to include Belgium, the Rhineland, Savoy, Geneva and Nice and the creation of dependent republics, the Great Nation could claim to have counterbalanced, if not compensated, the loss of colonies and freedom of the seas. For the policy of passing on the costs of such uninterrupted warfare to defeated or dependent states had paid healthy cash dividends. And if the crises of the Atlantic ports and their great trading families were to appear irreversible (American ships at Bordeaux fell from fifty-one in 1797 to zero in 1799), the prospects of expanding land markets for French producers looked promising.

In his relations with Europe, as in his reordering of France, Napoleon was to develop many of the policies already initiated under the Directory. Many, but not all. In two particular respects, Brumaire marked a rupture with the past. First, the generals were brought under control, as a unity of direction was imposed on France's external policies that had been lacking since the Jacobin Year II. In the second place, since the credibility of the liberation of peoples and popular sovereignty had been irrevocably compromised, new methods and policies of ensuring collaboration had to be elaborated to provide political and social stability for the new order Napoleon's France was imposing on Europe. The price paid for this was the definitive discrediting of pro-French local patriots and unequivocal popular hostility to the arbitrary, unregulated exactions and behaviour of French occupying forces.

NAPOLEON AND EUROPE

The conquest of Europe has always constituted the centre-piece of the historiography of the Napoleonic years. Nor could it be otherwise, given the prolonged sequence of military victories, the profound and often irreversible changes imposed on the political geography of the Continent, and the imagery of the triumphant hero so crucial to the fabrication of the Napoleonic myth. But within a historiography that has overwhelmingly privileged military-political events, interpretations of the motivations underlying Napoleon's actions and policies have differed radically, conditioned (like all historical interpretations) by the political beliefs and moral values of the periods and societies in which successive generations of Napoleonic experts have written.

Today few historians would claim that, from the outset, Bonaparte had a single plan in mind, whether for the rule of France or the settlement of Europe. Unequivocally influenced by the reforming ideals of the enlightenment, he remained hostile to the dogmatic systems of its more theoretical exponents, whose abstract coherence

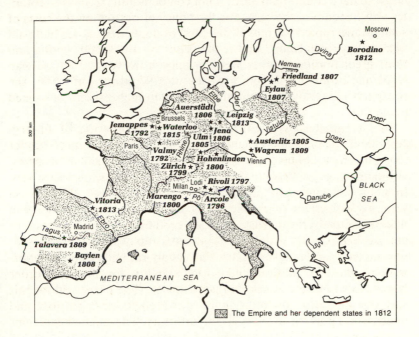

Map 1 Major Napoleonic battles 1792–1815

he regarded as inapplicable to the practical demands of government. 'You *idéologues*', he remarked in 1806 to Karl von Dalberg, prince primate of the newly created Confederation of the Rhine, 'act according to systems worked out in advance. As for myself, I'm a practical man, I seize events and push them as far as they will go'.[18] Such aphorisms, glittering like false gold in Napoleon's vast correspondence and the subsequent memoirs of contemporaries, have inevitably caught the eye of historians, often anxious to bolster a thesis; they need to be employed with critical caution, precisely because they were delivered by such a past master of audience and occasion as Napoleon. Nevertheless, the repetition over the years of certain themes, with innumerable minor variations according to the circumstances, offers a valuable indicator of some underlying tenets, prejudices and beliefs of this complex, secretive man who chose to spend so much of his life exposed to public view. 'Idéologue', for instance, was a favourite term of disparagement, extended from the original group of intellectual supporters of Brumaire whom he purged from public office in 1802, to all collaborators of philosophical bent suspected of insisting on their ideals. Napoleon remained firmly grounded in a practical, realistic, utilitarian approach to politics, eager and rapid to exploit every opportunity, in diplomatic matters as much as on the battlefield. There can be little doubt that he was describing a genuine conviction when he remarked, with unusual self-irony, that 'high policy is nothing more than good sense applied to great matters'.[19]

Such pragmatism permeated Napoleon's attitude to Europe, a continuous adaptation to changing circumstances, in which real or apparent successes laid the ground for a successive, ever more ambitious stage. Whatever contemporary English suspicions about the unlimited aims of the Corsican upstart, Bonaparte's policies and wars are best understood not as the unveiling over the years of a blueprint already in existence, nor as the obsessive pursuit of a single aim (such as the total defeat of Britain), but rather as successive phases rendered possible or (in Napoleon's eyes) necessary by the presence and behaviour of hostile forces. Nor can any one phase be described as the pursuit of a single dominant objective, for within each one different and often conflicting policies were inextricably enmeshed, while every successive phase inevitably included the increasingly contradictory load of the innovations and consequences of the previous stages. At most it is possible to note – as did contemporaries – that the continuation of the wars became ever more inevitable in direct relationship to Napoleon's expanding ambitions and self-confidence.

A convenient (albeit simplified) approach to Napoleon's policies in Europe is to separate his political from his economic aims. The former, elaborated in two phases, separated by the peace of Amiens, were concerned with the establishment of a political and then a dynastic hegemony, until 1806–7. The latter then played an increasingly dominant role, with the Continental blockade – at least in part a response to the British Orders in Council – becoming the centre-piece of the economic struggle with Britain.

The first phase, until 1802, marked no change from the Directory's policies. Nor was this surprising, given the prime role played by Bonaparte in forcing and extending the ambitions of the Directors, from the occupation of northern Italy and the treaty of Campoformio (October 1797) to the Egyptian expedition (July 1798). The latter episode, launched with as much insouciance as the initial Girondin war of liberation, combined a traditional anti-British policy – with its immediate threat to trade routes and its vague intimations of an invasion of India – with Bonaparte's romantic vision of an Oriental civilisation that merited modernisation. Such hopes had foundered with Nelson's destruction of the French fleet at the battle of the Nile (Aboukir: 2 August 1798). The basic contradiction of the irreconcilability of French imperialist ambitions with the achievement of peace not only remained, but also had worsened by Brumaire, with the advance of the forces of the second coalition across Italy and Switzerland. Initially, even the independence of initiative of the generals remained, as Bonaparte was unable to make Moreau accept his strategy of a rapid dual-pronged attack across the Rhine and Alps.

Military victories at Marengo and Hohenlinden (14 June, 2 December 1800) brought a general peace nearer – as in 1795 – with Habsburg Austria's enforced acceptance of French annexation of the left bank of the Rhine and Napoleon's settlement of Italy by the treaty of Lunéville (9 February 1801). Exploitation of a favourable international conjuncture by a now vigorous and unified French diplomacy momentarily promised a Continental coalition against Britain, with the Russian-led league of neutral states. Finally economic and political difficulties in Britain turned the mirage of peace into reality, with the treaty of Amiens, signed by a mutually suspicious Britain and France (25 March 1802).

It would be difficult to underestimate the importance of Amiens, as for the first and only time between 1792 and 1814 it ended the state of war between France and one or (usually) more European powers. General Bonaparte had displayed his capacities to make peace, the prerequisite for stability; grateful citizens voted overwhelmingly to transform the first consul's constitutional position into that of consul for life (2 August 1802). If British control of the seas was confirmed, with recognition of her conquest of Dutch Ceylon and Spanish Trinidad, France had achieved not only her natural frontiers (Belgium, the Rhineland left bank, Geneva, Savoy), but also a hegemony that extended far beyond them: the military occupation of Piedmont and the Batavian republic, the recognition of the Batavian, Helvetic, Ligurian and Cisalpine republics and territorial enlargement of the Cisalpine, the expulsion of the Habsburgs of Tuscany and Modena in favour of the Spanish Bourbons, for whom a new kingdom of Etruria was established (treaty of Aranjuez between France and Spain, 21 March 1801), tacit acceptance of France's right to interfere in German and Spanish affairs. Papal recognition, in the form of a Concordat (18 April 1801), consecrated France's new role in Europe.

But if Lunéville and Amiens testified to Napoleon's capacity to enforce a pacification on the European states, the very expansion of direct French control beyond her natural frontiers threatened the durability of the peace. Napoleon's actions increased the diffidence of his rivals and ultimately provoked the renewal of war. British commercial and manufacturing interests felt frustrated and threatened by the refusal to open the French market and by the colonial interest again displayed by Paris, with the cession of Louisiana to France by Spain (1 October 1800), Bonaparte's despatch of an expedition to reconquer San Domingo and Guadaloupe (February 1802), and renewed diplomatic activities in the direction of India. In Italy, Napoleon had assumed the presidency of the Cisalpine republic and provocatively changed its name into the 'Italian republic' (24–6 December 1801); Piedmont was annexed by France (11 September 1802), as well as Elba and Piombino, while Parma was occupied (October 1802). In Switzerland Napoleon imposed a constitutional settlement by military threat, which created a new republic of the Valais, controlling the Simplon pass, rectified the Geneva frontier in France's favour, and forced the federal cantons into an alliance with France (29 May 1802; act of mediation, 19 February 1803). In Germany, Napoleon incited Tsar Alexander's ambitions to play a leading role in Europe and exploited the territorial greed of German princes to weaken the Austrian emperor's authority as overlord. The infinitely complicated tangle of demands for compensation resulting from France's annexation of the Rhineland left bank was transformed, through able diplomacy, into a political opportunity to create, at the expense of the Catholic Church and the imperial free cities and knights, a limited number of southern German states and a Protestant majority of imperial electors, jealous of their independence and hence attracted, through hostility to Austria, into the French orbit (Rezes of Regensburg, 25 February 1803).

The renewal of war with Britain (May 1803) and Austria and Russia (August 1805) marked a new phase, in which the implications of the control of sea and land respectively by the opposing forces of Britain and France became reality. Whatever the reciprocal provocations, the underlying reason for the revival of hostilities between Britain and France, after so brief a pause, was the clash of conflicting imperialisms. Bonaparte sold Louisiana to the United States, partly to finance the invasion of Britain (3 May 1803). British naval superiority prevented Napoleon's army from crossing the Channel and definitively ended the threat with Nelson's destruction of the French and Spanish fleets at Trafalgar (21 October 1805). Control of the seas meant not only the development of British trade, particularly in Spanish America, but also harassment of neutral ships to the

Continent, and the ability to supply forces hostile to the French, as in Sicily or Portugal. But Britain remained impotent to challenge Napoleon's control of the land-mass of Europe, her major market.

The extension of the maritime economic struggle with Britain into the war on land against the third coalition was the direct consequence of Napoleon's continued affirmation of his power. Prussia was worried by the French occupation of George III's duchy of Hanover, bordering on its frontiers. With the kidnapping and execution of the duke of Enghien (March 1804), the unstable Tsar Alexander turned against Napoleon, whom he saw as a dangerous rival in Germany and the Ottoman empire. But above all Austria, in serious economic difficulties, was provoked into war by Napoleon's deliberate challenge to Habsburg imperial authority. By taking the title of emperor rather than that of king (18 May 1804), Napoleon asserted his European pretensions, with deliberate evocation of Charlemagne, whose authority had extended over Germany and Italy. If Francis II's immediate riposte was to proclaim himself hereditary emperor of Austria (11 August 1804), within a year he felt goaded into war by Napoleon's assumption of the title of king of Italy (19 March 1805), his annexation of the Ligurian republic, his direct administration of Parma, and his creation of petty principates at Piombino and Lucca for Elisa Bonaparte and her husband Felix Baciocchi (March–July 1805). Italy had been Napoleon's chosen ground to expand his territories and humiliate the Austrian emperor. With the outbreak of war against Austria and Russia, Napoleon's intention to extend and shift his influence and activities to Germany was confirmed by the alliance with the southern German states of Bavaria and Württemberg.

The spectacular victories over the Austrian–Russian armies at Ulm (15 October 1805) and Austerlitz (2 December 1805) and then – after Frederick William III's wholly unexpected declaration of war – over the Prussian armies at Jena and Auerstädt (14 October 1806) transformed Napoleon's vision of his role in Europe. The Carolingian empire of the west, oriented primarily towards Italy – to which Napoleon made deliberate rhetorical allusions – began to assume even more ambitious dimensions, with echoes of Charles V's realm extending across Europe. At the same time, Napoleon's very mastery of Europe convinced him of the possibility of compensating loss of control of the seas by imposing a land blockade against Britain. Both developments implied indefinite French presence across the Continent, until such time as the states and societies of Europe would recognise their debt to France by accepting its political and economic hegemony, and Britain would be forced to capitulate.

Austria's defeat meant her expulsion from Italy (treaty of Presburg, 26 December 1805): Venetia (given by Napoleon to Austria only eight years earlier at Campoformio), was annexed by the kingdom of Italy, Tyrol and the Trentino (hereditary Austrian lands) by Bavaria. The Bourbon dynasty of Naples, protégé of the Tsar, 'has ceased to reign', declared Napoleon (27 December 1805), who assigned the kingdom to his brother Joseph (30 March 1806). Of the former rulers of Italy, only the Pope survived and his protests were ignored with the occupation of the Papal ports of Ancona and Civitavecchia.

The policy in Germany represented a greater innovation, in the sense that Italy was firmly within the French sphere of influence, and for almost a decade Napoleon had manipulated the peninsula's political geography. In Germany, France traditionally had looked to Prussia as a counterweight to Habsburg Austria and Russia. The idea of encouraging a third, francophile force in Germany among the central and southern states had originated with Sieyès and Talleyrand under the Directory and had assumed material form with the Rezès of 1803. Until Austerlitz Napoleon was hesitant, frequently changing his ideas about Germany's future. Now he enlarged the territories of his allies, Bavaria, Württemberg and Baden. But the real novelty was his insistence, against the reluctance of the German princes, on the creation of the Confederation of the Rhine, of which sixteen princes formed part (12 July 1806), in place of the Holy Roman Empire (declared defunct by Napoleon on 1 August 1806). A central-southern bloc had been set up, with a population of over 7 million and Napoleon as its Protector; the initial intention of creating a new constitutional structure faded away, but the military commitment to provide France with 69,000 soldiers remained. The new sovereign rulers, various of whom proclaimed themselves king, constituted an effective counterbalance to Austria. Until Jena Prussia was left as the dominant state in the rest of Germany.

Prussia's defeat inevitably expanded Napoleon's ambitions. Russia's support for Prussia determined him not only to truncate the Hohenzollerns of their western territories, but also to use the kingdom indefinitely as a military base in order to pursue the war eastwards. Although the battle of Eylau (8 February 1807) was indecisive, the French victory at Friedland (14 June 1807) convinced Alexander to come to terms with Napoleon. The treaty of Tilsit (7 July 1807) marked the end of this renewed phase of war, with Napoleon at the peak of his power. In agreement with his new ally Alexander of Russia, Prussia was dismembered: its lands west of the

Elbe were assigned primarily to create a new kingdom of Westphalia, under Jerome Bonaparte, while its Polish provinces were turned into an independent grand-duchy of Warsaw, under the king of Saxony. Westphalia, Saxony and hence Warsaw entered the Confederation of the Rhine and were to function as military frontier posts against any future threat from Prussia or Russia; French armies remained garrisoned at Warsaw and in what remained of Prussia, which was subjected to payment of a massive indemnity. In exchange for promises of expansion into Swedish Finland and the Turkish empire, Alexander also ceded the Adriatic port of Cattaro and the Ionian islands to Napoleon. As important was the decision to exclude British trade, with the agreement of the two allies to force the neutral states of Denmark, Sweden and Portugal into this Continental federation.

All the elements of the Napoleonic imperial system were already in place before Prussia's unfortunate sortie of October 1806, and they were consolidated by Tilsit. Europe was to be reconstructed around a system 'of federated states, or a true French empire', in Napoleon's words. Within this federation, states could be made and unmade, sovereigns appointed or transferred, frontier lines shifted to extend French territory or to make adjustments between vassal states – all by the Emperor's decision, sometimes without even advising the rulers concerned. The Emperor's family was the prime beneficiary: his brother Joseph was appointed king of Naples (30 March 1806), his brother-in-law Joachim Murat grand-duke of Berg (15 March 1806), his brothers Louis king of Holland (3 May 1806) and Jerome king of Westphalia (18 August 1807). But allied rulers, such as Max Joseph of Bavaria or Dalberg, former elector of Mainz, were richly rewarded, as were meritorious generals, like Berthier, for whom the Swiss principality of Neuchâtel was created (30 March 1806). Arguably, Napoleon's desire to legitimise his dynasty by marriage ties with old ruling houses played a role in his intense involvement in Germany (in contrast to Italy, where he had chased out the only surviving dynasties of Savoy and Bourbon to the islands of Sardinia and Sicily): his wife Josephine de Beauharnais' family was married into the Bavarian and Baden ruling families, Jerome to that of Württemberg, and even the faithful Berthier to a Bavarian princess. Napoleon himself was to set aside Josephine in order to marry Marie Louise, daughter of the Habsburg emperor, in 1810. Although formally the allied states remained independent, their rulers were forced to collaborate in the Emperor's wars and to submit to his economic policies. This imperial system was a political, military, dynastic and economic federation of very unequal states.

The Continental blockade was a logical complement to the imperial system, which became possible precisely as a consequence of the new dimensions of Napoleon's military successes. The French attempt to exclude British manufactures dated back to the outbreak of the Revolutionary wars and had marked a high point of Directorial economic ambitions. British mastery of the seas implied not only a defence against invasion, but also a naval blockade of Continental ports and the ability to disrupt the crucial two-way trade with the colonies and Americas. Napoleon's progressive extension of land control paradoxically accentuated this sharp division of influence between the two rivals, as Britain attacked or seized the warships of allied or neutral states (Spain, Holland, Denmark, Naples, Portugal) and destroyed France's merchant marine. Through the campaigns of 1805–7 Napoleon achieved land-mastery over all northern and western Europe, except Sweden and Portugal, which provided him with the necessary conditions to reverse the relative relationship of power between the two countries by declaring Britain to be 'in a state of blockade' (Berlin decree, 21 November 1806). The assumption underlying the blockade, argued with increasing success by Montgaillard, was that, by closing all Continental markets to British exports, British tax revenues would fall drastically, its government would be unable to finance hostile coalitions or service its national debt and so ultimately would be forced to sue for peace.

In a spiral of reciprocity the measures were exacerbated on both sides: in response to the British Orders in Council (1807), the decrees of Fontainebleau and Milan (13 October, 23 November, 17 December 1807) extended the prohibition of imports to neutral carriers and to entire categories of colonial and manufactured goods regarded by definition as British, irrespective of their real place of origin. With the manifest failure of the blockade to bring Britain to her knees and the ubiquitous evidence of massive smuggling of British goods to the Continent, the system was tightened further by the introduction of prohibitive import dues at France's borders (decrees of Trianon and Saint-Cloud, 5 July, 12 September 1810).

Three aspects of the blockade need to be noted, because of their profound implications for the territories under French control. First, the blockade was not only a negative weapon of France's economic warfare against Britain, but also the basis of a positive project to open up Continental outlets for French products, as substitute – or indeed definitively alternative – markets for the lost colonies. Hence an underlying tension persisted in relations with allied or vassal states with competitive manufactures or other products. Secondly, the very mechanics of the blockade required the imposition of a customs line along not only the coasts, but also the inland frontiers. The manifest incapacity of the Customs service (despite the steady increase in personnel) to police such prolonged lines meant the deployment of regular troops, frequent disregard for legal procedures, and arbitrary modification of territorial frontiers. Inevitably this application of a tariff policy geared to French interests in the most narrow sense conflicted with the efforts to win over local populations to the model of French rule. Finally, if the blockade developed as a natural complement to the enlargement of the imperial system, in turn it became a propulsive element for the pursuit of ever more extensive control by military means.

It was the application of the blockade, in fact, that underlay the progressive transformation of the imperial system into the mirage of a universal empire. This is not to say that Napoleon's military expansionism was simply a response to the impossibility of sealing off the Continent to British products. Political elements were undoubtedly important in the decision to take over Spain; fear that Alexander was about to change sides explains the invasion of Russia. Nevertheless, success of the blockade, both to defeat Britain and to ensure France's economic markets, was ever more inextricably linked to political calculations, not least because such success was dependent on Russia's collaboration in controlling eastern Europe.

The invasion of Portugal (October 1807) was the counterpart to Alexander's invasion of Swedish Finland and Ottoman Turkey, agreed at Tilsit. The annexation of Tuscany and Parma to France (December 1807, May 1808), and of the Papal Marches to the kingdom of Italy (April 1808) met the requirements of both Empire and blockade, through direct administration. But precisely because military control of the Continent was believed to be the means to arrive at an effective stranglehold of Britain, the very dimensions of the land-mass to be controlled made the objective unobtainable. Thus the insurrections in Spain, following Napoleon's brusque replacement of the Bourbons by his brother Joseph (May–July 1808), initially seemed no more problematic than earlier popular resistance – as in Calabria – even after Dupont's defeat at Baylen (22 July 1808). The armies that Napoleon sent into Spain were relatively limited in size and contained a high proportion of foreign troops (Germans, Italians, Swiss and Poles), because the Grande Armée was required to keep control of eastern Europe. The terms imposed on Prussia (French occupation of key fortresses and limitation of its army to 42,000) and the apparent confirmation at Erfurt of the alliance with

Alexander (September 1808) appeared to ensure the control of eastern Europe. Nevertheless the displacement of the Grande Armée to Spain (November 1808) was the immediate cause of Austria's decision to renew war against France (1809).

The remarkable mobilisation of an army of 300,000 in Germany and, after the bloody check at Essling (21 May 1809), the victory of Wagram (6 July 1809) seemed to re-establish Napoleon's dominance. Control of Italy was completed with the deportation of the Pope and the annexation of the Papal States (May–July 1809). With the treaty of Schönbrunn (14 October 1809), Austria was forced to cede territory to Bavaria, Warsaw and Russia and was cut off from the sea with France's annexation of Trieste, Croatia, Carinthia, Istria and Dalmatia. These territories were reorganised as the Illyrian provinces (December 1809) in order to ensure cotton imports by protection of the caravans from Constantinople and to close the Adriatic coasts to Britain. It is possible that by 1810 Napoleon began to doubt his earlier dynastic policy, given the reluctance of his brothers to enforce the blockade.[20] His sudden marriage to the Austrian emperor's daughter, Marie Louise (2 April 1810) abruptly reversed his anti-Habsburg policy in Germany, but appeared to consolidate French control of central Europe. Empire and blockade again reinforced each other, with the annexation of Louis Bonaparte's kingdom of Holland (9 July 1810), and of territories belonging to both Jerome's kingdom of Westphalia and the grand-duchy of Berg, followed by that of the hinterland of the north German coast, including the Hanseatic ports (22 January 1811), and the Valais and Ticino canton (July 1810, January 1811). The greater part of Spain was removed from Joseph's control and placed under military governors (8 February 1810). By 1812 the Grand Empire had reached its maximum extension, over 750,000 square kilometres, divided into 130 departments, with 44 million inhabitants, besides the four Catalan departments, six Illyrian intendancies and twenty-four departments of the kingdom of Italy.

But the survival and consolidation of the imperial system depended ever more urgently on military victory. Wellington's ability to hold out and increasingly to circumscribe French control of Spain had the effect of a running sore, pinning down substantial French forces. Alexander of Russia's frustration with Napoleon grew, as he felt that the French were failing to give him appropriate support in Finland, the Ottoman empire and Persia. The denunciation of the alliance (31 December 1810) tore a rent in the Baltic end of the blockade. Once more only a decisive victory could permit Napoleon to reaffirm his hegemony. The invasion of Russia (May 1812 to March 1813), with yet another Grande Armée of nearly 700,000 men from twenty nations, proved the intimate dependence of the Empire on military success. Napoleon was unable to destroy his enemy, despite the victory of Borodino (7 September 1812), and his army disintegrated as it withdrew in the Russian winter. Alexander's decision to invade Germany was the direct cause of the renewed coalition of 1813, the abandonment of France not only by its traditional antagonists, but also by many of its allies and rulers created by Napoleon. The defeat of Leipzig (16–19 October 1813) led to the collapse of the Empire and Napoleon's abdication (6 April 1814).

The dramatic events of these intense years tend to mask the close correspondence between the internal evolution of France and that outside her frontiers. The ties between domestic and external developments were not only close but also reciprocally influential. At the political level, for example, the north Italian (Cisalpine) and Dutch (Batavian) republics adapted their constitutions to Brumaire and, at a second stage following Napoleon's assumption of an imperial title, were transformed into kingdoms. But, equally, the assumption of the title of emperor – an essentially domestic development – played a not insignificant role in the creation of the third coalition and the renewal of war. At the economic level, a similar correspondence can be identified. The struggle between France and Britain, which dominated the history of the Napoleonic years, dated back to long before the Revolution. Its imposition on the entire Continent, with the blockade, was a direct extension of France's domestic concerns; the determination to exploit France's military hegemony to open up markets for French manufactures provided a further example. In both instances, the attempt to resolve French economic domestic problems by turning to the territories under French control contradicted the ambitious efforts to implant by administrative fiat, outside her frontiers, a French model of modernity, which would sink roots and attract a broad and long-term consensus.

For however dependent ultimately on the army, Napoleon's hegemony of Europe was not (and could not be) dependent on military rule. The territories incorporated within French Europe were conceived of (with only marginal exceptions) as the constitutive elements of a new form of state and society that would characterise the new era. The new model was not born in the dawn of Brumaire, but developed over the years, in direct dependence on the evolution of Napoleon's concept of his own role. Hence the policies imposed on the conquered lands corresponded, according to their date of incorporation, to the phase of administrative restructuring within France herself, and changes in policies towards the external territories paralleled domestic changes. Contemporaneously, the very existence of this vaster terrain opened up new perspectives for Napoleon and his close advisers which influenced their choice of policies. In particular, they pointed towards a more intimate identification of France and Europe, most concretely identified in the ambition to create new ruling elites of service, which would cut across former national loyalties.

The profound belief in the possibility of creating a Europe in the image of France underlay Napoleon's reconstruction of Europe. How this utopian ideal was to be achieved and the contradictory tensions and forces that resulted from the attempts to realise it constitute the main theme of the following chapters.

2 The tools of conquest

I need bulwarks, because my confidence is more solidly built on
the strictness of the rule than on the character of men. I employ
many men, I hardly know any of them. Hence I must place my
trust in them. The safest way for me, but for them too, is to ensure
that they cannot abuse my trust.

> (Napoleon, 1811: *Mémoires du comte Beugnot*,
> Paris, 1866, vol. 1, p. 387)

As Napoleon's policies developed over the years, embracing ever
wider areas of Europe, so the tools of conquest – in terms of administrative mechanisms and personnel – were modified, adapted and
rendered more professional to meet the demands of an expanding
Empire. Much stress is placed in the historiography of Napoleon,
quite correctly, on his growing social conservatism, his shift away
from the egalitarian ideals of the Revolution towards inherited status
distinctions, a quasi-revivalist display of the aristocratic trappings of
the ancien regime or of the monarchical societies of his peers in
Austria, Russia or Britain. But often in-built into this explanation of
the social trajectory of the Napoleonic experience is the assumption
that such conservatism can be equated with a decline in quality. At
the deeper and longer-term level of the negative cultural effects of
constraints of conformity and excessive centralisation on initiative,
intellectual expression and possibly innovation, such an equation is
tenable – and was indeed affirmed at the time in the language of
liberty by Mme de Staël and Benjamin Constant. But at the more
immediate, practical, day-to-day level of creating and running the
Empire, the evidence that emerges from the immense documentation
and experiences of the small army of administrators argues against
such an assumption. For the most part, the cumulative experiences of

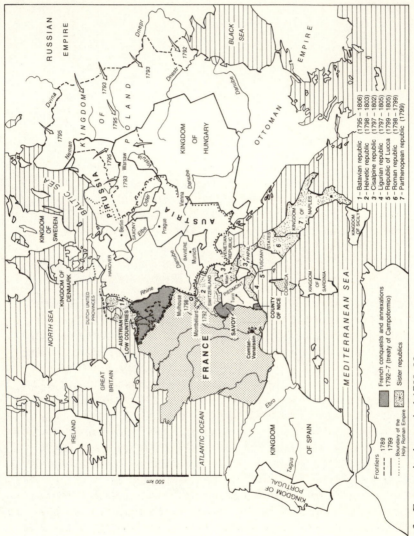

Map 2 Europe in the period 1789–99

Frontiers
- - - - 1789
———— 1799
········ Boundary of the Holy Roman Empire

■ French conquests and annexations 1792–7 (treaty of Campoformio)

▨ Sister republics

1 – Batavian republic (1795–1806)
2 – Helvetic republic (1798–1803)
3 – Cisalpine republic (1797–1802)
4 – Ligurian republic (1797–1805)
5 – Republic of Lucca (1799–1805)
6 – Roman republic (1798–1799)
7 – Parthenopean republic (1799)

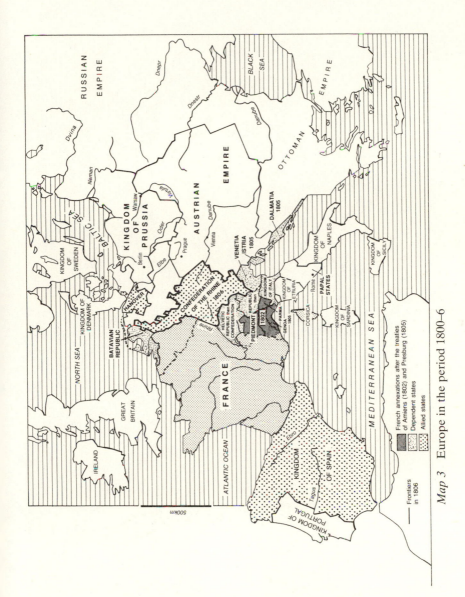

Map 3 Europe in the period 1800–6

Legend:

French annexations after the treaties of Amiens (1802) and Presburg (1805)

Dependent states

Allied states

—— Frontiers in 1806

Labels on map:

RUSSIAN EMPIRE

Dnepr

Dniestr

Dvina

BLACK SEA

OTTOMAN EMPIRE

Danube

DALMATIA 1805

AUSTRIAN EMPIRE

Neman

Vistula

KINGDOM OF WARSAW

KINGDOM OF PRUSSIA

Oder

Berlin

Elbe

Prague

Vienna

VENETIA ISTRIA 1805

KINGDOM OF NAPLES

KINGDOM OF SICILY

KINGDOM OF SWEDEN

BALTIC SEA

KINGDOM OF DENMARK

HANOVER

NORTH SEA

BATAVIAN REPUBLIC

Rhine

CONFEDERATION OF THE RHINE 1806

HELVETIC REPUBLIC (then CONFEDERATION)

KINGDOM OF ITALY

PIEDMONT 1802

PARMA 1805

GENOA 1805

KINGDOM OF ETRURIA

Rome

PAPAL STATES

CORSICA

KINGDOM OF SARDINIA

MEDITERRANEAN SEA

GREAT BRITAIN

IRELAND

ATLANTIC OCEAN

FRANCE

KINGDOM OF SPAIN

Ebro

Tagus

KINGDOM OF PORTUGAL

500km

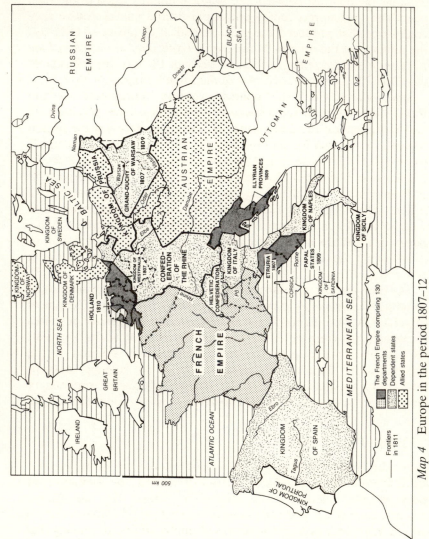

Map 4 Europe in the period 1807–12

The French Empire comprising 130 departments

Dependent states

Allied states

Frontiers in 1811

these years led to a progressive refining of the wheels of administration and of the selection of their human cogs. It is this that explains the contrast between the political-military crisis of the final years and the unprecedented and sophisticated administrative self-confidence that produced the great statistical enquiries of 1812–14, the minister of the interior Montalivet's *Exposition of the state of the Empire, presented to the Legislative Body* of 1813, or the minister of war Clarke's *Administrative atlas of the French Empire* of 1812.[1]

Since Tocqueville, the political rupture represented by the Revolution has been redimensioned by the insistence of observers and historians on the administrative continuity between the ancien regime, the Revolution and the Napoleonic experience. What tends to be ignored in these considerations of the long-term trend of the French state is the radical change of scale imposed by the expansion of France in the Revolutionary-Napoleonic period: the problems of organising an Empire of 130 departments with 44 million inhabitants were of a different order from those faced by the Constituent legislators in a France of 83 departments inhabited by a population of 27–8 million. Space, time and language assumed other dimensions in this new context.

The bureaucratic developments should be seen as a response to the rapid political changes imposed on Europe by Napoleon. Their most novel feature was the forging of an administrative corps and practices in the field, for there were few precedents to build on or react against, as had been the case in the early Consulate in relation to the Revolutionary decade. The composition of so far-flung a corps constitutes the main theme of this chapter. But some preliminary remarks are required about the allocation of responsibilities at Paris.

THE ROLE OF PARIS

After the initial, fertile period immediately following Brumaire, it is unclear how often Napoleon himself provided the initiative for administrative modifications. But it is certain that he always maintained a direct and close control over all proposals, and that he would intervene, even in the details of minor affairs, displaying that remarkable memory and knowledge of men, matters and milieux that so impressed his entourage and visitors. Prince Metternich, a hostile but attentive observer of the French emperor from the time of his nomination as ambassador at Paris in 1805, contested the reality of Napoleon's knowledge of his domain: 'A truth that is not sufficiently well known . . . is the shallowness of Napoleon's knowledge about a great part of the internal administration of his immense state. Above all, he understands nothing about trading relations'.[2] There is considerable evidence to support Metternich's judgement about the superficiality, indeed the simplicity, of Napoleon's economic ideas. But the very centralisation of the system, from its creation in the Year VIII until the abdication, with its insistence on hierarchical control of individual decision-making and nomination of officials, ensured that Napoleon was informed about personalities and administrative problems in all corners of his Empire to a degree inconceivable to bureaucrats or ministers of our times.

The price paid for such personalised centralisation was delay. Major progress had been achieved in modernising the land and water routes within France already before the Revolution. The difficulty was the absence of anything comparable beyond France's old frontiers (except in Britain). Napoleon's almost obsessive insistence on constructing roads, even across the Alpine passes, is proverbial and – like his extension of the Revolutionary telegraph lines – corresponded to military strategy and political needs. Every new route, as he observed in 1811, 'ensures and consolidates the reunion of these countries to the Empire and is hence a matter of prime importance'.[3] But with the extension of the frontiers, the heavy use to which the roads were subjected by increasingly frequent troop movements and the deployment of the Grande Armée ever further east, the problem worsened of how to force the pace of road construction in order to meet the ever more urgent pressures of administration and war. In fact, Napoleon tended to use special couriers, not just to coordinate military movements or announce a victory during his campaigns, but for all important matters. And such couriers, as Marbot recalled in his memoirs, might carry not just secret despatches, but silks for the empress imported illegally despite the Continental blockade.[4]

There was a fundamental incompatibility between Napoleon's constant mobility and the requirement of his authorisation for an infinity of minor administrative acts. It took fourteen months, for instance, for the hospital of Santa Maria Nuova at Florence to be granted permission by Napoleon to sell some houses it owned in order to pay its creditors.[5] Major decisions could be transmitted with remarkable speed, such as the decree to confiscate all colonial goods in the grand-duchy of Berg, signed by Napoleon at Nossen (between Dresden and Leipzig) on 8 May 1813, received by special courier at Paris on 14 May and by Beugnot, the minister responsible at Düsseldorf on 16 May.[6] But delay became ever more the norm as Napoleon was increasingly absent: between 1805 and 1814 the Emperor spent only

900 of 3,500 days at Paris;[7] and it was not accidental that so many major political and administrative decisions were taken in 1810, the only year he spent in or near France. With the Russian campaign the delays worsened. Authorisation for expenditure in Berg was granted by Roederer, the minister responsible at Paris, only for expenditure from January to April 1813 on 19 March, for May and August expenditure on 14 August, for June and July on 8 September, for September on 1 October, and never thereafter.[8]

It is this insistence on personal control irrespective of geographical displacements that gives an impression of fluidity to the channels of administrative communication along which the Empire was run. Napoleon's official visitations to one or another part of the lands he ruled directly or controlled (as distinct from, though sometimes connected to, his sudden, frightening appearances at the head of the Grande Armée) were like sharply accelerated versions of the stately progress of medieval monarchs or of the Emperor Charles V. He was at Bruges, Ghent, Antwerp, Brussels and Maestricht in July 1803, at Aix-la-Chapelle, The Hague, Cologne, Coblenz, Mainz, Trier and Luxemburg in September–October 1804, in Piedmont, the kingdom of Italy, Parma and Genoa in spring 1805, in northern Italy again in November–December 1807, at Erfurt in autumn 1808, in Belgium in spring 1810, in Antwerp, Holland and Berg in October–November 1811. Such occasions were marked by a sudden flurry of administrative activity, including the resolution of long delayed matters. For besides the continuous round of receptions, these visits regularly comprised intense sessions between Napoleon, the ministers and councillors of state he had brought with him and local administrators, in which individuals were praised or blamed, and decrees passed to relieve or develop the local economy and embellish the privileged city with new roads or promenades.

It is not always easy to understand why a particular issue should have left its documentary traces in one rather than another ministry or council. But the broad lines of responsibility at Paris relating to the territories outside France's pre-Revolutionary frontiers can be attributed within the twin parameters of functional specialisation and territorial status.

Functional specialisation – diplomatic, military or fiscal affairs, for example – was the least precise. For however direct and personal a control Napoleon exercised over political, diplomatic and generally all major decisions, he was meticulous in his demand for information, and often ready (particularly in his earlier years) to listen to the

opinions of one or more ministers, state councillors or mere functionaries, a practice that was formalised in Year X by the creation of a
privy council of changing composition. Diplomatic matters were
channelled exclusively through the ministry of foreign affairs (except
for major negotiations, which Napoleon dealt with personally or for
which he often nominated his own representatives). But their repercussions, for example relating to the economic blockade, could find
their way to the council of state, the privy council, the Customs
general directorate, the ministry of finances, the consultative general
councils on manufacturing and trade, the ministerial board of trade,
and elsewhere. Fiscal matters would primarily be processed and
prepared within the ministry of finances and the treasury, but –
depending on the object – could be the responsibility of the
Extraordinary demesne or the Customs. Military affairs belonged to
the domain of the ministries of war and war administration, but
involved the interior ministry over conscription and civil–military
relations. Most matters relating to legislation and public administration would be discussed within the council of state. In short, as one
would expect, a primary degree of specialisation oriented the regular
bureaucratic channels of communication between Paris and the world
beyond France's frontiers, although overlapping (and sometimes con-
flictual) spheres of competence and the creation of consultative and
interministerial councils, as well as Napoleon's specific instructions
and the repercussions of earlier decisions, could easily generate a
wider diffusion of paper and discussion. Above all, the expanding use
of the council of state by ministers cuts across any clear-cut image of
functional specialisation. Increasingly, as is evident from an infinity
of sources like Stendhal's *Journal*, the councillors of state were
transformed into all-purpose experts.

   Territorial status provides clearer distinctions, as the areas can be
grouped in apparently distinct categories. Thus the territories progressively 'reunited' to France – from Savoy and the Belgian Low
Countries to Italy, Holland and the Hanseatic seaboard – were
administratively treated in uniform manner as part of France, divided
in departments with prefects, and hence the responsibility of the
ministry of the interior. Only if these territories were subjected to a
special transitional regime, like the Tuscan junta, Parma or the
Illyrian intendancy, was responsibility provisionally assigned to
Gaudin, minister of finances. Holland was treated analogously on its
annexation in 1810, with the creation of a Council for Dutch Affairs
under Gaudin. At the other extreme, established states which survived France's military onslaught (primarily Russia, Britain and

Austria, and Prussia until 1806) remained within the exclusive domain of the ministry of foreign affairs.

In between these extremes, at least two further classifications can be made. In the first group can be placed the states assigned to members of Napoleon's family. Such states, whether already in existence like Naples or Holland or newly created like Westphalia, were formally independent, and hence merited a diplomatic representative and correspondence through the foreign affairs ministry. But Napoleon's exactions of troops and his reservation to his crown of substantial incomes in these states, as much as the Bonaparte family relationship, led to parallel channels of communication with the ministry of war, the Extraordinary demesne, and via Napoleon's copious personal correspondence with his brothers and brother-in-law.

The second group contained the states over which Napoleon claimed direct authority, either permanently or for a long period: the republic-kingdom of Italy and the grand-duchy of Berg. As absentee head of the Italian state, with a vice-president-viceroy at Milan, he maintained the formal distinction between his two domains by employing the foreign affairs ministry but, after the creation of the kingdom, insisted on the permanent presence at Paris of a minister (Aldini). Responsibility for relations with Berg had initially been placed in the hands of Gaudin, minister of finances, possibly because of the reserved crown incomes. With Murat's departure (1808) and the choice of Louis of Holland's 5-year-old son as grand-duke, Napoleon shifted responsibility for control of the administration of Berg to the minister-secretary of state Maret, and then (because of Maret's passivity) to Roederer, who was given the same status.

It is evident from these examples that even territorial status does not provide clear-cut distinctions about responsibilities at Paris for non-French territories. Military demands and the increasingly arbitrary attempts to enforce the Continental blockade involved the war ministries and Customs, who on occasion bypassed foreign affairs in their relations even with established allied states, such as Bavaria or Baden. The alliances imposed on these states, particularly within the Rhine and Helvetic (Swiss) Confederations of which Napoleon was Protector, and the reservation to the French crown of properties and incomes within conquered states multiplied the channels of communication with Paris. The allocation to favoured ministers of mini-states – Benevento to Talleyrand, Neuchâtel to Berthier – led to the utilisation of official channels (foreign affairs, war) for what was virtually patrimonial administration.

The facade of a rationally organised central administration with functional or territorial allocation of responsibilities at Paris for the effective maintenance of France's domination of Europe, masked a complexity that, far from disappearing, probably increased over the period, because of the conflicting expectations and demands made by the different branches of the administration. The result was not the confusion that might have been expected, but effective control, which can be attributed to Napoleon's personal role, the implacable demands of the military and the professionalism of the bureaucratic corps. It is difficult to impose a neat interpretative grid on such complexity, although it is easy to illustrate it, for example through the occasional irritation of a prefect in responding to the demands of different ministers about the same object, such as statistics on cereal production or public order. Far less tangible is the problem of how information was filtered, and at what levels, before it reached the Emperor. Indeed, in a deeper sense, one is forced to ask to what extent a socio-cultural filter operated throughout the system, constructing those very realities that Napoleon and his servants expected to find, whether about the nature of the territories under French control, the functioning of the economy, social behaviour or any other aspect of the organisation of society. It is a problem of considerable significance (and not only for the Napoleonic regime), as such information contributed in the process of decision-making. What is certain is that, following the retreat from Russia and the renewed formation of the anti-Napoleonic coalition, as French armies were pushed back across central Europe and Spain in 1813, control rapidly gave way to evidence of opposition and disorder. Worried local elites hastened to prepare for a pacific transfer of power on Napoleon's defeat.

The Parisian civil service remained almost exclusively French. The only ministry which contained a small proportion of foreigners or natives of newly annexed regions was foreign affairs, where the tradition of a specialised training at Strasbourg and linguistic skills encouraged the recruitment of Alsatians and Germans, such as Reinhardt and Bacher. In other ministries the enlargement of France's frontiers does not appear to have had any effect on recruitment. Nor is this surprising, given the small size of the ministries (the interior numbered only 220 employees in the late Empire), the strong influence of patronage and presence at Paris on chances of recruitment, and the opportunities and needs of employment in the new local administrations.

Nevertheless 'new' Frenchmen formed part of the constituted organs of government in the capital. Their presence was a deliberate political gesture, a consecration of the reality of the expanding Empire, for which Napoleon was directly responsible. A very general indicator of evolution of attitudes towards the incorporation of these new compatriots is provided by their presence in the legislative assemblies. Lambrechts, the sole Belgian senator in 1800, was sceptical about getting a compatriot appointed to the Tribunate: 'There is little hope, as they do not seem to be very generous in offering places to men from the annexed departments'.[9] There seem to have been none among the 120 members of the Tribunate appointed in 1800 or 1802, despite the annexation of Belgium, Geneva and the left bank of the Rhine (fourteen departments). In the Legislative body, membership became automatic in that all departments were represented (constitution of Year X). Although the departments of the annexed territories constituted one-third of the total number, the 22 per cent 'new French' members of the Legislative body between 1800 and 1813 represented a fair proportion, given that over half their departments became part of France only in the later years. A similar conclusion can be drawn for the Senate. Of the initial sixty-three senators only Lambrechts was born outside France (in Belgium) and he had served as minister of justice during the Directory; in sharp contrast, of senators nominated between the Year IX and 1813 over a quarter of the new members came from Italy, Belgium, Holland and Germany. Some of the French members of the Legislative body were prefects of annexed departments, like Frémin de Beaumont, who represented the Manche for ten years until he was appointed prefect of the Bouches du Rhin in 1810, or Sauzey, who was the first prefect of the Mont Blanc until his election to the Legislative body as representative of the same department in Year X. Successful French prefects were more often rewarded by their appointment as senators, like Viry, prefect of the Lys, Cochon de Lapparent, prefect successively of Vienne and Deux-Nèthes. The 'new Frenchmen' appointed to the legislative assemblies were overwhelmingly influential figures, politically or socially, in their countries of origin, like Durazzo, the last doge of Genoa, the Piedmontese noble Falletti di Barolo, the Tuscan minister and engineer Fossombroni or Schimmelpenninck, former grand pensionary of the Batavian republic.[10]

When Holland was annexed in 1810, guarantees were given of posts within the Empire: six senators, six councillors of state, two judges in the supreme court, twenty-six deputies of the Legislative body. Holland was unique among the incorporated territories, because of concern about the political reaction against annexation among a population with a proud tradition of independence, so soon after its previous remodelling into a Bonapartist kingdom. But there can be little doubt that in general Napoleon saw the presence of these new compatriots in the legislative assemblies as symbolising the unity and indivisibility of the French Empire. At the same time, their landed wealth and in most cases noble origins served to consolidate the conservatism of these bodies.

Membership of the Legislative body and Senate was a mark of honour and source of privilege, but hardly an onerous burden. Appointment to the council of state was a different matter, as it was the very core of the central administrative system, on which rested Bonaparte's affirmation of advancement through merit. Here too only Frenchmen seemed to have been appointed in the earliest years as councillors of state (or *maîtres des requêtes*), but from 1802 Napoleon included natives of the annexed departments: of 112 councillors, six were Italians, two Germans (including Dalberg) and four Dutch. The council of state was conceived as the seedbed of the future administrative class for the entire Empire, the civilian equivalent of the military academy. Nowhere is its importance demonstrated more clearly than in Napoleon's insistence on the presence of young nobles from the annexed departments among the auditors. From the creation of this category of trainees in 1803, Belgians and then Italians requested appointments; in 1811, of thirty-three nominations, fourteen were from the newly annexed Rome. As striking as the competition to enter the ranks of the auditors was Napoleon's overriding of the hostility to their appointment of the scions of leading Roman and Piedmontese aristocratic families, like Cesare Balbo. For a rigorous experience as auditor, initially at Paris, was regarded as ideal preparation for service in the field, not just in terms of professional training, but as a form of acculturation. The auditors were seen as crucial tools in the transmission of the values and hence the durability of the French Empire.

Paris was to play the role of imperial Rome, not just as the brain of an administrative body, but as its heart, drawing in and pumping out the life-blood of a culture which was assumed to have attained new levels. The boundless ambition and underlying ambiguity of this intimate mesh of political-administrative responsibilities and socio-cultural aspirations was reflected in the assiduous presence of the leading functionaries in the fashionable salons. From Pompadour to Mme Roland, Récamier and Josephine de Beauharnais, political sociability had characterised the Parisian salons. Whether official in tone (like Caroline Murat's), scientific (like Madame d'Helvétius at Autueil) or in opposition (like Juliette Récamier or Germaine de Staël), the Parisian salons were now frequented by a new imperial and European elite. The cultural legacy, beyond France's borders after 1815, was to be no less marked than the directly political experience.

THE MECHANICS OF OCCUPATION

How to occupy a country and what to do with it was a process that the French learnt by trial and error during the Revolutionary decade. In later years Napoleon built on these experiences, but continued to improve on the mechanics of the operation, introducing major variations.

The Convention, in a decree of 15 December 1792, proclaimed the abolition of feudalism in all the occupied territories, and despatched commissaires to prepare elections as the manifest proof of liberation. But already in these earliest years of hostilities, the logistic problems of warfare and the manifest reluctance of the populations to be liberated rapidly led French generals, like their superiors at Paris and the civilian commissaires accompanying the armies, to regard occupied territory as enemy territory. Two immediate consequences followed. First, the military commander felt free to requisition and exact what (at the least) he judged necessary to supply his army, and (at the worst) he believed could be extorted for his soldiers, his suppliers, his government and, last but not least, himself. Secondly, the commander, while asserting control over all state institutions, was reliant on civilian collaboration to facilitate his exactions, and hence normally reluctant to encourage the proposals of local patriots to purge the existing administrators or (worse) to set up new Revolutionary administrative structures. In addition, lack of experience, authority or concern often meant that a general in charge of an army was unable to control his subordinates, so that local pillaging and illegal exactions accompanied the official efforts to meet the demands for supplies and indemnities of the occupying forces. This was certainly the experience of the Belgian Low Countries and Rhineland in 1793–4. The creation of 'extraction agencies' (euphemistically called 'commercial agencies') in the Belgian and German territories in 1794, as of a 'military agency' in Lombardy in 1796, was essentially an attempt to cut out private initiative, since it weakened the ability of the constituted authorities to make the local populations pay their share of the military-imposed ransom. The

problem worsened in the Directory years because of the inability of
the government at Paris to control its generals.

Treatment as enemy territory was dependent on the formal status
assigned to each country by the French authorities. For, in theory at
least, the French troops would be evacuated once a new friendly
government (such as a sister republic) had been set up, or the
population had voted for reunion to France. Hence the pressures on
local populations to change their status were compelling. But local
voices, whether patriotic or desperate, were rarely heard, as they fell
foul of the conflicting ambitions or policies of French commissaires,
generals and Parisian politicians. Even where the patriots were able
momentarily to seize the initiative – as in Liège, the Low Countries or
Lombardy – they were soon constrained by the French occupying
forces. The very early experience of the patriots in the principality of
Liège can be regarded as paradigmatic of this process. Here the
popular societies had played a central role, with the French occupation in 1792–3, in setting up a provisional administration and
preparing a vote in favour of reunion to France, despite the ferocious
attacks on their commitment by a Convention commissaire, Publicola
Chaussard. In 1794, although both the municipal and the provisional
central administrations were re-established, the French commissaire
Frécine radically reduced their powers, and then, ignoring local
opinion, carved up the former principality into two parts, assigned
respectively to the nearby (and hence resented) authority of Brussels
and Aix-la-Chapelle.

In general, the change from simple military occupation to some
form of provisional civilian administration was usually the result of
the diminishing returns of military exactions. Thus in the Rhineland,
where there was an army of occupation of 100,000, a central administration was set up in 1794, consisting of equal numbers of French and
Germans. The administrative problem was complicated in the
Rhineland (on both sides of the river), because previously sovereignty had been divided between 101 petty states. In Lombardy,
after only a few months of occupation, Bonaparte accepted a central
administration of patriots as it facilitated the monthly payments for
his army.

The underlying problem was the uncertainty about the future in
each territory, about which local patriots, occupying generals, civilian
commissaires and the authorities at Paris could have different and
conflicting views. Thus the Belgian (and hence Liège) experience of
provisional administrations and 'extraction agencies' rapidly led to
annexation (1795), which meant not only the removal of military

exactions, but also a total rupture with the administrative practices of the past through the division of the territory into departments. In the Rhineland, on the other hand, the successive military administrators (Generals Custine, Hoche and Augereau) only tampered with the administrative structures, replacing the central administration with French-staffed general directorates (May 1796) to improve the flow of payments. Only after the peace of Campoformio (October 1797), when the Directory was convinced that the left bank would remain French, was military authority replaced by the appointment of a general commissaire, F. J. Rudler, to restructure the administrative, financial and judicial system in preparation for annexation. In yet another variant, the Directory accepted the Dutch patriots' creation of the Batavian republic (May 1795), but only at the price of annexing territory to improve the French frontier, payment of a huge indemnity and the maintenance of an army of 25,000 French soldiers. In Italy, provisional administrations were set up in Genoa and Venice, as subsequently at Lucca and Rome (1797–8). Only at a second stage was General Bonaparte prepared to transform the Lombard provisional general administration into a sister-republic, the Cisalpine (July 1797), which remained responsible for the maintenance of the French army; and it was similarly the initiative of a French general, Championnet, that allowed the creation of the Neapolitan republic (January 1799). The reluctance of the Directory to change the existing administrative structures in Italy was shown in the refusal to allow the Piedmontese patriots to overthrow their government, and then (December 1798) in its acceptance only of a provisional administration. In Tuscany, despite the sympathy of the French commanders Gaulthier and Schérer towards a change of regime, the Directory insisted on a purely military occupation (1799).

In the eyes of the local patriots, the proclamation of a republic signified the creation of an autonomous sovereign state. From the point of view of the Directory, the republics (apart from their possible diplomatic implications at a future peace treaty) merely constituted another experiment in the mechanics of occupation. Ultimate authority remained firmly in the hands of the military commanders. Some, like Masséna and Augereau, were legendary for their systematic pillaging. Irrespective of their personal greed, these military leaders, like the French civilian commissaires, intervened at will in the activities of the local republican authorities, writing and rewriting their constitutions, purging their assemblies, appointing new executive commissions, according to their political inclinations and the fluctuations in the life of the Directory. Whatever the political and personal antagonisms between military and civilian agents, Jacobins and moderates, in 1797–9 there was little difference in the operational techniques deployed by Generals Bonaparte and Brune and ambassador Trouvé in the Cisalpine, the agents Mengaud, Lecarlier and Rapinat in the Helvetic republic, the delegates Noel and Delacroix in the Batavian republic, commissaire Abrial at Naples, or General Masséna at Genoa. Only in Piedmont, where commissaire Eymar supervised the actions of the provisional government on a daily basis, can any variation be noted, when Eymar's successor Musset dissolved the government and (like Rudler in the Rhineland) began to reorganise Piedmont on a departmental basis in apparent preparation of annexation (1799).

By Brumaire, successive French governments had experimented with the mechanics of occupation and elaborated certain techniques. Purely military occupation, treating the country as enemy territory, was limited to the short term or to emergencies (such as Masséna's seven requisitions in Switzerland in five months of 1799). If occupation was prolonged, the standard practice was to replace the local administrators (many of whom had fled) by a provisional administration of patriots or less willing collaborators. The precise physiognomy of such provisional administrations varied, as did their titles, but the primary concern of the French representatives was to ensure collaboration, not demonstrations of independence. Up to this point these territories were certainly regarded as potential bargaining counters in a future peace. Wherever the extension of France's frontiers was seen as both desirable and feasible, the territory was restructured on French departmental lines, whether after annexation (Savoy, Belgium) or in preparation (Rhineland, Piedmont). Elsewhere the very plurality of sources of power under the Directory, at Paris and in the occupied territories, sometimes offered the possibility to local patriots to transform provisional administrations into new republics, under the sympathetic eye of the French general in command. The Directory adapted to this situation, sending out members of the legislature as commissaires with extensive powers to control both generals and republican administrations. Their success was normally greater with the latter than the former. But the very conflict of power continued to offer a political space for the local patriots, without providing any stable prospects for the future of the republics.

Napoleon, after Marengo, could exploit two advantages in the reoccupied territories lacking to his predecessors: unity of command (in contrast to the previous diffusion of power) and a degree of support from the local elites (because of the discreditable behaviour of the old regimes during their brief restoration in 1799–1800). His immediate solution to the administration of these territories was to employ as model the constitution of the Year VIII, just as the Directory had turned to the constitution of the Year III. In Piedmont, the Cisalpine and Liguria executive government commissions and legislative councils were set up (June–July 1800). But the real power was placed more firmly than ever in the hands of French representatives – Generals Jourdan and Dejean in Piedmont and Liguria, army inspector Petiet in the Cisalpine – who acted as virtual proconsuls, combining military and civil authority, receiving orders directly from the First Consul, presiding over the meetings of the executive commissions. Within a year (April 1801) the military control was formalised in Piedmont and Liguria by transforming them into the 27th and 28th military divisions of France, even though neither of them had yet been annexed.

Three alternative methods were employed during the Consulate in the search for stable solutions to the control of foreign territories. Piedmont was 'prepared' for annexation by the nomination of a general administration under General Jourdan, responsible for introducing the entire French machinery of government (April 1801). Within a month, prefects had been appointed to the six departments. To assist Jourdan and his council of six, experts were imported for the more specialised branches of administration: A. J. Hennet, a financial bureaucrat who had served under Necker, G. A. Jourde to set up the new judicial system, General Wirion to establish a gendarmerie, the bishop of Amiens to sort out the ecclesiastical hierarchy. For political reasons annexation was delayed until 11 September 1802, the local population being informed two weeks later. Jourdan, too republican for Napoleon's taste, was replaced by the conservative General Menou. As in the Rhineland, where the extraordinary authority of a general commissaire continued until Year X, although prefects had been appointed already in Year VIII, a two-tier system was continued until 1805, with both Menou as administrator-general and regular prefects, creating ambiguities over the respective responsibilities of the minister of the interior and the administrator-general. Piedmont provided the model for future annexations.[11]

The second method, apparently as definitive, was the creation of republics under direct French rule. Here too northern Italy provided the experimental field. Consultation of local notables, with the summoning to Lyon of carefully selected figures of the Cisalpine republic, was the consular version of proclaiming consensus. The creation of the Italian republic (January 1802) with Napoleon as president, a Constitution and entirely native administration under Melzi d'Eril based on the French prototype, and the maintenance of a French army at the new republic's expense, seemed to offer a viable solution in the form of a vassal state that could be restructured in the French image. The refusal of the Ligurians to go to Lyon, through their fear of being swallowed up in the new Lombard state, perhaps explains why Napoleon gave them a separate constitution, with a legislative council, electoral colleges and senate, but under the firm control of the French representative Saliceti (June 1802). The uncertainties and disadvantages of their status (trade with Piedmont was hit by a new tariff barrier, obligations were imposed to provide soldiers and sailors for France) encouraged enthusiasm for annexation, as had been the Piedmontese experience.

The third method was less direct – an attempt to ensure control of foreign territories without the difficulties of occupation. In the case of Holland, the Batavian republic was replaced by a more traditional collegial regency, which restored power to the former urban oligarchies and Orange aristocrats (September 1801), while imposing the obligation on the Dutch to maintain an army of 18,000 men. In Switzerland, Napoleon proposed a more original formula, carefully avoiding further annexations or commitments by ensuring the return to power of the former cantonal oligarchies in a 'mediation' which he guaranteed as Protector. In return the Swiss were committed to supply France with a regular military contingent (1803). The Swiss precedent was to be repeated on a far grander scale in Germany, where the invention of the Confederation of the Rhine among (initially) sixteen states, with Napoleon as Protector, confirmed and indeed extended the territorial sovereignty of the participant members, while committing them to recruit 63,000 soldiers for France (1806). In both instances, the shadow of Napoleon's protection acted as an effective substitute for direct intervention, the Grande Armée was ensured of substantial contingents, and the example of state modernity provided by France encouraged emulation among the dependent rulers.

The creation of the Empire and Napoleon's military triumphs of 1805–7 raised the techniques of occupation to a new level. Annexation became a skilled art, as repeated recourse was made to it. With the annexation of Venetia in 1806, local notables were appointed as special commissaires, a temporary measure until the nomination of experienced prefects from the kingdom of Italy. Already in 1802, on the death of the duke of Parma (whose state had been ceded to France by the treaty of Aranjuez, March 1801), the French resident, Moreau de Saint-Méry, was appointed administrator-general for the unusually lengthy transitional period of four years (October 1802 to January 1806). It was presumably the revolt at Piacenza (December 1805) that decided Napoleon to 'prepare' the territory for annexation, with the appointment of a special 'administrative prefect', Nardon (1806–8). The diplomat Champagny was first sent to prepare the annexation of the Ligurian republic. But he was immediately followed by the former consul Lebrun and a team of experts to create three new departments (June–September 1805). On the Piedmontese model of a two-tier structure, Lebrun was to remain governor-general of Liguria for two years, alongside the three prefects. With the annexation of Tuscany (December 1807), Dauchy was first appointed as administrator-general with specialised staff transferred from the Piedmontese departments, then Menou was sent as military commander and head of a provisional junta of experts to establish the French system. The members of the Roman *consulta* charged with an identical task following the annexation of the Papal States (May 1809) were partly the same as those of the Tuscan junta (Gérando, Janet, Balbo). With the annexation of Holland (1810), the aged Lebrun was once more employed as lieutenant-general to set up the prefectoral system, then staying on – as previously in Liguria – as governor-general (1811–13). Special intendants were despatched to absorb the three Hanseatic departments on the North Sea (1812), and French *commissaires* were sent to set up four departments in Catalonia in 1812, in the widespread expectation that the region was to be annexed.

In many ways, the most interesting example of the mechanism of annexation is that of the Illyrian provinces, created out of territories seized from Austria in 1809. Ruled by a governor-general (Marmont, then Bertrand), an intendant-general of finances (Dauchy, then Chabrol) and six intendants, despite a decision in April 1811 to assimilate the area to the French system of government, Napoleon was forced to accept its practical impossibility. Culturally and ethnically remote from the French experience, at the very frontiers of civilisation, the Illyrian provinces were assigned a special status, neither a simple military occupation nor rapid annexation, but necessitating adaptation at a much slower pace than the three months prescribed to Rudler in the Rhineland or the seven months given to Gérando in Tuscany.

Besides annexation, the Empire innovated in terms of techniques of occupation through the elevation of Napoleon's family to new and old thrones. These Bonaparte states resembled the republic-kingdom of Italy more than the allied states of the Rhine Confederation. For, although formally independent, Berg, Naples, Holland and Westphalia, like Elisa's petty state of Lucca and Berthier's principality of Neuchâtel, had French advisers and ministers, were subjected to military contingents, and above all were obliged to adopt the French machinery of government. Indeed Berg under Murat and even more Jerome's new kingdom of Westphalia were expected to become model states whose example would be followed by their neighbours. Precisely because he regarded these family states as an extension of the Empire, Napoleon saw no reasons for formalities (even consultation) before interfering in their affairs, as Louis of Holland discovered when he lost his throne, and Joseph of Spain when Napoleon created military administrations in Catalonia, Aragon, Navarre and the Basque country. Spain was a special case, since the unending war inevitably subordinated civilian administration to the military. But it is evident from Napoleon's ample correspondence with his kin sovereigns that he would brook no discussion of the subordination of their states to France, not only in terms of political hegemony, but also as a cultural model demanding close imitation. If Joachim Murat, alone among Napoleon's family, was able to affirm expressions of independence, this was primarily because by these years the emperor was distracted by other, more pressing problems in distant parts.

Continuous warfare, as well as the economic blockade, explains the renewed importance of military occupation in the later years. Increasingly Napoleon sent in his generals to impose a military administration. Sometimes, when an extended though temporary occupation was anticipated, civilian administrators might be appointed – like the prefects Thiébault and Tournon at Erfurt and Bayreuth in 1810, who were instructed not to make any administrative changes. Elsewhere military occupation could lead to subsequent institutional changes, although without removing the presence of French troops, like the creation of the grand-duchy of Warsaw (1807) or the annexation of the Hanseatic cities (1812). Mostly, military occupation was seen as a deliberately heavy-handed method of ensuring payment of indemnities by a defeated enemy. This necessitated the presence of civilian administrators, like Bignon, imperial commissaire in charge of the conquered Prussian provinces in 1806 and of occupied Austria in 1809. Nowhere was this policy clearer than in Prussia, where French forces remained after Jena until 1810, then returning in February 1812 to use the humiliated state as supply base for the Russian campaign. The distinction in the handling of Austria and Prussia is significant. Napoleon never proposed depriving the Habsburgs of their core territories, nor even apparently tried to subordinate this traditional enemy within France's direct sphere of influence. Prussia, on the other hand, was treated brutally and deprived of its most 'Europeanised' territories (Poland), as a punishment for the irresponsible behaviour of the Hohenzollerns in 1806. It seems likely that Napoleon never wanted to absorb eastern Europe. By these final years, his involvement in Germany and eastern Europe was so predominantly geared to warfare, that military occupation, rather than other techniques of administering territories, had inevitably returned to the fore.

The range of methods adopted to administer French-dominated territories provides the clearest evidence of the continuing uncertainty and ultimate inability to find a definitive solution to the mechanics of occupation. This failure to identify and refine a single model of occupation rendered inevitable the personal intervention of the Emperor and his direct agents. In a sense, the return to military occupation – in which Spain acted as a precocious standard-bearer – can be seen as cutting the Gordian knot, a simplified, exasperated and appropriately belligerent means of resolving the issue. Each variant in the mechanics of occupation carried with it immediate and longer-term implications in the relations between occupiers and occupied. For the establishment and consolidation of an expanded Empire, indeed of a Europe modelled on France, depended on the possibility or impossibility of a prolonged dialogue. Military occupation negated dialogue.

THE GENERALS

If Napoleon was the most civilian of military rulers, who owed his undeniable popularity in the Consulate years to his qualities as administrator and peace-maker, he was a general and under no illusions that the durability of his regime and its ability to sink roots was ultimately dependent on military strength. The army remained the essential tool of the spread of French control and influence. Hence, given that the upkeep, administration and logistics of the army constituted the military counterpart to the mechanics of occupation, one could expect to find a broadly similar pattern of evolution, growing professionalisation and centralisation. In fact, the parallelism does not hold good, essentially for two reasons. The first relates to the very essence of Napoleonic warfare, which rendered ultimately impossible the centralisation of military logistics above the level of the individual army corps. The second was the relative indifference of the Emperor to major aspects of military administration. The latter point may appear somewhat paradoxical, given the significance of military attributes in the Napoleonic myth. There is little reason to doubt contemporary descriptions of the general's capacity to arouse boundless enthusiasm and loyalty as he moved among his soldiers at the Boulogne camp or on the battlefield. And he was intensely interested (and interfering) in every detail of military uniforms, which symbolised so well his values of hierarchy and glory. But his enthusiasms were selective and rarely extended to the humdrum details of army administration, as can be illustrated by a rapid survey of the main sectors.

Recruitment of armies was always a matter of crucial importance, which (as will be discussed later) demanded central control in terms of its volume, regularity and methods of enforcement. But, although subject to the war ministries and involving army officers, it was essentially a responsibility of civilian administrators – the prefects.

The strategy of campaigns was even more centralised, in the person of Napoleon, whose orders were transmitted to the army commanders by his minister of war and faithful and efficient chief of general staff Berthier. But this very strategy, which lay at the core of Napoleon's military genius, denied the possibility of an effectively centralised administration of the armies. For the Napoleonic campaigns were structured around sudden, rapid movements of armies, often over very long distances, whose unexpected convergence took the enemy by surprise, so facilitating the decisive mass attack. For this reason it made no sense to set up an overall, central intendancy for the military forces, but only intendancies at the level of the individual army corps. The 1805 campaign in Germany involved seven army corps, Murat's cavalry corps and the Imperial Guard (180,000 men), the 1806 campaign in Prussia six army corps and the Guard (160,000 men), the 1807 campaign in Poland seven army corps, two cavalry corps and the Guard (150,000 men), the 1809 Austrian campaign ten army and one cavalry corps, besides the Guard (200,000 men), the 1812 invasion of Russia twelve army and four cavalry corps (530,000 men).

If strategic and tactical reasons underlay this unexpected but real lack of centralisation, Napoleon's notorious disinterest in the practical details of the logistics of his armies helps explain the tardiness and relative paucity of development of appropriate structures for their supply and administration. A ministry for war administration had been created in 1802, under Generals Dejean (until 1810), Lacuée (until 1813) and Daru, but its responsibilities remained essentially limited to the coordination of the activities of the individual army intendancies, the general state services (*régies*) (for the provision of bread, meat, forage and hospital services), transport and clothing.[12] The intendants-general, successors to the Jacobin representatives on mission and Directorial army commissaires, were meant to act as the counterbalance to the army commanders, but already under the Directory had failed to contain the pillaging of such generals as Masséna and Augereau. In the Napoleonic years, their performance was better but certainly failed to keep up with the needs of the troops, who continued to be inadequately equipped, ill-clothed and often underfed, with their wages overdue. Napoleon was far from unaware of these inadequacies, but never got beyond the denunciation of civilian suppliers he expressed to Dejean in 1807: 'Our armies will never be organised until there is a single administrator, until everything is military. . . . Until then we shall continue to be at the mercy of rogues like those we know too well'.[13] But it is questionable whether even militarisation would have been successful, given that appointment to posts within these intendancies was heavily dependent on recommendations, particularly by generals, more so than in most other fields. Stendhal owed his position as war commissaire in 1806 to his cousin Pierre Daru, then intendant-general of the Grande Armée.

Compared to the intendants-general and their staff of intendants and *commissaires aux guerres*, three other services responsible for the regular administration of the armies enjoyed a better reputation, not least because of Napoleon's interest in their effectiveness. First, a carefully chosen inspectorate of officers was responsible for the development of artillery. With the exception of Marmont, their names – Songis, Lariboisière, Eblé, Sorbier, Drouot – do not figure on the roll-call of military glory recognisable by later generations through the literature of the Napoleonic legend and the street names of Paris. But Napoleon never forgot his origins as an artillery second lieutenant, indeed he recalled it proudly at a banquet in honour of Tsar Alexander at Erfurt. Secondly, a distinctive and well-paid corps of inspectors ('*inspecteurs aux revues*') was created in 1800 in order to carry out regular reviews that the numbers of soldiers actually present corresponded to the numbers declared by their officers. Finally, a special body of military paymasters was set up, appointed by and exclusively responsible to the ministry of the treasury (not the war ministries), and subjected to detailed and rigorously applied regulations (1805) to keep them independent of the army staffs. Napoleon's close supervision of this corps was such that in 1808, while engaged at Bayonne in forcing the Bourbon dynasty to cede him the kingdom of Spain, he took time off to dismiss the paymaster of the army of Dalmatia, Duliège, and confiscate his deposit and possessions for irregularly granting funds to Marmont.[14]

It is not surprising that these highly specialised services should have attracted more administrative attention than the army intendancies, as they dealt with matters about which Napoleon was particularly sensitive – artillery power, the strength and smartness of his regiments, and honest accounting. Mindful of his initial training, Napoleon was increasingly concerned to develop the firing power of his armies, particularly to compensate for the decline in the proportion of experienced veterans in the army. He took a personal interest in reviewing the turnout of the regiments. Marbot recalled how he would ridicule commanders for their inadequate knowledge of their troops.

> Besides the standard questions about numbers of men and horses, armaments, etc., he threw a host of unexpected question at them, for which they were not always prepared. For example: 'How many men have you taken from a given department over the past two years? How many carbines produced at Tulle or Charleville? What's the average age of your soldiers? of your officers? of your horses?' Such question, always delivered in the most peremptory, abrupt manner, accompanied by a penetrating expression, disconcerted many a colonel. But a hesitating reply was ill advised, as Napoleon mentally put a black mark against the officer'.[15]

As warlord and head of state with an almost kitchen economy concern to balance the budget, for Napoleon the review inspectors performed an inestimably valuable task in not making him pay for non-existent troops – even if he seemed resigned to a decline in their efficacy after the initial Consulate years ('They make me pay for all the dead soldiers', he complained to Mollien, minister of the treasury in 1808).[16] The army paymasters, sticking to the letter of their instructions, retained his confidence, in contrast to the intendants. Hence it was not surprising, when the administration of conquered territory was changed from military government (under a general) to civilian, that the responsibility should have been given to review inspectors or military paymasters rather than intendants-general, or alternatively to councillors of state. Daru, in charge of exacting war indemnities from Austria in 1805 and Prussia in 1806, was councillor of state and review inspector before being appointed intendant-general of the Grande Armée for the Russian campaign; his immediate subordinates during the Prussian occupation were the paymasters-general Estève and La Bouillerie and the chief review inspector Villemanzy.

If army administration failed to develop the bureaucratic complexity, sophistication and pride of place of that of civil society, army leaders retained the primacy in Napoleon's hierarchy of values. Given his career, his obligations towards a number of them with the coup of Brumaire, and his permanent reliance on military victory, this is hardly surprising.

There can be no doubt that military valour, in its most classical sense of a highly individual quality, was regarded as a praiseworthy attribute. Of the 2,248 generals of the Revolutionary-Napoleonic wars, 230 were killed, while 1,235 accumulated a total of 4,055 wounds; six army commanders were killed in battle.[17] Oudinot (who died aged 80) fought in all the major campaigns except the Peninsular wars between 1800 and 1814 and was wounded twenty-three times. He can be regarded as representative of the professional soldier, a loyal man of action not well suited for other functions: when ordered by Napoleon to occupy Neuchâtel as a new French territory in 1806, he gave a brief speech, reported by a local bourgeois as 'well prepared in the French manner and delivered in the style of an authentic grenadier leader'.[18] Unlike many of his peers, Oudinot was honest and punctilious in his behaviour towards the populations of the territories he occupied, maintaining strict control over his soldiers, even paying for his board and lodging. Napoleon always remembered bravery in battle, particularly when it tilted the balance, and was generous in his largesse on the field and after. He retained a sneaking respect for the swaggering comportment that sometimes accompanied such courage, even for those whom he disliked, like Augereau (as he recalled at St Helena):

His height, his manners and his language, all made him seem a braggart. But he was far from being one, after he found himself gorged on honours and riches – which, to boot, he grabbed for himself in every possible way.[19]

Even if advancement was no longer so open as in the early years of the Revolution, when most generals achieved their rank before they were 30, the army continued to offer great possibilities, not only through the continuous state of warfare, but also because of the patronage of senior officers. Kinship and marriage alliances grew stronger within this military caste, perhaps the defensive mechanism of parvenus or political trimmers, as Georges Six has argued.[20] Berthier's two younger brothers became generals; Davout, who married the sister of Pauline Bonaparte's husband General Leclerc, helped a brother and uncle to become generals, while a cousin's husband became a colonel; two Clary sisters married Joseph Bonaparte and Bernadotte, while the son of the third sister became a general and the two daughters married the future Marshal Suchet and General Saligny. Bessières, Beurmann, Beylié, Damas, Dumas, Lanusse, Wimpffen and many others were families with two brothers as generals. Six has estimated that at least 240 generals were fathers, sons, brothers, uncles, nephews, cousins, fathers-in-law, sons-in-law, brothers-in-law or husbands of widows of other generals.

While nepotism assisted a military career, personal contact with Bonaparte and alignment with his meteoric political career were even more important. The crucial moments were those of his early years – the Army of Italy, the Egyptian campaign and Brumaire. Careers were made or broken in those years, dependent more on attitudes adopted than on strictly military achievement. For example, Berthier, Bessières, Lannes, Andréossy, Bertrand, Marmont, Murat and Duroc were close to Bonaparte in all three episodes and were appropriately rewarded. Masséna, Suchet, Clarke, Brune, Sébastiani and Bernadotte established or consolidated their careers in Italy. The Egyptian expedition forged particularly close ties, which were to last through the Empire. The future paymaster-general Estève's career began there; Davout, who was presented to Bonaparte by Desaix and immediately despatched to Toulon to prepare the Egyptian expedition, owed his spectacular career to this. Junot and Menou were repeatedly offered career opportunities by Napoleon, despite the excesses of the former and mediocrity of the latter. It would be tedious to prolong the list.

As revealing are the instances of officers whose careers were broken by attitudes judged unacceptable by Bonaparte's close entourage. General Damas, Kléber's protégé in Egypt, was accused by Menou, after his patron's murder, of the defeat at Canope (21 March 1801) and was disgraced, along with his brother, also a general. Reynier, Damas' superior at Canope, was placed under arrest by Menou and subsequently exiled to Italy. Napoleon himself oscillated in his willingness to distinguish military capacities from personal or political prejudices. He persecuted Moreau and distanced Jourdan from a political role, because of their consolidated reputations as republican generals; Macdonald was removed from his post in command of Versailles four days after Brumaire, then kept at a distance and disgraced after defending Moreau in 1804; Miollis was removed from active service after voting against Bonaparte's nomination as consul for life. Gouvion Saint-Cyr, on the other hand, who refused to make his soldiers swear the oath of loyalty to the consuls after Brumaire or to allow them to join in the highly organised appeals to Napoleon to become Emperor in 1804, had an important, albeit bumpy, career, and was finally appointed marshal in 1812. Grouchy, who protested against the consulate, was deployed actively throughout the period, even if he was appointed marshal only during the Hundred Days. Even Augereau, who initially opposed Brumaire, enjoyed a successful career with ample material rewards, once he rallied to Napoleon.

For officers who had fallen foul of Napoleon or his closest followers, or disagreed with his trajectory, service in the vassal states offered the major outlet, at least until the later years, when the military demands of Spain, Germany and finally Russia led to their recall. Some had chosen to move voluntarily into this outer circle, like Martel, aide-de-camp to General Fiorella in the Army of Italy in the 1790s, who followed his general to serve the Italian republic and kingdom; or the younger General Damas, who entered Louis of Holland's service in 1806, resigned over Holland's annexation, moving on to Jerome of Westphalia, in whose army he was killed at the battle of Moscow (Borodino) in 1812; or the former mercenary General van Hogendorp, who became minister of war in the kingdom of Holland, before returning to Napoleon's service with its annexation. Others requested permission to serve in these vassal states in the hope of returning to favour. Thus Macdonald, after his disgrace over the Moreau affair, was allowed to enter Joseph of Naples' service in 1807, and then that of Eugene de Beauharnais in 1809, before his role at Wagram got him a marshal's baton; Reynier became minister of war at Naples before his recall to the Grande Armée in 1809; Miollis served in the army of the kingdom of Italy and in this capacity was ordered by Napoleon to occupy Rome, in 1808, where he remained until 1814; Michaud entered Louis of Holland's service in 1806, was recalled by Napoleon as governor of the Hanseatic cities, but because of his excessive rectitude was soon removed, and ended his career in Jerome of Westphalia's army.

The great majority of this multitude of generals enjoyed a regular and undistinguished career, which (appropriately) has left little trace in the historical record. Among the more able – or more powerfully sponsored – Napoleon chose to use some in three roles which demanded different capacities than the purely military: as commanders of occupied territories, as administrators, or as diplomats. These roles were not mutually exclusive, for some generals in the course of their careers fulfilled two or, like Brune, even all three of such functions. Their employment by Napoleon responded to the accelerating demands imposed by the dynamism of the Empire, as well as reflecting the importance assigned to the military.

Little need be said about military occupation, as its very repetition must have accustomed commanders to its techniques, which became increasingly regulated. The underlying principles – maintenance of public order and exaction of taxes – implied strict control over the comportment of the soldiers and continuity of administrative operations. Typical were Napoleon's orders to Oudinot for the occupation of Neuchâtel:

> You must go to Neuchâtel and take possession of this principality in my name. You will order that all taxes continue to be raised as normal. You will take care not to change the customs barriers that separate Neuchâtel from France. . . . You will confirm all the authorities in office. . . . You will ensure the maintenance of good discipline. You will settle your troops so that they can rest. You will speak well of Prussia. You will print and display the following proclamation: 'In the name of H.M. the Emperor and King, my sovereign, I have taken possession of the principality of Neuchâtel, which the king of Prussia has ceded him. The troops under my command will maintain strict discipline. On the other hand, they must be welcomed by the inhabitants with appropriate sentiments.' You will change nothing in the administration until I give you new orders.[21]

The clear concern to obtain at least passive acceptance by the population – a tenet first applied explicitly and effectively by Brune in his pacification of the *chouan* departments of western France in 1800 – reflected the negative experiences of the revolutionary occupations and the permanent worry over undisciplined soldiery.

If the generals appointed to act as governors of cities or larger territories regarded their post as temporary and transitional, particular conditions of warfare offered possibilities to commanders to transform military occupations into more prolonged and complex structures of administration. This was the case of Calabria, where the difficulties of repressing the revolt led to the delegation of civilian authority by Joseph to a special commissaire, combining military and civilian powers, with the authority to report judicial abuses (such as the acquittal of captured 'brigands') and make appointments to local offices. Above all, it was characteristic of Spain, where the inability of the French armies to inflict a decisive defeat on Wellington and the guerrilla forces led to a dual system of administration, divided between Joseph and the more successful generals, with Napoleon's connivance.

The Emperor's unilateral decision of 8 February 1810 to place Catalonia, Aragon, Navarre and the Basque country under military rule in effect subordinated his brother's authority to that of the generals. General Barthélemy, for example, ignored the protests of the civilian intendant at Santander, Aldamar, in exacting 300,000 francs to cover the costs of his troops, and then imprisoned the unfortunate administrator of the *rentes* for trying to carry out his duty. The two most successful military leaders, Marshals Soult and Suchet, acted as virtual viceroys for nearly three years in Andalusia and Aragon. In an attempt to reaffirm his authority, Joseph sent a commissaire with special powers and the rank of minister to Andalusia, but this royal representative, count de Montarco, rapidly identified himself with Soult. Suchet disciplined his troops, ensured honest public accounts and regular justice and reopened the academy of Zaragoza; but he refused to accept the nomination by Joseph's government of a councillor of state and three prefects to administer Valencia. Such were the possibilities open to ambitious generals in special circumstances at the periphery of the Empire. The consequences could be disastrous, as the military and personal rivalries of these proconsuls effectively destroyed the unity of action required to defeat the exceptionally tenacious enemies in the Peninsula. Marbot, aide-de-camp to Masséna in 1810, recalled disconsolately Suchet's failure to assist Saint-Cyr, Victor's lethargy in supporting Soult's invasion of Portugal, the refusal of Ney, Reynier, Soult and Bessières to accept Masséna's authority.[22]

Employment as administrators would seem to have been more appropriate to the talents of military officers. Inevitably, some of the generals closest to Bonaparte were appointed to the council of state in the early Consulate: Caffarelli, Admiral Bruix, Dejean, Mathieu Dumas, Gouvion Saint-Cyr, Bernadotte (replacing the uncomfortable Brune), the former deputies Lacuée and Jourdan. As France's territories expanded, the skills of officers in specialised branches were put to good use. Bertrand was sent to Bavaria in 1805 to train its army. General Wirion, commander of the gendarmerie in the Sambre-et-Meuse army in 1794, was responsible for setting up the gendarmerie in the nine departments of newly annexed Belgium (1795–7), then in the Rhineland departments (1798), Piedmont and the Cisalpine (1801). His colleague General Radet, who had reorganised the gendarmerie in the Midi in 1798 and then throughout France in 1804, carried out inspections of the gendarmerie in Piedmont and Genoa, descended on Naples in 1806 to set up its gendarmerie, repeated the exercise in Tuscany in 1809 and then Rome (where he was personally responsible for arresting the Pope), before moving on to the Hamburg gendarmerie in 1811. Chasseloup-Laubat, commander of the engineer corps in the Army of Italy (1796, 1799) was responsible for the fortifications in northern Italy (1801–5, 1808–9) and Holland (1811).

But irrespective of specialised skills, with the Consulate the responsibilities of commanders of military occupations began to be extended officially to include the installation of the new civilian structures of administration that characterised absorption within the Empire. Napoleon's brother-in-law, General Leclerc, was sent as governor-general, combining military and civil authority, to St Domingo, where he died (1802); Jourdan was appointed administrator-general in Piedmont (1801); Menou, Jourdan's successor in Piedmont (1802), was subsequently appointed commander of the Italian departments (1805), governor-general of Tuscany (1808) and then of Venice (1809); Marmont was both army commander and governor-general of Dalmatia (1806–8) and then of the Illyrian provinces (1809–11), as was his successor Bertrand (1811–12); Davout was governor-general of the grand-duchy of Warsaw (1807) and then of the Hanseatic cities (1810). In contrast to the later 1790s, when generals had set up and intervened in civilian administrations often against the orders of the Directory, the conjunction of military and civilian authority in the person of a general was congruent with the techniques of expansion of the Empire. Between the authority of these governors-general and that of the viceroys in Spain, the distinction was not one of effective power, but of a legitimation conferred by the confines of the Empire. Outside these confines, France was represented officially by its diplomats, who – in extreme cases of areas of prolonged warfare like Spain – were replaced by military viceroys; inside the constantly redrawn lines of annexation, military governors-general were nominated to meet the same needs. Increasingly, these military representatives of Napoleon required civilian experts.

THE DIPLOMATS

The diplomats constituted a substantial and distinctive group, like the generals, although their numbers were always far smaller: career personnel at the ministry at Paris never rose to more than 55 (or 75 including translators and temporary employees), diplomats in the field averaged around 130, with a further 250 in the consular service.[23] The cost of the diplomatic service was little more than 1 per cent of the French budget throughout the Napoleonic period. In some respects these figures provide an accurate reflection of the subordination of the normal channels of international relations during these years. But they are misleading as an indicator of the importance of the functions assigned to diplomats in the Napoleonic vision of the world.

The ministry of foreign affairs had been badly disrupted during the Revolutionary years because of its identification with the ancien regime in terms of functions and aristocratic personnel. By the end of the Jacobin Year II, France had only four accredited diplomatic representatives, all in neutral states. Under the Directory, Delacroix, Talleyrand and Reinhardt reconstructed the professionality of the ministry, but by Brumaire there were still only eight posts abroad. France's diplomatic representation fluctuated along with Napoleon's manipulation of Europe's political geography, expanding or contracting according to the state of peace and extension of the Empire's frontiers. But the relationship was fairly loose, since the extinction of sovereign states consequential upon the expansion of the Empire was partly compensated by the creation of vassal states, and because Napoleon and Talleyrand tended to maintain the traditional ancien regime pattern of representation, despite the political changes. Thus, out of a total of twenty-nine diplomatic posts in 1802, there were nine in Germany, besides Berlin and Vienna; later, eleven posts were accredited to Rhine Confederation states; in Italy, where Napoleon progressively swallowed up the former states, he maintained a diplomatic mission at Lucca, his sister Elisa's mini-duchy, as late as 1809. The number of consulates (responsibility for which had been transferred from the ministry of marine to foreign affairs in 1793) remained stable at ninety to ninety-five until 1810, despite annexations and the interruptions of war, as posts were maintained or newly opened to monitor the economic blockade.

Appointment to the ministry or to posts abroad, among diplomats as with generals, was strongly influenced by family patronage and recommendation. Roederer's son was one of Talleyrand's three personal secretaries; consul Lebrun, minister Chaptal, even Lafayette gave a helping hand to protégés or kin; diplomatic bureaucrats in service, like Caillard, assisted their relatives. Professional continuity had survived through the Revolutionary years, particularly in the persons of Alsatians and Germans, often trained at Strasbourg University, like Reinhardt, Otto and Bacher. Their presence certainly assisted the professional and linguistic competence of the diplomatic representation in Germany throughout the period, just as the earlier experiences as consul of Hauterive and Dhermand facilitated the commitment to reconstitute an ample consular network.

The concern to provide specialist training certainly existed. A school of oriental languages to train interpreters or *drogmans* (1795) was maintained at Paris and Constantinople. Hauterive was responsible for a school for aspiring diplomats (April 1797): the pupils needed to know French, Latin, one or two modern languages and the geography of universal history; they were to be taught public law, modern political history, the constitutions and 'statistics of states', and above all analysis of reports in order to form judgement and acquire method and style; they were to serve in both the ministerial bureaux and abroad. But in practice, less than one-third of these 'aspirants' made a career in the service, as advancement (a note from the ministry observed in 1805) 'depends entirely on the connections their relatives have with the persons responsible for nominations or with the political agents themselves, who normally obtain satisfaction if they ask that their protégés accompany them on their political missions'.[24] An attempt to extend to the diplomatic service the use of the council of state as a training ground for a future professional class by reserving posts of legation secretaries to auditors (1806) was effectively reversed by the ministerial *éminence grise*, Hauterive, who utilised it to obtain nomination as auditors for some young diplomats already in service. In practice, there was no bureaucratic development of professionalism – except for linguistic requirements – but a professionalism acquired in the field by a core of long-serving diplomats, like Reinhardt, Bacher, Helflinger, Jacob or Siméon. In the consular service, especially in the earlier period of reconstruction, the stress on experience, continuity and local knowledge – and hence on family ties – was even greater; only in the later years of the Empire did military events prise consuls out of their favoured posts in Spain and Portugal to the cold north German coasts.

Personal appointment by Napoleon, in so small a corps, inevitably played a disproportionate influence on career prospects, as he chose men without previous diplomatic or consular experience. The results could be disastrous, as in the case of Chateaubriand, nominated secretary of the legation at Rome on the recommendation of Fontanes and Napoleon's sister Elisa. Chateaubriand later complained that his duties were as insignificant as those of an office-boy in a prefecture. But this was hardly surprising, given his disregard for diplomatic protocol, his predilection for royalist exiles, his romantic identification with the myth of Rome, and his conviction that he was predestined personally to reconcile Christianity and politics. As the ambassador, Cardinal Fesch, wrote in irritation to his nephew, the First Consul Bonaparte, Chateaubriand was 'a man launched by a faction, a Doctor who wants to dogmatise, a writer incapable of satisfaction just from producing books'.[25]

Initially the major beneficiaries of Napoleon's personal choice of diplomats were the generals. To represent France diplomatically with military men was a logical sequence to the coup of Brumaire – and in some cases compensation for aid received. In twenty-nine diplomatic postings, seventeen generals were named under the Consulate as head of mission, and eleven during the Empire. Between diplomatic and consular posts, seventy-one officers were named as heads over the entire period. During the brief spell of general peace in 1801–2, virtually all the ambassadors or plenipotentiaries were generals – Beurnonville in Berlin and then Madrid, Brune at Constantinople, Andréossy at London, Clarke in Florence, Mathieu Dumas at Naples, Jourdan at Milan, Gouvion Saint-Cyr at Madrid, Hédouville at St Petersburg, Lannes at Lisbon, Macdonald at Copenhagen, Ney at Berne, Turreau at Washington. Many of them insisted on bringing a full military 'household' with them, causing some friction with the ministry of foreign affairs about responsibility for the costs. Other generals, particularly close to Napoleon, were sent on special missions: Duroc to Berlin, Basel, Vienna, St Petersburg and Copenhagen; Savary in 1805 to Alexander I as a cover to spy on the Austro-Russian forces.

Many of these generals were ill-suited for their diplomatic duties, and some clearly preferred the battlefield. Gouvion Saint-Cyr floundered amidst the diplomatic intrigues of Madrid of 1801–2; Ney found himself a diplomat *malgré lui* as military commander in Switzerland, through the failure of his civilian predecessors to work out a viable constitutional settlement. Brune, like Lannes, tried to shorten his term of office. Junot at Lisbon, like Gardane at Teheran, simply abandoned their posts when they heard that the fighting had started again.

On occasions these military diplomats were used to impress the

Court to which they were sent: almost all the ambassadors to Constantinople were generals, starting with Brune. Some, under the Consulate, acted as virtual proconsuls, like Dejean at Genoa or Jourdan in Piedmont. In other cases, their military qualifications fitted them particularly to report on potential enemy forces, like Andréossy at Vienna in 1806, who was accompanied by the future General Mériage as secretary; both of them were to return in 1809 in military command of Vienna. Very few were used repeatedly as diplomats, to the extent of abandoning their vocation: Beurnonville, ambassador at Berlin (1799) and Madrid (1802), was then retired to the Senate; Andréossy, a military engineer, served as ambassador in London (1802–3), Vienna (1806) and Constantinople (1812–14); Caulaincourt, Talleyrand's protégé, was regarded as particularly suited as an ancien regime noble to be ambassador at St Petersburg (1807–11), subsequently becoming Napoleon's foreign minister (1813–14). All in all, Napoleon's initial experiences of using generals as diplomatic representatives would seem to have made him gradually more wary of their suitability.

Increasingly, with the return of émigré families, especially from 1810, aristocrats resumed their traditional role in the diplomatic service: between 1800–8 and 1812–13 the proportion of aristocratic heads of missions rose from one-third to 60 per cent, and at all levels noble diplomats tended to be younger than non-nobles. The expansion of the Empire marginally increased the aristocratic element, as Napoleon appointed the Piedmontese San Marzano to the embassy at Berlin and the Belgian Mercy-Argenteau to Munich. Turnover tended to be limited, advancement prospects uncertain, particularly given these exogenous influences. One consequence was that many able men, in both the diplomatic and consular services, preferred to turn elsewhere. Fauvel, vice-consul at Athens, was unperturbed, given his passion for archaeology. For the young Roederer, foreign affairs was only a staging post, before his appointment as auditor and then prefect; Marivault and Jordan followed a similar path. The young Siméon, after postings to Florence and Rome, took service (like his father) under Jerome of Westphalia; Jacob moved his career to the kingdom of Italy; Chateaubriand and the young Portalis, both promoted rapidly to Rome and Ratisbon, abandoned the service. The most senior of the consuls, Coquebert, after serving in Hamburg, Amsterdam, London and Dublin, made his career in the ministries of the interior and commerce.

Napoleon never underestimated the importance of the diplomatic service in France's international relations. Stipends of foreign affairs bureaucrats were higher than for corresponding grades in other ministries; bonuses were given for successful negotiations, as well as honours and titles. Outward display was of importance to uphold France's prestige and justified expense: Andréossy, as ambassador at London, received 240,000 francs a year, Caulaincourt at St Petersburg 480,000 in order to maintain an appropriate style. Napoleon granted Talleyrand's successor as foreign minister, Champagny, additional funds, as 'my intention is that my minister for foreign affairs should have more livery, ostentation, servants and ceremony than the minister of the interior'.[26] Great stress was placed on the quality of the highly visible social activities at the embassies, with fêtes and receptions: Madame Lannes' balls at Lisbon were renowned.

The diplomats served the customary two functions of their trade – as sources of information and as agents of their country's policies – but in a more specific and integrated manner than was the norm. Despite Napoleon's correspondence with his generals in the field and his family sovereigns and his use of experts and spies on special missions, diplomatic reports remained his main and most regular source of information about the external world. Napoleon insisted on daily reports from the minister, as well as the texts of all important despatches; at one moment he even demanded to see all the diplomatic correspondence, although he soon accepted the need to filter the mass of paper within the ministry. As the demands for information steadily increased, the department reminded its representatives 'that they should neglect no detail, however small, if it can shed light on the state of the country, the spirit of the Court, the character and attitudes of influential persons'.[27] The demands on the consuls were even greater: no doubt bowing to the statistical fashion of those years, in 1802 Talleyrand sent a circular to all consuls, asking for periodic commercial statistics, with a model questionnaire specifying the information required, sometimes dating back to 1792. Following the blockade decrees of 1806 ever more frequent reports were demanded on the state of commerce, shipping movements, trading practices, food supplies, grain prices, monetary exchange rates and smuggling.

High priority was obviously placed on military information. The Cadix consul-general sent detailed reports on the movements of British squadrons in 1805; Ornano, consul-general at Cagliari, reported on the Sardinian army and the island's fortifications, should Napoleon decide on an invasion. In 1805 Otto at Munich and Bacher at Ratisbon sent precise information about the position of the

Austrian armies that enabled Napoleon to trap them at Ulm. In 1811–12, Bignon, resident at Warsaw, made up for the inability of the ambassadors at St Petersburg, Caulaincourt and Lauriston, to send reliable information on the Russian forces by setting up a network of Polish spies in Russia's western provinces.

The most continuous function of the diplomats, besides reporting information, was to act as instruments of propaganda. As Hauterive stated in 1812:

> One of the responsibilities of the ministry of foreign affairs, whenever hostilities commence again, is to prove that France has always faithfully fulfilled her commitments to peace and that the crime of aggression must be imputed to the governments against whom she is at war.[28]

Regular circulars were sent to all legations outlining the French viewpoint. Military victories, the solidity of the imperial regime, Napoleon's personal popularity, the lies of allied propaganda about the impact of the Spanish war on French opinion, were main themes of the diplomats' united front.

In allied or satellite states, diplomats were expected, sometimes even encouraged, to play a more leading role. At Danzig, Massias, jointly with the military governor Rapp, employed the *Danziger Zeitung* as a means to rally opinion. At Warsaw, Bignon was officially responsible for recruiting and equipping Polish troops, besides his indefatigable involvement in guiding the creation of the new state's administrative structures and persuading the faction-ridden nobility to work together. In general, the diplomats' responsibilities in dependent states were to ensure respect of the blockade and regularity in payment of subsidies and recruitment of troops. In neutral states, besides the traditional role of winning a favourable attitude towards their country, on occasions they reverted to earlier expertise: when British fleets attacked Copenhagen (1801) and Constantinople (1807) the French ambassadors, Generals Victor and Sébastiani, hastened to organise their defences.

Napoleon's ambitions necessitated an active diplomatic and consular corps, not just in Europe, but in the Levant, the United States and even further afield. The recurrent mirage of the Orient, as much as the need to neutralise Russia, explains not only his consistent concern for representation at Constantinople (where generals were thought more likely to impress the divan), but also the despatch of Sébastiani on a secret mission to Egypt and Palestine already in 1802, missions and a legation at Teheran (from 1805), even the nomination of consuls to the Cape and Macao (1802). Given Napoleon's highly personal direction of foreign affairs, his diplomatic representatives enjoyed virtually no autonomy. At most, like Sébastiani in Turkey or Alquier in Sweden, they were pawns in a vast game of chess whose credibility could be burnt by sudden changes of diplomatic alliances. In his relations with states that remained at least formally independent, Napoleon's diplomats, like his generals and senior bureaucrats, were expendable tools of conquest.

THE PROFESSIONALS OF ANNEXATION

Repeated seizures of territory on the scale of Directorial-Napoleonic France required personnel with particular political and administrative skills to absorb them. A rapid glance at the careers of some representative figures involved in the mechanics of occupation offers some insight into the gradual emergence of a class of civilian professionals, convinced of the potential of modern administration and expert in its application. As always, neat classifications break down before the realities of the overlap of functions and the highly personalised careers of individuals under Napoleon. But a study of the men responsible for the civil administration of occupied territories merits attention.

Many of the officials involved in the multiple forms of occupation of the consular and imperial years gained their initial experience as members of the Revolutionary assemblies sent into the field as commissaires.[29] François-Joseph Rudler had served in the Legislative assembly before transforming the left bank of the Rhine into four departments of France; A.-F. Miot de Mélito, a *feuillant* in 1792, was commissaire at Florence, Rome and in Corsica in 1795, minister-plenipotentiary in Piedmont in 1796 and despatched to Holland in 1798; Ange-Marie d'Eymar was a deputy to the Estates-General before serving as commissaire to the Cisalpine republic in the Year VI and to the provisional administration in Piedmont in 1798–9; the notorious Antoine-Christophe Saliceti, fellow Corsican and patron of Bonaparte, was also a deputy to the Estates-General, as well as a member of the 1792 Convention, who acted as commissaire in Corsica, Oneglia and Genoa between 1793 and 1797, and intrigued unofficially at Genoa, Florence and Rome in 1798–9. With the exception of Saliceti, almost all these politicians had opposed the Jacobins and some had had to flee or hide during Year II.

Besides the assemblies, alternative paths of experience were service in a ministry or an army, or previous experience abroad. Claude Petiet, whom Napoleon nominated to govern Lombardy in 1800–1, had started his career as an ordnance officer in the army in 1790 and had served in both the Directory Legislative assemblies and as minister of war. Charles-Etienne Coquebert de Montbret, who was to have a brilliant career as head of the statistical bureau in the ministry of the interior and then secretary-general of the ministry of manufactures, had started as consul at Hamburg for nearly ten years before the Revolution and was to be employed by Napoleon in the delicate posts of consul at London during the peace of Amiens and then as general commissioner to establish the excise system on shipping on the Rhine in 1805.

By Brumaire, most of these men were aged about 40 (the oldest, Eymar and Petiet, were born in 1747 and 1749; all the others between 1755 and 1762). They owed their appointments after Brumaire to their previous experience, or because of the patronage of the inner circle close to Napoleon. Thus L. A. Fauvelet de Bourrienne, whose reputation rests on his suspect memoirs and his corrupt practices as chargé d'affaires at Hamburg from 1805 until his clamorous dismissal in 1813, had started his career in the embassy in Vienna in 1788, continuing to serve in Leipzig and Warsaw until 1792, but owed his progress to his position close to Napoleon as personal secretary at Leoben in 1797, then at Campoformio, on the Egyptian expedition, and in Italy in 1800. J. A. M. Agar, count Mosburg, owed his entire career to his fellow citizen from Cahors, Murat: commissaire with the provisional administration in Tuscany in 1801, member of the Legislative body for the Lot department in Year XII, he accompanied Murat on the 1805 campaign, became chief minister in his duchy of Berg, followed Murat to Naples in 1808 where he was minister of finances, and got imperial recognition of his Berg title as comte Mosburg through the direct intervention of Caroline and Murat in 1812. F.V.J. Lespérut, a friend of the *idéologue* Volney, was secretary to General Berthier during the Consulate, briefly secretary-general of Berthier's ministry of war and appointed to the Legislative body in 1802, before moving into the entourage of Elisa Bonaparte Baciocchi as administrator of her new duchy of Piombino in 1805; recalled by Berthier to act as governor of his principality of Neuchâtel (1806), he reported to Berthier at the general headquarters at Warsaw, but was snatched by Napoleon to act as administrator-general of finances in occupied Silesia (1807), returning to Neuchâtel only in 1810.

Lespérut's experience is revealing of the career mobility of those able to hold the favour of powerful patrons. He moved essentially in what could be described as the outer circle of service, in the new states created by Napoleon. To be employed in the outer circle was not an unambiguous proof of success, nor was it without its dangers. Jean-Claude Beugnot had been recommended by General Beurnonville to Lucien Bonaparte after Brumaire and had played a major role in the creation of the prefectoral system, then serving ably as prefect of the Seine-Inférieure department (1800–6) before being called to the council of state. As minister of finances in the new kingdom of Westphalia he felt particularly exposed because of the conflicting orders of Jerome and Napoleon and returned to Paris within a year; as commissaire and minister of finances at Berg, he felt cheated when Roederer was appointed as his superior and secretary of state in 1810 and requested (in vain) to be transferred to Holland. Joseph Bonaparte's entourage at Naples was heavily marked by Frenchmen who had fallen into disgrace: the former Jacobin P. J. Briot (a protégé of Lucien Bonaparte) was intendant in the Abruzzi, Saliceti (whom Napoleon mistrusted, but who had once acted as Joseph's secretary) was minister of police. Roederer himself, who had rewritten the Cisalpine constitution, but had then fallen out of favour in 1802 and been retired to the Senate, was appointed as minister of finances at Naples only through Joseph's insistence. Faipoult de Maisoncelles, who had a chequered career in the Revolutionary years, culminating as Directory commissaire contesting General Championnet's creation of the Neapolitan republic, had been dismissed from his post as prefect of the Belgian department of Escaut (1808) and was only saved by Joseph, who appointed him councillor of state in Spain. Gérando found himself removed from the list of councillors of state, while serving as commissaire in Catalonia in 1812, like Siméon in the duchy of Berg.

For the military, despatch to these outlying vassal states could also be a sign of disfavour and risky in its consequences. Marshal Masséna, temporarily out of favour with Napoleon through his financial malpractices, constantly demanded his recall from Naples. General Reynier, who had killed in a duel his former superior officer in Egypt, was exiled to Naples. General Damas had been retired in 1803, arrested with Moreau in 1804 and managed to remake his career only through Murat's insistence that he was the ideal man to create an army in Berg. General Lamarque refused to follow Joseph from Naples to Spain as it meant resigning from the Grande Armée: 'I wish to remain French'.[30] Whether or not Napoleon refused to grant the Bavarian chief minister Montgelas' request for the services of General Bertrand,[31] it seems probable that such service in a vassal state would have harmed his subsequent rapid career, which was to end with his personal accompaniment of the Emperor to St Helena.

Service in the new vassal states was ambiguous: it could signify equally a sign of promotion in a promising career, recall from the oblivion of previous disgrace, temporary banishment, or permanent exile into the outer circle. Despatch to territories where Napoleon intended to maintain direct control, by contrast, became an increasingly professional affair. Sometimes continuity had been ensured by the appointment of the transitional administrators as the first prefects, like Shée, Jolivet and Jeanbon-Saint-André in the Rhineland in 1800; the same method was to be employed with the transformation of Parma into the department of the Taro by Nardon (1806–8), and the creation of the Valais into the Simplon department (1810), where the diplomatic resident Derville-Maléchard became prefect. Expertise became a requirement, with teams being sent in to adapt the existing systems to French structures at successive annexations. In Piedmont in 1801–2, French technicians of finances, the judicial system, the gendarmerie and ecclesiastical matters were joined by Prina, the future minister of finances in the kingdom of Italy. When Liguria was annexed in 1805, not only was the former consul Lebrun sent to head the team, but so too was the minister of finances Gaudin, who was subsequently to be despatched to Holland in 1811 with the same task of reorganising the financial system. Daru, intendant-general of the civil list, was made responsible for the administration and exaction of the huge indemnity imposed on conquered Prussia in 1806. Coquebert de Montbret, who had served in Amsterdam and was an acknowledged expert on Customs and Excise, was detached from the ministry of the interior on a special mission to Holland after its annexation to organise the new Customs line.

By the middle years of the Empire, service in the newly occupied or annexed territories became a step in the career of young auditors, often in place of a sub-prefecture. Bruguière de Barante's vocal dislike of his posting as intendant to Danzig, Warsaw and Silesia (1806–7) led to his downgrading as sub-prefect, before promotion to prefect. Rouen des Mallets was intendant of Ragusa and Carniole in the Illyrian provinces for two years (1811–13) before appointment as prefect; Stassart was intendant of the Tyrol, Elbing, Königsberg, east Prussia and Berlin (1806–7), before becoming sub-prefect and then prefect; Cesare Balbo was secretary to the junta absorbing Tuscany and the *consulta* annexing the rump of the Papal states (1808–10);

Nicolai was intendant at Vilna (1811–12) before becoming prefect of the Piedmontese Doire department.

The growing professionalism was reflected in linguistic expectations. If some of the older French ministers serving in the vassal states – like Agar and Beugnot in Berg and Siméon in Westphalia – did not know German, by the later years language became one of the necessary qualifications. Italian, still the language of culture, seemed to have presented no problems. But in Germany, the need for personnel in the new Hanseatic departments and the continuous occupations led to a major shake-up of French diplomatic representatives in 1811–12.

There had emerged a category of senior bureaucrats of territorial occupations, skilled in the art of inducting newly annexed regions into the French methods of administration, and able to pass on their expertise to the young auditors who accompanied them. A few examples are sufficient to illustrate the point. L. J. E. Dauchy, a moderate of the Estates-General and Directory assemblies, who had served as prefect in the Aisne and Piedmontese Marengo departments, and as councillor of state since 1802, was proposed by Eugene de Beauharnais as prefect of the newly annexed department of the Adriatico (Venice). He was then appointed administrator-general of finances and domains in Dalmatia in 1806, intendant for the treasury in the junta responsible for assimilating Tuscany in 1808, and then intendant-general in the Illyrian provinces (1809). F. L. R. Mouchard de Chaban, whose competence as a prefect successively in the Rhineland Rhin-et-Moselle and Belgian Dyle departments led to his nomination as *maître des requêtes* in 1802, was appointed to the Tuscan junta (1808), then as intendant of the interior and finances in the Hanseatic departments in 1810 and intendant-general of finances of the 32nd military division (north Germany) in 1813. J. M. de Gérando, who had fled from the Terror to Naples and then from the Fructidor purge to Germany, was seconded from the ministry of the interior to assist in the annexation of Genoa in 1805, the Tuscan junta in 1808 and the Roman *consulta* in 1809, returning as councillor of state until he was once more sent into the field as intendant for upper Catalonia. C. F. Lebrun was sent successively to Liguria (1805–7) and Holland (1810–13) to supervise their absorption into the Empire. The reluctance of the young auditor Balbo to serve in the Tuscan and Roman special commissions of annexation was anomalous. H. C. F. Barthélemy enthusiastically seized the opportunity offered by his knowledge of German to serve in a newly absorbed Hanseatic department; A. Petit de Beauverger specialised in the North Sea area, as secretary-general of the commission responsible for the organisation of the Hanseatic departments (1810–12), before his appointment as prefect of Ems-Occidental (1813).

The pace of annexation had produced its professional specialists, senior bureaucrats of the absorption of conquered territories. Few if any were appointed specifically with this purpose in mind. Most had acquired experience in the council of state, where it was not uncommon for its members to be employed in specialised services or ministries.[32] Nevertheless, if initially their deployment in occupied territories was the outcome of their duties and skills within the normal course of administration, they developed into a specialist group. With exemplary rapidity, they rendered the areas under their control administratively similar to France, before handing over responsibility to the prefects. It seems likely that their physical presence in the territory was as important as their professional training in order to achieve such radical restructuring. The counterproof is offered by the principality of Neuchâtel where virtually nothing was changed in eight years: its ruler, Marshal Berthier, never set foot in it, while his representative Lespérut spent only a few months there intermittently. The accumulated experience of these senior bureaucrats presumably would have been passed on to the generation of auditors. Time was lacking and was abruptly brought to a halt by military defeat.

THE PREFECTS

Assimilation to the cultural model of France, and even more absorption within its frontiers, was recognised as a lengthy process. If military means were necessary to impose French hegemony, only civilian rule could achieve the broad social consensus on which the solidity of the regime necessarily rested. Like their Revolutionary predecessors (or most imperialist ideologists), the most convinced of the Napoleonic elite do not seem to have regarded the ultimate achievement of a new Europe fashioned in the image of France as a chimera, but to have accepted that it would require a new generation to overcome the deep-rooted superstitions and prejudices inherited from the past. In the meantime it was the task of the administration to create the conditions which would facilitate and accelerate the process of acculturation.

The prefects personified this responsibility. Obviously they could not act alone, nor were they judged omnicompetent. Local collaboration was essential for the functioning of the administration, from sub-prefects to judges, from financial agents to mayors. In the satel-

lite states – like Bavaria, Holland or Warsaw – French presence
(apart from the military) was normally limited to diplomatic representation and temporary missions by experts; even in the
Bonaparte family kingdoms (except for Naples), French advisers
were not more than a handful. The role of these local elites, whether
in the annexed territories or the formally independent states, will be
considered later. For the present, in this discussion of the tools of
conquest, it is necessary to look at the composition of the prefectoral
corps responsible for administering the annexed territories.

Between 1800 and 1814 306 prefects were nominated; we have
details of the careers of 281.[33] Political patronage inevitably played a
major role in the initial appointments, given the rapidity with which
ninety-seven prefects were chosen: about twenty prefects had studied
or served with Napoleon in his youth, seven had belonged to the
scientific commission of the Egyptian campaign, two had been diplomats in Italy. The Beauharnais clan, Lucien Bonaparte as minister of
the interior (aided by Beugnot), Talleyrand, General Clarke and the
two Consuls Cambacérès and Lebrun exercised considerable patronage, while family and personal relationships played, as always, an
important role. In later years, patronage and kin remained important, but their effects were more diffused.

Politically, the prefects were men of the Revolution, few of whom
had administrative experience before 1789. Over 40 per cent of all
prefects had belonged to a Revolutionary assembly, but inevitably as
the years passed the proportion dropped; by 1807 it was 38 per cent,
by 1813 only 23 per cent. Socially, although bourgeois prefects always
remained a majority (61 per cent over the whole period), the proportion of nobles grew already under the Consulate and early Empire
with the return of the émigrés and the substantial increase in the
number of posts (23 per cent in 1800, 31 per cent in 1804, 39 per cent
in 1808, 41 per cent in 1813). It seems likely that, as in the diplomatic
service, these nobles made careers more rapidly than their bourgeois
peers; it is certain that they were given preference in nominations to
the more important departments.

But whether noble or bourgeois, administrative capacity was
always of prime importance. About sixty prefects of the initial list had
been members or presidents of departmental administrations, or
commissaires of the Directory supervising these local administrations, or mayors of large cities. Over the entire period, 32 per cent
of the prefects were recruited from the administration, having previously served as sub-prefects, secretaries-general, intendants of
occupied territories, bureaucrats, diplomats or consuls; 20 per cent

came from a legal background; the military provided 12 per cent of the prefects. As Whitcomb has shown, there was an increasing professionalisation of the prefectoral corps, with the proportion recruited from the administration rising from 15 per cent in 1802 to 41 per cent by 1811 and 47 per cent by 1814. A substantial number of initially nominated prefects were dismissed in the first three years, and major turnovers occurred again in 1810 and 1813, in the latter cases specifically to make way for younger qualified men. Over the entire period the average years of administrative experience of the prefects rose steadily – from 2.4 years in 1800 to 6.5 by 1805 and 10 years in 1812 – whereas their average age fell from 48 years (1808–10) to 45 following the turnovers of 1810 and 1813. As in other fields, it was the auditors who emerged as an increasingly important group: forty-two auditors in all were promoted to prefect, by 1813 one in four of the prefects came from their ranks.

Given these overall traits of the prefectoral body, it is useful to enquire whether the annexed departments were in any way distinctive. The language of 'reunion' preached uniformity, the transformation of the annexed territories into departments similar in all respects to those of 'ancienne' France. Later historiography, particularly of these annexed regions, often lamented that equal career opportunities were not available. In fact, only 32 prefects, or 12 per cent, came from outside France's pre-1789 frontiers, although the 43 annexed departments constituted one-third of the total 130 in the Empire. Among these thirty-two, the largest contingent came from Italy – thirteen or 5 per cent of all prefects (although the Italian departments numbered 11 per cent of the total) – followed by nine Belgians (3 per cent, with 7 per cent of the departments), seven Dutchmen (with the same number of departments), one German (eight departments) and two Swiss (one department, but with Geneva in another). The comparison worsens if the length of period of departmentalisation is taken into account, for the Belgians had become French since 1795, the Rhineland Germans in 1800, the Piedmontese since 1802, whereas the Dutch only in 1810. It is evident on these figures that the Germans in particular were discriminated against.

More significant is an analysis of the policy over appointment to prefectures within the annexed departments themselves. Of the total 281 prefects, 98 or 35 per cent were responsible at some stage for one of the 44 annexed departments.[34] The proportion who originated in these territories was remarkably high – of the total thirty-two 'new French' appointed as prefects throughout the Empire, twenty-five served in these new departments, equivalent to one of every four prefects. There was evidently a deliberate policy of favouring such appointments, whose evolution can be traced through successive phases. Initially only Frenchmen were appointed. All the seven prefects who served in the two departments of former Savoy and Geneva were French, as were fifteen of the sixteen who served in the four departments of the Rhineland left bank. The twenty-eight prefects who administered the nine Belgian departments included only two Italians and one Belgian. With the annexation of Piedmont, the policy seemed to change: of twenty-two prefects, nine were Italian, all except one from the former Sardinian state; two of the nine prefects of the three Genoese departments came from Genoa. But with the later annexations in central Italy, such consideration for local appointments vanished, with only one Italian (and then from a different state) out of nine prefects. In Holland, because of the particular circumstances, policy changed again, with seven Dutch and four Belgian appointments, compared to only three French. In the Hanseatic departments, evidently for linguistic reasons as well, three Belgians were appointed, alongside two French.[35]

A closer look at the twenty-four 'new French' prefects throws further light on the underlying policies. In Piedmont, the initial appointments to all six departments were of Italians, all except one from Piedmont or the ex-Sardinian county of Nice; in three departments the second nomination was also of a Piedmontese. Two of these prefects, Angelo Gandolfo and Carlo Giulio, were professors at the University of Turin; Giulio had been a member of the so-called 'Jacobin' triumvirate that collaborated with Jourdan. Giulio Robert, who died in office as prefect of the Tanaro department in 1803, had been a member of the Italian deputation to Paris during the 1798–9 retreat of the French armies, in the provisional administration in 1800, and Piedmontese minister to the Cisalpine government. Others came from noble families, often leading ones – like Giovanni Francesco San Martino della Motta or P. A. Biamino Arborio – but always with some previous political or intellectual qualification that brought them to the attention of the French authorities and explained their willingness to serve. Thus San Martino, a botanist, was a member of the Academy of Sciences, who had formed part of the provisional government in 1800 and of the municipal administration of Turin in 1801. Vittorio Federico Ercole della Villa di Villastellone, who had been chamberlain to the king of Sardinia, was nominated by Berthier to the Piedmontese Legislative assembly in 1800 before his appointment as prefect to the most important department, that of the

Po, where he served for four years. Giovanni Lorenzo Degregory di Marcorengo had taken a law degree, travelled widely in France, England and Germany before the Revolution, and been among the first in Italy to experiment with balloon air flights; he had already collaborated with the French in Year VII as commissaire in the Sesia tribunal, and became sub-prefect of Biella after Marengo, before his appointment as prefect of the Stura department, where he also served for four years, before his elevation to the Senate (1803) and as imperial count (1808).

With the annexation of the Ligurian republic, Napoleon nominated the most distinguished aristocrat, Gerolamo Durazzo, to act as prefect of Genoa as guarantee of a smooth transition; Durazzo had been a member of the executive committee and took constitutional responsibility with the return of the French in 1800, and had been appointed as the last doge of Genoa in 1802. The same stress on continuity is visible in Holland, where the initial Dutch prefects had all served Louis of Holland's administration as *landdrost*, usually for at least two years. Some, like P. Hofstede, had a more varied experience, as provisional secretary-general (1805) and *landdrost* successively of two provinces, Drenthe (1807) and Overijssel (1809); or C. G. Hultman, *landdrost* of Maasland in 1808, nominated prefect of the Vaucluse in 1810 before his appointment as prefect of the Bouches de Meuse.

Other 'new French' prefects had already entered French service before they were employed in their country of origin or neighbouring areas. Thus Biamino Arborio, who was initially appointed as a councillor of the prefecture in his home department of Sesia, was nominated sub-prefect at Lille and then Douai two years later, before his rapid promotion as prefect of the Stura department in 1803. P. C. G. de Coninck-Outrive had started his career in similar fashion as councillor of the prefecture in the department of the Lys, before his appointment as prefect of the Ain in 1802 and then of the Belgian department of Jemappes in 1805. To stress the distinction of national origin in these instances is somewhat arbitrary, for there is little to distinguish the career patterns of these 'new French' administrators from the 'old' French, except in linguistic capacities; even in this respect the Alsatians were as well qualified. Thus de Coninck, on the basis of his initial experience in the Ain, was evidently regarded as an able administrator whose origins and linguistic skills could be put to best use in the northern seaboard: from Jemappes, he was appointed successively to the Dutch department of Bouches de l'Escaut (1810) and then to Hamburg, capital of the Bouches de l'Elbe department (1811). But there was little to distinguish his career from that of S. L. J. Jannesson, an Alsatian (nine years de Coninck's junior), who started as councillor of the prefecture of the Haut-Rhin department, was appointed sub-prefect of Deux-Ponts in the Rhineland department of Mont-Tonnerre (1807) and then promoted as prefect of the northern Dutch department of Ems-Oriental (1810); Jannesson's family relationship (brother-in-law) with the Belgian auditor, count d'Arberg, may well have helped the latter's appointment as prefect of the Bremen department of the Bouches du Weser (1811) and then of Jannesson's original department of Mont-Tonnerre (December 1813). But if de Coninck and Arberg provide examples of 'new French' who continued to be deployed in regions with which they could be presumed to have a special affinity, this was hardly the case of Biamino Arborio, who was transferred from the Stura to the Belgian Lys department (1811), perhaps on the assumption that he had acquired knowledge of this northern French region during his early service as sub-prefect in the neighbouring department of the Nord. Arborio's career was paralleled by that of the Belgian B.-J. Holvoet, who started as a councillor in the prefecture of his native Lys department in Year XI, was appointed *maître des requêtes* in 1810 and director of the tobacco monopoly in 1811, before his appointment as prefect to the 'old' French department of the Loire (1812). The careers of Arborio and Holvoet were essentially similar to those of Frenchmen, who were transferred between 'old' and 'new' French departments, like C. Cochon de Lapparent, prefect of Vienne after Brumaire, who was transferred, to his despair, to the department of Deux-Nèthes; or A. Jubé de la Perelle, a member of the Tribunate in the Year VIII, prefect of the Doire (1808), and then of the Gers department (1813); or P. A. F. de Lezay-Marnésia, prefect of the Rhineland department of Rhin-et-Moselle (1806) and then of the Alsatian Bas-Rhin (1810).

A few of these 'old' French prefects were born in nearby regions. This was particularly marked among the Rhineland departments. Thus Lezay-Marnésia was born in the Jura; N. S. Simon, prefect of Roer (1800), was born at Colmar; J. C. F. de Ladoucette, born at Nancy, was transferred as prefect from the Hautes-Alpes to Roer (1809); J. Bexon d'Ormschwiller, prefect of the Sarre, was born in the Moselle area; and his successor, M. X. Keppler, in the Bas-Rhin. Such a choice of prefects of local origin is comparable to that of Flamands in the Hanseatic departments, based on linguistic and possibly cultural reasons, whereas the Italians and Dutch nominated as prefects in their home areas were appointed as a manifestation of continuity. Elsewhere, relative vicinity of birthplace to location of service would seem to be coincidental, and in any case far less significant than other factors, such as previous experience: Ange-Marie d'Eymar was not appointed as first prefect of the Genevan department of Léman because he was born at Forcalquier in the Basses-Alpes, but because as representative of the Directory in the Cisalpine republic and at Turin he had acquired considerable knowledge and contacts within the region.

The common denominator to the prefects in the new departments was experience, particularly in the administrative field. It was not unusual, particularly in the early annexations (Savoy, Belgium, Rhineland), for men to be appointed in their fifties, like Ange-Marie Eymar (b. 1747), prefect of Léman 1800–3, whose experience dated back to the Estates General.[36] Indeed in the earlier years young appointments were the exception, where administrative experience and often political contacts explained the rapid promotion. Thus P. J. M. Boucqueau de la Villeraie (b. 1773), a Belgian lawyer, had been actively pro-French since the Year II and had demonstrated his qualities as commissaire of the Directory with the central administration of the Sarre (Years VI–VIII), until his appointment as prefect of Rhin-et-Moselle at the age of 27 (1800). Even in these early appointments, under the Consulate, a majority of the prefects had already served at least two to three years in an administrative capacity, and some had a prolonged political-administrative past. Thus, Alexandre de Lameth, a deputy to the Estates-General and émigré from 1795, had already served as prefect of Basses-Alpes since 1800 before his appointment to Rhin-et-Moselle in 1805; Pierre Loysel, a deputy of the Legislative assembly, the Convention and the Council of the Elders, was employed in the registration and demesne department from the eve of Brumaire until his appointment as prefect of Meuse-Inférieure in 1802 and then of the Po department in 1805; the Ligurian G. B. Roggieri, who had first met Bonaparte at Campoformio, had been the Genoese representative at the Cisalpine, member of the Ligurian Legislative assembly in 1800, minister of foreign affairs of the Ligurian republic from 1803 until annexation, when he became prefect of Meuse-Inférieure.

Some prefects were obviously regarded as particularly suited or skilled in the administration of the new departments, as they were transferred from one to another, like Loysel and Coninck, or Lameth who moved from Rhin-et-Moselle to Roer (1806) and then to the Po department (1809). B. V. de Chauvelin, who had served for six years as prefect of Lys (1804–10), before his appointment as councillor of state, was then despatched to Catalonia as intendant-general in 1812.

Of the ninety-eight prefects who served in the new departments, ten were appointed successively to two departments and two (Lameth, Coninck) to three.

During the imperial years, the period of administrative experience before appointment tended to lengthen for prefects of the annexed departments, as elsewhere. Increasingly use was made of auditors, which tended to reduce the age of prefects. Of the 112 appointments of prefects in the 44 departments, one-third (37) were of men who had already served as prefect elsewhere, and a notably higher proportion who had served as sub-prefects or in equivalent positions. Of these prefects, twenty had begun their careers as auditors, of whom seventeen were nominated from 1808 (six in 1813). By these later years, the experiences of the annexed departments did not differ significantly from the overall pattern of the Empire, where (as Whitcomb has shown) the period of previous administrative experience increased, contemporaneously to a slight fall in average age, through the steady increase in the number of auditor-trained prefects.

It is in the earlier years that the policy towards the new departments shows its specificity in the care displayed from the outset in the choice of prefects. Unlike many departments of 'ancienne' France, very few of the initially appointed prefects were changed rapidly. In the twenty-eight departments annexed before 1808, three of the first prefects died in office within three years, three others were promoted, and only two were moved out of administrative responsibility; in all other cases, including the immediate successors of the defunct prefects, the prefects served from between three and thirteen years. Stability was characteristic of prefectoral rule within the annexed departments, already firmly established by the end of the Consulate and consolidated during the Empire. The only major changes that can be observed are clearly related to overall policy. Thus, in preparation for the annexation of the Ligurian republic (spring 1805), policy towards the entire bloc of Piedmontese departments was reconsidered: the three surviving Italian prefects were removed, and the department of the Tanaro was suppressed, with its prefect transferred to the new neighbouring department of the Apennins. The replacement of the two prefects of the departments in former Savoy in 1810 formed part of the far larger turnover of that year that affected the entire Empire.

The prefects were not the sole agents responsible for absorbing the new departments into the French system. Napoleon regarded his generals in the thirty-two military divisions that incorporated groups of departments as an important check, and sometimes counter-balance, to the civil authority of the prefects. He and his ministers regularly sent out specialists into these new departments for a range of purposes. Thus, engineers, mining experts and trade specialists were despatched to regions of the expanding Empire in order to assess economic potential.[37] With the blockade, agents were sent out to explore how smuggling could be checked, like the Customs inspector Catineau La Roche in the Illyrian provinces in 1810 and in Italy, Germany and Switzerland in the following years. At one point or another, almost everywhere, spies, like Pellenc in Illyria, were sent to report on both the administered and the administrators. As the Empire grew, the complexities of its administration and the contradictions resulting from the attempt to impose an essentially single and static model became ever more evident. The prefects, as the central cogs of this wide-flung machine, were the most exposed to the pressures.

The tools of conquest had been forged over the years as an inevitable response to the repeated experiences of conquest and occupation. At Paris the cultural benefits of the French model were never placed in doubt, but constituted a shared assumption which explains the unusually corporate unity of vision and which was translated into a remarkable *esprit de corps*. But unity of vision and of administrative action regularly ran up against the bedrock of regional diversity, whether historical, cultural, economic or social. The experiments of different mechanisms of control were conceived as means to create and consolidate acceptance or support, but provoked expressions of independence. As the frontiers of the Empire expanded, the pressing insistence on centralisation was contradicted by autonomous comportments at the periphery. It is to these contrasts between unity of vision and diversity of practices, between the language of centralisation and the realities of the periphery, between control and independence, that we need to turn in order to understand the Napoleonic conquest of Europe.

3   The practices of conquest: administrative integration

To organise is a word of the Empire.
(Balzac)

Even before the French armies moved in, the states they subverted
were in a condition of crisis that rendered them vulnerable. From the
Austrian empire to the Dutch United Provinces, from Bourbon
Naples and Spain to the Swiss Confederation, the rulers of the ancien
regime states were confronted by social tensions which only too easily
coagulated around the ossified political and administrative structures
they upheld or tried to reform. Revolt had already been repressed in
the Austrian Low Countries and Dutch republic, before it turned into
revolution in France, and flickered, threatening to catch fire, over the
following decade in a multitude of localities, often unaffected directly
by French arms (although not by the menace – or promise – of the
French example). The plots and risings in southern Piedmont,
Arezzo and Pistoia, Schaffhausen, Valais or Zurich, as in the cities of
Mainz or Naples, were supremely local in their origins and expression, even if they were symptomatic of a far broader and diffuse
social malaise and discontent. The disasters of occupation, or pressures of war on states such as Spain, Portugal or Venice which bought
their peace or neutrality, absorbed the particularity of such tensions
into generalised resentment against rising and ever more arbitrary
fiscal exactions. In territories occupied by the Directory armies,
wherever peasant risings exploded – above all during the retreat of
1799 – they were interpreted by the French without reference to the
underlying economic and social causes specific to each context. At
most the risings were acknowledged as expressions of resentment at
the unregulated conduct of the soldiery; more commonly, they were

attributed to the influence of priests and reactionary local notables, manipulating religious superstition and traditional ties of respect and dependence.

To what extent were the French authorities aware of the social and economic crises of the territories they occupied, particularly in the specificity of their local contexts? In the earlier years of the Revolution, wherever tensions had climaxed in political revolt, there is ample documentation that information and rumours about such episodes circulated widely at Paris, where they were transmuted into elements of the domestic political struggle. Nor could this be otherwise, given the presence of political exiles and enthusiasts. Many of the 40,000 Dutch who had fled their country to escape the repression that followed the failure of their revolution in 1787 went to Paris. On the other hand, riots, demonstrations and risings against bread prices, urban speculators or feudal exactions during the Revolutionary decade – as in Guipúzcoa, Piedmont or Calabria – were interpreted in purely political terms. The inevitable lack of detailed local knowledge combined with the high level of politicisation to obscure perception of deeper social or economic processes, be they the decline of the Dutch economy or the antifeudal struggle of Catalan peasants.

After Brumaire, characteristic of the Napoleonic years was the determined effort to collect information about the territories and peoples under French rule as an instrument of government. There was a need, in the words of Adrien Duquesnoy, who bore much of the responsibility for formalizing statistical enquiries in the Consulate years, not only for a regular flow of information about economic matters and administrative arrangements but, even more, 'adequately precise details about the habits, prejudices, opinions, customs and energy of the inhabitants, so that the Government can determine the appropriate measures of surveillance, repression, encouragement and protection to obtain the best results in each different locality'.[1] The correspondence of the administrators at all levels – from the sub-prefects as much as from the governors-general and senior officials – are replete with descriptions and explanations of the areas and societies for which they were responsible. But here too, now that politics had become administration, the information was structured in categories that fixed knowledge into administrative modules. The formal mould into which the information was ordered and presented, by its very insistence on a uniform matrix, distanced and inhibited the possibility of analysis of social and economic relations in localised contexts. At the same time, it encouraged an indulgence in platitudes about social characteristics, an anthology of commonplaces culled from the *philosophes* and economists of the enlightenment, sometimes updated by the more recent writings on the science of man and progress of civilisation. In lieu of explanation, social groups and entire peoples were allocated to an appropriately labelled and preformulated box, as 'idle' or 'industrious', 'superstitious' or 'enlightened', 'feudal' or 'civilised', and so forth.

Such indifference towards an analysis of the social reality was not accidental. The concerns of the Napoleonic administrators were not those of the scholar (even if the more exceptional among them, like Chabrol or de Gérando, displayed marked scientific interests). They were of an eminently practical nature, often sustained by a genuine, albeit utopian faith in the possibility of arriving at a well-ordered society. To achieve this end, two complementary routes were indicated. On the one hand, the experiences of the Revolutionary decade, including those in occupied territories, imposed an obligatory and negative reading: they provided clear signposts of what was to be avoided, especially divided authority, uncontrolled political expression and social conflict. On the other hand, the French system of administration, progressively elaborated over the years, constituted a standard and increasingly mandatory model, whose application was expected to produce a stable and modern society, freed of the dross of the past.

THE RESTORATION OF ORDER

Virtually every state brought within the French sphere of influence carried with it a legacy of recent disruption. Perhaps the only exceptions were the electorate (from 1806 kingdom) of Bavaria and the tiny Swiss principality of Neuchâtel. In the former, from the accession of the young pro-French elector Max-Joseph in 1799, the leading minister Montgelas accelerated a reforming tradition, then applying the new system to the territories periodically granted to Bavaria by grace of Napoleon. In the latter, ceded to Napoleon by the king of Prussia in exchange for Hanover (1806), Lespérut, representative of the newly enfeoffed Prince Berthier, warned against precipitous change precisely because of the stability of the society: 'One must be cautious about changes with a people which is happy with its laws and tends to believe that this is because of these laws'.[2]

War, invasions, occupations, dismemberment of territory, punitive indemnities, economic upheaval, sometimes change of regime, were the causes of the disruption. They were experiences not only of the 'sister republics' of the Directorial years, from the Batavian to the Parthenopeian, but also common to defeated states like Spain and Naples, to regions annexed by France, such as Belgium, the Rhenish left bank, or Holland, as much as to politically remodelled states, like the Rhine and Swiss confederations or the grand-duchy of Warsaw. They were experiences that spanned the entire Napoleonic period, from the termination of the Batavian (1801) and creation of the Italian republic (1802) to the occupation of Spain (1808) and the annexation of the Hanseatic ports and Swiss Valais (1810).

Whether in territories annexed by France or heavily subject as satellite states, the administrators called to mark a break with the past were confronted with two major consequences of the previous years. First, the deliberate dismantling of political and administrative institutions within each state, or their progressive decomposition under external pressures, had created a political vacuum, in which power effectively devolved from the centre to the periphery, where the local patriciates and landowners, traditionally incorporating authority, wealth and reasonably continuous presence, reaffirmed the authority of municipal and provincial institutions. Secondly, the political experiences of these years had created deep divisions among the elites, often as profound as those resulting from the Revolutionary struggle in France. Where there had been a change of regime followed by a repressive restoration – as in Belgium, Piedmont, Lombardy or Naples – the bloodshed and persecutions had added a new dimension of vendetta to the political enmities between patriots and conservatives, enmities which already too easily coincided with long-standing feuds between local factions and families. Even where there was no restoration, hostility and divisions ran deep among the elites, whether through the direct experience of revolution – as in the Batavian republic – or its indirect consequences, in the form of economic crisis and political humiliation, as in the pro- and anti-Godoy factions in Spain or the resentment of the smaller bourgeoisie of Bremen against the city patricians. Perhaps only in the states newly created by rapid military victory out of formerly separate sovereignties – like the grand-duchy of Berg, the kingdom of Westphalia or the grand-duchy of Warsaw – was there no time for such divisions to sink root; although here, more than elsewhere, local authority and power was entrenched.

Confronted with these legacies, the immediate tasks confronting the new administrators were the restoration of order, the affirmation of political authority and the acquisition of local collaboration. All three tasks required knowledge of the area.

The systematic collection of information was regarded as forming an essential prerequisite to effective administration by Brumaire. The great statistical topography of the departments of France, initiated by the Directorial minister of the interior, François de Neufchâteau, and actively pushed forward by his consular successor, Chaptal, gave official consecration to the widespread optimism of intellectual and political circles in the possibility and desirability of collecting and ordering information on every aspect of the human environment. This massive enterprise, which at its peak (1802–3) involved the activities of 20 per cent of the personnel of the economics division of the ministry of the interior and represented an attempt to engage the collaboration of the local intelligentsia, was to flag in the increasingly pragmatic and secretive environment of the Empire. The preparation and publication of a statistical topography for each department had proved too slow, whether as political propaganda (to demonstrate the progress since 1789) or as information that could be of immediate practical utility.[3]

If a failure as a utopian intellectual project, the experience of the statistical topography not only remained, but also acquired a more all-embracing status as the central discipline in the elaboration of a science of administration. The collection of data about the resources, economy and society of the department provided the administration not only with factual knowledge as a preliminary to policy decisions, but also a regular check on the correspondence of administrative norms to social evolution. For C. J. Bonnin, 'through the knowledge of facts, governments will search for remedies appropriate to the needs of nations'.[4] For de Gérando, statistics provided a method and procedure of observation, analysis, comparison and synthesis, which was essential to ensure that the administration avoided arbitrary actions and exercised its functions in the public interest. Statistics provided the legitimising of the new role of the administration in its relationship with society. Administrative action, as de Gérando put it, signified

> the rights of society as much as the principle of power exercised by the authority that represents it. The law regulates administrative action; the interests of society are its rule and its aim. Private interests are like a deposit held on trust by Authority, marking its limit.[5]

It would be difficult to overestimate the pervasive influence of this intimate, at moments almost symbiotic relationship between statistics and administration. If Napoleon had little patience for the more metaphysical aspirations of the statistical exponents, nobody ever doubted his devouring thirst for facts. Beugnot, sent with other experts to examine how to organise the newly created kingdom of Westphalia, began his report:

> Sire, When those of us who lived at Paris received Your Majesty's orders, you insisted that we provide you with details, an abundance of details. It was your way of informing us that the simplest features of Westphalia were a matter of great interest to you; and that it would never be importunate to speak to you frequently about your peoples.[6]

Napoleon's avidity for factual information, with which he importuned one and all, formed part of his public image. But it was consistent with his insistence, out of public view, that his administrators acquire first-hand knowledge.

The obligation on prefects to carry out an annual tour of their departments – which Napoleon extended to the kingdom of Italy with his reorganisation of the administration in 1805 – was merely one aspect of what by then had become standard practice. As occasion demanded, special agents were despatched across the Empire and beyond its frontiers to draw up statistical assessments of the potential of resources (including those in territories not yet under French control) or to investigate the malfunctioning of branches of the administration. Where specialised knowledge was required, such enquiries were entrusted to men with appropriate skills, such as Héron de Villefosse, who was appointed 'general inspector of mines in the conquered territories' in Germany, or the engineers Baillet and Gallois in Piedmont and Liguria.[7] More generally, the ability to collect and present information in statistical form, according to requirement, was regarded as normal procedure, part of the standard training of aspirant prefects, like the auditor Plancy, who was sent to the Belgian departments in Year XII (1805) to assess the likely shortage in the cereal harvest.[8]

Given this widespread faith in the statistical collection of information within the administrative mind at Paris, it is hardly surprising that French prefects should have insisted in such an exercise of style even when it was apparent that it could be of little practical value, nor that similar beliefs should have prevailed outside France's frontiers. Chaptal's grandiose project had embraced all the departments of France. By 1805, of the total 111, 25 constituted new territories incorporated by France: statistical memoirs were compiled by at least

47 prefects, including a remarkable one on Montenotte by Chabrol de Volvic, future prefect of Paris. The annexed regions were particularly well served, with memoirs on Savoy, eight of the nine Belgian departments and three of the four Rhenish ones.[9] Years later, when the fashion and method of compiling statistics had changed fundamentally, from the large-scale description to the regular collection of data on individual sectors of the economy, the intendant-general of the interior of the newly annexed Dutch provinces, F. J. B. d'Alphonse – who as prefect of the Indre had already produced one such memoir – still felt the urge to draw up a vast statistical 'General survey of Holland' in 1,364 pages.[10] Nor was he alone: the prefect of a Catalan department, Alban de Villeneuve, prepared a 'Statistical, historical and administrative memoir providing a description of the administration of the department of the Bouches de l'Ebre before the war, the changes it has experienced since the war and its state on 1 January 1813'. In form and content a replica of the Chaptal statistical memoirs, it rests as a monument to the power of established modes of thought, even when rendered anachronistic, unrealistic and impossible to complete by the conditions of war:

> The destruction of the archives, the flight of the most enlightened persons, the ignorance, mistrust or ill faith of those who have stayed, and last but not least the difficulties of communications have and for a long time will continue to impede the completion of a work of this sort.[11]

The Netherlands offered repeated examples of the collection of statistics as a necessary part of the administrative process. The major effort made by the last Batavian government (1798–1801) to centralise the administration was inevitably complemented by wide-ranging statistical enquiries, previously inconceivable in the context of provincial independence; under Louis Bonaparte, the French pattern was adopted of regular reports on economic activities. In the kingdom of Italy, the passion for statistics was so great that public officials, like Scopoli, minister of education, and private scholars, like Vincenzo Cuoco, launched projects as ambitious as Chaptal's departmental topography. In Naples, Murat tried to replace the assumptions about the country's wealth (which at best relied on old investigations of enlightenment reformers like G. M. Galanti, at worst on prejudiced guesses) by the solid facts of statistical enquiries. The frontiers of French influence were signposted by the outward march of statistics, like those ordered by Marshal Suchet in 1810 as military governor of Aragon, as he settled in for a lengthy stay. Perhaps the most intriguing example of the success of the French model of 'state statistics' was the 1806 short-lived decision by Prussia (which possessed its own distinguished and autonomous statistical tradition) to set up a bureau of statistics in imitation of the Parisian one; Jena truncated the experiment.

The restoration of order required both less and more than the statistical collection of information could provide. In the immediate instance, the solution to disorder was armed repression; over the longer term, the destruction of banditry necessitated a knowledge of kin and communal networks that escaped official administrative sources, and usually the police.

The wars and upheavals of the Directorial years were inevitably accompanied by the breakdown of order in the countryside. Bandits and bands were no new phenomenon, and their repression had been utilised by late-eighteenth-century governments as a means to extend central authority by the creation of militarised patrols. Wherever there were frontiers – and hence smuggling – unlicensed carrying of arms was common and the presence of bands hardly less so. But banditry or brigandage was not confined to frontier areas. It was traditional in the mountainous areas of the Mediterranean, where it was normally contained within the local structures of power. In times of major crisis of state authority, factionalism destroyed the consent underlying the exercise of local authority and banditry increased, as in Calabria, the Pyrenees and the western Alps. Where large armies existed, military defeat encouraged the rapid diffusion of banditry through disbandment and desertion, as in Piedmont, Lombardy, Naples and Spain, or later, during the Napoleonic débâcle, across northern Europe.

The restoration of order was given high priority during the Consulate as, in practice and symbolically, it constituted a necessary condition to win the support of landowners and peasants. Where whole regions defied authority – as in the Vendée and Calabria – military force was used. Hoche's tactics of isolating and destroying the bases of the counter-revolutionaries in the Vendée were deployed with some success by Masséna against the brigands in Calabria; at first Napoleon assumed that a similar response would be adequate in Spain. Elsewhere – initially in the departments of the French Midi, Piedmont and the Italian republic, then in every new territory conquered by the French – the most obtrusive manifestations of banditry were rapidly suppressed by the creation of a corps of military police,

the gendarmerie, recruited locally and stiffened by a leavening of
seasoned French soldiers. General Wirion organised the gendarmerie
in the Belgian departments, the Vendée (following Hoche's military
campaign) and Piedmont, where he insisted with the Parisian
ministry of war on a large enough force of veterans of the Italian
campaigns. Protection of the main roads and patrols in most turbu-
lent areas were normally adequate to restore order relatively rapidly
– as in Belgium, Piedmont, the Italian republic or Tuscany.

The effectiveness of the repression of bandits and brigands was
dependent on the scale of the phenomenon and the attitude of the
local population. In Calabria, the difficulties of penetrating the in-
accessible Sila mountains, the vicinity of British-controlled Sicily and
the collusion of large numbers of landed proprietors encouraged a
vigorous brigandage: long after Masséna's military repression, the
gendarmerie General Manhès was deploying three mobile columns to
fight pitched battles with bandits. In Catalonia, the distinction between brigands and guerrillas was often a fine one, and rendered the
restoration of order permanently fragile: for patriotic resistance en-
veloped and cloaked episodes of simple banditry, while hostility to
the French was so widespread that it proved impossible to create a
gendarmerie. By contrast, in Piedmont even tightly organised bands
near the Ligurian border, like Scarzello's at Narzole, were ultimately
destroyed when local support was withdrawn. If salt smuggling could
never be eliminated, as Napoleon himself acknowledged,[12] the active
cooperation of local landowners, organised as national guards, had
restored a tranquillity to Piedmont by 1808 which remained undis-
turbed even when French power collapsed in 1814. Presumably the
apparent absence of banditry of a serious nature further north in
Europe – from the Rhineland to Berg, Westphalia, Holland and the
Hanseatic departments – can be explained in terms of the rapid
handover or seizure of power, the established authority of local
elites, and the presence of substantial military forces. In these
regions, the main concern of the gendarmerie (as also in Piedmont or
the kingdom of Italy) was to enforce conscription and search for
smugglers.

The safety of citizens in their persons and property lay at the very
core of the Napoleonic settlement. It constituted the complement to
the Revolutionary affirmation of the monopoly of public power by
the state. It implied respect for the due processes of law. In the light
of the gross infractions of respect for legality of Napoleonic rule –
from the kidnapping and execution of the duke of Enghien to the
practices of conscription – such a statement may seem to ring hollow.

Extreme situations were regarded as justifying extreme solutions. Thus military tribunals were employed in the repression of revolt or what was defined as brigandage (an elastic term, which made the accused liable to the additional, serious offence of association). But even such an exceptional procedure could backfire – as in the failure to convict those accused of responsibility for the Bologna revolt of 1802 or the judicially debatable suppression of the Scarzello band in 1808 – because of inadequate knowledge of criminal law.

There can be no doubt about the constant concern of the civilian administrators to protect the citizens from arbitrary actions. At a general level, respect for the private sphere of citizens acted as an ultimate but effective constraint on the expansive aspirations of the administration. In the day-to-day handling of affairs, the tendencies of those directly responsible for the maintenance of order to ignore or infringe the legal rights of citizens was a continuous source of friction. Whether inside or outside imperial frontiers, there was a litany of protests from prefects and rulers against the abuses of the military or corps like the gendarmerie, Customs officials and officers of the alcohol and tobacco monopolies (*droits réunis*), with quasi-military functions and comportment. In Piedmont, the readiness of the governor-general Menou to impose collective fines or quarter gendarme mobile units on villages suspected of collaborating with bandits was opposed by the prefect and overruled by the minister of the interior in 1807, because this punished the innocent with the guilty. D'Auzers, head of the police in Piedmont, condemned the comportment of the tax officials in 1809:

> I am inundated by complaints against the *droits réunis* . . . some of their petty agents are gallows birds, recruited from the dregs of society. . . . They entangle the peasants in a maze of laws or regulations that these poor wretches cannot hope to know or understand; they threaten them with legal proceedings, they frighten them too, even over the most simple matters and . . . by the use of such odious means, exact a sort of tax on ignorance and weakness.[13]

In Lombardy, the viceroy Eugene ordered the chief judge to respect the rights of individuals accused of involvement in the 1809 risings: 'I shall say no more than tell the Minister that the circumstances do not justify the violation of due forms and hence I recommend he ensure that respect for procedure and prosecution of the guilty march together'.[14] The Dutch were shocked by the behaviour of tax officials and gendarmes following the annexation of their country. As Gogel complained, 'The Dutch public has always been accustomed to being treated according to the letter of the law'.[15] The reconciliation of the maintenance of order with respect for legality was essential for the civilian administrators as an affirmation of political authority. It represented a precondition of the search for a social base of acceptance, if not of collaboration.

From the outset, the new administrators of the territories annexed by France or set up as sovereign states were dependent on local collaboration. There was rarely, if ever, any lack of administrative personnel at the middling or lower levels. On the contrary, the immediate and pressing problem was how to reduce the exuberant number of public employees, which was a common feature to the former regimes, whether or not affected by revolutionary upheavals. In France, after Brumaire, Lucien Bonaparte had slimmed down the ministry of the interior from 345 to 66.[16] Melzi, vice-president of the Italian republic, found the administrative offices of the Cisalpine swollen with politicians persecuted or deported during the Austrian restoration. Beugnot observed of Westphalia that 'administrative posts are the old perquisite of a class of poor nobles. Such posts have multiplied far beyond the need'.[17] Joseph of Naples, reporting to his brother, immediately noted that 'the great scourge of this country is the wholly excessive number of employees; I shall be obliged to discharge many of them'.[18] In fact, his administrative reforms threatened half the civil class with unemployment.

The difficulties confronting the new administrators were of a different nature: how to choose collaborators who would be at one and the same time politically impartial, administratively capable and willing to serve.

The political divisions of the previous years made social reconciliation a prime necessity for future stability, as Bonaparte had demonstrated in consular France. The same conditions prevailed in virtually all the regions annexed by France, as well as the newly conquered states, with the exception of Germany, where only the Rhineland had been seriously affected by the Revolution. The patriots and politicians of these countries, disillusioned by the Revolutionary fragmentation of authority or adapting adroitly to new times, were ready to support an administration with extensive executive powers, even at the expense of political representation. Isaac Gogel, the idealist of 1794 and determined but frustrated minister of finances of the Batavian republic of 1798–1801, by 1804 was calling for

an energetic government which . . . does not have to be in conflict
with subaltern bodies and which is not obstructed by every kind of
provincial claim, but is limited only by some rules and may proceed freely so long as it does not infringe them.[19]

The problem was that various of the new leaders appointed by
Bonaparte – Melzi as vice-president of the Italian republic, Menou as
governor-general of Piedmont, Schimmelpenninck as grand pensionary of the Netherlands – were hostile to the patriots and maintained
that the employment of men too openly identified with the previous
governments would frighten off the moderate and conservative landowners and notables. Melzi was obsessed with the need to make a
break with the past, vetoing candidates who had served in the
Cisalpine assemblies or (even worse) been deported by the Austrians
in 1799. The experience of the Batavian republic was still recent
enough in 1805 for Schimmelpenninck to agitate the spectre of 'anarchists'. In reality, at least in the states where the restoration governments of 1799 had displayed their persecutory zeal for vendetta, a
more likely reason for the reluctance to serve of the hitherto politically neutral was prudence – at least until Bonapartist rule proved its
durability. As the years passed and the Napoleonic star continued to
rise, the problem seemed to disappear. Fear of so-called 'Jacobins'
was of major importance in Belgium, Piedmont, the Italian republic
and Switzerland; by 1806 Joseph was appointing some genuine
Jacobins to posts in Naples (including Bonaparte's early patron
Saliceti as minister of police). In Spain, where the patriot experience
of the 1790s had never occurred, it was fear of popular vengeance
that effectively discouraged collaboration with the French. But the
suspicion and resentments that resulted from the attitude of leading
families and individuals towards collaboration were to mark the years
of the Restoration, as evoked so tellingly in 'The Chartreuse of
Parma'.

Where patriots were excluded, it became even more difficult to
appoint capable and willing men, particularly at the higher levels.
Melzi's correspondence with his foreign minister Marescalchi at Paris
is replete with complaints about the reluctance of wealthy, noble
landowners or urban patricians to accept appointment as prefects.
Some were so wealthy that the not insubstantial stipend of
20,000–24,000 lire was only a relative attraction. Most refused because of the obligation to move to a different department, giving
priority to their family and administration of their patrimony. In the
end, a substantial proportion of Melzi's aristocratic prefects soon

resigned or were removed through incompetence, as were the Venetian nobles appointed by Melzi's successor Eugene de Beauharnais.[20]

Melzi's experiences were reasonably typical, even if he complicated them by his hatred of Jacobins. Reluctance to serve if this required physical displacement was general, as it had been initially in France too. Nor was such reluctance restricted to prefectures. Appointments to posts as judges were declined for identical reasons, as a judge at Alessandria (Piedmont) explained his refusal of nomination to the appeal court at Genoa: 'Given my personal situation, under no circumstances could I distance myself from my country and leave my properties and family. . . . This promotion would be nothing but a misfortune for me and would bring me to destitution'.[21] Moreover, administrative capacity was not easily detectable from the personal friendships, family loyalties or exercise of patronage that lay behind perhaps the majority of early appointments; which explains the unusually high proportion of replacements in all states, including Brumairean France. The result was that in departments and states with previous revolutionary experiences, like Piedmont, the Italian republic and Holland, posts in the police and civil judiciary tended to be thronged with patriots. In countries without such experiences, like Venetia, Naples, Berg or Spain, it often proved difficult or impossible to recruit the respectable (and respected), particularly to the more onerous or less prestigious offices. In Berg, the nobles were unwilling to serve as judges, as this required legal training and hard work, according to Beugnot. In the city of Naples the police were accused of being agents of one noble clan, the Cassano.[22]

The situation was aggravated, particularly in the first round of appointments in each newly administered region, by the preference given to Frenchmen. In Belgium there was resentment at the exclusion of locals; perhaps this was the reason for the initial appointment of Italians (including locals) in Piedmont – many of whom were soon replaced. Only in the Dutch departments annexed in 1810 was there a notable continuity of personnel from Louis' reign, as a sop to the strong tradition of national independence. Throughout the annexed departments, preference was given to Frenchmen for the senior posts in the financial administration and criminal judiciary. Outside the Empire, the situation was if anything worse, given the contempt for locals of many of the senior French in charge of the territories and the expectations of their compatriots of jumping on the bandwagon of the new administrations. In Italy, Holland, Berg, Naples and Westphalia, the protest was unanimous against Parisian pressure (backed by French generals stationed in the territories) for appointments of Frenchmen. Only in Spain was their presence necessary, given the unwillingness of local elites to serve. Eugene in Italy and Louis in Holland resisted most effectively; Murat threw fits of fury at the 2,000 requests for posts he had received at Paris in 1811.[23]

These difficult relations between occupiers and occupied were never satisfactorily resolved, not just because of the relative brevity of French rule, but perhaps even more because of an increasing reluctance of Napoleon and his followers to reconcile Parisian certainties with local expectations, despite the protests of his relatives and administrators in the occupied territories. There was an impatience with local inadequacies, expressed revealingly by the young Stendhal in his private journal, after two years spent in Brunswick attached to the French war commissiares (1806–8):

> My attitude towards the people of this country has been typical of that of a young man, of a true Frenchman, criticising to their face what seemed to me criticisable, as if they were philosophers without prejudices, and even letting them glimpse my contempt for their heavy dullness.[24]

MODERNISATION OF THE STATE

Brumaire had occurred as a response to the demand for effective authority. The propaganda of its victors attacked elected assemblies and eulogised undivided authority. The inevitable consequence was a deep shift in the concept of representation. Demonstration of popular sovereignty through the right to vote, already battered and manipulated under the Directory, was reduced to the symbolism of the Napoleonic plebiscites and the infrequent exercise of indirect elections by a suffrage limited to the wealthy and educated. Elected representatives were deprived of legislative authority, and summoned to meet for restricted periods in a consultative capacity. At the departmental level, however, at least in the early years, they retained an important function – that of expressing public opinion. For Adrien Duquesnoy, who was responsible for coordinating the activities of the departmental general councils, such an institution

> had the precious advantage of providing the government with the pure expression of public wishes and of making it know the

thoughts of the departments. Such an institution constantly enlightens the government about the results of all the acts which emanate from its authority and reports the opinion of the administered, about both the men who have been invested with some power and the different public services. It is an institution that cannot but perfect the administration in all its parts.[25]

Duquesnoy's vision of the complementarity of the roles of a central directive administration, incorporated in the ministry of the interior, and a multitude of local elites, each the expression of public opinion in a single department, soon faded before Bonaparte's increasingly authoritarian self-confidence. The departmental general councils ceased to present *cahiers de doléances* and were confined, under the prefect's direction, to limited fiscal responsibilities of tax allocation. At most, as Molé, Napoleon's minister of justice, later reflected, their representative function was performed (in an even more discreet manner) by the Legislative body: 'it consisted, generally speaking, of men less independent than worthy, and above all less servile than peaceable, and so could serve Bonaparte as a monitor, since there was no brake'.[26]

With the disappearance of any institutional expression of public opinion, increasingly the administration claimed to represent the nation. The entire philosophy of Napoleonic rule was based on the assumption that a modern and efficient administration was implicitly identified with the most responsible and progressive opinion in society, and that – precisely because it possessed the power of the state – such an administration could create a framework that would accelerate the development of a stable and productive society more effectively than any elected representative body. Napoleon, in his customary expeditious manner of settling matters which in his opinion had already generated too much theoretical hot air, informed the newly created Italian state legislature (1805) why conventional representation was outdated:

> Political liberty, which is so necessary to the State, does not consist of this sort of multiplication of authority, but in a visibly stable and secure system of good administration. Once the royal treasury has been separated from that of the nation, so that the King cannot use the Nation's coffers for himself; once a Legislative body receives annual accounts of the expenditure of the funds it had assigned, once it has decreed the necessary new funds, political liberty is guaranteed.[27]

The context of Napoleon's utterance was the resistance of the leading councillors in his kingdom of Italy to the abolition of the departmental assemblies. The episode is symptomatic of the difficulties experienced in exporting the French model of administration. For if the model was single, the multiplicity of societies to which it was applied meant that the fit was rarely perfect. 'The knowledge of facts' was the bureaucratic answer. But for reasons of history, administrative practices, tradition or simply prejudice, even the most enlightened subjects somehow did not always seem to accept the reasonableness of the proposals. Behind the impatience of the French and the often frustrated evasiveness of their local correspondents was the objective difficulty in each of the territories of the entrenched presence of juridical categories and institutions that were ill adapted to the new French laws.

The demarcation of space presented a delicate problem in all the areas where French authority was established or its influence accepted, precisely because it incorporated the difficulties and often the impossibility of reconciling the new and the old concepts. To redesign the territory of a state in new administrative units conformed to the French experience not only in practical terms, but also as a symbolic gesture of rupture with the past. But space has always constituted an object of jealous attachments and material prerogatives, capable of opening new wounds or reviving slumbering rivalries. Hence it is not surprising that the determination to rationalise boundaries should have aroused opposition, nor that, at the lower level of the communes where territory, interests and identity were most intimately linked, such rationalisation should often have been rejected.

In the areas annexed by France the redrawing of internal frontiers constituted a deliberate attempt to break with previous political identity. In the case of former provinces, like the Austrian Low Countries, Savoy or the fragmented territories of the left bank of the Rhine, the transformation into departments was straightforward: Savoy became the department of Mont-Blanc, the nine Belgian departments were easily drawn up as they corresponded to the main cities of a highly urbanised region. Where entire states or capitals were swallowed by France – Liège, Piedmont, Genoa, Tuscany, Holland, Rome, the Hanseatic ports – the division into single military divisions and multiple departments became the exclusive terms of reference in official and public documents. The pride of the former capitals was assuaged by tacit recognition of their pre-eminence as the first among equals. But this was little recompense for the patriots of Liège, capital of the Ourthe department, whose former principality was truncated, despite their protests, to the advantage of Dyle. Geneva, formally reduced to capital of Léman, was allowed to conserve privileges unknown elsewhere in the Empire, more because of its unique prestige in late-eighteenth-century Europe than for its economic importance. Rome was given the title of second capital of the Empire, which not surprisingly was regarded as insulting by the nobility of the former capital of Christianity. But Catalonia, whose latent sense of national identity was stimulated by the French occupation, was divided into four departments, with its administrative capital even displaced from Barcelona to Gerona.

Political overtones thus coloured the division into departments, which constituted the essential unit for all purposes of administration. Less desirable, because of its negative consequences on social reconciliation, was the major discontent generated among the smaller cities by the new administrative divisions. Attempts to soothe provincial feelings were made by proposing the formation of numerous subprefectures. But for reasons of administrative costs their numbers were rapidly reduced: in Piedmont from thirty-one to twenty-one (1801). The choice of Hamburg, Bremen and Osnabrück as capitals of the Hanseatic departments on the Baltic offended Lübeck, Oldenburg and Lüneburg (1810).

Outside France a distinction needs to be made between newly created states and those which continued to exist but where the regime was changed. In the former, carved out of the territories of various states with radically different institutions and administrative practices, departments and sub-prefectures were created. In Berg and Westphalia, their boundaries were marked – as in France eighteen years earlier – by attempts to achieve a rational balance between space and population, where administrative centres would be within reasonable access of all inhabitants. In the republic-kingdom of Italy, where historical traditions remained strong, the same pattern and problems emerged as in the annexed departments of France: on the one hand, official ostracism of all references to earlier 'national' identities, with the division into departments of the former territories of Lombardy, the Papal States and Venetia; on the other, discontent of urban oligarchies at Bologna and Venice, offended at their relegation to the level of other departments.

The experience of the states whose political identity was maintained without rupture is revealing of the sensitivity of the administrators towards the rhetorical and emotive appeal of local identity. In

Naples, Joseph stressed the continuity with the previous regime, accepting the provinces created by Zurlo in 1801 and employing the traditional terms of districts, compartments and universities for the sub-divisions, with intendants in place of prefects. In the Netherlands, the attempt of the centralising Batavian republic of 1798–1801 to eliminate the historical identity of the provinces by the creation of new departments barely lasted two years; and when King Louis reintroduced departments, he paid attention not to change the boundaries of the provinces. In Frankfurt, the ruler of the new grand-duchy, Dalberg, took care to create departments whose boundaries respected the historical prerogatives of the cities (1810). In Bavaria (where there was no change of regime), Montgelas, enthusiastic and active reformer in the Bonapartist mould, waited until the apparent security of the peace of Tilsit to consolidate the enlarged kingdom by the abolition of all the old names except Bavaria and the creation of new administrative units, on the basis of statistical enquiry into their geography and population.

The French model of administration was hierarchical and centralised. It assumed, as Roederer expressed it with that penchant of politicians for recent scientific terminology, that 'the executive chain descends without interruption from the minister to the administered and transmits the law and the government's orders to the furthest ramifications of the social order, with the rapidity of an electric current'.[28]

At the centre, the council of state combined legislative and judicial functions with political advice; the ministry of the interior was responsible for all administrative matters except in those sectors for which a specific ministry existed. Alongside the interior, war (for which Napoleon created three ministries) and foreign affairs, finances represented the most important ministry, which under Gaudin's uninterrupted direction retained total autonomy from all other branches of the administration. The central administration grew in size and complexity over the years, in consequence of the wars and the growth of the Empire. Auditors and *maîtres de requêtes* were added to the council of state, the number of ministries increased to twelve; under Montalivet, the ministry of the interior rose to about 220 staff.

In the departments, prefects and sub-prefects represented the administration. Directly responsible to the ministry of the interior, their very role as sole representatives of central authority inevitably involved them in functions relating to other ministries, over conscription (war), public opinion (police), religion (cults), the economy (manufactures and commerce), or matters affecting the judiciary (justice) or revenue (treasury). In fact, since appointments to posts or honours were based on the names proposed by the prefects, all ministries (except foreign affairs) were to a degree reliant upon them. However comprehensive the prefects' responsibilities, their jurisdiction did not extend over all the representatives of the state. The generals in charge of the thirty-two military divisions of the Empire acted not only independently, but also on occasion in rivalry with the prefects. The judiciary, from the tribunals and assize courts in all departments to the thirty-seven appeal courts and the supreme court at Paris, responded to the minister of justice, in homage to the Revolutionary principle of the separation of powers. The numerous financial employees responded to their hierarchical superiors and turned to the prefects only for support in carrying out their duties. The police, including the directors-general at Rome and Amsterdam and the directors responsible respectively for the Piedmontese and Tuscan departments, were subject to the minister of general police, whose authority also extended over the thirty gendarmerie legions. In theory separated by the precise nature of their responsibilities, in practice the presence of these officials in the departments easily generated friction or conflict with the prefect, because of overlapping spheres of competence and the impossibility, to a greater or lesser degree, of any of them acting without his knowledge and involvement.

It was the duty of this army of functionaries to ensure the rapid execution of those general laws and specific measures by which the government intended, on the one hand, to complete the Revolutionary task of liberating the economy and society from obstacles to free initiative, and on the other hand, to force the pace – within the legal limits of a respect for property and persons – in the direction of its own model of modernity. To the student of the Napoleonic civil administration, there can be no doubt about the care and seriousness with which the laws and decrees were discussed and prepared, any more than about their lack of novelty in terms of the juridical and economic ideas circulating since the later eighteenth century.

The most publicly spectacular measures had already been passed in the earliest phase of the Revolution. Napoleonic legislation was elaborated in the more discreet environment of the council of state and the ministries. But, like the Revolutionary reforms, it derived directly from the pre-Revolutionary discussions, both within and outside France. This can be illustrated by the two most radical initiatives of the Napoleonic period – the reordering of finances and the legal codes. The separation of finances from the administration was not merely the consequence of the bankruptcy of the French monarchy and Revolutionary governments, nor of Bonaparte's obsession with kitchen accountancy; it reflected the well-established Habsburg late cameralist distinction between policing (in the eighteenth-century sense of legislation and administration) and public finance. Similarly, the civil code took so long to elaborate and was relatively so ill-balanced because of the differences and opposition of juridical ideas, which were finally resolved by Bonaparte's imposition of a compromise, 'a transaction, a badly estimated quotation', in Molé's words.[29] The civil code consolidated the social changes that had already been achieved in France, consecrating absolute property rights (to which the code dedicated 1,776 articles, compared to 515 articles regulating persons). The criminal code was more regressive, not just because of the greater difficulty in revising criminal law in the absence of any equivalent to Roman law, but because Napoleon (unlike his eighteenth-century predecessors) was more concerned with affirming the state's monopoly of the administration of criminal law (expressed in the code of criminal procedure) than with the content of the law itself.

There is no need to repeat the litany of Napoleonic legislative and administrative reforms which have left so profound an impression on the subsequent evolution of France. What is of concern here is the determination to export the entire corpus of these reforms and the reactions they aroused. Given the differences in intellectual traditions (as well as languages) that characterized the numerous states and societies where such an attempt was made, the cultural shock was necessarily profound. There was also a fundamental difference in the recent political experiences of France, with its unreneged decade of Revolutionary change, and other European countries. Elimination of intermediary corps and privileges that impeded a direct relationship between the state and individual citizen and the free circulation of goods, confiscation of ecclesiastical property and achievement of a balanced budget through rationalisation of the fiscal system and land cadasters, abolition of the guilds and economic individualism, codification of the sources and procedures of law to achieve legal equality – to name only the most important aspects of the reforms – appeared so new in the areas of French expansion only because they were introduced or imposed on states and societies that to varying degrees were still functioning with the norms of the ancien regime.

Within the annexed territories, French administration and laws were introduced with ever briefer periods of adaptation: nearly eighteen months passed between Piedmont's 'preparation' for the French system under General Jourdan (April 1801) and its annexation (September 1802); Lebrun was given six months to adapt Liguria (1805), as was the *consulta* responsible for Rome (1809); within six weeks of the decision to introduce French legislation into the Hanseatic departments, the imperial printing office produced copies of complete collections of French laws and decrees in French and German that amounted to 32,000 volumes.[30] More interesting as illustrating the attractions and difficulties of exporting the French model of administrative centralisation are the experiences of the states within the Napoleonic sphere of influence. Three themes provide illuminating examples: centralisation, fiscal reform and the civil code.

A centralised structure of administration was the aspiration of all eighteenth-century regimes. Hence it is not surprising that councils of state, prefects and sub-prefects should have been adopted (with minimal variants in form and terminology) with alacrity by the rulers of these states. The problems of translating these structures into the exercise of power can be located on the one hand in the effective authority of the prefects and, on the other, in the degree of autonomy of the lowest level of the new organisation, municipal administration.

In the Italian republic, where Melzi enjoyed a notable degree of autonomy, the prefects' authority was potentially restricted by the presence of two lieutenants, chosen among the local notables, and effectively counterbalanced by a departmental administration with vaguely defined powers and real financial control. There can be no doubt about Melzi's tendency to identify with his peers of the urban patriciates. However, he saw an objective need to reconcile the new French institution of the prefect with the traditions of local self-government by oligarchies whose powers had been reinforced by the Habsburg reforms.[31]

In states with federalist structures, like the Low Countries or Swiss confederation, the same problem presented itself even more acutely. The unitarian patriots of the Helvetic republic (1798) had invented prefects even before Brumaire. But they lacked the strength to break the hostility of the merchant and professional bourgeoisie of the cities, who returned to power with Bonaparte's restoration of cantonal autonomy in the Mediation of 1803.

The Dutch experience initially seemed to follow a similar trajectory: in a country whose national independence was equated with provincial and municipal autonomy, the energetic patriots of

1798–1801 managed to set up only the embryo of a French-style structure, with national agencies at the centre and local commissioners who proved incapable of exacting the obedience of the town regents. The following years of the Regency of State (1801–5) witnessed the full restoration of the urban patriciates. As Gogel complained:

> The present government succeeds in combining the worst . . . by having an infinity of governments all endowed with constitutional laws and separate powers, so that the departmental councils dispute with the government and the towns and communes with those first councils. All power is disposed to self-extension.

It needed the bankruptcy of the cities, through falling revenues and a rising wave of pauperism, for the Dutch burghers to accept the dependence of local administrations on central government.[32]

Fiscal reform was the touchstone of Napoleonic modernisation of the state. It signified the emancipation of the state from the throttle-hold of spiralling public debt that characterised the ancien regime governments and consecration of its role as sole tutor of legal equality through the fair distribution of taxes. Precisely because it touched so many interests, of individuals and categories, its implementation was massively difficult. Roederer, former member of the Constituent assembly's taxation committee, as Joseph's minister of finances in Naples, was fully aware of the immensity of the issues, which he described as 'not so much a question of the administration of finances but rather the creation of an administration'. The only method was to utilise the existing fiscal mechanisms through which to introduce the new system: 'I departed as little as possible from the practices of the Revenue office and its agents. . . . The basis for every projected tax already existed at Naples, the form I proposed to adopt came from France.'[33]

Not surprisingly, given the common enlightened matrix, there were many points of similarity between the French model of public finances and taxation and those of reforming states such as Lombardy, Tuscany, some Swiss cantons, and even Naples (as Roederer observed). The comprehensive reform of the fiscal system in the Netherlands, which the great finance minister Gogel finally managed to impose in 1806, and which spread the burden of taxation more uniformly between provinces and among social groupings within each province, owed more to Gogel's earlier abortive reform of 1801 than to the French. The existence of such earlier or contemporaneous reforms rendered assimilation to the French system easier, particularly in the Consulate years, when the pressure of taxation was still contained. Elsewhere, as in Germany, the impact of the French reforms was immediate and radical, in that it implied the separation of public from domain or Crown revenues, the destruction of feudal privileges and the compilation of land cadasters. For Roederer, always an optimist, the land tax destroyed feudalism and encouraged smallholdings in Naples. In Poland, Illyria and parts of Germany, however, feudalism remained so strong that it prevented the effective functioning of the French reforms.

In the end, the French model of public finances was adopted, albeit with variations, in virtually all Continental states except Russia and the Ottoman Balkans. Public finances were legally regulated, fiscal administration was restructured, budgeting was introduced, unified and rationalised and simplified systems of public expenditure, revenue and debt were adopted. Over the longer term, these reforms laid the bases for modern systems of public finance. But at the time, their impact and success was far from uniform. A general reason for this was the rapidly rising increase of demand on revenue to meet the military requirements of Napoleonic hegemony. In all the states public debt – the cause of the breakdown of ancien regime finances – increased vertiginously, particularly from 1806–7. In the kingdom of Italy, revenues increased by 50 per cent between 1805 and 1811, while the deficit rose from 1 million to 5 million lire. In the German states, the increase of the public debt was on an even greater scale. If direct taxation remained structured around the land and moveable property taxes and trading licence (*foncière*, *mobilière* and *patente*), the number, pressure and proportion of indirect taxes relative to overall revenue rose steeply. Some of these taxes, like that on salt or customs duties, were common to all states; others, like the French tobacco monopoly, were applied only in some states, such as Berg. But everywhere their collection incited official abuse and popular hostility. It was not coincidental that Customs and *droits réunis* officials, alongside gendarmes, were the object of popular assaults at the moment of collapse of Napoleonic rule in 1813–14; nor that the only minister to be murdered by a mob was Prina, Gaudin's counterpart in the kingdom of Italy responsible for public finances.

It seems likely (although it is still virtually impossible to demonstrate, in the absence of detailed studies of its impact on the distribution of wealth) that in their adoption of the French fiscal system, these states replicated its structural inequalities, possibly on a greater scale. Land cadasters were compiled with great haste, once Napoleon urged their completion in 1807, sometimes with the assistance of

French technicians, and almost certainly far less thoroughly than in France. Once again, the effectiveness of reform – in this instance the distribution of the land-tax – was closely tied to the collaboration or obstructive capacities of the landowners and local administrators. In regions where feudalism was strong (even in Naples, let alone in Bavaria or much of Germany), fiscal reforms were impaired and distorted, at the expense of the socially weak.

For Napoleon, the civil code possessed universal value. He brooked no delays in its introduction in the territories he annexed and exerted notable pressure on family and friends in favour of its adoption. He ordered its introduction into the grand-duchy of Warsaw, Hamburg and Danzig. On 31 October 1807 he instructed Joseph and Louis that 'from 1 January the Napoleonic code becomes the law of their peoples'. Champagny, his foreign minister, explained to the rulers of Bavaria, Hesse-Darmstadt and Baden that the code

> is an object of study and admiration throughout Europe by every-one concerned with the science of laws. . . . It is not just a great empire that feels the need for a uniform legislation. There are few states, even small ones, where the differences in customs do not create difficulties for transactions and damage the execution of justice in civil matters. This is even truer for Germany than for other countries. Many states and provinces formerly ruled accord-ing to their own laws and those of the Holy Roman Empire are now under a new rule and united to other states with an entirely different legislation. Hence the adoption of the Napoleonic code will be a blessing for the peoples of these states as it will eliminate the variety of customs that rule them.[34]

Napoleon, in his more imperious moments, aspired to iron out and render uniform laws, customs and practices. After all, as he explained to Louis, the Romans had imposed their law on their subject peoples, why should not the French do the same with the Dutch?[35]

Precisely for the same reasons his brothers and allies resisted his urgings. In Westphalia, his writ ran free. In Holland and Naples, Louis and Joseph finally submitted, but modified sections of the code which conflicted with local juridical principles and practices. Beugnot proposed to introduce it gradually into Berg; when he was overruled and the code took effect with less than two months' advance notice, the local mayors resigned in mass against the obligation personally to view all corpses and newborn babes.[36] Baden accepted the code, with modifications. Bavaria and others within the Confederation of the

Rhine resisted, pointing to the example of the Prussian code of 1794 as an alternative model. A jurist, von Allmedingen, expressed the general reluctance in a highly Germanic form: 'Perfect laws are the beautiful and free forms of the interior life of a nation: they come out of life itself. The Civil code has not come out of the life of the German nation.'[37] Introduction of the code was impossible without reorganisation of the judicial system. The one and the other touched so close to the orderly functioning of civil society that even reforming Bavaria took care not to adopt them.

ADMINISTRATION AND SOCIETY

Administration could yield its positive effects only through a detailed knowledge of society and its leaders. Statistical enquiry was the instrument to provide the factual information about society – the resources, economy and institutional organisation of an administratively delimited area. The range of such enquiry could be extended, given the ethnographic curiosity about the science of man and earlier stages of civilisation, to descriptions of social practices and even physical appearance. But the observations remained extremely general, as they were predominantly confined to the behaviour of the common folk, by definition anonymous. The conduct of elites was normally too familiar to require comment, except in so far as it related to the public sphere. Their attitude towards the French, their level of education or religious prejudice might merit a prefectoral note, but not their forms of sociability except in so far as these contained implications for the conduct of the administration.

On the other hand, effective administration also demanded the identification of those individual members of the local elites who were judged to possess particular qualities. Napoleonic rule displayed an unquenchable thirst for lists of persons deemed worthy of attention because of their wealth, family, reputation, talents or other merits. Such lists were essential for a multiplicity of purposes – to appoint to administrative posts, to classify the richest and most respectable, to gauge attitudes towards the regime, to identify economic entrepreneurs or philanthropists, or (most common of all) to present the names of those from whose ranks would be chosen the members of representative or consultative councils at all levels. The departmental lists of the thirty or the six hundred paying the highest taxes, of the sixty 'citizens distinguished by their civil and private virtues', or 'the most outstanding' or 'remarkable persons', of the candidates for appointment to the judiciary, the communal, sub-

prefecture and department councils, to the local consultative
chambers of arts and commerce and bureaux of philanthropy, to the
imperial guards of honour, were compiled to meet the demands of
central government.[38] An expanding and ambitious administration
knew no bounds to its search for personal information about the
elites. By the later years of the Empire the ministers of police,
Fouché and Savary, asked the prefects for 'personal and moral
statistics': 'For reasons of social order, the government needs to
know who are the most influential persons. Since, in general, wealth
is the basis of the greatest influence, it is of interest to the government
to identify all the rich families, without exception', including information about unmarried daughters and their likely dowry, their
physical appearance, qualities and religious principles.[39] In this case
at least, such police files remained incomplete, partly through the
reticence of the prefects to violate the privacy of respectable citizens
beyond the immediately practical needs of administration.

While these lists were ordered by the central government, they also
acted as a means of acquiring knowledge of local notables essential to
a prefect for the smooth discharge of his responsibilities. The annual
tour of the department which formed part of the prefect's duties
served the same purpose. It enabled the functionary to assess the
public spirit through his personal contact with those regarded as
opinion-makers in an essentially static society. Who these leaders
were and how they were to be approached was specified with unusual
precision by Di Breme, minister of the interior in the kingdom of
Italy, in his instructions of 1807:

> Furthermore, they shall ensure that they get to know those per-
> sons whose capacity, morality and attachment to the government
> indicate that they will be best able to discharge the duties of
> podesta, mayor or registrar. . . . Prefects will pay particular atten-
> tion to find out about public opinion. . . . They will ensure that
> they get into conversation with various persons and lead them
> to explain their attitude frankly and in confidence. . . . In each
> commune, they will note those persons who have most influence
> over the common-right peasants; and will take care to find out
> whether they are attached to the government, through sentiment,
> principles or other reasons, or if their conduct makes them suspect
> of contrary opinions. Above all they will obtain the most exact
> information about the behaviour and opinions of the parish priests
> and other ministers of religion, whose ministry puts them into a
> position to be useful, if good, or harmful, if bad.[40]

Knowledge of the reputation and comportment of local opinion leaders was the prerequisite for gaining their acquiescence and, if possible, their active involvement in the administration. For wherever a new regime was set up, it required the consent and collaboration of leading personalities. The Cisalpine notables were summoned to Lyons in 1801, like the Genoese senators to Milan in 1805, the Spanish grandees to Bayonne in 1808 and the Dutch ministers to Paris in 1810, to provide a fig-leaf of responsible opinion to decisions that had already been taken; they were the Bonapartist sequel to the faked plebiscites of the Directorial years. Such grand notables constituted a handful of personalities known to Bonaparte and his advisers for reasons of political career or social prestige. Their future attitudes could not easily be judged from their behaviour during such artificial and browbeating meetings.

More substantial and necessary was the commitment of leading local figures to act within their own countries as catalysts for acceptance and support of the new regime. Melzi in the Italian republic, Schimmelpenninck in the Netherlands, Bülow in Westphalia, Nesselrode in Berg, even Rougemont in tiny Neuchâtel, performed such a function. In Naples faction ran so deep that Joseph's appointment of great nobles like the Cassano clan alienated other leading figures. In Spain, the fragmentation of the elites in the years before Bayonne meant that the pro-French, like Azanza and O'Farrill, were few and isolated. To obtain the visible participation of personalities with a widely accepted reputation, usually from a leading aristocratic or patriciate family, was of major importance. The collaboration of reforming ministers of earlier political experiences, such as Zurlo and Ricciardi in Naples, Gianni in Tuscany, Cabarrús in Spain, was an inadequate substitute as, whatever their commitment, they were politically isolated and usually socially insignificant through lack of appropriate kin and influence. Murat in Naples was forced into increasing reliance on the military. The failure of the French administrators in Spain, whether serving Joseph or in Catalonia (albeit under the particular conditions of war), was highlighted by the absence of collaboration of local notables.

In France, from Brumaire, the operational words in the search for stability were 'amalgamation' (*amalgame*) and 'rallying round' (*ralliement*). 'Amalgamation', or its synonym 'fusion', was an ambiguous term, as it implied not only reconciliation of the political opponents of the recent Revolutionary years, but also an end to the social divides of the ancien regime. The ideal way to achieve amalgamation was through a military or civilian career, where Jacobin and servative, noble and non-noble, would work together in the service of the state. But the ideal was not always realisable, and the Napoleonic administrators were satisfied with less committed attitudes which could be interpreted as evidence of 'rallying round'. It is evident that the transformation of the French republic into an Empire, soon followed by the creation of a host of courts outside and within the imperial frontiers, offered new and attractive possibilities of *rallie-ment* to the old aristocratic families, with the relatively few exceptions of those obstinately faithful to the former dynasties. But reputation requires time to sink roots. Much effort was expended by Napoleon and his propagandists to counter the recurrent sense of instability engendered by his international adventures. 'Announce my imminent arrival at Naples', Napoleon wrote to Joseph two weeks after the latter's occupation of the southern Italian capital, 'Naples is so distant that I cannot promise you that I shall get there; but for both the army and the peoples of the country, there is no harm in announcing that I'm coming'.[41] Every victory appeared to reinforce *rallie-ment*, with the most distinguished nobles and patricians, even those of staunchly dynastic loyalties – in Piedmont and Belgium, Naples and Holland, as much as in France – accepting court office or appointment as mayor of their local city. But every renewal of war as regularly revived suspicions and potential withdrawal: 'The moment that a campaign starts is always marked by plots', were the resigned, cynical words of the police commissaire of Cuneo to the prefect of the Stura in July 1809.[42]

It is useful to distinguish between career and non-career posts. The establishment of administrations on the French model meant not only the dismantling of the old offices, but also new career opportunities. Prina in the kingdom of Italy employed nearly 250 within his ministry of finances in 1805, the ministry of the interior over 100;[43] by 1810 the central administration had expanded to some thousands. In Holland, Bavaria, Westphalia or any other of the states where administration was modernised, there was a corresponding creation of career posts. Ministry of finances officials operating in the departments of the kingdom of Italy numbered over 5,000 already in 1805. In the absence of detailed research in local archives, it is impossible to calculate precise figures for posts in the departments. But on the basis of the incomplete listings of the published almanachs of four annexed departments – Mont-Tonnerre for 1808, Léman and Escaut for 1811 and Arno for 1813 – it is clear that, taken all together, administrative, financial and judicial posts were numerous and increasing in number.

The prefectures and sub-prefectures were the most contained, with 20 to 45 employees; the judiciary (including justices of the peace) normally recruited between 80 and 120; while the total of employees responsible for revenues ranged from 120 to over 300; public works, civil engineering, the postal service and various other responsibilities easily added on a further 30 to 60 posts, education 25 (Escaut) to 40 (Geneva); besides the police and numerous low-level jobs.[44]

Despite individual hesitations, the patriots of the republics continued to offer their services, even with the change to monarchy. There is a continuity of personnel, for example, at the higher levels of ministers and prefects, from the Dutch patriots of 1787 through the Batavian republics of 1798–1801 and 1805–6, to Louis' kingdom of 1806–10 and the annexed departments of 1810. At the intermediate and lower levels of career posts, there would also seem to have been no shortage of candidates. Italy or Germany had experienced a major expansion of higher education in the previous decades: Pavia university had about 150 students in the 1760s and a thousand in 1788; in Germany there were some 2,000 to 3,000 'writers' in 1766 and about 11,000 in 1806.[45] In Poland, where the educational level was markedly lower, a school of law and administration was founded in order to train functionaries, chosen primarily from the poor nobility.

The problem was one of access, particularly in states like Naples where previously the educated class had depended on a plethora of underpaid but official sinecures. Patronage was all important, especially in the newly annexed departments and the satellite states in Italy, where there was forceful competition from Frenchmen. Perhaps linguistic difficulties, as much as deliberate policy, ensured the reservation of most career posts to locals in the German states and Holland. Even so, the growing professionalism of the administration – and presumably the age structure of those in office – made access increasingly difficult. Giuseppe Tornielli, prefect at Novara, warned his younger brother Gaudenzio that there was no possibility of employment without a long, unpaid apprenticeship:

> Prefect Caccia di Romentino's brother is a good example: after nearly two years of apprenticeship in this prefecture, he was unable to get paid employment, as the first to be placed are those left out with the introduction of the new system. He has abandoned the career he had embarked on.[46]

The problems for the new rulers above all related to the non-career posts that constituted the base of the administrative pyramid. It was at this level that the prefect's lists should have served to identify the appropriate candidates. The matter was of crucial importance for the effective introduction of French practices in newly annexed regions, as it was often difficult to recruit with adequate rapidity the professional technicians of local government. Two years after Venetia was annexed to the kingdom of Italy, the new prefect of the department of the Tagliamento, Giovanni Scopoli, reported that:

> The communes are all in the greatest administrative disorder, because few have a revenue office, and no land registrars or other administrative directors were set up in the cantons, so that everything is entrusted to the mayors in a new country, with a multitude of completely new laws.[47]

The complaints of the prefects and sub-prefects were universal about the impossibility of finding candidates with appropriate qualifications for the rural communes and small towns. There is little doubt that, at least within the Empire, the demands made on local administrators were on a different level from those of previous governments, whether in terms of responsibility for taxation, maintenance of communal roads, registry of births, marriages and deaths, or sanitary measures. Lack of adequate private means, education or reputation were the explanations the prefects put forward, often to justify the continuing dependence on the local parish priest. The attitude of the new authorities towards these parish priests was ambivalent, inevitably so given the suspicion and respect attributed contemporaneously to the Church. The local clergy was mistrusted as potential catalysts for reactionary opposition to the new order – and often fulfilled this function where religious conservatism was the norm, as in the ex-Papal Marches in Italy, or in regions of the remodelled German states where Protestantism or Catholicism had formerly excluded toleration. However, the parish priests were also needed by the new administrators who utilised them as public officials for the civil registry and were often dependent on their role and prestige as intermediaries between the state and the local community.

In reality, the comments of the prefects revealed the limits of the lists of the good and the worthy that were compiled so assiduously. They often masked an uneasy sense of their ignorance of the hidden complexity and moral assumptions of kin, neighbourhood, property and working relations that characterised life at the local level, whether in an Emilian village, a Westphalian seigneurial village, the Zeeland dykelands or a Catalan peasant community. For willingness or reluctance to assume responsibility often depended on attitudes that were extraneous to the new order, and the new issues that now appeared were only gradually mediated into terms and interests of relevance to the local leading families. In the small town of Werden in Berg, the local notables forced the resignation as mayor of the local innkeeper, who was judged to have stepped out of place.[48] In southern Piedmont, the refusal of royalists to serve alongside patriots was not simply political, but covered longer-standing local family rivalries; after years of French rule, the same men would unite as natives of Mondovì to attack an outsider, 'who has little consideration for local men'.[49]

In the newly annexed departments, the French authorities were aware of the dangers of being sucked into such introspective local affairs. Two examples can be given – the redrawing of communal boundaries and measures of administrative policing (*haute police*). Abstract rationality and the practical needs of cadastral measurements for fiscal purposes argued in favour of rectifying the illogical confines of communes. In Piedmont, the prefects applied themselves with dedication and tact to negotiate between communes for exchanges of territory or settle age-old disputes. Such was the wasps' nest that their endeavours provoked that finally the council of state itself decreed the boundaries should be left untouched.[50]

A similar caution was displayed in the use of measures of *haute police*, punishment imposed by the administration without trial, in response to requests from local officials or even individuals. *Haute police* was used by the French in Piedmont or Tuscany as an instrument to achieve calm or reconciliation where unrest or divisions existed between or even within families. Acceptance of the impartiality of the French as an outside authority was an essential condition of *ralliement*. The evidence of success was to be found in the slow acceptance – first in Belgium and the Rhenish departments, from 1806–7 in Savoy and Piedmont – by leading noble families of appointments as mayor of a city or president of the departmental electoral college.

It would be inaccurate to conclude that reluctance or resistance was universal at the local level. There were always some who were convinced of the advantages and opportunities offered by French rule, particularly among purchasers of national properties or the free professions. But the particularity of the problem of imposing the new administrative system at the level of commune and sub-prefecture was the traditional impermeability of local notables to abstract calls to rationality or duty, the relatively greater importance of private over public concerns.

The consequences for the model of modernising administration were significant. The application of general measures intrinsic to the new system could nullify all the efforts at impartiality and careful cultivation of local personalities: religious equality and Jewish emancipation were resented by the landowning nobles of Westphalia, subordination of the Church was resisted by Catholics in Belgium or the former Papal States. The abolition of feudalism was a direct challenge to the dominant class of landowners in Naples and Berg, as in Poland and Valencia: Calabrian landowners might be prepared to serve in the provincial guards out of fear of peasant risings, but this usually marked the limit of their collaboration. The greater the shock of the measures introduced by the new administrations in terms of the socio-economic conditions to which they were applied, the lesser the willingness of the local notables to accept formal responsibilities. It is hardly surprising that there should have been a reluctant but widespread readiness to serve in local government in Holland under Louis Bonaparte but not in the grand-duchy of Warsaw under Frederick Augustus of Saxony.

Readiness to collaborate, however, often implied, on the one hand, negotiation of the conditions of service and, on the other, tacit acceptance by the authorities of exceptions to the uniformity of their rules. Bonaparte always insisted that 'men change in relation to their position, especially those with talent and foresight who best calculate the future', observed Melzi regretfully.[51] But if men adapted to the responsibilities of their post, some managed to adapt the post to their own advantage: ex-Count Ippolito Lovatelli of Ravenna refused appointment as prefect since it meant leaving his home base, but accepted employment as prefectoral lieutenant at nearby Forlì, where his position strengthened his and his cronies' hand in cornering the market in the purchase of national properties.[52] In the Rhineland, there was far greater collaboration by nobles in the Bas-Rhin department, whose income depended on their properties, than in the adjacent Mont-Tonnerre and Sarre departments with a wealthier ex-court and service nobility.[53] In Valencia, the price Marshal Suchet paid for the collaboration of the local noble landowners was the maintenance of feudal dues, which they exacted with the support of French troops.[54]

The alternative to compromise was recognition of the practical impossibility of making the administrative system function effectively at the local level and hence acceptance that, in some respects, it would be subject to unavoidable limitations. How could this be otherwise when a Baron Kettler regarded his nomination as mayor of

Münster as a joke and continued to act as in the good old days before the arrival of the French?[55] Whereas complaints of lack of qualified candidates in rural areas would seem to be common to all areas, whether in or outside imperial frontiers, compromise or resignation at the impossibility of adapting local notables to the expectations of the new administrative spirit would seem to be characteristic primarily of the satellite states. In contrast to Baron Kettler, Barthélemy, a young and ambitious sub-prefect in the newly annexed German department of Bouches de l'Elbe, when confronted by the insolence of the mayor of Lüneburg (who had held the office for the twenty-five years of Barthélemy's life), firmly put him in his place, with the virtuous self-confidence of an auditor fresh from Paris.[56]

Multiple examples could be cited of the inability of the reformers outside the Empire to impose their standards at this most intimate level of village and town, each instance specific to the local context and mentality. In the kingdom of Italy, prefects failed to control the expenditure of smaller communes: the village of San Salvatore, the minister Di Breme discovered, was exacting a local land tax at the level of 178 denari per scudo, where the legal limit was 3 centimes (or about 8 denari).[57] In Holland the abolition of the guilds – which Gogel regarded as a decisive struggle of the forces of light against those of darkness – did not prevent Amsterdam from denying a Jew the right to trade in glass, porcelain and mineral water.[58] Outside the Empire, even the French administrators most sure of their mission recognised the difficulties of convincing opinion. The price of collaboration was acceptance of limits. In foreign territories even convinced local reformers, appointed as ministers or prefects, might identify with the interests of the notables, like Carlo Verri, prefect of the department of Mella, who sided with the patriciate of Brescia in opposing a new cadastral measurement of their urban properties.[59] As Beugnot recalled, he had no choice in Berg but to abandon municipal government to Nesselrode as

> a means of softening the foreign yoke in the eyes of the Germans was to propose for that part of the administration that required daily activity a man of repute who spoke their language, shared their tastes and even their weaknesses, and whose comportment corresponded to all their prejudices.[60]

THE CONSTRAINTS OF PHYSICAL AND SOCIAL SPACE

The administrative model of France – initially including the major reforms of the Revolutionary decade incorporated by the Consul Bonaparte, and then in its successive amplifications – provided the obligatory reference point throughout continental Europe. Even hostile powers like Prussia followed the Napoleonic experiments in state-building with close attention. The Prussian ambassador in Westphalia, Küster, reported to Frederick William III with admiration at the early and rapid progress of the creation of this new state (October 1808): 'The main feature is the felicitous unity of the administration in place of the previous heterogeneous elements of states; its simplicity, rapidity and energy cannot fail to achieve full success'.[61]

In the earlier years, there was recognition of the need for prudence in the introduction of reforms derived from the French archetype. Even in the annexed departments, there was a process of trial and error in the imposition of the French system: in his instructions appointing Lebrun as governor-general of the former Ligurian republic (10 prairial Year XIII/29 May 1805), Napoleon stressed 'the experience I had in Piedmont of the false operations that were carried out there'.[62]

Outside French frontiers, there was cautious recognition of the difficulties. Melzi enjoyed an unrivalled degree of autonomy, partly because Bonaparte's preoccupations with sorting out France in this most fruitful period of the Consulate subordinated his attention for the Italian republic. As Marescalchi reported to Melzi on 17 December 1802:

> I don't always succeed, even in the two days . . . when I'm allowed to visit him, . . . in discussing calmly with the consul . . . without some urgent matter interrupting us. So an affair can be delayed from audience to audience and sometimes, because it's clear that he gets irritated if I remind him, I put the matter to him yet again, but this time in writing; but he only replies when he wants to.[63]

But lack of time was not the only reason. Napoleon intervened in the Netherlands in 1805 to impose Schimmelpenninck at the head of a French-style centralising administration, which brought together moderate Batavian republicans and Orangists in a recognisable *amalgame*. But the Emperor then kept in the background, lending his support only for major issues like Gogel's tax reform. When he created the grand-duchy of Berg for Murat (1806), he followed developments closely, but advised caution against the wholesale application of the French administrative machinery.

However, increasingly the French system was imposed or urged on prefects and allies as a model that brooked little modification or delay, except in the light of political (which normally meant military) exigencies. As always, the change was neither abrupt nor definitive; it was not the clear-cut application of a blueprint, but a progressive exercise of pressure. Thus, outside imperial frontiers, the insistence on close conformation to French practices was most visible initially in the region where Napoleon exercised direct sovereignty – north-central Italy – with the creation in 1805 of the kingdom of Italy (often called the Italic kingdom), whose administrative structures were immediately revised to reduce the anomalies of Melzi's republic. The kingdom of Holland (1806–10) provides a transition case, where in the earlier years Napoleon's constant recommendations to his brother Louis that he should take over the French system were accompanied by a practical acceptance of the often substantial differences of the Dutch reforms. By contrast, Napoleon was more insistent with his brother Joseph, possibly because of the widespread prejudice that the Neapolitans were less civilised: the 'semi-barbarians' of Calabria, 'savages of Europe', the *lazzaroni*, the rabble of the capital city, were not to be won over by conciliating their feelings, but only by threatening them immediately with cannon, as he himself had done at Cairo, and then imposing firm French rule.[64]

The change in style and insistence was marked by 1808 and became absolute by 1810. The time allowed administrators and prefects to impose French laws and procedures in the new departments in Tuscany, Rome, Holland and the Hanseatic coast shrank to a few months. From 1808 the Emperor was constantly urging Murat in Naples, Louis in Holland, Roederer and Beugnot in Berg, to hasten the adoption of the French system. Eugene de Beauharnais in Italy was informed by his stepfather that he would brook no disobedience; Jerome in Westphalia was presented with the *fait accompli* of a constitution and administrative package.

Napoleon's representatives and close collaborators expressed his belief that France was offering other states the possibility of enjoying the benefits of her success in creating the pattern for the future, without suffering the pains of its revolutionary parturition. The experienced diplomat Otto reported from Munich in May 1808:

> The entire Bavarian administration is convinced that this kingdom, which is so closely united to France by the most sacred

political ties, must assimilate all its institutions with ours; . . . all the cogs of government, which have already produced such marvellous effects in France, will be introduced step by step into this country, which will profit from our experience without undergoing the shocks that preceded the glorious reign of H.M. the Emperor.[65]

In fact, allied states alone, like Bavaria and Baden, were able effectively to resist the pressure and filter the French model, selecting and adopting those elements that seemed most appropriate to local needs, despite Napoleon's attempts to convince the member states of the Rhine Confederation into accepting his civil code and a French-style constitution.

The crucial year was 1810, during which Napoleon attempted to tighten and centralise control domestically by statistical enquiries in the economy, the creation of the Imperial University and the new decrees of the Continental system. It is hardly surprising that the counterpart should have been intolerance of deviations from the French example. By 1812, even in war-bound Catalonia, the solution to old ills was new administration, as the prefect Alban de Villeneuve observed in his otherwise banal explanation of Spanish decadence:

> The principal causes of the depopulation of Spain are war, famines, . . . the incursions of pirates, the vast landholdings of lords and church, the expulsion of the Jews and Moriscos, ecclesiastical mortmain, the great number of individuals who embrace the religious life, forced labour, begging, the natural sloth of the inhabitants, and at bottom an internal and inveterate ill that derives from bad government.[66]

By 1812 Napoleon's conviction that he possessed the administrative formula for stable rule was so profound that, as his Grande Armée advanced into Russian Poland, he immediately tried to organise the territory into departments.[67]

Napoleon's growing insistence on the uniform application of the French model was inevitably matched by increasing resistance. Space and the vitality of the European past worked against its feasibility. The immoderate presence of the French aroused resentment. Military and economic exploitation ultimately contradicted administrative integration.

All the administrators responsible for introducing the French system were agreed about the need for a gradual approach in the new territories. Physical space and social organisation worked against the practicality of the immediate adoption of the entire French system. An underlying sense of the backwardness that resulted from the irregular process of civilisation surfaced in platitudes about the character of the different peoples – the docility of the Tuscans, the feudal mentality of German seigneurs, the idleness of Spaniards and Neapolitans, the stolidity of the Dutch. Time was needed to provide the necessary material conditions and to counter the prejudices of the local populations. The tyranny of physical geography could be overcome through knowledge of the terrain, construction of new roads and bridges and state monopoly of the postal system. In the meantime, military repression of brigands and personal administrative inspections served as preparatory measures: 'I believe that the true system to follow in a country where there is need to ensure uniformity in the methods and where there is little change in posts is few directorates and many inspections', Roederer advised Joseph in his kingdom of Naples.[68] Napoleon agreed with Joseph that immediate suppression of the mendicant orders was dangerous and accepted that the introduction of the metric system required time. For Beugnot, in his report to Napoleon on what was needed to structure Westphalia, the social organisation of feudalism imposed the gradual introduction of reforms:

> for the feudalism that exists in your state of Westphalia is not the weak and almost extinct feudalism that existed in France in 1789, where one could only observe privileges and honorific rights. Here feudalism is part of the social order, it is at its roots. . . . All reforms must be slow and measured: this is one of those matters where time is required for success.[69]

Murat's councillors in Berg, Agar and Nesselrode, were cautious about reform of municipal administration, first experimenting in the capital Düsseldorf, with the appointment of an executive Stadt-Direktor and only slowly extending the solution to other cities.

Even more than graduality, adaptation of the French model to the historical, social and institutional particularities of each state became the central issue in dispute. Napoleon did not deny the existence of such particularities, only the method of dealing with them. Ever more forcefully, he reprimanded his relatives and representatives for their desire to conciliate the local populations. Lebrun was castigated for suspending the conscription of sailors at Genoa, Joseph mocked for trying to win the sympathy of the *lazzaroni*. From the height of his power, Napoleon drew on his experiences to conclude that, as the key to conquest was the application of an established sequence of military operations, so standard procedures existed for the consolidation of new regimes, including harsh repression of the inevitable insurrection.[70] 'Peoples are not governed with weakness, which only draws misfortunes on them', he told Lebrun.

> Did you hope to govern the people without discontenting them first? . . . *You know well that in matters of government, justice signifies force as a virtue.* As for those who say that this will make the Genoese discontented and push them to behave badly, for me this is unacceptable language. I know their weight and worth.[71]

It was this indifference to popular reaction that led him initially to underestimate the strength of Spanish hostility.

His respondents, for their part, did not deny that the French path to modernity was the best and indeed the only (or at least the inevitable) one. Like the Emperor, they were convinced of the benefits of a council of state and prefects, of statistical enquiries and free circulation of goods, of industrial exhibitions and urban embellishments. They shared his conviction that the mechanisms through which society operated could be understood and controlled: it was a question of identifying the leaders and ensuring their acquiescence. Even in Spain, Joseph's ministers thought it would be possible to negotiate an end to opposition, as it was led by local notables who were their relatives and friends.[72] Where they differed from him – even before conscription and the Continental system of the later years rendered administrative modernisation irrelevant as a means of integration – was in their assessment of the dangers of discontent, and their conviction that concessions to national susceptibilities would prove more effective in consolidating their rule.

Causes of friction were multiple, inevitably so given the infinity of local situations; the final ruptures between Napoleon and the relatives he had raised to thrones resulted from the untenable strains of war and blockade. But the impossible dream of a uniform administrative system probably forced the satellite rulers into stronger affirmations of identification with their peoples than might have been expected. Joseph and Louis Bonaparte, Murat and even young Jerome were genuinely concerned, like Melzi before them, to revive or create national pride: 'To uplift a humiliated nation, one has to imagine it today as it will be tomorrow', reflected Joseph in 1806.[73] Nothing could have been further from Napoleon's thoughts: for him, the morrow belonged to states modelled on and in the service of France.

The faithful reproduction of the French administrative system touched on sensitive nerves. It is significant that the aspect which aroused greatest hesitation and resistance was that of the new legal codes. For the adoption of a new legal system was not limited to retraining practitioners of the law; it affected profoundly day-to-day practices, established conventions and ingrained prejudices. In Naples, the civil code was modified to avoid too sharp a break over inheritance and dowry practices. In Westphalia, Siméon wanted to adjust the penal code to local usages. In Holland, Reuvens insisted that the codes be adapted to fit 'our institutions, our physical and moral situation, our manners and customs'.[74]

Only the allied states, like Bavaria, were able to adopt a more gradualist and controlled approach, experimenting with reforms by their application in specific localities, modifying articles of faith of the French system (such as the regulation rather than the abolition of the guilds), quietly abandoning what was regarded as unrealisable, such as the French legal and judicial system.

Resistance to adoption of the French administrative model was undoubtedly heightened by its association with the intrusive presence of Frenchmen. The military commanders and officers, stationed in the eleven military divisions covering the annexed departments, in the five divisions in the kingdom of Italy, or in the satellite states, were a constant source of friction with the civilian authorities. Their suspicion or contempt for the local inhabitants (including their elites) hardly encouraged good relations. Whether pro-patriot (like Masséna in Naples) or conservative (like Menou in Piedmont), they tried to exert pressure in favour of appointment of French civilians. The prejudices of some of the leading French administrators pushed in the same direction. According to Roederer, French functionaries worked even without pay, Neapolitans expected pay without work: 'it's the division of leisure'.[75] Beugnot expostulated that the Germans were 'convinced that the French constitutions are worthless and that they serve their country well by opposing when possible, hampering when they cannot oppose, and delaying when they cannot hamper'. For the young Stendhal, the only lively personality in Brunswick was a Jewish banker.[76] A minor figure like Pierre Legarde, director-general of police in the Venetian departments, argued that:

A people destined to be dependent on France for a long time cannot be governed by its own men, as they have an interest in paying as little as possible and hence are always inclined to hide the country's resources and protest that the taxes are too high.[77]

Far from encouraging such self-interested propositions, the administrators and rulers of the new regimes resisted the recommendations
and urgings from Paris and locally to appoint Frenchmen. Naples was
exceptional, regarded as potentially wealthy and legitimate booty;
but even here Joseph and Murat argued strongly in favour of employing locals; the constitution of 1808 specified that all offices be reserved to Neapolitan subjects. Melzi had already refused to give in to
French pressure, whether from Paris or military commanders. In
Germany and Holland, Beugnot, Siméon and Lebrun insisted on the
need to reserve the posts to the local elite in order not to create
unemployment and discontent. Napoleon accepted that only Poles
could hold office in the grand-duchy of Warsaw. The hostility against
French office-seekers was often out of proportion to the numbers
actually employed. But resentment at their possible employment
hardly assisted administrative integration.

Roederer, one of the most experienced administrators of foreign
territories, was a convinced exponent of French administration,
which he regarded as the solution to the problem of maintaining
equality and stability without oppression. In 1810 (the year of the
tightening of control), he wrote to Napoleon:

> A characteristic of your government is to conduct affairs through
> institutions and not to rely on men endowed with arbitrary power.
> You have thus given the lie in your immense Empire to the grand
> theory that asserts that great empires are incompatible with
> moderate government, since it was thought impossible to govern
> distant provinces without sending and being an oppressor.
> Because you cannot answer to your peoples for so many agents,
> you have institutions that answer for them, and they answer to you
> for the institutions.[78]

Despite Roederer's optimism, the problem remained, that the excellence of the institutions was in practice dependent on the men who
made them function. Inevitably not all lived up to expectations, even
among the French. In Calabria, the local commanders sold exemptions from service in the civic guards. The prefect Barthélemy
recalled that his first superior Reiset (in whose office he had been
placed at the age of 14 by a friend of his stepmother's family) laid the
basis of his fortune by using his position as general tax collector at
Colmar to speculate against French currency: he used to cross the
Rhine, carrying bags of 2,000 louis d'or – symbol of Napoleonic
monetary stabilisation in 1803, officially quoted at 20 francs – which

he exchanged at Frankfurt at a profit of 50 to 60 centimes per coin. Thiébault recorded that in Spain the paymasters-general of the armies in like manner profited from the funds under their control, which they used to lend at high interest rates.[79] Corruption was rife among Customs officials at every frontier, particularly where smuggling became a full-time business, as at Strasbourg or Hamburg. Nor were such weaknesses limited to lower-level officials. Military leaders continued to abuse their positions for private profit: Brune demanded half a million guilders and got 80,000 as a 'gift' when he left the Netherlands in 1799; Napoleon was furious with Masséna for extracting 3 million francs illegally from the local administrations with the occupation of Venetia in 1806 and insisted that he disgorge them.[80] Bonaparte's artillery school comrade Bourrienne, as consul at Hamburg, turned the Continental system to his private advantage, accumulating at least 1 million francs from illegal licences, before Napoleon ordered an official investigation in 1810. Talleyrand's penchant for bribes was notorious throughout Europe.

It would be inaccurate to conclude that the Napoleonic administration was vitiated by corruption. It is difficult to imagine a regime holding power over an extended period without scandals or individual examples of corruption, which naturally figure prominently in contemporary memoirs. The Napoleonic administration upheld high standards, partly in reaction to the lax permissiveness of the Directorial years, far more out of a genuinely collective sense of professionalism and duty (besides the importance attributed to administrative controls). Such isolated cases of private profit from public service essentially only dirtied minor cogs in the vast machine – except for the administrative machinery of the Continental system, which was seriously clogged up.

More serious a constraint on the smooth running of this massive, sophisticated complex was the scarcity of local men imbued with the skills and convictions of the French functionaries. As Beugnot commented gloomily: 'It's already a great deal to take our institutions to neighbouring peoples, but it always remains a difficult matter to form men for these institutions, until the time arrives when they will be born from the institutions themselves'.[81] This was particularly evidenced in the refusal (or inability) to accept the new bureaucratic lines of communication, which (it was believed) could be short-circuited by personal contacts. Where new administrations were still in their infancy, outside the Empire, such practices were not uncommon. Precisely because of the accentuated centralisation, access to decision-makers was crucial. Without such access, causes could easily be lost or in any case drag on forever. On occasion, Napoleon could act the medieval monarch as embodiment of justice: a peasant deputation from the Dortmund countryside in Berg (advised by a liberal lawyer) waited outside the gates of St Cloud and finally managed to present a petition against their feudal lord to the Emperor in person.[82] More generally, citizens and officials sought for the means to sidestep the functionary directly in charge by appeal one or more steps above: a mayor appealed to the prefect, ignoring the sub-prefect (as at Lüneburg), a prefect to the head of state, ignoring the ministry of the interior (as at Brescia).[83] Everywhere local notables sought for means of access to Paris and especially to Napoleon: Berthier, as prince of Neuchâtel, received regular requests for intervention with the Emperor; the nobles of Valencia appealed directly to Joseph against Napoleon's abolition of seigneurial rights (though in fact they then continued to be exacted).[84] Dutch democrats, like Gogel and Verhuell, denied access to the French government during the collapse of the Regency in 1804, turned to Marshal Marmont.[85] Marshals had a special line to Napoleon.

Such initiatives were not without their dangers, at least for functionaries: Chateaubriand's ostentatious ignoring of protocol at Rome was used as an excuse for relegating him in punishment for his protest at the execution of the duke of Enghien; Francesco Angiolini was dismissed because of his critical comments about his superior in Dalmatia, Vincenzo Dandolo; the mayor of Brussels, Rouppe, was not only dismissed but also exiled for his resistance to orders from Paris and appealing to public opinion by printing his version of the issues at dispute.[86] For private citizens, little was to be lost by such attempts to bypass the normal channels of the new administrative system. Patronage and contacts already played so important a role in access to the bureaucracy that they continued to be considered as normal practice for the favourable resolution of issues at dispute. Nevertheless, such initiatives are revealing of an issue of more general significance: the problematic relationship between administrators – who asserted the novelty and institutional impersonality of the new machinery of government – and the administered, whose persistence in attempting to exercise traditional methods of personal influence on decisions was indicative of a cultural attitude of diffidence.

THE CONTRADICTIONS OF INTEGRATION

It would be hazardous to maintain that Napoleon's concept of the state remained unchanged. The identification of the administration with the state, by the very fact of the continuous extension of the former, implied changes in the concept of the latter and expansion of its role. It is only too easy to point to the radical shifts in the institutional arrangements Napoleon imposed on France and the satellite states or to the contrast between some of the constitutional norms and the practices of government to conclude that there was no consistency, merely the political contingencies and propagandistic benefits of the moment. Nevertheless, there can be no doubt that Napoleon always regarded the institutional organisation of the state as the only sure means of laying foundations (in the Machiavellian sense of '*gittar fondamenti*'). It is equally clear that in the organisation of the state he held firmly to a few fundamental ideas, mostly derived from the pre-Revolutionary critique of the ancien regime: equality of citizens before the law, control and accountability of public finances, absolute property rights, legal protection of individual initiative, secularisation of the state, participation in public affairs open to all elites, who were defined by wealth, education and comportment. The science of administration, through which these concepts were to be translated into practice, was probably the most recent and certainly the most novel of Napoleon's ideas about the state.

Until the marked tightening of control in 1810, Napoleon's vision of the relationship between society and the state contained elements of the ancien regime concept of representation, however reduced and controlled in reaction to the Revolutionary experiences. In the late ancien regime, the political ideas of sovereignty of the people had conflicted with the social practices of organic representation by status and group. Now the concept of popular sovereignty had been totally abandoned, whereas organic representation was revived under different names. From the first constitution (the Brumairean model of Year VIII) to the last one (grand-duchy of Frankfurt, 1810), representation was restricted to specific categories of the populations, whose selection procedures were kept as distinctly separate as those of the former Estates-General. Political representation of groups was an old idea among French political theorists, elaborated, for example, by the Huguenot Hotman in the sixteenth century. The Bonapartist categories constituted what were regarded as the elites or opinion leaders of each particular society; they represented both the description of its social composition and Napoleonic assumptions about specific groups whose influence or contribution merited recognition. Landed proprietors were always present and were often given a greater share of representation; in terms of wealth, the category was defined broadly, so as to include relatively modest proprietors. Manufacturers and merchants equally constituted a general category. In the republic of Italy, an additional electoral college was created of *dotti*, presumably because of the reputation of the intellectuals in the Lombard reforming tradition and universities; *savants* and artists were similarly recognised with an electoral college in the constitutions of Bayonne, Naples and Berg, where jurists in particular enjoyed considerable prestige. In the Spanish, Neapolitan and Polish constitutions, the traditional power of nobility and clergy was recognised by the creation of colleges reserved for them.

In terms of parliamentary democracy, the limited powers and restricted and contorted electoral procedures – which in some cases (Spain, Bavaria, Berg) were never even put into practice – reduced Napoleonic representation to a mere simulacre. Only in Warsaw, highly conscious of its recent parliamentary tradition, did the diet express animated and on occasions effective criticism of the executive. But it would be a mistake to dismiss the constitutions as mere window-dressing. They were drawn up either as the basis for the creation of a wholly new state (Italian republic, Westphalia), where representation of the new 'national' entity complemented administrative efforts to overcome regionalist and particularist tendencies; or as a means of legitimising the new political power through the participation of powerful and potentially dangerous social groups (Warsaw, Spain, Naples).

The constitutions (with the exception of the republic of Italy, created immediately in the image of France) belonged to a particular moment of the Napoleonic trajectory – 1807 to 1808 – when military and diplomatic successes brought nearer the mirage of French hegemony over Europe. It was the moment when Napoleon signed his decrees emperor, king and protector 'by the grace of God and the constitutions'.[87] Napoleon personally dictated the draft of the constitution of the grand-duchy of Warsaw, before assigning the new state to the king of Saxony. The Polish constitution of 1807 was the model for the new kingdom of Westphalia, was closely imitated by Bavaria and was the basis of discussions for representation in Berg. The Spanish constitution of 1808 (copied by Joseph as his parting gift from Naples) was again personally supervised by Napoleon at Bayonne, in a manner closely resembling his patronage of the Italian constitution of 1801 at Lyons: in both instances, his concern was to render the leading notables coresponsible, and hence to legitimise the reordering of the state. From 1810 more authoritarian methods of administrative centralisation were judged the most effective path to the future. But in the earlier years, above all at the peak of his success, constitutions were an integral part of Napoleon's perception of how to lay foundations, the counterpart to the modern administration, the bridge between state and society through their expression of what Napoleon defined as liberal government.

Nowhere was this expressed more clearly than in the creation of the kingdom of Westphalia (1807). More confident than ever that his genius enabled him to empathise with the wishes of the peoples of Europe, Napoleon explained to Jerome, with a dose of rhetoric, how good government would win the affection of his new subjects:

> What the peoples of Germany impatiently desire is that individuals who are not noble and have talent should have an equal right to your consideration and employment; that all forms of serfdom and intermediary ties between the sovereign and the last class of the people should be wholly abolished. The benefits of the Napoleonic code, the publicity of procedures, the creation of juries will all be distinctive characteristics of your monarchy. Let me spell out my thoughts to you completely: I count more on the effects [of such reforms] than on the greatest of victories in extending and affirming your monarchy. . . . The peoples of Germany, of France, Italy and Spain want equality and liberal ideas. I have been leading the affairs of Europe for some years now and I have become convinced that general opinion is against the buzzing of the privileged. Be a constitutional king. . . . This way you will find that you have the strength of opinion and a natural ascendancy over the absolute kings, your neighbours.[88]

Given Napoleon's ambition to demonstrate, through the kingdom of Westphalia, the possibility of creating a model state, his insistence on the appropriate ways to attract social support is not surprising. Perhaps more interesting in this son of the Revolution is his identification of such means with the attack on privilege of 1789, albeit now tempered by more recent liberal constitutional ideas.

In a peaceful world (and Napoleon's administrators, even in Spain, envisaged such a world, almost till the end), it might have been possible to judge how far this massive experiment in modernisation was feasible and what changes it induced at the social level. But it was never a 'pure' experiment, as it was increasingly vitiated by contradictory exigencies.

The fundamental social conquests of the Revolution, wholeheartedly incorporated in the Napoleonic model – abolition of feudalism, free exercise of individual activities and circulation of goods, full property rights – were introduced most effectively in territories subject directly and for an extended period to French rule. Within these territories, the local avant-garde often shared a common cultural tradition, sometimes an earlier reforming experience, which rendered less radical the imposition of the new French system on societies where feudal and corporative structures had vanished or lost their force. When French administrators negatively described a society they came into contact with as displaying the characteristics of an earlier stage of civilisation, they expressed the differences, in their eyes, between societies which, however imperfectly, functioned like their own and those that seemed to equate to an earlier phase of the evolution of France: 'One would have to go back four or five centuries to find such examples in France', exclaimed Beugnot about feudal rights in Westphalia.[89] Not only Piedmont, Lombardy, Tuscany or Holland, but even Savoy, areas of Belgium and parts of the Rhine left bank where seigneurial rights still survived, were societies which the French felt they could 'read' without excessive difficulties. They also happened to be geographically close to France, which explained more widespread knowledge (from cultural and commercial contacts and the Directorial wars) and permitted more direct and continuous pressure.

Southern Italy, Germany, Spain and then Poland and Illyria were more distant and less known. At times the reports of the French administrators read as if they were explorers. They identified feudalism as the dominant social system of regions or even the entire area of these countries and recognised with shock that it could not be destroyed at the stroke of a pen. Hence their insistence on the graduality of reform. At the same time, juridical respect for property was strong among ex-Constituent deputies, like Beugnot and Roederer, or members of the civil code commission, like Siméon: serfdom was unacceptable, as a personal obligation; but distinctions needed to be made (as in France, in the days following the abolition of feudalism on 4 August 1789) between feudal and property rights. In Naples, where ex-Bourbon reformers like Zurlo welcomed strong French government as the means to destroy feudal power, a feudal commission was created – unique in Europe – to sort out the division of feudal lands between their former owners and the communes.

Elsewhere, particularly in Germany, the new or reforming rulers preferred compromise. In Berg and Westphalia, as in Bavaria, Frankfurt and Hesse, only personal serf obligations were abolished, while seigneurial dues required redemption by the peasants. The distinctions were often vague and local tribunals supported the lords. The peasants in these states, most surely aware of the successful abolition of all seigneurial rights in France and then in the (formerly German) Rhine left bank, continued their legal battle for years, sometimes with the support of French administrators, like Siméon. The result was to discontent the seigneurs, without winning the support of the peasantry. Bacher, the experienced chargé d'affaires at Frankfurt, reflected that, since the nobility and regular clergy would never support 'the new order of things', the governments 'in the end would be forced to admit that they were politically obliged to favour the redemption of rights in order to gain popularity and win the support of the rural population'.[90] In Spain, war conditions and the need to raise revenue persuaded Suchet to ignore the Emperor's decree abolishing feudalism. In Poland, Napoleon did not even propose to abolish noble privileges.

The contrast between the decisive determination of the French within the annexed departments of the Empire and the cautious pragmatism with which they approached the abolition of feudalism in Germany and Poland cannot be explained simply in terms of awareness of the greater social dimensions of the issue. It also resulted from practical exigencies of the wars and the political situation. Since Napoleon's initial invasion of 1796, Italy had entered definitively into the French sphere of influence: hence the Neapolitan feudatories could be attacked with vigour as the kingdom formed part of the future configuration of Europe. Napoleon's control of Germany was both more recent and less sure, particularly as he moved further east. Its future lay with the model states of Westphalia and Berg, perhaps in due course of Warsaw. But time was too short to risk the immediate opposition of the local nobility. Given the example of French procrastination, it was not surprising that even reforming states in the Confederation of the Rhine, like Bavaria, should also have progressed slowly. The strategic demands of international politics and war worked against the effective abolition of feudalism, thus undermining a central social pillar of the Bonapartist construction of the new state and society.

This was not the only contradiction of the civil project of integration. It is a commonplace of historiography that the end of the republic marked a conservative shift in Napoleon's evolution. The implications of the proclamation of the Empire went far beyond questions of style or of international politics. It led directly, on the one hand, to the abandonment of the concept of equality, with the creation of the new imperial nobility and, on the other, to an erosion of the financial independence of some of the satellite states, with the reservation of revenues for the benefit of the new dignitaries. Both nobility and endowments will be discussed in more detail on pp. 174–84. For the moment, it is enough to note that the new titles and entailed revenues fell almost exclusively outside the frontiers of the Empire. The principalities and duchies created by Napoleon from 1806, first in the annexed Venetian territories and throughout the Italian peninsula, then ever more heavily in Germany, as well as in Switzerland and Poland, created exceptions to the administrative unification of the satellite states and even left political enclaves within their territorial sovereignty, like the former Papal possessions of Benevento and Pontecorvo in the kingdom of Naples, transformed into duchies for Talleyrand and Bernadotte.

Napoleon's purposes in creating a nobility did not signify the abandonment of his ambitions to construct a new society. On the contrary, as he stated in his message to the Senate setting up the first duchies: 'He had been guided principally by the great idea of consolidating the social order and his throne, which was its foundation and base, and creating corresponding centres of support for the great empire'.[91] But the existence of an ever more numerous class with material and honorific privileges (30,000 had been admitted to the Legion of Honour by 1814) could not but work against the principles of legal equality central to the administrative concept of the state and reinforce the resistance of the landed aristocracies to the abolition of their seigneurial dues in the dependent states.

The practical consequences were directly contradictory to the aim of integration. Nowhere was this seen more clearly than in the kingdom of Westphalia, which had been created explicitly as a model state, the excellence of whose administration would win the support of the population and invite imitation throughout Germany. Napoleon's reservation as military entails of half the Crown allodial domains destroyed all possibilities of balancing the state budget and funding the necessary reforms and new administrative structure without exercising inequitable pressure on the population. The right of military conquest was deliberately deployed by Napoleon as adequate justification for ignoring the principles and practices which Jerome's functionaries had been appointed to administer: 'These domains belong to my generals who conquered your kingdom; that is a commitment I took towards them and which nothing can make me abandon'.[92] A principle systematically applied by Napoleon as essential to reconcile the local elites was the acceptance of at least a substantial portion of the public debt of their predecessors by the new regimes. But in Westphalia it was rejected in favour of the holders of endowments: 'I know that there are donees whom one would like to make responsible for the debts of their predecessors, whereas I gave them their properties free of all expenses'.[93] A convention was imposed (10 May 1811) which exempted the entailed lands from all taxes and charges, requisitions or billeting, and set special conditions for the redemption of feudal tithes.[94] To all effects and purposes, the 943 beneficiaries of Napoleon's generosity in Westphalia enjoyed extra-territorial status that frustrated the uniformity and equality of every administrative measure. Westphalia and the former British Crown state of Hanover were the most heavily burdened with Imperial endowments. But the total 30 million francs' revenue received by nearly 5,000 beneficiaries was drawn almost exclusively from the territories under French control outside the Empire.

Military and political priorities were always in conflict with the necessarily long-term and patient efforts at consolidating support through administrative action. The boundaries imposed on some of the new states, usually for strategic reasons, denied the necessary continuity of territory and hindered economic activity. In the republic of Italy, the traditional frontier area of the Lunigiana, between Tuscany and Liguria, was almost cut off from the rest of the state in the interests of a military corridor. Beugnot strove continuously but ineffectively to bring together the northern and southern parts of Berg, which were connected only by a narrow strip of land, and to obtain an uninterrupted stretch of territory along the Rhine as a major trade route between Holland and southern Germany. Napoleon was impervious to arguments of the rationalisation of territories of states outside the Empire: with the annexation of Holland in 1810, he also absorbed the neighbouring areas of Berg, with a quarter of its population, in order to rectify the French customs line.

As imperial ambitions expanded, so the military and fiscal pressures on the satellite states increased, contradicting and jeopardising the regularity and normality of civil administration. In 1808 Mosca, prefect of the Reno department in the kingdom of Italy, commented on the positive effects of the new system,

as the new political and administrative institutions gain in solidity, so the tranquillity and confidence of the populations seem to grow proportionately, as they understand the advantages of this progressive settlement of things which is now happening so eventfully, after many years of muddled opinions.[95]

The success of the Napoleonic project could emerge only through the peaceful application and progression of the new administrative structures and training of a professional bureaucracy. Conscription and fiscal exactions distracted and disrupted the efforts of the ever more skilled functionaries throughout French-controlled Europe. By 1810, faced with the reluctance of his brothers to enforce his crippling demands, Napoleon attempted to reconcile the contradictions of his policies by insisting ever more on centralisation and uniformity. Spain provided the paradox of this final phase, with the unending insistence on the possibility of creating the modern state by civil reforms negated by the demands of war, but still partly implemented, at least in Aragon, under the military administration of Suchet.[96] The dogmatic insistence on a theory of civil administration which in practice was applicable only under military rule highlights the contradiction of integration by the later years of the Empire.

Administrative integration was seen as the sequel to military occupation and the means to create a new relationship between state and society. Through the restoration of order and modernisation of the state, the Napoleonic functionaries expected to win the support of the elites – the opinion-makers of society – and acceptance by the mass of the people. The possibilities of success of such a project were contradicted by the military demands of the wars and Napoleon's insistence on an increasingly rigid centralisation. At the same time, the responses of the populations to the imposition of administrative integration inevitably modified its practices. These are the main themes of the following chapters.

4   The practices of conquest: exploitation

> The Romans gave their laws to their allies. Why should not France insist on the adoption of her own?
>
> (Napoleon to Louis Bonaparte, 13 November 1807)

The French administrative project, as theory and practice, reached its high point in the very years of the political-military crisis of the Empire. Social psychologists and some historians of war have argued that the greater the pressure, the higher the capacity to respond of individuals and social organizations. It is a hypothesis that tends to concentrate on the short term, ignoring the prolonged after-effects on individuals and groups. In the case of Napoleonic Europe, the smooth oiling of the French administrative machine effectively enabled Napoleon to wage ever more bloody battles and continuous military campaigns, and to conceive of the feasibility of forcing the European land-mass into the corset of the Continental blockade. Compared to the world wars of the twentieth century, Napoleon's struggle against Britain and the coalitions never reached the level of total war. Absolute exclusion of British goods from the Continent did not also mean a policy of starving the British into submission; the immense waste of human life in battles was never accompanied by the destruction or, even worse, extermination of enemy civilian populations. Technology did not provide the means, and mentalities had not yet transferred to the 'enemy' the fanatical conviction of evil.

Nevertheless, if the professionalism of the bureaucracy ensured the more or less efficient application of France's economic policy and conscription for her armies, both blockade and wars destroyed the very bases of the administrative project. For the bureaucrats, the presence and influence of France in Europe derived from its identification with a particular form of progress – the modernisation of more backward societies through administrative guidance. It was a project intimately linked to the universalist values of the Revolution, corrected of their excesses. It depended on the force of example that could be expressed only in peaceful conditions over an unspecified but certainly not brief period of time. It was this that justified integration within an expanding empire and the export of French theories and practices of good administration to neighbouring states. The very premises on which the administrative project was based were denied by French economic and military policies. For the one and the other inevitably signified the exploitation of the material and human resources of the territories within the French sphere of influence. At every turn, the economic and military practices of conquest negated the advantages of administrative modernity, to the frustration of the prefects in the annexed departments and councillors in the satellite states.

War and the blockade, it could be hoped, would be of limited duration. But the same years when their impact was felt most heavily were also those in which the most central values of the administrative project were challenged by the steady diffusion of social privileges. These were the years when the military offered an alternative model to that of the civilian administration, when the introduction of an imperial nobility denied the equality of citizens, when Napoleon's practices of distributing state revenues as largesse to his relatives and favourites destroyed the viability of such model states as Westphalia. From 1810, as the blockade tightened, the wars accelerated and social privileges increased, the impossibility of reconciling the practices of integration and exploitation came to the surface.

ECONOMIC POLICY

The Revolutionary legislators possessed a body of theories about how economies functioned unprecedented in quantity, range and level of sophistication. They were of the essence of the *philosophes'* debate and some propositions had inspired radical changes in policies under reforming ministers and princes like Turgot and Peter Leopold of Tuscany. In the initial dismantling of the ancien regime by the revolutionaries it would be difficult to overestimate the importance of the ideas central to French and Scottish economists like Quesnay and Adam Smith and the multitude of other theorists. The study of economic theories during the Revolutionary-Napoleonic period has attracted far less attention than enlightenment theorists or the utilitarians and political economists of the Restoration. But without

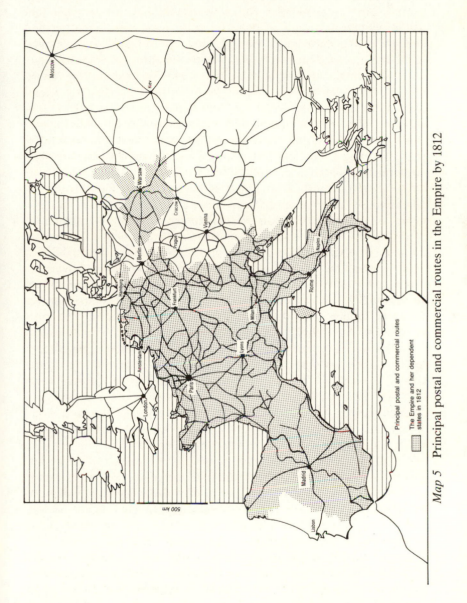

Map 5 Principal postal and commercial routes in the Empire by 1812

doubt the fundamental concepts inherited from the late eighteenth century – from individualism to the natural order or invisible hand of the market, from utility to the role of exchange, from rapidity of circulation to economic interdependence – were influential, not only in the theorising of the *idéologues*, but as part of the mental baggage of the French administrative class. Nor could this be otherwise, given the extensive overlap in personnel between the worlds of the scientists and French officialdom.

Nevertheless, in the Napoleonic years theoretical debate about the workings of an economy appears to have lost its pride of place. In part, this may have reflected Bonaparte's impatience and growing intolerance of abstract reasoning; in part, it was doubtless an aspect of the compression of autonomous discussion that resulted from the dilatation of an ever more conventional official wisdom. But as important was the divergence between the concerns of economic theorising and the objectives of economic policy. For the axis of the theoretical debate had always been the analysis of the national economy, whereas the unprecedented conditions of continuous warfare distorted the established framework of policy decision-making within the national economy by enhancing, on the one hand, the role of the state and, on the other, the relationship between the national and the international economy.

Private initiative and property remained articles of faith for official representatives, which were seen as marking clear limits to state action. Even at the peak of the administrative drive for economic statistics, in 1812, a prefect could explain his failure to provide detailed figures on forges in that they 'have to be obtained from private individuals over whom I have no power, who are free to reply or not without any possibility of my compelling them'.[1] In theory, the role of the state was primarily to remove the obstacles and create the conditions for a self-regulating internal market based on initiative and competition. This was the purpose of the early Revolutionary prohibition of corporations and workers' coalitions (1791), as of the later Napoleonic attempts to regulate out of existence collective rights in the countryside through a rural code (1811–14). It explained the creation of institutions for the diffusion of technological knowledge, like the Conservatory of arts and crafts (1794). It underpinned the great statistical effort of the ministers of the interior François de Neufchâteau and Chaptal (1797–1804), for whom the public availability of regional data was to serve as a stimulus to economic activity and entrepreneurship.

In practice, however, the state was forced into an ever more active role through the consequences of both Revolutionary legislation and war, and in response to the demands of manufacturers and traders. During the Revolutionary decade, the state found itself responsible for manufactories abandoned by émigrés; at the same time, it was forced to extend its control over whole sectors of the economy, like metallurgy, in order to supply the armies. For their part, manufacturers and traders gave few signs of appreciating the value of statistical data, whereas they never ceased to appeal for state aid. Ministers and bureaucrats were under continuous pressure to impose protective tariffs, provide subsidies, guarantee large-scale orders or constrain foreign competition. In this sense, the Continental blockade, at least initially, constituted a logical extension of the function attributed to the state, rather than a turning-point in economic policy. At the same time, it represented the economic counterpart to the role the administration assigned itself in modernising society: with the blockade, the state claimed the right to force the pace and direction of the new European economy, although (as in other fields) it remained ultimately dependent on the willingness of its collaborators – the entrepreneurs – to seize their opportunities.

The leading importance of the relationship between the national and international economy derived directly from the wars. Economic theories before (and after) the Revolution were premised on a condition of peace, necessary for the analysis of the domestic factors of production, distribution and consumption. The realities of the Revolutionary-Napoleonic experience denied such an assumption. The immediate implication of war with Britain and the coalition powers was the sharp diminution and rapid loss of commerce with the colonies, previously the fastest growing sector of the French economy. The wars and naval defeats throttled trade with the British, Spanish and soon the Dutch empires. Initially neutral, especially American, ships ensured some continuity of traffic with the colonies, albeit at a lower level. By 1798 the English fleet had effectively interrupted Atlantic exchanges; the revival following the peace of Amiens proved ephemeral. The consequences for the French economy were multiple. The collapse of colonial trading repercussed on the general level of economic activity throughout the country, affecting agricultural exports, manufactures and processing and re-export of colonial goods. France's external balance of payments deficit deepened, thus rendering French currency vulnerable to enemy rumours and bankers' speculations in financial centres like Amsterdam and Hamburg. The wars affected the economy ambivalently, on the one hand disrupting normal economic activities and generating inflation, on the other, opening up new opportunities and the possibilities of new markets.

The immediacy and persistence of the crisis of colonial trading and the recurrence of wars led to a profound reorientation of the structure of the French economy. The south-west, whose prosperity had been developed around the Atlantic trade, was affected most deeply, with the deindustrialisation that resulted from the dislocation of its activities. Elsewhere the new conditions produced extremely varied responses within the different sectors, industries and regions. Some traditional industries, like linen and hemp, declined with the closure of the colonies and subsequently the fall in naval demand for ropes and canvas; others, above all cotton, expanded and modernised in the absence of British competition. Paris asserted its primacy as the banking centre and cotton capital of the country. River and land transport and inland entrepôts gained in importance. In contrast to the uncertainties of the 1790s, the agricultural sector ceased to be a source of concern for most of the Napoleonic years, until 1812. Against this reassuring background, trading and manufactures assumed and were to retain a new level of importance for policy-makers, because of the structural shift of direction of the economy towards the Continental land markets, away from the Atlantic seaboard.

The Revolutionary decade had been marked by inflation and state bankruptcy, as well as the crisis of foreign trade. Napoleon, whose ideas about economics were traditional and at times primitive, responded by a rigid monetarist policy, alongside measures to boost exports and production. Such policies were basically contradictory, as the monetary and budget measures had deflationary effects on the economy. Fearful of the inflationary dangers of paper currency (after the only too recent experience of the *assignats* and the Directory's bankruptcy), Bonaparte restricted circulation to the metallic monetary mass; he inhibited the level of loans and hence the potential contribution of the new Bank of France as a source of credit. State finances were considered in terms of their political implications and regarded as entirely separate from the needs of the economy. The budget was to be balanced from year to year, as deficits (which were only officially recognised in 1811) were seen as putting at risk public confidence. The correspondence between Mollien, minister of the treasury, and Napoleon shows clearly the Emperor's unawareness of the negative consequences on the general level of economic activities of such rigid accountancy, or of how fiscal requirements could affect the capital market. When the tobacco monopoly was established in

1811 to boost revenues, the minister of the treasury Mollien commented bitterly at how it drained liquidity: 'all available capital at the moment is utilised in the securities demanded by the tobacco monopoly administration. . . . One should first of all decide whether fiscal needs or trade are more fundamental to an empire.'[2]

Nevertheless, if Napoleon was less sophisticated than many of his advisers in his understanding of economic mechanisms, he was vigorously decisive in his support of French manufactures against the British. His policy developed that advocated by Delacroix during the Directory, in the imposition of favoured market outlets for national products outside France's frontiers, as much as in the exclusion of British manufactures. Whatever the opinion of the theorists about leaving the national market unfettered so that it could achieve its natural harmony, in the international economy such liberal ideas were rejected out of hand. The economic world view of Napoleon and influential publicists like Montgaillard remained essentially mercantilist – a static concept of a fixed stock of wealth, in which the increase of France's share implied a diminution of that of her eternal enemy, Britain. Not all Napoleon's advisers were in agreement. Some, like Chaptal or Coquebert de Montbret (both significantly with scientific leanings), were opposed to highly protective measures. Chaptal, before his appointment as minister of the interior, affirmed:

> It is not true, despite general belief, that prohibiting the entry of foreign goods will benefit our national factories. Such a ban results in three major inconveniences: firstly, it deprives the State of customs revenue; secondly, it encourages smuggling; thirdly, it deprives our manufacturers of the stimulus of competition.[3]

Such liberal views, still respectable during the Directory, were soon to sound as rarefied as voices in the desert. Economic competition became part of a larger struggle, expressed in military metaphors and equipped with weapons of war. Already during the Directory, war by corsairs had become a major industry. American consular sources estimated (no doubt with gross exaggeration) that French and Barbary corsairs had seized 3,000 British vessels in the Mediterranean between 1793 and 1800.[4] In 1798 Schimmelpenninck privately confessed his conviction that the French government lay behind the systematic attack on ships reaching Dutch ports:

> I am more and more convinced in these unhappy circumstances that the system of French privateering is so organised and in such a formidable and extended state that an announcement of the arrival

and landing of a neutral ship . . . is now synonymous with a confiscation.[5]

Nothing came more naturally to Bonaparte than the active encouragement of such a policy. For, as Metternich perceptively observed to Stadion in 1808,

> he has supreme contempt for the status of the merchant and confuses industry with usury, trading with monopoly and profit with theft. I'm sure that he thinks he is trading by means of his corsairs. He protects them because he regards them as military merchants and their ships as nobler shops than those of peaceful citizens.[6]

After Trafalgar and the definitive loss of any hopes of naval victory, the corsairs represented the sole means of challenging British control of the seas and an effective weapon against neutral ships smuggling illegal British manufactures to the Continent. As late as 1811 a Corsican privateer, Pollan, was able to defy British naval surveillance of the Catalan coast.[7]

Napoleon's methods in boosting national manufactures and trade were characteristically brusque and authoritarian. Political pressure and legislative intervention were regarded as appropriate weapons through which French trade would replace the lost colonies with the territorial markets of Continental Europe. Trade could be disciplined like armies, as Chaptal later recalled: 'he presumed to manoeuvre it like a battalion and demanded that trade submit as passively'.[8] States within the French sphere of influence were to be persuaded to offer preferential treatment to French goods, while Customs barriers were erected to protect French manufacturers against English competition. Such a policy was not new, but dated back to the war with Britain and the anti-French coalition. Nine Customs laws to exclude British goods had been decreed between 1793 and Brumaire, seventeen more before the 1806 imposition of the blockade, compared to six subsequent measures. If the immediate purpose was to extend the military and naval war against Britain into the industrial and commercial spheres, the longer-term aim was to enable France to replace Britain as the workshop of the Continent. Even before the blockade, there was an awareness of the need to gain time behind protective barriers in order to catch up with Britain's technological superiority. As the preamble to publication of the official Customs tariff of 1804 stated: 'Foreign industry will be driven back from our territory for as long as is needed for French factories to make good their losses and consolidate their establishments'.[9]

Within this project of a grand Continental market, Germany necessarily played a central role, not only because of the potential promised by its population and pre-1789 commercial relations, but also as a crossroad between north and south, west and east, Europe as far as Russia, which was reflected in the importance of the great fairs of Leipzig and Frankfurt. In Geoffrey Ellis' words, the Rhineland became the hub of this new pattern of international trade, which explains the importance of the Rhine's navigation convention of 1804 negotiated by Coquebert de Montbret among the rival cities along its banks. Italy was initially of importance as a supplier of foodstuffs and primary materials for industry (hides, oil for soap, wool, cotton and above all raw silk); but increasingly it was seen as an additional, even a substitute market to compensate for the failure of French manufactures to replace British goods against local competition. Spain and Portugal, like Holland, were considered essential for access to their colonies; their importance declined sharply with the British blockade of their ports and the military struggle. It is misleading to compare the relative importance of the different regions of Europe as trading partners of France in terms of the official figures, because of the continuously shifting frontiers and scale of smuggling. But French agricultural exports to northern Europe, according to Champagny in 1806, were three to four times greater than to the south; all French exports to Italy (excluding the annexed departments) were only about half those to the German Rhenish Confederation between 1806 and 1810, but rose to 65–75 per cent in 1811–12.[10] There can be little doubt that the Mediterranean declined in importance relative to central-northern Europe, albeit never so disastrously as the Atlantic seaboard.

The economic consequences of this policy of tariff discrimination against British goods, combined with political-military pressure on the European states, were extremely varied, both within France's frontiers and in the other states. The frontier distinction, in economic terms as in so many other ways, is a crucial one, as Customs barriers were applied in a single direction – in favour of French manufactures – long before the Continental blockade. Thus the Italic republic had been browbeaten into a Customs treaty with France that privileged some French imports already in 1803. The duchy of Berg, whose manufactures were often similar to English products (textiles, haberdashery, ironmongery), was forced to negotiate with the Directory tariff reductions on its exports to France, which were progressively lost, until they ceased by 1806–7. On the other hand, inclusion within France's frontiers offered access to the largest unified market in Europe for Belgian, Luxembourg and Alsatian cotton and iron producers. The major exception to such possibilities (at least before the annexations resulting from the blockade) were the Piedmontese silk weavers, whose production and outlets were deliberately sabotaged in order to protect Lyons' monopoly.

The political imposition of frontiers and their continuous modification had immediate and profound consequences on regional economies. The absorption of Belgian Brabant within the French republic deprived the pipe-makers of Gouda of Ardennes clay and Dutch brewers and distillers of Flemish hops, grain and coal. The complementarity of economic exchange on the two sides of the Rhine was abruptly broken. Augsburg commission agents suffered from the new barriers on the traditional trade routes between Italy, northern Germany and eastern Europe. Piedmontese wine producers lost access to their traditional Lombard markets in the kingdom of Italy. Woollen cloth production in the Italian Marches, incorporated in the kingdom of Italy, fell with its severance from the good quality wool supplies of Lazio. Zinc and lead mines in Carinthia lost their markets in Austria with the creation of the Illyrian provinces. The examples could easily be multiplied. But if well-established regional patterns of production and trading were thus dismembered by political means, new economic areas were created by precisely the same artificial measures. The new state of Berg created in 1806 brought together for the first time the coal-mines and metal forges of Mark and Berg. Within France's frontiers, a new industrial region was created, stretching from Liège and Verviers to Aix-la-Chapelle and Cologne. The annexation of the southern Black Forest by Baden gave its manufacturers an elastic labour supply.

The repercussions of the French-imposed reorientation of European manufacturing and trade were multiple and in many ways unforeseen. For even where the frontiers introduced discriminatory policies, they could not prevent the transfer of entrepreneurs, capital and techniques from south Alsace and north Switzerland; German and Swiss entrepreneurs introduced advanced cotton technology in Lombardy, Piedmont and Naples.

Napoleonic efforts to force the pace of French manufacturing and trade were probably effective until 1806 and in the early period of the blockade. In aggregate terms, French foreign trade increased significantly from the disastrous years of the 1790s wars: total trade, estimated officially at about 1,000 million francs in 1787–9, had fallen to under 500 million in 1797–9 and rose to over 900 million in 1804–6.[11] Woollen and cotton cloth, iron and steel increased in volume of production and in some cases modernised technologically. But the very protection from British competition that encouraged French manufacturers played an analogous role in the development of rival industries outside France. For many of the same factors operated in like manner inside and without France's frontiers.

As with France, there was a direct relationship between entrepreneurial activity and size of internal market: the Munich beer industry benefited from the enlargement of the kingdom of Bavaria to 3.5 million inhabitants; Lombard woollen cloth production increased in the republic (then kingdom) of Italy, whose population rose from 3 million to 7 million; the Rhenish Confederation led to Customs agreements between some of its states, to the benefit of Baden cotton production; Saxon cotton manufacturers gained access to a market of 3 million with the creation of the grand-duchy of Warsaw under the king of Saxony.

As in France, many of the entrepreneurs in these other states remained closely tied to the state. There were few who relied on traditional export markets, like the great cotton entrepreneur Oberkampf or the Prato woollen fez manufacturer Mazzoni. Mining and metallurgy, whether in the Ruhr, Bas-Rhin, the Aosta or Brescia valleys, gained from the constant military demand for armaments. The demand for woollen cloth and tanned skins was related directly to the provision of uniforms and shoes for soldiers. The sharp contraction of navies and merchant marines was immediately reflected in the crisis of rope and canvas producers, in Holland and Genoa, as in lower Normandy.

The blockade encouraged the development of industries capable of taking advantage of the protection provided by the new measures and competing effectively with French producers outside the Empire's frontiers. For price differentials and transport costs now worked against the competitivity of French products. Mechanization of cotton spinning spread rapidly in Berg, Baden, north Switzerland and Saxony. The productivity level of Mulhouse printed cottons was far lower than that of Belgian producers within the Empire; Berg and Saxon cottons, according to the prefect Chaban, cost 20 per cent less than those of Brussels. A French manufacturer like Oberkampf actively tried to open up new export markets, but he was unable to compete against Swiss and south German printed cottons.[12] Woollen cloths from Bohemia, Saxony, Hesse and especially Berg undercut the cheapest French cloth from Verviers, Montjoie and

Aix-la-Chapelle: 'the abundance of raw materials and the low cost of labour prevent other factories from competing against the factories of these countries'.[13] The failure of the economic project to create a vast land market for French manufactures in place of the lost colonies was to become ever more apparent with the development of the Continental blockade.

THE CONTINENTAL BLOCKADE

The decrees of Berlin (21 November 1806) and Milan (23 November, 17 December 1807) raised the economic war with Britain to a new level. Since Brumaire, Bonaparte had insisted that his allies exclude British goods. He had negotiated preferential trade treaties with Naples (1800), Spain (1801, 1803), Portugal (1801), Russia (1801), Turkey (1802) and the Italic republic (1803, 1806). These complementary policies of impeding British trade and encouraging French exports had been pursued by clearly delimited measures, which still left ample scope – within the limits of repeated bouts of warfare – for the continuation of existing patterns of international commerce, and for trade with the colonies, carried in particular by neutral ships. Following the peace of Amiens, the merchants and shipbuilders of the Atlantic ports, financed by Parisian bankers, had invested in a restoration of the pre-Revolutionary colonial oriented economy; even as late as summer 1806, with the renewal of diplomatic contacts with Britain, many turned their hopes overseas. But on each occasion the outbreak of war led to a sharp commercial crisis, as in 1803 and 1805, with loss of ships, interruption of colonial trading and bankruptcies.

French manufacturers and merchants were insistent on the need to find alternative markets. From 1805 Oberkampf took active steps to find new outlets in Italy, the Belgian departments and Holland. The Marseilles chamber of commerce stressed that the Italian and Spanish markets were needed to replace Santo Domingo:

> The loss of our main colony must attribute an ever higher value to the outlets that our factories and manufactures still hold in Europe. . . . It is in the interest of France to supply, if not the totality, at least the greater part of all the manufactured articles that Spain consumes and supplies to her colonies.[14]

The Berlin and Milan decrees appeared to offer the means to meet the demands of the business community. First, they extended the prohibition and seizure of goods from Britain or her colonies to all

French-dominated Europe, even to Russia after Tilsit; then, in reta-
liation to the British Orders in Council, the same principle of confiscation as prizes was extended to all neutral ships with British licences
or products. Initially the measures aroused considerable expectations, as they followed the defeat of Austria and, most recently, of
Prussia. Whether or not the British economy would collapse through
the glut of over-production caused by closure of her major markets,
the French-controlled Continent was protected from competition.
Political pressure or military force (it was assumed) could enforce
obedience, as with the invasion of Portugal (1807). The markets of
Europe lay open. In the words of an advertisement of the wholesale
metal dealer Deloche in 1807: 'What prospects cannot be imagined
for our trade today, now that political and friendly relations have
turned Germany, Holland, Spain and Italy into vast fairs where
France will always find a certain sale for her surplus industrial
products?'[15]

No economic policy could satisfy all interests. The blockade accelerated cotton mechanisation and production. But cotton printers like
Oberkampf experienced constant difficulties in substituting Indian
cottons with 'national' fabrics of equivalent quality, and even more in
ensuring adequate and regular raw cotton supplies from Brazil
(through Portugal), the United States, southern Italy and the Levant.
In fact, while raw cotton consumption in France doubled between
1785 and 1809 from 4,000 to 8,000 metric tons, it quintupled in
Britain from 8,000 to 42,000 tons. With the re-establishment of peace
on the Continent in 1807 many inland areas of the Empire – Paris, the
Lyons area, Belgium, the left bank – enjoyed economic expansion
until 1810. French export of cotton products increased tenfold in
these years, and silkstuffs, woollens, mixed textiles, metal and luxury
goods all benefited. By contrast, the Atlantic ports definitively lost
their lifeline of neutral shipping: American ships entering Bordeaux
dropped from 121 in 1807 to 6 in 1808; and traditional outputting
industries, like linen, persisted in their irrevocable decline.[16]

The success of the blockade depended on Napoleon's capacity both
to keep out British goods, and to ensure adequate alternative supplies of foodstuffs, raw materials and manufactures. In the event,
neither of these conditions was met. According to Camille Perier,
sent to Germany by the interior minister Champagny in 1807–8,
British cotton yarn and sewing cotton was still 16 per cent cheaper
than French yarn nine months after the introduction of the blockade.[17] His explanation was stockpiling by importers. But sealing off
the coastal areas proved an arduous and impossible task, which

stimulated the ingenuity of traders to circumvent the law. Smuggling became a highly organised commercial activity of major proportions. A major reason for this was the inability of the French to substitute British supplies of raw or semi-finished materials.

At the same time, as we have already noted, the very conditions of protection encouraged the rapid expansion of textile firms in Germany, Prussia and Austria which competed successfully against the French. Many of the German states, according to the military expert Jomini in November 1806, were hostile to Britain and ready to respond to some form of joint Customs agreement. But the blockade, for Napoleon and his advisers, was conceived of only as a very unequal partnership, with no serious consideration of reciprocity. France's allies, even the satellites, were formally independent and hence able to set up their own Customs policies. In a world of protection, liberal ideas were impractical, as the free-trader Bavarian minister of finances, Hampesch, reluctantly recognised.[18] Champagny recognised the problem as early as August 1807, when he urged Napoleon to insist on free passage or extremely preferential transit and import duties for French goods in the Confederate states. Germany was not only a market, but also the obligatory route for exports of wines and spirits, silkstuffs and luxury goods, fashion ware and quality woollens to Poland and Russia. It is hardly surprising that the German princes refused to accept French propositions and only in individual cases submitted under pressure, reluctantly and partially, to lower tariffs on French exports to their states. The effect of this first phase of the blockade on trading relations with Germany and eastern Europe can be illustrated by the examples of the two major western German states, Berg and Bavaria, and of Poland.

Berg was of major importance in pre-Revolutionary Franco-German economic relations, both as a manufacturing centre of textile and metal products, and as the export route for German manufactures to France. Hence it was particularly vulnerable to French protective tariffs, the more so as many of its manufactures were similar to those produced in Britain. The effect of the blockade was to impose duties on Berg goods of up to nearly three times their value. Murat supported his manufacturers' appeal for special treatment (as under the Directory), but to no effect. Berg entrepreneurs searched desperately for alternative markets. They sent a deputation to Napoleon (which finally caught up with him at Warsaw), asking for preferential treatment for textile exports to Italy; momentarily he agreed, but within months, on his return to France and Italy, had revoked his decision. Northern German trading relations became more important and Berg textile manufacturers resisted, despite rising wage levels, till 1809. But then the crisis came. Appeals for transit concessions across France to Spain and Portugal were rejected. The result was an attempt to compensate the manufacturing crisis by a huge increase of trade in smuggled British goods which transited across the country towards France, Switzerland and Italy.

When Napoleon absorbed Holland within the Empire in 1810, he also annexed northern Berg to the south of the Dutch border, with nearly a quarter of its 1 million inhabitants. The 4,000 industrialists of this small state of Berg, now land-locked, its exports blocked not only by France but also by its German neighbours, were induced by the blockade measures of 1810 to appeal for reunion with France as the sole solution. The episode revealed the real interests at stake. The Berg manufacturers argued, somewhat disingenuously, that the absorption within France of Belgian textile manufactures at Verviers and Aix-la-Chapelle had not lessened production at Louviers, Sedan or Elbeuf, nor had Crefeld silk and cotton ruined Lyon's monopoly: 'The struggle against England's mercantile tyranny can be sustained only if the industrial states are themselves privileged'. For the Cologne chamber of commerce, across the Rhine in the department of the Roer, despite ten years of tariff discrimination, Berg competition remained too keen. In a remarkable admission of inferiority, the manufacturers successfully urged the prefect to keep their Berg rivals out of their protected French and Italian markets, as

> We conclude that: (1) our labour costs must be higher than on the right bank of the Rhine, as our labourers work less and spend more than those of Berg; (2) our goods are of a lower quality than those manufactured in the grand-duchy because, since our workers no longer find subsistence in the convents, they only work out of necessity, whereas Berg workers strive to make their products as perfect as possible; (3) as a result, our factories could not withstand the competition of those of the grand-duchy of Berg, if it were annexed to the French empire.[19]

Berg, like the kingdom of Italy, was directly dependent on French authority. Bavaria, by contrast, was France's major and most loyal ally, not just in Germany. So long as Napoleon's preoccupation was the coastal blockade of British goods, Bavaria benefited: sugar-beet and tobacco production increased, optical glass was manufactured at Munich, textiles at Augsburg, calico printing, pins and needles and ceramics at Schwabach. The 1806 measures, because they applied to the kingdom of Italy, were a direct threat to Bavaria's traditional exports and transit trade to Italy. Max Joseph was surprised at Napoleon's rigidity, since Bavaria had continuously given way to demands for tariff concessions on French wines and manufactures. The Italian and Bavarian ministers, Marescalchi and Montgelas, negotiated a trade treaty, which confirmed the French prohibition of British goods, but reciprocally reduced Customs duties by 50 per cent (2 January 1808). Champagny convinced Napoleon to annul the treaty, not only because Bavarian woollens were too competitive for the French, given 'the proximity [to Italy] of Bavarian factories, their cheap labour, their perfect knowledge of consumer tastes', but also because Bohemian, Moravian and other German cheap cloths would be exported to Italy under cover of the treaty.[20] The consequences for Bavaria were dramatic but not disastrous. Economically, Bavaria responded in kind: she introduced her own protective tariff in 1809, mechanised and expanded production for her large internal market, and exploited her geographical location to obtain advantages in the new transit route of raw cotton from the Ottoman empire imposed by Napoleon on Austria after Wagram (1809). Nuremburg experienced a new age of prosperity as the centre of Bavarian manufacturing exports and even colonial imports. But politically the breakdown of trade with Italy was a major cause of the revolt of her recently acquired territory of Tyrol in 1809.

The vitality of the Polish economy depended on its exports of cereals from Danzig to western Europe, overwhelmingly to Britain. The decrees of 1806 and occupation of Danzig by Marshal Lefebvre (1807) led to a sharp inversion of the formerly favourable terms of trade, as wheat exports collapsed. The result was disastrous for the already indebted Polish landowners and catastrophic for the peasants, who fled the land. As elsewhere in the Continent, the protection provided by the blockade opened up opportunities, especially for textile entrepreneurs: Saxon cottons and Silesian woollens expanded into the Polish market. The protectionist tariffs introduced by the government of the new grand-duchy of Warsaw encouraged investment and expansion of national production of woollens, mines and distilleries. French manufacturers were unable to compete with such cheap textiles, while their traditional luxury exports – such as wines and silks – presumably suffered with the rapid decline in income of Polish noble households.

As evidence mounted of the inability of French entrepreneurs to take over the central role of British manufactures in Germany and eastern Europe, the Mediterranean assumed increasing importance as a reserved market. The initial hopes of the Iberian market rapidly vanished with the difficulty of access to the Portuguese and Spanish empires and popular resistance in Spain. The major objects of trading, constantly endangered by guerrillas and bandits, were food supplies for the French armies and import of colonial goods to France. It is hardly surprising that such trade should have been monopolised by a well-established Perpignan merchant, François Durand, who gained immunity for his mule trains across the Pyrenees by supplying both French troops and their enemies: 'his profits are so enormous that they touch on the indecent', commented the Spanish authorities.[21]

Italy inevitably became the focus of interest. Italy supplied between 50 per cent and 75 per cent of French raw silk and organzines. With annexation, Piedmontese silk production was colonised, as Lyons insisted on a monopoly, not only for its own manufactures, but also – since it never utilised more than half Piedmontese production – as an entrepôt for re-export of the surplus to central Europe. As a precautionary measure, the head of the Parisian bureau responsible for manufactures, C. A. Costaz, vetoed the transfer to Prato (in the annexed department of the Arno) of models of textile machinery, lest Prato entrepreneurs emerged to challenge established French manufacturers.[22] The kingdom of Italy was subjected to similar pressure, particularly with the imposition of the preferential trade treaty of 1808, which gave the monopoly of cotton imports to French producers and confirmed the high tariffs on Lombard and Venetian exports to their traditional trading partners – Switzerland, Austria, Bavaria and the German states. It was precisely this policy of turning the Italian peninsula into a subordinate market for French manufactures that precipitated relations between Napoleon and Murat at Naples. For Murat, like the princes of the Rhenish Confederation, reacted against France's ever more peremptory imperialistic economic policy by imposing his own highly protective tariff barrier in 1809. Cotton, woollen and silk factories were set up in Naples by foreign entrepreneurs with government support and orders; raw cotton production rose in three to four years (according to the American consul in 1815) from 5,000 to 20,000 bales.[23]

The ability of the French government to enforce the blockade depended on a range of only partly controllable factors: absence of military campaigns, British hostility towards neutral shipping, relations between different corps of the administration, the level of commitment or corruption of individual bureaucrats, the degree of resistance of France's allies and local populations to the dislocation and deprivation caused by the blockade. When the positive factors tended to converge – as in the first half of 1808, when active warfare was confined to Spain, President Jefferson prohibited American trading, and the coasts were closely guarded – the result was a downturn in British foreign trade. At other times, laxity of surveillance led to the immediate revival and increase of smuggling, with the support of the British navy.

Smuggling, by definition, is impossible to quantify, as confiscations are not necessarily proportionate to the quantity of goods illegally transferred. But its structure, topography and intensity in these years are well documented. Alongside supply of armies and speculation in national properties, smuggling offered the major possibility of making large fortunes. A graphic description is offered by Winn, an American merchant in Malta, in a letter to his partners of 1 August 1808:

> The Rebecca arrived here 23 ult.° and sails again tomorrow with your humble servant on board for Trieste. I take $10,000 on board myself in Sugar and Coffee, and the Brig is filled up on freight. . . . As I am to be convoyed to and from . . . I consider the risk but very trifling. The principal danger, I fear, is in port. . . . I don't fear the Austrians, but the French may make a sudden move and take Trieste, or they may march an army and frighten the Austrians into these measures, and then farewell to the little Rebecca and $10,000 . . . the temptation is so great I can't resist it. . . . Should I be fortunate, and find the markets in the state they were in at the date of the last advices, I shall make from 100 to 150 per cent.[24]

Malta was one of a series of islands in the Mediterranean – like Sicily, Corfu and Vis in the Adriatic – occupied and deployed by the British as depots for colonial goods and manufactures to be smuggled on to the mainland. Portuguese ports served the same purpose on the Atlantic coast. But Holland and the northern European coasts were inevitably the most attractive for British producers. Coquebert de Montbret, who had a broader experience of European trading than anyone in the imperial administration, had argued that the only effective means to win over Holland was a genuine customs confederation linking France, Holland and Italy: 'Holland will never be brought to reject English merchandise; it is a trading country, not an industrial one, so that it is wholly in its interest to handle England considerately'.[25] The open collusion between the Dutch government, bankers and traders was insufficient to restore Dutch prosperity and cost Louis his throne in 1810. But French pressure, before and after 1810, merely shifted the epicentre of British activities further east, to Danish Tönning in 1807 and then to Oldenburg and then Altona, just outside Hamburg. Heligoland became the North Sea depot for British goods, with Frankfurt as the distribution centre. Bourrienne, the French representative at Hamburg, sold over 150,000 authorisations for the export of illegally imported goods between August 1807 and December 1810, at fixed rates of 0.25 per cent to 0.50 per cent the value of the merchandise; he was estimated to have made 1 million francs out of this private initiative, which implied the export of goods worth 200 million to 400 million francs, or 60 million to 120 million annually.[26] It is hardly surprising that colonial cotton, sugar and coffee continued to circulate in Germany, Switzerland and Austria at prices often lower than at Paris, even after the 1810 decrees. As the North Sea coast became more difficult for smuggled goods between 1810 and 1812, British ships increased their activities in the Balkans and Adriatic, even clearing the Illyrian coast of corsairs in order to win the goodwill of the local merchants. Bacher, the minister at Frankfurt, noted the immediate effect of the Trianon decree (5 August 1810) imposing prohibitive entry duties into France:

> Since the coasts of Holland and the Hanseatic cities as far as the Oder are no longer as accessible as in the past to colonial goods and merchandise, it is claimed that such traffic now takes a new direction. All the routes that lead from different points of Russia, on the one hand towards Prussia, on the other towards Poland and Moravia as far as Vienna, and from the Ottoman provinces into the Austrian empire, have been successively activated for English goods unloaded in the Levant ports. It is said that the Danube will replace the Rhine as the canal through which the states of the Rhenish Confederation will be able to obtain supplies in the future.[27]

In many regions smuggling offered the possibility of relatively high earnings, whether for the trader or the worker. Gaudoit of Caen, officially a lace merchant, imported illegal British goods worth probably 750,000 francs between 1801 and 1808, from London via Amsterdam or Rotterdam to Düsseldorf or Frankfurt, on to Paris, whence they were redistributed to Bordeaux and Strasbourg. The Rothschilds emerged as leading bankers at Frankfurt, London and Paris by financing illegal trading and working both the British and French licensing systems contemporaneously. Along the Rhine, a smuggler could earn 12 to 24 francs for one night's transport, when an agricultural labourer's daily wage was 1 to $1\frac{1}{2}$ francs. In Roussillon, each trip across the Pyrenees was worth 10 francs, compared to the 3 francs of a day-labourer. In Hamburg, where a pound of coffee sold at 12 sous more than at Altona, the insurers offered 4 sous per pound to each carrier; the distance was so short that they could make ten to twelve trips a day; the authorities estimated that some 6,000–10,000 persons smuggled coffee, sugar or other goods every day, of which not more than 3–5 per cent was confiscated.[28]

Nevertheless, it would be erroneous to conclude that the measures to enforce the blockade were mere window-dressing. They were never wholly effective, nor could they be. They were sabotaged within the very ranks of the French administration for reasons of corruption or rivalry: the denunciation by Eudel, the Customs director at Hamburg, of the lack of commitment of the military commander, General Morand, hardly differed from the hostility of the military and civil authorities in Roussillon towards his colleague Boulouvard, responsible for Customs on the Catalan frontier.[29] But that the decrees had a sharp effect, where French power could police them, is reflected in the differences in insurance rates paid for illegal British goods: only 6–8 per cent of value in Hamburg in 1808–9, along the Rhine they had risen from 6 per cent in 1800 to 10 per cent in 1801–2, 26 per cent in 1807–8, 30 per cent by July 1809, and up to 50 per cent by 1811; the rates for American ships to Naples rose from 15 per cent in 1809 to 25–30 per cent by 1811.[30]

The 1810 decrees of Saint-Cloud, Trianon and Fontainebleau (3 July, 1 August, 10 and 18 October) aimed at tightening the pressure on British exports by a wholesale onslaught on illegal British goods, strengthening the privileged position of French manufactures by raising imperial and Italian Customs tariffs still higher, and turning smuggling to the advantage of the French treasury by issuing licences for agricultural (and then silk cloth) exports and imports of necessary raw materials. Such propositions were contradictory. For example, the decision to authorise (in return for payment of a 40–50 per cent tax) the sale of prizes seized by corsairs and of the stockpile of colonial goods confiscated in Holland weakened the market for French manufactures over the short term. The licensing system, which it was hoped would deepen American discontent with the arbitrary action of the Royal Navy, effectively provisioned Britain with desperately needed wheat, while failing to provoke the United States into a rupture of relations with Britain until too late, in mid-1812. The major crisis in France of 1810–11 was directly related to the new level of economic warfare launched by the decrees and annexations. But in broader geographical terms, the authoritarian application of the blockade, so blatantly in favour of France, distorted the normal flows of trade, diminished the level of economic activities throughout Europe, diverted capital from industrial investment into trading and smuggling, and worsened relations at all levels between France and the states and peoples within her sphere of influence.

The consequences of the new measures for trade flows and economic activities were immediately visible in all regions. The axis of traffic on what had been Europe's main waterway, the Rhine, which had moved north–south with the import of colonial goods from Holland, was reversed as colonial imports dried up and were replaced by wood for construction and heating sent north from Baden and Württemberg. Far more widespread were the negative effects of Napoleon's decision (12 November 1810) to establish a French-controlled cotton route from the Ottoman empire in order to replace overseas cotton supplies and thus damage both Britain and France's Continental competitors. From 1 January 1811 the established Levant route – from Salonika via Austria, Germany and Switzerland to Cologne, Mainz, Coblenz and Strasburg – was replaced by caravans that crossed Macedonia and Bosnia and the Illyrian provinces to Trieste, then bypassing Austria via Bavarian territory and the kingdom of Italy to Piedmont. Sismondi, secretary to the Geneva chamber of commerce, protested at the losses caused by so abrupt a change, and in general at the impossibility of trading under continuously changing regulations:

> It is a question of trading with a country with whom correspondence is slow and unsure, where there is a minute number of men with the appropriate knowledge and where all information is difficult to obtain. Hence trade has a basic need of time in order to change its former direction; it needs time above all because it has suffered from so many ruinous shocks which have terrified all speculators. . . . For some time now the financial laws of France and all the countries subjected to it have lacked all stability. . . . Commercial speculations are based on the existing order, whatsoever it is, and on the belief in its duration, so that every shock produces a disruption of private wealth, the ruin of mercantile enterprises and universal discouragement.[31]

The industrial crisis of 1810–11 was caused by the immediate slump in trading outlets. As stocks built up, bankers and merchants tightened credit terms and raised interest rates, leading to bankruptcies of small firms and speculators in all major cities, from Paris and Lyons to Amsterdam, Rotterdam, Hamburg and Basel. Some industries within the Empire recovered, holding or even increasing production in 1812–13, like the cotton firms of Mulhouse and the Belgian Bauwens at Passy, or the coal-mines of Jemappes. The Italian market undoubtedly gave a respite to French manufacturers, like the cotton printers of the Parisian region and the Haut-Rhin. But by these years French protectionism had become increasingly inward-looking. Holland and the Hanseatic cities, although annexed by France, continued to be excluded from her markets by the new Customs barriers until October 1812. The results were disastrous: the closure of the ports to colonial goods meant the collapse of Dutch processing industries. Hamburg, which had replaced Amsterdam as the financial centre of the Continent since the years of the Consulate, used its wealth to redeem confiscated British goods and relieve the poverty of its citizens by a sophisticated charitable system.

Outside France's frontiers, the effects were everywhere negative and in some cases disastrous. Within the Rhenish Confederation, many of the states sought protection and above all public revenue, on the model of France, through tariff barriers. Others, like Austria, in practice failed to apply the 1810 decrees, thus further disadvantaging states like Berg, whose textile workers migrated to Austrian Moravia and Bohemia. In the kingdom of Italy, the crisis of over-production that resulted from the blockage of market outlets was so widespread that by August 1811 Montalivet was paradoxically suggesting to Napoleon that contraband exports of silk to Britain be encouraged. It would be advantageous, he wrote,

> to authorise the smugglers at Dunkirk to carry organzines to England. Their operations will be extremely active again in a month or six weeks' time as the nights grow longer. This sort of trading is a normal activity, practised at all times, the outlets it procures are important.[32]

It is always difficult to assess the responsibility of political measures in economic conjunctures. The blockade, even after 1810, cannot be compared with the total economic warfare of 1939–45. Nor can the crises of specific industries or regions be ascribed necessarily to the blockade: Dutch industry and trade was already in decline before the 1790s; labour costs in Berg textile firms were already making production uncompetitive before 1810. Movement of entrepreneurs, capital and workers and the spread of mechanisation in textiles and mining, in Lombardy and Piedmont as in Berg and Saxony, was facilitated by the blockade and survived the short-run crisis of the final years of French domination. The Napoleonic-style Customs union, because it was so one-sided, diverted trade rather than creating it. But it led to a heightened awareness of the advantages of protection, as a form of defence against unequal industrial competition, as a source of public revenue, as a means of reducing the administrative costs of government. Administrative rather than economic reasons explain the initial creation of the *Zollverein* in Restoration Germany.

If the economic consequences of the blockade thus need to be nuanced, there can be no doubt about the negative social consequences. The blockade sowed doubts, aroused resentment and even led to revolt. Within France, manufacturers as loyal as Oberkampf protested at 'the tyranny or, more exactly, the piracy' of the French generals in Spain.[33] The public burning of confiscated British manufactures in 1812 – worth 2 million francs in Amsterdam, 500,000 francs in Hamburg, 200,000 francs in Frankfurt – outraged the bourgeois sense of property. Above all, the behaviour of the corps of Customs officers, whose numbers had increased from 12,000 in the Year V (1796–7) to over 35,000 by 1810, aroused hostility at every level. In July 1809, 300 French Customs officers crossed the Rhine and cut off all communications between Holland and Berg without consulting the rulers and administrators of these two formally independent states; Jerome of Westphalia experienced similar contempt for his sovereignty. The Danish representative at Hamburg, Rist, noted the indignities to which the Customs officers subjected the ordinary folk:

> The Customs was no longer satisfied with stopping the carriages and searching them at their convenience . . . ; pedestrians were also subjected rigorously to body searches, and those less well dressed were touched all over; even women of a better class were subjected to this.[34]

In Berg, economic crisis and unemployment led to open revolt by industrial workers in January 1813. The hostility of the local population was compounded by the behaviour of the Customs officials, as they attempted to perform the impossible task of sealing off the imperial frontiers between Holland and the grand-duchy, and searched houses in the inland cities to rout out deposits of illegal goods. It was hardly surprising that Customs and *droits réunis* officials, together with gendarmes, should have been the chosen object of popular attacks when French authority collapsed. Their comportment negated the bureaucrats' dream of winning support through the superior quality of their administration.

CONSCRIPTION

Conscription, wherever it occurred, touched the most sensitive nerve of individuals, families and communities. It was an intrusion in private and social life, it could destroy the equilibrium of the family economy, it threatened delicate balances of interests within small communities based on trust by the arbitrary choice of who should depart. Above all it was novel in its annual regularity.

The pre-Revolutionary armies and navies of Europe – with the partial exception of Prussia – were composed of more or less willing volunteers, mercenaries who had chosen a career to which entry was incomparably easier than to the guilds. Popular fear of enrolment and diffidence towards soldiers was reinforced by a climate of opinion which, by the later eighteenth century, was hostile to the deep-rooted exaltation of military prowess that had accompanied and character-ised European societies since feudal times. The enlightenment insist-ence on values of rationality, order, humanitarianism, tolerance and peace argued against military service. The noble officer, in his ignor-ance, superficiality and arrogance, symbolised the negative attributes of a privileged caste, chosen butt of the *philosophes*' scorn. Economic criticism of the wasteful cost of armies, of their distraction of useful hands from gainful employment, combined with Rousseau's ideal of the citizen in arms. Contempt for the common soldier or sailor, recruited from the dregs of society, combined with horror at the brutality of his treatment.

The Revolutionary army marked a rupture with this past in terms of scale and social composition. Previously cost had acted as a decisive constraint on size: in the 1760s, Prussia and France, the states with the largest armies, maintained 160,000–170,000 troops; in 1789, the French line army amounted to about 165,000 men. Although mercenary, the armies had become increasingly 'national', to avoid the expenses of distant recruitment, so that even the foreign regiments of the French army (with the exception of the eleven Swiss ones) consisted for over 90 per cent of Frenchmen. Peasant resent-ment against the obligatory militia system that supplemented the professional regiments perhaps explains why the volunteers were drawn primarily from the urban poor. The French army in 1789 was thus markedly out of line with the overall distribution of the population, including 60 per cent urban artisans and shopkeepers and only 20–25 per cent peasants.[35]

The National Assembly had abolished the militia system and had rejected conscription in favour of a small professional army. But between 1789 and 1791 the army was in danger of disintegrating, as soldiers deserted and, after the king's flight to Varennes, officers emigrated or retired. By January 1791, the line army was 20,000 short of its authorised strength of 150,000. By the end of 1791, about 6,000 officers, or 60 per cent of the officer corps, had emigrated; by April 1794, 87 per cent of officers on active duty in mid-1789 had left the service.[36] With an increasing sense of urgency, the Revolutionary assemblies were forced to rebuild the army. The entire organisation was restructured: the number of units and officers was reduced, a far more humane system of military justice was introduced, new regulations about battle training and tactics were issued. The officer corps was overwhelmingly restocked, with the promotion of non-commissioned officers, initially by examination, but increasingly on the basis of their years of service. The nation was called to arms, with repeated appeals for volunteers between 1791 and 1793, serving as separate units alongside the line army, until they were merged in February 1793.

The new army was young – 60 per cent were aged 18 to 25 – and with little experience of service: one-third of the soldiers had served less than one year in February 1793, and two-thirds under four years. But it was an army that now increasingly reflected the social composition of the nation, with two-thirds of the line soldiers, rising to 80 per cent in the 1793 mass levy, from the countryside. If the soldiers were inexperienced, their officers, including the non-commissioned, were overwhelmingly veterans. The fact that the new officers were closer to their men than any ancien regime corps, with a deep and shared patriotic motivation, goes as far towards explaining how a fighting army was forged so rapidly as the readiness of the officers to adapt their tactics to their new combat experiences.

Increasingly, the appeal to patriotism failed to produce the required numbers, while volunteers withdrew after a campaign. Quotas were imposed on departments, culminating in the August 1793 mass levy which made all unmarried able-bodied males aged 18 to 25 liable to service for a limited period. In this Jacobin year of emergency, the army reached a peak of 750,000 men, which was to be surpassed only in the later Napoleonic years. Under the Directory, numbers were falling fast through desertions, death and disease, and it was this sharp decline that explains the Jourdan-Delbrel law of September 1798 which made military service obligatory. The law stated: 'Every Frenchman is a soldier and has the duty to defend his country'. The minimum age of the five 'classes' was now raised to 20, and service was to be for five years. The municipalities were ordered to draw up the lists by year of birth or class, while a review committee was to examine or reject the unfit and those smaller than 4 foot 9 inches (1.57 metres).

There can be no doubt that the authorities were aware of the difficulties of enforcing the new system. Pierre Daru, secretary-general of the ministry of war in the early Consulate, recommended in 1802 that the choice of those actually enrolled be left with the local communal authorities as a means of softening what was recognised as a hated measure:

> The distribution is entrusted to the magistrates most immediately charged with the interests of the people. Such magistrates are necessarily domiciled in the place where they exercise their current functions and have a greater need than anyone to retain the respect of their fellow citizens; the disinterest of these municipal magistrates is a sort of guarantee of their honesty and independence.
>
> . . . The author of this draft law thought that to decide the method of choice would render the law more rigorous; that the only way to soften it was to take local circumstances into account; that it was impossible to solve the problem of justice and uniformity; that it was necessary to provide the people's magistrates with a clear sign of confidence; that surveillance of the interested parties was sufficient guarantee of the equitable distribution that is hoped for; and, finally, that wise regulations were sufficient to prevent the abuses that are rightly feared.[37]

However, control was increasingly taken over by the direct representatives of the central government: communes were grouped into cantons under the sub-prefect's control in order to weaken personal favouritism in the identification of the unfit in each new class; the prefect and military officers formed ambulant recruiting commissions; the prefect and sub-prefect replaced the local councils in the repartition of the levy between the arrondissements and communes.

Initially no substitution had been allowed, but with the failure of Jourdan's first levy, drawing by lot was accepted. At first, those registered as poor had been discharged without obligation to find a replacement, but this was apparently ignored or dropped. Substitution became a matter of money, with marked variations between departments, but rising everywhere to between 3,000 and 7,000 francs. Because of abuses, a series of modifications were introduced, in order to avoid the use as substitutes of men liable for future service or for conscription in other administrative areas: by 1806 substitutes could be drawn only from those who had not been chosen from the five preceding classes within the department. With the characteristic thoroughness of the Napoleonic administration, all the modifications were finally incorporated into a lengthy single regulation in 1812.

This immensely complicated and difficult process of raising mass armies was a constant and growing concern of administrators in both France and the allied states. Overall numbers remain uncertain, partly because they refer to different definitions of the armed forces, and partly because the base years employed to calculate overall aggregate numbers are not always the same. In 1807 Napoleon decided to calculate for himself the size of the French armies under Louis XIV as a comparison with his own forces. He arrived at a figure of 546,000 in 1692, considerably higher (after the Jacobin effort) than the Revolutionary and Consulate figures, which were mostly under 400,000; only in 1808 did such a general estimate for the French army rise to 500,000; and it was then to increase sharply from 1809, with the intervention in Spain and then the Russian campaign, rising to a maximum of 1,100,000 under arms in May 1813.[38] The levies in France, between the Year VIII and 1813, officially demanded 2,835,000 men, with the pressure increasing from 1808, rising by 1812 and 1813 to nearly 50 per cent of the registered classes liable for service.

The overwhelming superiority of France's population relative to that of other nations and its youthful age structure (with three-quarters of the 28 million under the age of 40 in 1789) help explain why Napoleon boasted that there were no limits to the numbers of men he could raise. Historians have compared conscription in imperial France to that of the First World War of 1914–18, concluding that the weight of the former was far less, removing under 7 per cent of the population (36 per cent of the cohorts liable to conscription). But the vast documentary evidence in the administrative records, especially the prefects' reports, leaves no doubt that contemporaries regarded conscription as an unmitigated evil, to be resisted by all means. The rules of the game about physical disabilities, marriage, clerical status and above all purchase of substitutes, which offered considerable scope for evasion, were compounded by passive resistance and open collusion by local authorities, who covered up for those who failed to turn up to the examination or conscription lottery.

With due statistical zeal and closer correspondence to reality than in fields where private collaboration was essential, the head of the conscription bureau of the ministry of war, A. A. Hargenvilliers, drew up tables specifying the size of levy in each department, the number rejected as physically handicapped or too small, and the differences between the numbers of those called up, despatched and actually enrolled into the army, attributable to desertions at the various stages.[39] An average of one in three of the recruitable classes was rejected as unfit between 1798 and 1809. Of those chosen, to 1804–5, 8.7 per cent were judged draft evaders (*réfractaires*) as they failed to turn up, and a further 33.5 per cent subsequently deserted. In the nine Belgian departments, the proportion of evaders rose from 10.7 per cent (till 1804–5) to 42.4 per cent in 1805–9, while that of deserters fell from 49.3 per cent to 14.8 per cent.

Local studies uniformly document the general hostility to conscription under the Directory, extending well into the Napoleonic years. As Alan Forrest argues,[40] the opposition from the peasantry – which exploded at its most spectacular in the Vendée rising – reflected the sharp shift in the composition of the French army from an urban to a heavily peasant one, a shift accentuated by the practice of substitution, which tended to diminish the presence of reasonably wealthy (and hence primarily) urban families. The experience of such widespread hostility made the authorities hesitant about imposing conscription in some regions, both in France and the satellite states. Thus the Vendée was initially exempted from the Jourdan law; its attempted imposition in the Flemish departments led to a peasant revolt (1798). In the kingdom of Naples, Joseph Bonaparte never imposed conscription, while Murat, when introducing it in 1809, kept it initially at the very low proportion of one in 1,500 inhabitants (compared to one in 500 in the early years in the Belgian departments). The more recalcitrant among the newly annexed departments (in Belgium, the left bank of the Rhine and elsewhere) tended to be given lighter quotas in the initial conscription levies, though this was then adjusted in subsequent years within each region. Similar difficulties were experienced in the coastal areas: Lebrun hesitated immediately to introduce conscription of sailors in Liguria, although by 1810 rougher methods were being used in the Hanseatic ports. In mountainous frontier areas, like the Pyrenees, the Piedmontese Alps or Neuchâtel, battalions of chasseurs were allowed; but they tended to desert across the frontiers.

Analysis of resistance to conscription shows definite regional variations. As one would expect, the evaders were most numerous in areas where the physical terrain facilitated evasion, in mountainous, heavily forested or frontier areas. Religious or ethnic differences sometimes counted, which explains the greater opposition in the Flemish departments like Escaut, compared to French-speaking Belgium. By contrast, in areas where there were strong pre-Revolutionary traditions of military service – as in the northern and eastern frontier regions of France, the Swiss cantons, Sarre on the left bank of the Rhine, or the Monferrato in Piedmont – conscription proved far easier, even in the early years. It is probably such discipline that explains the positive response to conscription in a poor, wooded and mountainous department like the Sarre. Desertion after enrolment, usually on the march to the military depots, would not seem to display any particular pattern of regional differentiation, presumably because the conscripts had finally accepted their lot.

'Insubordination', the official description for evasion of conscription, steadily diminished over the years. The turning point can be dated in 1805–6, coinciding with the end of the period of Napoleon's reorganisation of his army. In the Rhine left bank departments, desertion accounted for about 10 per cent of the annual levies between 1800 and 1805, falling sharply to under 2 per cent in 1806–10, with 1809 as a crisis year for the authorities, because of the imposition of a supplementary levy; from 1811 such pre-conscription resistance virtually disappeared, even though these were the years with the heaviest levies. Only in the final débâcle in 1813 was there a sharp rise in the number of deserters among serving soldiers. The Belgian departments followed a similar trajectory.

Such a development is paradoxical, as the enforced removal of men for an indefinite duration, if not permanently through death, touched the most sensitive nerve of the familial and communal organisation of daily life. There can be no doubt about the massive hostility of the populations in the early years both in France and the allied states: in the kingdom of Italy, conscription was enforced only by virtual press-gangs. It seems likely that the increasing efficiency of the administrative machine accustomed the people to obedience. The passive resistance of entire communities was certainly broken by transferring their administrative responsibilities to the sub-prefects and prefects. The resentment against substitution as a discriminatory measure of wealth would appear to have diminished as the annual levies enrolled ever larger numbers, as brothers, friends and entire classes of age were marched away. There are instances of self-regulation, where the conscripted justified or denounced their peers who had failed to turn up. At least in the heyday of the Empire the Church gave its support to the authorities, with parish priests preaching obedience. Amnesties had some effect. But ultimately it was the use of force against recalcitrant conscripts that ensured obedience: spies, billeting and above all mobile columns broke the back of insubordination, arresting 63,000 in 92 departments between 1810 and 1812. To this can be added great care in obeying the letter of the law, not least through fear of sparking off mass popular revolts, such as occurred in the Tyrol in 1809. The recaptured deserters were then despatched to safe locations, like the isle of Elba, where they were trained with notable professionalism.

Within France's frontiers, conscription had been forced into acceptance by the civilian population – whether French, Flemish, German, Swiss or Italian – as an unpleasant but inevitable fact of life. A bureaucratic machinery had been developed, whose methods could be applied to newly annexed regions like Holland and the Hanseatic cities, whose populations were still recalcitrant: Napoleon despatched Réal, a councillor of state, to Holland and his military aides-de-camp to Germany in 1811 to enforce obedience to conscription and round up evaders.[41] Outside the frontiers, it proved more difficult to develop similarly effective techniques.

Napoleon introduced conscription wherever he assumed direct control – in the Italian republic in 1802, Berg in 1807, Holland and the Hanseatic departments in 1810. The only exception was at the extreme periphery of the Empire, the south-eastern frontier of the Illyrian provinces, where French civilisation met the once threatening Muslim Ottoman empire. Here, in military Croatia (as it was described), the Austrian system of permanent military collective settlements (*zadruga*) was left in place. Elsewhere the Emperor insisted that his dependants and allies raise armies for his wars. A prime reason for the creation of the Rhenish Confederation was to obtain an abundant supply of German troops. For, as he advised Murat, newly nominated duke of Berg: 'According to French practice, troops cost too much; Bavarian style, they are much cheaper'.[42]

The rulers of the satellite states were also anxious to create their own armies, some – like Eugene de Beauharnais and Murat – because of their military vocation, others – like the Polish nobles – as a pledge of their independence, all because it would reduce the crippling cost of maintaining French troops on their soil. Everywhere they ran into the difficulties already experienced by the French, but with variations which are revealing of the different traditions and social structures.

A problem common to many of these countries was how to raise troops rapidly without an appropriate administrative structure, at a time when neighbouring states were in the same predicament. Two long-established solutions were tried: enrolment of convicts and sometimes orphans, and recruitment of prisoners and deserters from other armies. The Neapolitan contingent to Spain in 1807 consisted of convicts and captured brigands; when Napoleon demanded a further contingent of 3,000 for Germany in August 1812, they were taken from the Vicaria prison and were of such poor quality that 1,000 were sent back.[43] The Dutch, a people of naval bellicosity with a horror of landed warfare, traditionally bought mercenaries, German by preference. The size of army Napoleon demanded from his brother Louis (30,000 to 40,000 men) created multiple repercussions, because of the Dutch refusal to introduce conscription (except for orphans); instead, they offered high pay and bonuses to encourage Dutch volunteers, while enlisting Germans and Swiss and Prussian prisoners held at Mainz and elsewhere on the left bank. The result was that when the Berg administrators tried to meet their commitment of 5,000 soldiers in 1807, they found that Dutch recruiting officers had preceded them. General Damas, appointed by Murat to create the new Berg army, sent his recruiters to the military prisons in Nancy and Dijon to enlist prisoners; but because the Spanish, Swiss, Dutch and Poles had already been taken, they managed to raise only 800 and were forced to turn their attention to neighbouring Hesse. Berthier, newly created prince of Neuchâtel, decided there was no need to introduce conscription, given the tradition of military service, and in this same year (1807) forbade recruitment of his subjects by other states. When the kingdom of Westphalia was created, also in 1807, van Hogendorp (until recently Dutch minister of war) arranged for the soldiers originating from the ex-Prussian territories of Westphalia and re-cruited by Holland to be transferred to Jerome's service.[44] The same pattern of fishing in neighbours' pools could be observed in Italy: evaders and deserters who fled across the border from the neighbouring French departments found themselves conscripted in the Italian republic; Neapolitan recruiters for Joseph tried to persuade soldiers to desert from Beauharnais' army. Murat's prolonged hesitation in introducing conscription in Naples (1809), and the practice of convict supplementation derived from the resistance of the landed barons and worry about the reaction of the *lazzaroni* of the capital. But the danger of recruiting convicts or captured prisoners was that they deserted so rapidly. Colonel Noguès created a Westphalian regiment mostly of Prussian, Austrian and Russian prisoners; when he took them to Hamburg in 1808, he lost thirty a day, bribed by the British and Russian ambassadors.[45]

Conscription created massive resistance and evasion everywhere, except where there were earlier traditions of military service, as in Switzerland or at Mainz where the Elector had already introduced it. Resistance was particularly marked in regions which previously had been specifically exempted from conscription, as in Mark, formerly Prussian, now part of Berg. But where the social structure remained heavily seigneurial, conscription could never succeed, because of the dependence on the landed owners. In Bavaria entire social categories were exempted when conscription was introduced in 1804–5, and only with the invasion of 1809, and then with the heavy demands of 1812, was the system tightened.

Elsewhere, as in the Italic republic from 1803, Venetia from 1806 or Holland from 1810, the familiar pattern of flight, self-mutilation, local collusion and heavy-handed bureaucratic measures was the order of the day. In regions where banditry had been common, as in southern Piedmont or Calabria, evaders and deserters were seen as reinforcing their numbers and structures, and certainly did so with the collapse of French power in 1813. Elsewhere, particularly where the priests preached obedience and resignation, as in Venetia, evaders tended to give up, at the most after two to three years, through the material difficulties of living in hiding, dependent on kin and friends. Those who could afford them bought substitutes for their sons; but besides the rising cost, there was the danger of desertion by substitutes: one unfortunate citizen of Padua paid four times, as the first two deserted and the third was then drawn by lot for the reserves. In 1813 Napoleon illegally conscripted those who had bought substitutes.

As in France, violent methods were deployed to overcome resistance. Villages, towns, even a city like Milan, were surrounded by troops and subjected to house-by-house searches, with the arrest of all males of conscript age. Once captured, they were rapidly marched away from their local areas, to diminish the chances of desertion. Jacquin, a veteran in service since 1798, recalled how he marched from Brittany to Turin in 1806 in order to be close at hand to receive recruits from Provence: 'there was no way of getting any of them to Brittany, as they deserted en route through fear of being embarked on ships. The recruiting non-commissioned officers responsible for accompanying the detachments arrived at Vannes, as it were, alone'.[46] Jacquin's experiences within France were applicable throughout Europe, wherever there was conscription. In Catalonia desertion was as continuous a drain on recruitment to the Spanish armies as ever it was to the French. Even patriotism had its limits, particularly in a region whose population had previously been exempt from conscription. The French prefect at Lerida could not be accused of wishful thinking when he wrote: 'They detest military service and it's only by force that they can be torn from their families to serve in the rebel bands'.[47]

ARMIES

Mathieu-Louis Molé, descendant of a dynasty of magistrates and the most civilian of Napoleon's ministers, had no doubts that Napoleon was happiest when he was with his soldiers:

> The Army above all was the object of the First Consul's care and his warmest concern. The fortnightly reviews that he held at the Carrousel and in the courtyard of the Tuileries were famous throughout Europe. The beauty of the troops and the precision of the manoeuvres were not what attracted most attention. One came to see Bonaparte in his element, amidst such rich and elegant uniforms he was recognisable in his single-toned dress, his small hat without braids and, if it was raining, his grey overcoat. When the troops were assembled, he dismounted and walked among the ranks. He stopped in front of each soldier, examined his uniform, called those he recognised by their name – and there were always a large number – recalled the occasion on which they had distinguished themselves, accepted their requests with good grace but without committing himself to any of them. In my opinion, in no other role did he reveal himself so directly, nor display more ably and profoundly the art of leading men.[48]

Napoleon upheld and magnified the tribute rendered by the Revolution to its defenders. Indifferent to the tiresome details of military logistics and administration, to the point of often leaving his soldiers without pay, food or adequate clothing and shoes, he never wavered in his conviction that armies were only as good as the quality of their men. If a marshal's baton was no longer carried in any private's sack, soldiers and non-commissioned officers could still make careers, so long as they possessed a minimal education.

Veterans continued to be lodged and honoured at the Invalides, as before and during the Revolution. The widows and orphans of soldiers killed in battle could expect assistance, the wounded received pensions. The recognition of obligations by civil society towards the military once they had ceased to fight was without parallel in Europe.

Officers received particular attention, to the point that Napoleon personally followed their promotions, even at the level of lieutenant and captain. But the favours lavished upon the officer corps did not derive purely from the Emperor's passionate interest in the ceremonies and ritual of the parade-ground. In the hierarchical philosophy of the regime, officers were crucially important for at least three reasons. First, because in the confusion of the battlefield, victory depended, even more than on the officers' bravery, on their 'talent' – and by talent was understood technical instruction in the art of war. Secondly, the role of officers in the world of the military was seen as corresponding to that of the elites in civil society: the example of the few was necessary, if not sufficient (for good order and discipline were also required), to ensure the proper comportment of the many. Thirdly, service within the officer corps was seen as the means of overcoming the divisions inherited from the past, whether between the aristocracy and the bourgeoisie, or between the old and new citizens and subjects of France.

Instruction became increasingly important as the key to promotion, alongside number of years in rank and bravery. Indeed, officers sometimes got together to pay 'military teachers' for lessons in mathematics, map-reading and foreign languages.[49] Promotion in the artillery and engineering corps was virtually dependent on examinations. The stress on technical expertise, so characteristic of the Revolutionary-Napoleonic experience, was not confined to France, but remained strong in Italy: the military academy at Modena had long-established traditions; at Naples an engineering school was set up; if the outstanding Piedmontese artillery school was suppressed on annexation, its personnel continued to collaborate in French military schools and the *école polytechnique*, as well as the University of Turin.

Military schools and academies were of importance not only to provide appropriate instruction and discipline to the future officers, but also to 'amalgamate' the elites in the service of the state. They were to act as the military equivalent of the auditors in the council of state, training grounds for the most able young, where talent supported by wealth replaced birth. It was not surprising that Saint-Cyr and La Flèche were imitated in the allied states. The University of

Pavia in the kingdom of Italy was transformed into a military academy. Max Joseph of Bavaria and Louis of Holland both set up military schools; given the military reluctance of the Dutch, it was not surprising that in their school discipline was attenuated and education accentuated. For Lacuée, the military schools would unite the future elite of the Empire more effectively than the state schools organised by the Imperial University; the list of prize-winners at Saint-Cyr in the Year XI included boys from annexed Italian and German departments.[50] The creation of elite corps in the armies served the same function. The guards of honour and velites restricted to the nobility and wealthy, whose social exclusiveness attracted volunteers, were introduced into the kingdoms of Italy and Naples, on the model of France.

The entire ethos of society shifted dramatically away from the critical attitudes towards the army of the enlightenment. Honour became the key concept, in the fullness of its military connotations. 'Even for a Frenchman it is difficult to explain with precision what honour is', Pierre Crouzet exhorted the pupils at Saint-Cyr soon after Austerlitz, citing the examples of Bayard, Duguesclin, Turenne, Jeanne d'Arc and – curiously – the Dutch Barneveldt.

> Facts, far better than words, can define and prove its existence. Honour, gentlemen, is the second religion of the French warrior. . . . Sons of our heroes, consider your august Emperor as your father: overwhelmed by his benevolence, you owe him your blood. . . . For him you must live, for him you must die: to sacrifice your life for him is to sacrifice it for honour itself, which has never had a more noble image on earth.[51]

The cult of individual glory and a romantic image of the military life were again leading values, as can be seen in Stendhal's *Journal* of his military campaigns in these years, as much as in his later novels.

There is considerable evidence that the families of the notables, not only in France, but also in the annexed regions, responded to the appeal of a military career. In Paris, the sons of merchants, landowners and rentiers volunteered alongside students, merchants' assistants, notaries' clerks. In the Belgian departments, there were initially over 2,600 volunteers and velites, or nearly 4 per cent of the conscripted in the Years VII to XIII, although the numbers fell dramatically in the following years (523 in 1805–9). In Neuchâtel, the leading families sent their children to Berthier with the advice: 'In the career you are about to enter, he is the most powerful protector that you could possibly meet. It is essential that you be one of the first to volunteer'.[52] Despite the hostility to conscription, a military career – which remained genuinely open to all the talents, given the unrelenting demand – had become a symbol of prestige, a channel for social promotion, even a pledge for the national aspirations of Poles and Italians. Only the Spaniards rejected the intimate association of honour with the Napoleonic armies, attributing it rather to their own independence.

This remarkable identification between Napoleon and his military exploits was fundamental to the creation and success of the Napoleonic myth. The iconography of this myth was quintessentially military, from the paintings of Gros and David of the military hero at Arcole, crossing the St Bernard Pass, at Austerlitz, Wagram or Eylau, to such monuments as the Colonne Vendôme or the Arc de Triomphe; while the great French (and non-French) literature of subsequent years was imprinted with a predominantly military image of the hero. The myth was deliberately and assiduously cultivated by Bonaparte through the publication of propaganda, from his earliest command – with the *Courier of the Army of Italy* (1797) – to the *Bulletins of the Grande Armée*, which circulated everywhere, from salons to schools. As Alfred de Vigny recalled:

> Our teachers never stopped reading us the bulletins of the Grande Armée and our cries of 'Long live the Emperor' interrupted Tacitus and Plato. Our tutors resembled heralds, our classrooms barracks, our recreations manoeuvres and our exams military reviews.[53]

Of the three constitutive images of the Napoleonic myth identified by Jean Tulard – the young hero, the master of the world, and the proscribed exile – two were military. It is this disproportionate weight of military success in the Napoleonic myth that helps explain why the image of the Grande Armée remained so deeply rooted in nineteenth-century French literature: Hugo, Dumas and Nerval were all sons of Napoleonic officers, who – like Vigny – had avidly read the *Bulletins of the Grande Armée* in their youth.

How far the actual experience of soldiers and officers corresponded to the romantic image of military life would merit a longer discussion than is possible here. F.-J. Jacquin, the son of a Franche Comtois peasant, who was conscripted in 1798 and fought repeatedly from Zurich to Ulm, Essling and Wagram, jotted down a travel notebook of his movements.[54] He received his first uniform only after thirteen months, and his company refused to march from Bayonne to Spain in

1801 until they received their backlog of eleven months' pay and new shoes. His notebook reveals what was undoubtedly the most common experience of soldiers in Napoleon's armies – marches across huge distances, alternating with periods in the barracks. He marched an average 6 leagues a day (or 24 kilometres), but when necessary would cover 10–11 leagues. He marched across Switzerland, Germany, Prussia and Austria in 1799–1800, across France in 1801 to Salamanca, where he stayed only twenty-eight days before hastening up to Brest. In October 1805, from Vannes in Brittany he crossed northern France and Belgium by forced marches to Nijmegen in Holland in ten weeks, resting for two weeks before retracing his steps (presumably lighter on equipment) in five weeks. Within months, he marched from Vannes to Chambéry in six weeks and then slowly across the Alps to Turin with his recruits. Late in November 1806 he hastened by forced marches across the Po plain to Bergamo and Brescia, and then via the Trentino across Germany, marching 9–14 leagues a day, to Saxony and Pomerania on the Baltic (July 1807). After a leisurely walk back to France, he was given sixteen days' leave in the December snows to visit his family for the first time in eleven years. By 1809 he was marching through Austria and in 1811 was stationed in Holland.

Officers rarely marched (unless their horses were shot). Their abundant memoirs, on which the Napoleonic myth was fed, mostly recall battles, great men and the quality of their lodgings. For many, like A. Noguès, one of three martial brothers, military activity appears as the sole purpose of life: 'When offered . . . employment at Court, I replied that I preferred battlefields in Germany to standing around like a crane in antechambers'.[55] The ferocity of the war in Spain and the débâcle of the Russian campaign made at least some officers confess to less bellicose feelings. Nevertheless, alongside the bravado, a constant theme of these memoirs, is the nagging sense of rivalry, of petty injustices in the attribution of awards or promotion. Jacquin's disgust at being passed over for the Legion of Honour is at one with the acid criticisms of Thiébault, Marbot and innumerable other officers that acknowledgement of true valour should have been subordinated by marshals like Davout and Masséna and lesser generals to personal favouritisms and clientelistic considerations. For the price of honour – a consequence of its renewed centrality in the values of the time – was how to obtain its public recognition.

Personal experience of participation in the Napoleonic wars remains opaque, but was undoubtedly profound. The armies acted as a melting pot for both officers and soldiers, forcing the recruits through the artificial conditions of military life into a prolonged socialisation that cut across linguistic and geographical boundaries. The linguistic problems should not be underestimated. Noguès, who served Louis in Holland, explained somewhat complacently the failure of the French General Gracin to put some Dutch regiments through their paces in a review ordered by Bernadotte: 'In fact he did not know how to issue his orders in Dutch and instead of saying *gueswinde pas* (quicken pace), he pronounced *chuinte pas*, which means *pig pace*'. But Jacquin, who spoke only French, when he found himself alone in an Austrian village, managed to persuade the hostile peasants that he was not really their enemy.[56] The numbers and nationalities of the men who fought in or against Napoleon's armies ensured that the campaigns would enter the collective memory of vast numbers of families, in a manner subsequently paralleled only by the First World War. It would appear that for many, particularly the officers, the sense of making history more than compensated for the disappointments and discomforts. Even so unusual and sensitive an officer as Stendhal – who not only read all the time and was bored by the company of his peers, but also witnessed the bloodshed of the 1809 Austrian war and the burning of Moscow – retained his admiration for this military epic.

Napoleon had concentrated on the reorganisation of his armies between the peace of Amiens and Austerlitz. The aim of such a reorganisation was to strengthen their strategic flexibility, by increasing the autonomy of the individual armies under a single supreme command, which could always summon them at short notice to march rapidly across Europe during campaigns. All the armies depended on the core of Revolutionary or Consulate veterans, who disciplined the recruits as they marched them to their bases and tempered their performance on the battlefield. But as the demands on the troops grew heavier, their quality declined. From about 1806 the proportion of troops with experience of the Revolutionary wars dropped rapidly. In consequence the manoeuvres under fire, which were central to Revolutionary and Napoleonic tactics, proved less possible and the later battles became ever bloodier: 8,000 were killed at Austerlitz (1805), 30,000 at Wagram (1809) and Borodino (1812), 25,000 of a total army of 72,000 at Waterloo (1815). Napoleon tried to compensate for the inexperience of his infantry by strengthening the role of the artillery, but his arsenals were never able to produce enough guns. Even worse, despite the major improvements in field surgery introduced by Larrey and Percy, the inadequacy of the medical services meant a far greater toll of death through disease and hospitalisation than on the actual battlefield. Napoleon's contempt for human life, masked by his charismatic presence among his soldiers, was ultimately responsible for the débâcle of the Grande Armée.

A consequence of Napoleon's need for ever larger military forces, combined with the decline in the numbers of veterans, was an increase in the numbers of soldiers provided by the satellite states. The Napoleonic armies had always contained many 'foreigners', just as the forces of the satellite states included French officers, and all armies utilised captured troops. Service in Napoleon's armies offered prestige and greater career prospects, particularly in the Grande Armée, the army directly commanded by the emperor. 'French' generals included seventy Italians, thirty-two Poles, fifteen Swiss, eighteen Dutch, ten Belgians, twenty Germans and nineteen Irish and English. French armies of course included conscripts from the annexed departments. In the absence of detailed studies (except for Belgium), it is impossible to know with any precision what proportion of the total forces these represented. The nine Belgian departments provided 90,000 to 100,000 soldiers by between 1798 and 1809, the six Piedmontese departments about 95,000 between 1802 and 1814.[57] Napoleon deliberately and systematically incorporated such new Frenchmen within the existing regiments and battalions, in order to prevent the development of significant 'national' armies. Piedmontese proposals for a national guard were blocked and only volunteers were allowed to remain in Piedmontese regiments. Given the legendary reputation of Swiss soldiers, the refusal to allow the formation of a federal army, and even a Swiss military school, was perhaps inevitable. Instead, the autonomy of the cantons was stressed by allowing each its own militia; the contribution of the cantons to French armies may have amounted to 20,000 men.

The policy towards armed forces in the satellite and allied states was more ambivalent. On the one hand, such armies might be used as the basis to create or reinforce a national identity. After all, this was one of the functions of the imperial armies, as Napoleon angrily reminded Lebrun when he failed to conscript 15,000 Genoese sailors: 'I repeat, only when I shall have sailors aboard my ships will this country have become wholly French'.[58] On the other hand, allied armies were essential for the wars. A condition of the creation of the Confederation of the Rhine was that its states supply 63,000 men. Of these, Bavaria was responsible for 30,000. To forge an effective Bavarian army, Montgelas had asked Napoleon for a French general 'sufficiently firm to command the Bavarian officers and sufficiently moderate not to humiliate them':[59] under H. G. Bertrand, Napoleon's faithful companion from Egypt to St Helena, Bavarian forces increased from 16,000 in 1804–5 to a peak of over 62,000. Westphalia was committed to an army of 25,000. In Germany, Napoleon seemed to have had few worries about the possible hostility of such allied armies, even (after their defeats) of the Austrians and Prussians, who were committed to provide 30,000 troops each for the Russian campaign. In Holland, he must have realised that his demands were unlikely to be met, as the initial figure of 40,000 (1806) was dropped to 30,000 or 35,000. In Italy, instead, Napoleon consistently frustrated the ambitions of Melzi and Murat to utilise their armies in order to achieve a more independent status. Only in Poland was he prepared to exploit the explicit identification of army with patriotic independence: such was the conviction of the Poles that their future depended on Napoleon's victory that they were even ready to fight in Spain; the 30,000 Polish troops of 1807 had become 60,000 by 1809 and 100,000 on the eve of the invasion of Russia. The proportion of foreign troops steadily increased by the later years: they constituted over half of the Grande Armée that invaded Russia (500,000 to 600,000 men). Overall, the contribution of soldiers from outside France's frontiers to the Napoleonic armies amounted to perhaps 1 million men.[60]

The cost of these armies was crippling. Napoleon was always confident that he could make war pay, not only by encouraging his armies to live off the land during campaigns, but also by exacting huge indemnities from his defeated enemies and making his allies pay the heavy maintenance costs of the French armies on their territory. Gaudin, his minister of finances, claimed that the campaigns of 1806 and 1807 covered one-third of France's budgeted expenditure, in addition to the maintenance costs of her troops abroad. Austria's two defeats led to indemnities of 350 million francs, a large part of which was spent on the victorious occupying forces, but which yielded the French treasury 120 million francs; the indemnities imposed on Prussia amounted to 515 million francs, of which 220 million francs were paid to the war treasury and a similar amount spent on the occupation forces. But not all such impositions were exacted – Portugal paid only 7 million of the 100 million francs demanded in 1807 – nor were all campaigns profitable. The Spanish war was a constant drain, and the Russian campaign was catastrophic. The deficit in the French budgets from 1811 was due overwhelmingly to war: military expenditure rose from 40 per cent of the budget total in 1806 to 58 per cent in 1813. Even more, as Jean Gabillard has shown, in an economy where state borrowing was refused on principle and a rigid metallic currency system imposed, the military campaigns had serious deflationary repercussions on the French economy and bore much of the responsibility for the crises of 1805–7 and 1811–14.[61]

In the satellite states, the cost of the armies was even more crippling, as they related to both French forces and their own troops. The French army occupying the kingdom of Naples in 1806 numbered 40,000 (of whom a substantial proportion came from the kingdom of Italy), whereas Joseph estimated an army of 24,000 as the maximum the country could support. Murat was committed to provide 16,000 infantry and 2,500 cavalry by the treaty of Bayonne. Between 1808 and 1811 the revenues of the kingdom of Naples rose by 50 per cent, but army and navy expenditure increased from 60 per cent to 80 per cent of the total budget. Westphalia was committed to make a substantial financial contribution to Napoleon's war campaigns, as well as to pay for a French contingent of at least 11,000 to 12,000 men, until it raised its own army of 25,000. Beugnot estimated that Westphalia's state revenues could not rise above 34 million francs, while the war contributions would cost 31 million francs and the maintenance of an army of 25,000 a further 11.5 million francs. The Dutch national debt rose from 1,163 million florins to 1,475 million florins between 1806 and 1810, almost wholly through military costs.[62] It would be otiose to insist further. One of the great successes of Napoleonic administration, in all states under French influence, had been the rationalisation of public finances, resulting in substantial increase of revenues. The benefits were lost, as all states experienced a spiralling of expenditure directly caused by military requirements, from 1811 at the latest. The demands of the armies created public poverty, at the same time as they offered unparalleled opportunities for private wealth to suppliers and speculators.

Political scientists today point to the Revolutionary-Napoleonic years as marking (in some though by no means all respects) the beginnings of the professionalisation of the military: they point in particular to the creation of mass armies through conscription, the centralisation of supreme command with delegation to autonomous units, and the end of the caste system of officer recruitment.[63] It is easy to identify such elements in Napoleon's aims and practices. What are not normally discussed are the methods of imposition of such practices or their compatibility with the civilian ideal of administration. Conscription has already been discussed. It is worth noting that, at the officer level, if the army continued to offer a career open to talent, this was truer for the French than for the others, as too many French officers viewed the satellite armies as providing alternative opportunities for quick advancement. This may have been worse in Italy than elsewhere, but certainly the presence of French officers in the kingdoms of Italy and particularly of Naples was a source of constant friction. More in general, the behaviour of military commanders, not only outside France, but also within the new territories – of which Davout in the Hanseatic departments offers a prime example – outraged impotent civilian administrators.[64]

Gaetano Mosca considered that the subordination of the armed forces to civilian authority was among the most distinctive and crucial features of European civilisation. He attributed this to the integration of the officer corps within the ruling elites, contemporaneous to the rigid class divisions within the armies. Military intervention in the political life of post-Napoleonic Spain offers the most obvious exception to this generalisation about the history of Europe since 1815. But the pre-eminent role assigned to the army and the privileges given to the officer corps in Napoleonic society itself must raise questions about the nature of their subordination.

SOCIAL PRIVILEGE

Aspirations to social equality had flickered and died like fireflies in the summer's night of the Revolution. Long before Brumaire, equality had been restored – but in restrictive manner – to the sphere initially assigned it by the deputies of the National Assembly – a political weapon against privilege, defined juridically as equality before the law. The Consulate succeeded not only because it imposed political stability, but also because it ensured continuity with the social identity of the Directory: ownership of property marked an ever sharper divide from the labouring classes. The very insistence in identifying those regarded as notables at every level, the listings drawn up repeatedly by the administrators for this purpose, the terminology employed to describe their qualities, are all revealing of the strictly hierarchical representation of society under Napoleon. In the heyday of the Empire, in 1810, over 100,000 notables were classified by the prefects in tables of candidates judged suitable for membership of the departmental and sub-prefectural electoral colleges.[65] The revenues attributed to them ranged widely, from over 50,000 francs to under 500 francs, reflecting the low level of wealth in many departments. Landed property was the common denominator of all professional categories, whether these notables were defined as 'proprietors', 'farmers', or 'functionaries', 'merchants' or members of the liberal professions. One-third was described as proprietors, but since a large proportion of those listed as belonging to local administrations (18 per cent) were also dependent on their landed incomes, the category of landowner covered probably half the total number of notables; the functionaries were the next largest group (16 per cent), more than the liberal professions (14 per cent) or traders and manufacturers (11 per cent). These were Napoleon's 'masses of granite', who were to hold together 'the grains of sand-dust' of the ordinary people by their example, connections, wealth and influence; from their ranks were chosen the men of 'talent' to serve the state in civilian or military capacity.

There was a strong continuity in professions between the notability of ancien regime France and that of the Empire: if the most senior officials of Louis XVI's administration and army had vanished, the middle ranks retained their natural place among the ruling elites. But this continuity extended beyond occupations to social positions and wealth: most of the wealthiest landlords were nobles. In France, their strong presence in the departmental listings of the top twelve land tax payers (1802) reflected the remarkable resilience of the old noble families in the face of the persecutions and confiscations of the previous decade. In the annexed territories and satellite states, the very absence of the intense Revolutionary experience ensured the continuing influence of the great aristocratic families, whose wealth was based on land. Naturally this was not the case in regions where great estates had never been characteristic, such as Savoy, Haut- and Bas-Rhin or Léman, nor did it apply (except in the Orangist northern provinces) to mercantile societies like the Dutch. But in the Piedmontese departments in 1810, for example, 114 of the 150 names in the lists of the 30 'most heavily taxed' were ex-nobles, while in the Italic kingdom three-quarters of the electoral college of the 'proprietors' were the old nobility. Further east in Europe, supremely in Poland, there was never even any pretence at challenging the continuity of aristocratic political and social power.[66]

To conclude from this that little had changed from the ancien regime would be erroneous. If great landed families had survived the vicissitudes of political upheaval, they had still lost their fiscal privileges. The weight of the land tax remained highly disproportionate between departments, and even the radical decision to introduce the theoretically impartial cadaster (1808) was weakened by local opposition. But equality before the law meant equal liability to taxation, as well as access to landownership and to careers unhampered by legal restrictions.

Nevertheless, already under the Consulate, one sector of society was regarded as more equal than others – the military. Recognition of individual acts of military valour by the award of arms of honour dated back to the Directory. The Legion of Honour (19 May 1802), forced through the council of state by Napoleon despite the reservations of some councillors, was justified precisely in terms of recompense of honour. For Roederer, it was a means of shifting power away from the Brumairean notability of the electoral colleges to Bonaparte, on whom nominations to the Legion depended. The Legion was given a military and hierarchical structure (organised in fifteen cohorts, with grand officers, commandants, officers and legionaries) and was presented as a means of strengthening cohesion in a society atomised by the Revolution. It was expected, Lucien Bonaparte told the Tribunate, that 'this happy system of union established among the legionaries will hopefully spread through society'.[67] To facilitate the effectiveness of this collective military injection into civil society, the knightly Order was entailed with national properties worth 76 million francs. From the outset (as in the creation of *'sénatoreries'* for particularly meritorious senators in 1803), an income was assigned with each title. The purpose was to ensure that the beneficiaries enjoyed adequate financial means to uphold publicly attributed status, while avoiding the danger of creating a hereditary class. In practice, the rapid and continuous inflation of nominations reduced appointments to a sign of distinction, with an income guaranteed to keep the legionaries, irrespective of their social origin, above the labouring classes. From the initial 5,000 awards, the Legion grew to over 11,000 in 1805 and 38,000 by 1814. But, from its outset, the Legion remained an almost exclusive reserve for the military. In 1814 only 1,500, or under 4 per cent, were civilians, mostly leading dignitaries of the regime.[68] Lucien Bonaparte's sibylline phrase at the moment of the creation of the Legion of Honour perhaps masked an unconfessed hope that the corporate ownership and military organisation of the Order's estates would act as an embryonic model for a future French society. Napoleon, at his most self-confident, attracted by the example of the Roman empire, even tried to imitate the deployment of legionaries as a means contemporaneously to defend and stiffen society, particularly in the border or new territories. Initially (1802) he proposed to establish ten landed settlements, each with 400 veterans, retired because of their wounds; two experimental camps were opened at Alessandria in Piedmont and Juliers in the

Rhineland. Confirmation of the military settlements of Croatia, the *zadrugas*, may well have been encouraged by similar sentiments. In the same vein, 6,000 respectable dowries were offered in 1810 to induce veterans to marry and reproduce.[69]

There can be no doubt that, as Napoleon became more conservative over the years, his preference for the military became more marked. Victorious war offered officers and soldiers multiple opportunities for income supplementation, hierarchically structured according to grade. The enormous fortunes of favourite marshals – some of whom, like Berthier, Masséna and Ney, accumulated official incomes of 700,000 to over 1,200,000 francs annually – were the result of Napoleon's generosity, not to speak of his normal willingness to turn a blind eye to the 'voluntary donations' they extracted in occupied territories. But apart from military campaigns, the military were granted solid material benefits and growing social prestige. The officers received stipends that, particularly at the higher grades, compared very favourably to those of the civilian administrators. Over 4,500 wounded soldiers and officers were given incomes ranging from 500 francs to over 4,000 francs. Despite the civil code, officers' property was given protection against seizure, free education was enjoyed by their daughters, scholarships to military schools were given to their sons (and from 1812, exclusively to them). Retired officers were employed in the civil administration, especially at the lower levels, as head clerks in the police, Customs and financial administrations, where presumably the requirements of discipline and force particularly suited their military qualifications.[70]

The duke of Wellington recalled an imperial France that, in his old age, had already acquired the blurred and inaccurate contours of a mythical past:

> That country was constituted upon a military basis. All its institutions were framed for the purpose of forming and maintaining its armies with a view to conquest. All the offices and rewards of the State were reserved in the first instance exclusively for the army. An officer, even a private soldier, might look to the sovereignty of a kingdom as a reward for his services.[71]

Wellington's memories were coloured by his experiences in Portugal where, to someone of his aristocratic and military background, his French opponents – Junot, Soult, Masséna – may well have seemed upstarts who had risen from the ranks. Nevertheless, his comment, however exaggerated, confirmed a contemporary impression difficult to refute. Under the Empire the military had acquired the visible characteristics of a privileged caste. In official ceremonies, the officers insisted on and ultimately won precedence over their civilian counterparts. Their uniforms set the tone for civilian administrators. Their marriages were controlled by the minister of war to ensure they did not demean their standing.

From France, the privileged position attributed to the military spread outwards across Europe. This was hardly surprising, given the high proportion of generals who ruled or governed territories – from Murat and Eugene de Beauharnais to the marshals in Spain and Germany – not to speak of the plethora of French officers seeking to make careers in the satellite states. Nor could it be otherwise in a country like Poland, where the aristocratic officers of the vastly expanded army could legitimately assert that the nation's newly recovered independence was primarily dependent on military valour. Perhaps more unexpected, and certainly misplaced, was Louis' decision to affirm Holland's autonomy in the military sphere by the sudden nomination of Dutch marshals. As General van Hogendorp, minister of war, recalled: 'It was absurd and pointless to create six marshals for a small state like Holland'; the only effect was to irritate Napoleon by the implicit challenge to his exclusive monopoly of such promotions.[72] The social origins of the officer corps in the different satellite states would merit study. One can confidently surmise that, while the local nobilities lost their monopoly (except in Poland), outside France the officers lacked the genuinely popular component that had characterised the French revolutionary armies. Whether in Holland or Italy, Bavaria or Poland, the military set the tone for society, through their parades and uniforms as much as through their exorbitant demands on public resources. Indeed, within states like Naples and Spain the endemic threat of war in regions such as Calabria or Valencia led to a virtual militarisation of society, where the senior civilian administrators were often former officers, taxes were collected by the army, and the donning of uniforms throughout the civil administration symbolised the presence of the state.

If the military was encouraged to affirm itself as a caste, the nobility was deliberately created as an accompaniment to the Empire. The assumption of the imperial title required a Court and the assignation of appropriate titles to the sovereign's family. In the one and the other case the protocol of the ancien regime was assiduously copied. Even more symptomatic of the blatant desire to affirm the hierarchical order of an imaginary past was the juridical language employed to decree the grant of principates and duchies as grand fiefs of the

Empire to Napoleon's relatives and a few favoured generals and ministers (1806). The concept of primogeniture through the male line adopted for these fiefs, with reversion to the Crown in the absence of legitimate heirs, incorporated the ideal of what was seen as the original model of feudalism, as it was imagined to have existed in Carolingian times, purified of the accretions and corruptions of later ages. The same neo-gothic imagery can subsequently be found in the oath of fealty sworn by the new nobles, who vowed as true knights 'to march to the defence of the *patrie* on every occasion that its territory is threatened or that His Majesty goes forth at the head of his army'.[73] An excellent example, if ever there was, of a terminology replete with meanings shifting in significance from contemporary to imagined past in its references to '*patrie*', 'territory' and the king 'at the head of his army'.

The creation of a nobility (March 1808) was more than either a logical development from the initial principates or a means to reward the great and favoured. Titles consecrated the hierarchy of function, with level of honour corresponding to administrative grade: ministers, senators, councillors of state, presidents of the Legislative body and archbishops were counts; presidents of electoral colleges and of the highest tribunals, bishops and the mayors of the thirty-seven 'good towns' were barons. Progress in the service of the state could be publicly acknowledged by elevation from chevalier to baron. Prefects and generals could be rewarded by nomination at different points in the hierarchy of titles, according to Napoleon's estimation of their service.

At the same time, a title could be made hereditary on condition that the holder entailed his estate to guarantee an appropriate level of income, as well as demonstrate his reputation and standing. The aim was to create a new nobility that would replace and absorb the old aristocracies. The discretionary power of concession of heritable titles functioned as a weapon both to protect the social exclusiveness of the imperial nobility, and to divide the ranks of the old families of great name who remained aloof from the regime.

Napoleon's concern to rally the old nobility to himself was one more aspect of his growing conservatism. As consul, his policy had been clear: on the one hand, to offer legal guarantees of person and property to those who were prepared to accept the new France, on the other, to reduce to impotence impenitent royalists by terrorism (the kidnapping and execution of the duke of Enghien) and confiscation of émigré properties. With the consolidation of his power, the prestige of service to the state attracted the younger generation of nobles. The old aristocracy had almost vanished from the 1802 list of notables, where it represented only 3 per cent; but 58 per cent of the prefects in 1806 were ancien regime nobles, as were one-third of the sub-prefects and mayors.[74] The creation of new noble titles, while the old remained abolished, was both a deliberate challenge and a veiled suggestion to the old families that it was time to rally openly to the regime. Pasquier, who came from their ranks and was the leading figure in the new Council for seals of nobility, warned them:[75]

> Those who are called by their wealth, name or condition to play a useful role in public life too often deceive themselves into believing that their abstention attracts attention to them and gives them a real importance. Should a reaction arrive, of any sort, it is not to them that the government would ever appeal. It would turn to the men of action, to those whose acts or words could carry the strength or means to be truly useful, to those who have followed the current and are not some twenty years behind the times.

From 1810 discretion gave way to open pressure as Napoleon, now married to Louis XVI's niece, Marie Louise, demanded open obeisance from all the nobles, even the most nostalgic. The brusque change in approach can be detected in all directions. In a long note dictated on 14 June 1810, the Emperor recognised that without the participation of the old families, the imperial nobility 'would never convince those who formerly enjoyed the prerogatives of nobility to forget'. He proposed a hierarchy of privileges and titles to attract them. 'Give support to the present dynasty, get people to forget the old nobility, that's the end to reach'.[76] The insistence on entails and adequate income to live in a manner appropriate to status was carried to the point of granting regular subsidies to the poor nobles of Tuscany and Genoa (1810). An independent charity for poor pregnant mothers, taken over in the Empress's name, became the occasion to attempt to rally the grand old families via their philanthropically minded wives (1810). The nobles of the newly annexed departments were given the opportunity to request titles in place of those they had enjoyed before annexation (1811). Most sinister, the minister of police, Savary, asked prefects for a listing of the unmarried daughters of the leading families, with comments on their qualities and dowries (1810–11). As Savary explained:

> Such information is all the more necessary as most of the old families only seek to ally among themselves because they are persuaded that they can revive and give greater brilliance to titles that the government does not recognise and which today are no

more than the recompense granted to those who gave considerable service in the civil career. . . . They believe they would lower themselves if they united with families whose fathers have shed their blood so gloriously for their country.[77]

The imperial nobility numbered about 3,350, the greater part of whose titles were granted between 1808 and 1810. The lion's share went to the military, 59 per cent of the total, rising to 80 per cent of the chevaliers; 22 per cent were leading functionaries (councillors of state, prefects, bishops, magistrates) and 17 per cent notables (senators, members of electoral colleges, mayors); there were few scientists, artists, manufacturers or merchants. If the 'grand old world' successfully resisted the conscription of its daughters (only about ten of whom married into the new nobility), it rallied increasingly to the regime: 950 (or one-third) of the new titles went to ancien regime families, of whom 680 came from within France's pre-Revolutionary frontiers. In a satellite state like the Italic kingdom, where 227 titles were created, the proportion of military among its new nobles fell to 10 per cent; although old families constituted 70 per cent, this was more the automatic result of the posts they held than clear evidence of 'rallying round'.[78]

The creation of this new nobility, whether to reward the military and civilian servants of the state or to absorb the old aristocracy, was oriented primarily towards 'old' France. This is not to ignore the fact that non-French generals and aristocrats from the annexed departments were ennobled, nor that nostalgic nobles persisted in their passive resistance to rally in territories like Piedmont, Lombardy or the former Papal States. It is not accidental that of the 285 titles given to the leading families of the annexed departments or satellite states, 170 should have been given to Italians, compared to 70 granted to the highly committed Poles and a mere handful to the other nationalities. Indeed, of the five members of the council created to examine applications for titles and entails, San Martino was a Piedmontese of ancient lineage.

Nevertheless, Napoleon's concern was quintessentially with the France divided by the Revolution. In his visions of grandeur, the *ralliement* of the ancien regime great families assumed a central role of legitimising his dynasty. Hence his readiness to allow Murat and Joseph to recognise the old nobility in the monarchical states of Naples and Spain, as the grand-duke of Warsaw recognised the Polish magnate families and Jerome the old families of his Westphalian territories. Begrudgingly, Napoleon allowed them to create their own nobilities, but took care that their titles remained inferior to those of France. 'Kings shall not have the right to name princes; such a right is inherent to the imperial crown', he reprimanded Louis, whose proposals to create a Dutch nobility seemed to him inopportune in a country with such strong republican traditions: 'My institutions do not exist to be turned to ridicule'.[79] Joseph's elevation of General Salligny as duke of San Germano in Naples and then grandee of Spain was placed in proper perspective by the Emperor's appointment of the same general as a French baron. Napoleon was happy to exchange nominations to chivalric orders with an established dynasty like that of Bavaria, but was reluctant to recognise the orders instituted by Louis or Murat. In the federative system he had created, as contemporaries from its outer provinces, like van Hogendorp, observed:

> secondary states attached to France (governed by Napoleon's brothers or others) were not allowed to take any measures, to create any institution, above all military, which was not in keeping with the principles of government of the grand empire, head of the confederation.[80]

Yet the possibilities of success of Napoleon's policy of a 'fusion' of old and new nobility in France depended directly on the existence and integration of the Empire and federative system. This was illustrated unequivocally by the imperial policy of entails and donations that underpinned the heredity of titles. From the outset, in 1806, the titles assigned by Napoleon were located in the satellite or annexed territories. The principates and duchies were located initially in Venetia and central Italy, then in the kingdom of Naples and Germany. The Emperor of the French, heir to the Revolution, carefully avoided employing the toponymy of France for his new dukes. Equally, the incomes that went with the titles were no longer available in France, since the greater part and the most worthwhile national properties had already been alienated. Newly conquered territories offered the obvious solution. A condition of the cession of Venetia to the kingdom of Italy was that one-fifth of its revenues, as well as national properties to the value of 30 million francs, were attached to the new fiefs; a further annual income of 1.2 million francs was set aside for distribution to generals, officers and soldiers designated by Napoleon. After Tilsit, the same policy was employed on an ever larger scale. State revenues and national properties were reserved, above all in the German states, in order to guarantee entailed incomes and donations to select members of the new nobility and others (for donations were also given without titles).

The distribution of such personal largesse was guarded jealously by Napoleon. The two large volumes in which the names and amounts were listed 'he always kept on the corner of his table', recalled his cabinet secretary Baron Fain;

> when the Emperor wanted to distribute some endowed incomes, he himself calculated them, keeping his eye on what he had already donated. . . . After turning a number of pages of the great book, he stopped and looked at me: 'Aha, old chap', he said, 'I've found you one! Here you are! Ten thousand francs' income in Pomerania! Let it not be said that I've forgotten my secretaries.'[81]

By 1814 Napoleon had made grants to 4,994 persons, at a cost of nearly 30 million francs a year. The greatest part went, inevitably, to the military: 824 generals received 1,261 grants, worth over 16 million francs, while the smallest gifts (nearly 3,000, of 500 francs) went to soldiers and officers wounded in the wars. At the top of the league, Napoleon's relatives and favourite marshals, such as Paolina Borghese, Berthier, Ney and Davout, in all 486 recipients, or 10 per cent of the total, shared 28 million francs' revenue, or 80 per cent of the total.

No relationship existed between the geographical location of the properties from which the endowments were derived and the titles to which they were tied. Ney, duke of Elchingen, for example, was given revenues in Westphalia, Hanover, Trasimeno, on the consolidated debt of the Italic kingdom and the Rhine *octroi*.[82] It is possible that such wide, apparently haphazard distribution reflected Napoleon's intention of tying the material interests of his generals to the future of the Empire. It is certain that all territories were regarded as equal sources of revenue for entails and gifts – so long as they lay outside the frontiers of pre-Revolutionary France. For the beneficiaries, this created problems (and protests) in obtaining the money promised them. For the countries from which the revenues were exacted, Napoleon's policy of reserved donations was at the least onerous, at the worst – as in Westphalia – catastrophic. Nearly a thousand beneficiaries were guaranteed 7 million francs, or nearly 20 per cent of Westphalia's public revenues. Friction and unending lawsuits resulted from the demands of these absentee owners of entailed national properties that they be allowed to retain the privileges and seigneurial rights abolished by the civil code and laws that Westphalia had adopted in imitation of France. No better example could be given of the unresolvable contradictions between the modernising ideals of integration of the French administrative class and the practices of exploitation that accompanied the expansion of the Empire.

5   Responses to conquest

The peoples we are dealing with are too ignorant, too distant from
civilisation and above all too poor for us to hope to succeed all at
once.

(Lareintz, intendant of Ragusa, 1 March 1813,
Archives Nationales, Paris, F 1ᵉ62)

If they are of a different lineage . . .

(Goya, Los desastres de la Guerra, no. 61)

The premiss of the French vision of the new state and society,
administratively modern and socially integrated, was the legitimacy
of the exercise of governmental authority. Napoleon and his collaborators never doubted their freedom to act on behalf of the rights and
interests of those they governed, to apply rational decisions and
procedures on the basis of carefully collected information. Their
exercise of power was rarely arbitrary, for they genuinely respected
rights of property and persons and observance of due processes of
law. The self-confidence of the Napoleonic functionaries in the possibility of applying uniform norms to the diversity of territories and
peoples where they established rule or control was great.
Nevertheless they never denied the complexity of the societies for
whom they assumed responsibility, nor the reality of a multiplicity of
pre-existing sources of power. They recognised that acceptance of
their procedures and values required trust and collaboration on the
part of those they regarded as men of influence in society. They
acknowledged that the imposition of so comprehensive a new set of
rules would inevitably clash with many established practices, which
had emerged from and expressed often long-accepted values.
Perhaps only the most experienced of the senior functionaries of this

imperial enterprise – a former *idéologue* like de Gérando or a sceptic like Lebrun – appreciated that the very extension of the arena of action opened up by the continuous outgrowth of political frontiers generated an equivalent, indeed a disproportionate difficulty in translating norms into practices.

What is certain is that the French civilian administrators sought actively to involve the local elites in their experience as the necessary condition of success, ultimately the only sure means of sinking roots and ensuring the viability of the new model. They recognised the interdependence between their actions and the comportment of those they identified as the opinion leaders in each society. They sought to coopt such elites, they exploited and manipulated shared values as a means of building up confidence and ultimately trust, they accepted the need to transact, according to the demands of each locality, person or group. We have discussed the limits to such efforts imposed by the very heterogeneity of space and history, as well as the contradictions created by military and economic exploitation. But the Napoleonic analysis of society, precisely because of its static quality, constrained the capacity of the administrators to understand how the changes they were introducing modified existing attitudes, preferences and values, at the same time as introducing new elements, in an unending dynamic of changing social relations that questioned the very bases of their efforts, blocked or distorted the penetration of their ideas, and in some instances aroused armed resistance.

For the historian, the Napoleonic experiment in administrative integration offers a unique possibility in modern history to explore the moment of exercise of political and social power, because the state identified itself to an unusual degree with a single, unifying model. For exactly the opposite reasons, it is difficult to offer as complete or satisfactory an interpretation of the responses to the introduction of this model. For such responses were quintessentially local, the old and new expressions of different levels of cultural identity, social relations and constellations of power. The interaction between a state power that imposed itself with unprecedented thoroughness, and the thick structures of numerous societies of varying dimensions can be fully apprehended only by a worm's eye view, an approach that holds firmly to the local context and examines the relationships and interdependence between a plurality of powers at different levels and from different perspectives. A multitude of such studies are needed, not a single chapter in a study concerned to draw out the overall structures and mechanisms of the Napoleonic conquest of Europe. Nevertheless, it remains possible to sketch at least some of the range of responses. Such responses inevitably varied, not only because of the relative liberty of individual choice, but also in terms of their significance for the differing structures and forms of organisation of family, communal and social life. The responses are most visible not only at the political level of collaboration, withdrawal or resistance, but also where the utilisation of the new economic opportunities offered by the Napoleonic regime have left ample traces in the documentation. Less immediately apparent, but no less important for an assessment of the capacity of the new model to penetrate the inner structures of communities and societies, are the responses expressed in the forms of religious and lay sociability and patterns of social relations. A discussion of these themes, however brief, offers another dimension to our understanding of this experiment in imposed integration, as well as a means of gauging its success.

COLLABORATION

The Napoleonic analysis of society only partially adhered to the conventional image of the pyramid. In reality, all societies – for the Napoleonic administrators – were dichotomous, consisting of elites and 'people'. The 'people' was always ignorant, normally passive and rationally unknowable. Its ignorance was not only proof of its inferior status, but also surviving evidence of an earlier stage of civilisation. Its passivity resulted from the bonds of obedience and deference inbuilt into family and social relations, and was likely to be upset only through prolonged hunger or subversive incitement. It was unknowable precisely because its comportment corresponded to the irrationality of earlier ages, described and dismissed in (usually dichotomous) platitudes about unchanging social characteristics: thus the 'people', always regarded as an anonymous mass, was 'industrious' or 'idle', 'superstitious' or 'enlightened', 'feudal' or 'civilised'.[1] At most, the ties of influence and dependence that explained the functioning of all societies (and their pyramidal form) were deployed to explain the behaviour of even the most primitive and ignorant. As Napoleon instructed Joseph after his occupation of Naples in 1806: 'The *lazzaroni* must have leaders; these must be made responsible for all of them.'[2]

Such judgements could claim a distinguished lineage, from Montesquieu back to Montaigne and earlier. But the functionaries' sense of remoteness from the people was accentuated by two aspects of the Revolutionary-Napoleonic experience. On the one hand, the perennial gulf between the labouring poor and the propertied classes was deepened by the very stress on property of the new regime. On the other hand, the destruction of conventional institutional inter- mediary bodies, such as guilds or confraternities, had the unexpected consequence of removing traditional channels of communication – and hence of mediation – with the people.

Dependence on the elites was accentuated by this difficulty in reading the codes of the people. The only alternative – to which the administrators were forced to resort more often than they wished – was the parish priest. The insistence in drawing up lists of notables and the very criteria employed in selecting those judged worthy of public recognition confirmed the centrality of the role of the elites as opinion leaders and mediators of opaque societies. Property, now reaching down into the social structure to incorporate artisans and wealthy peasants, often beneficiaries of the sales of national proper- ties, was regarded as the most effective tie to the social order. Reputation, even more than wealth, was essential as it signified family and local roots, essential elements in ensuring the esteem and proper comportment of the peasantry and respectable poor. Public service was the seal of commitment to the common good, irrespective of political regime. If 'talent' – professional competence – had acquired a novel weight in the choice of administrators and magis- trates, its definition at the local level was negotiable, because of the importance of obtaining the collaboration of the provincial elites. The notables were crucial mediators at all levels, as exclusive source of information for the statistical enquiries, as representatives of local opinion, and as leaders whose political opinion would influence the lesser ranks of society. The dependence of the administration on their collaboration was the greater in the newly annexed territories, where the stock of intimate knowledge that derived from long familiarity was inevitably lacking.

Given this analysis of society and recognition of the role of the elites, what was the response of the latter? Outside the Empire, at the very top of the social hierarchy, Napoleon had made a special appeal to personalities distinguished by reason of family, wealth or political position. Why did a Melzi, a Schimmelpenninck, a Bülow or a Cassano agree to assume leading roles? We do not often have their direct testimonies, which in any case need to be read critically as they were written after the débâcle, usually in self-defence. But a brief glance at some of their careers suggests replies.

Francesco Melzi d'Eril, a wealthy and educated Lombard aristo- crat, brother-in-law of the Milanese reformer Pietro Verri, had met

Bonaparte in 1796 and was untainted by association with the Cisalpine republics. Vice-president of the Italian republic, with greater authority than his successor Eugene or any other head of state nominated by Napoleon (except Murat), this whiggish patrician was convinced of the need to forge a modern and stable state socially based on enlightened, moderate, wealthy landed proprietors. At the same time, he translated into secret diplomatic negotiations his utopian hopes of restoring independence to a Lombard-dominated north Italian state. Although removed from effective power with the transformation of the republic into a kingdom, he willingly accepted the honours that were showered upon him, was personally responsible for the selection of the new Italian nobility and reaffirmed his belief in an independent state at the moment of Napoleon's abdication.

The Dutch grand pensionary, Schimmelpenninck, a lawyer involved in politics since the troubles of 1784, representative of Amsterdam in the 1795 revolution and envoy of the Batavian republic at Paris and London, saw his role as saviour of his country. A committed patriot and moderate, he believed he could retain what was best in the Dutch republican tradition by reversing the centralising drive of the radical patriots and negotiating the independence of his country directly with Napoleon. His failure in the one and the other proposition led to his opposition to the creation of the kingdom of Holland, but not to his nomination to the French Senate after the annexation of 1810.

These two contrasting examples point to the principled belief in the possibility of retaining, if not independence, at least some form of identity, alongside the conviction – shared by Melzi and Schimmelpenninck with the French administrative class – of the need to modernise the state. Once involved in the affairs of state, whatever their disappointment and disillusion, they were irretrievably identified with the Napoleonic regime and ready to accept its rewards. Similar motivations of a personal sense of capacity and public duty in a moment of national crisis, inextricably enmeshed in the temptations of playing a primary role in the administrative modernisation of a new and potentially more powerful state, no doubt explain the role of other leading landed aristocrats such as Bülow in Westphalia or Nesselrode in Berg – just as in the case of Stein and Hardenberg in the enemy kingdom of Prussia.

It would be simplistic to pretend that these motivations were shared by all. In the tiny principality of Neuchâtel, the driving concern of the chief magistrate Georges de Rougemont was to neutralise rather than to encourage rapid and radical administrative change. In the kingdom of Naples the acceptance of the interior ministry by the duke of Cassano was correctly viewed as the appropriation of political power by a factious clan within the aristocracy. Nevertheless it is reasonable to conclude that acceptance of office by leading personalities at the moment of the loss of independence was based on a genuine belief in public duty combined with a (usually excessive) sense of self-importance. In many ways the counterproof of this was the decision of the Spanish *afrancesados* to join Joseph's government. Against all the evidence of their impotence and isolation, they collaborated with this new French king because of their fear of revolution and social anarchy, their faith in monarchy and constituted authority, and their belief in the need for political and social reforms: 'An extraordinary revolution will improve the existence of the monarchy, establishing it on the solid foundations of reason, justice and power', wrote Moratín.[3] These were sentiments shared by their constitutional opponents at Cadiz. It was their misfortune that the realisation of their expectations, which had been demonstrated in the administrative practices of so many other states, was destroyed almost before it could take shape in the fire of popular resistance.

The sense of participating in a most successful and important experience of reformism was not of course restricted to these leading personalities. It was shared by many of the old reformers, discredited or frightened by the revolutionary upheavals of the previous decade, who now returned, some in their old age, to governmental responsibility: Zurlo in Naples, Gianni in Tuscany, like Cabarrús in Spain, were symbols of the continuity that these reformers saw between the work of the enlightened despots and Napoleon. They were few, because age and disillusionment had taken their toll. Far more numerous and active were the intellectuals and 'technicians', mostly of recent decades.

It was hardly surprising that civil and military engineers, cartographers, scientists and educationalists should have collaborated freely and often enthusiastically with the French administration. 'Useful' science enjoyed a privileged relationship with the political class from the outset of the Revolution, and many of the leading scientists – from Chaptal and Laplace to Berthollet and Cuvier – continued to play a central role throughout the years of the regime. The Egyptian expedition, with its 167 scientists and artists, gave Bonaparte an aureole of intellectual sensibility that he was never to lose. Administrative modernisation included a vast programme of infrastructural works and scientific research, from the great roads and bridges that were among Napoleon's most lasting legacies, to mechanical, chemical or medical investigations for the improvement of manufactures and the art of warfare. The very size of the administrative class, within and outside France's frontiers, offered possibilities of career and sometimes, within limits, of experimentation, with far greater assurance of support than under even the most favourably disposed of the former enlightenment governments.

Many examples could be given. In Piedmont, when Charles Emanuel IV abdicated, the entire corps of 106 artillery officers opted to continue their careers in the French army. In the kingdom of Naples, the military academy of the Nunziatella, which had been reformed in 1786 but closed in the reaction of 1799, was immediately revived under its founder, General Giuseppe Parisi, who successfully urged the creation of a Scuola Politecnica to rationalise the teaching of mathematics and engineering in both their military and civilian applications. The Tuscan scientist Giovanni Fabbroni, whose career had suffered during the obscurantist years of the kingdom of Etruria, pleaded and intrigued incessantly after Tuscany's annexation until he was finally appointed inspector of civil engineering for the Italian departments. The careers of the Saluzzo di Monesiglio in Piedmont were exemplary of the adaptability of even aristocratic families of old lineage but a scientific mentality to seize the opportunities offered by the new regime to further their own struggle to introduce modern values against the provincial conservativism of their peers. The four sons of Giuseppe Angelo Saluzzo, artillery general, scientist and co-founder of the Academy of Sciences, chose different career paths, both military and civilian, which enabled the family not only to collect honours, but also to play a guiding role in the restructuring of the educational system.[4]

Such examples, all related to the field of engineering, come from Italy. It may be that there was greater collaboration among Italian scientists and 'technicians' than, for example, among Germans; if so, this was less through national differences than for reasons of the different dimensions and cultural traditions of the states that fell under French control within the two areas. But collaboration among the most technically prepared was far from restricted to Italy. In Holland, the financial expert Isaac Gogel swallowed his republican principles in order to force through his fiscal reforms under Louis Bonaparte and Napoleon; and Adriaan van den Ende utilised Louis' support to set up a nation-wide system of primary education that aroused the admiration even of the French Cuvier in 1811.[5] If the Napoleonic embrace stifled private and individual initiatives, in compensation it offered unprecedented opportunities to preach and practice cherished theories and principles to those who were willing to reciprocate by official involvement.

Collaboration, however, was not a matter primarily of leading personalities or scientists, but of elites. The sources, so lavish in their information about the identity of the elites, are more ambiguous in their evidence about the nature of collaboration. Refusal to collaborate could appear to be dangerous in some instances, such as when Napoleon ordered his brother-in-law Prince Borghese, governor-general of Piedmont and Liguria, that he should take

> measures to ensure that the pupils chosen for Saint-Cyr go there promptly, of their own free will or under threat of being disinherited and their properties confiscated. The prince should adopt the same measures to ensure that those nominated auditors go to Paris forthwith. . . . These wealthy Piedmontese families try to keep out of the way, but I want to force them to come to Paris.[6]

Nomination to a post might have no practical consequences, as in failure to turn up to vote in electoral colleges. Acceptance of appointment could mean many things, from barely veiled disapproval to energetic commitment, or indeed a changing experience, from the former towards the latter. The very ambivalence about motivation has offered fertile terrain for one of those less helpful historical debates, replete with references to mental reservations, based more on nationalist susceptibilities and facile psychologisms than on reliable evidence. For while there can be no doubt that at certain moments, among some groups and in specific areas there was a generalised reluctance to collaborate – as for instance at Hamburg after its annexation, among the clergy in some Belgian departments or the former Papal States, or probably in most annexed territories in 1813 – the weight of recent research points to the conclusion that after initial difficulties, the policy of *ralliement* was successful. Whatever the resistance to Napoleon's later policy of forcing the pace of social fusion by the creation of an imperial nobility and attempted marriage alliances, at the administrative and honorific level the French regime had won acceptance – at least as long as its presence seemed solid and permanent.

Military service as officers, with its connotations of glory and prospects of rapid career, attracted the younger generation, to the point of creating tensions and ruptures within noble families who had retained their distance from the new regime. From the outset the

French had worked actively to reintegrate the officers of former enemy armies who wished to continue service, or to ensure them pensions, overriding the opposition of the democratic patriots. It was important, in regions like Savoy where military service characterised the nobility, to avoid the opposition of suddenly unemployed and usually poor nobles. We do not know how many accepted in Savoy, but it is reasonable to assume that this old aristocracy remained hostile. However, gradually, examples appear of young sons who threatened to run away from home unless they were allowed to volunteer. Three of the four Verger brothers from the Tarentaise (Savoy), whose father had been killed in 1794 fighting in the Piedmontese army, were to die in Russia in 1812. The provost of Breslau Cathedral, Ch.-Th.-Frédéric de Regnauld de Bissy, saw the death of his 21-year-old nephew Bon de Regnauld in Spain almost as inevitable retribution for his lack of filial respect: 'He insisted on joining the military against his father's wishes, threatening to run away if he was not allowed to volunteer: and now here we have the result.'[7]

To fight under Napoleon could mean the search for glory at more than the individual level. It could signify the transformation into action of that broader aspiration towards a national identity which – like the concept of glory itself – formed constitutive elements of the new romanticism. If there is little evidence that Belgians, Dutch or even Swiss saw military service as a path towards the forging of national identity, such a sentiment was certainly present among some of the more literary-minded Italians and Germans who fought in Napoleon's armies – as it explained the commitment of many of the young Spaniards who resisted the French so bitterly in defence of their independence. In such contradictory instances, there was an intimate link between military valour and national independence.

Even without such longer-term ideals, the evidence is overwhelming that the image of Napoleon as military hero functioned as an effective catalyst for the young elites. Even during the Emperor's final, brutal reconstitution of his armies in 1812 and 1813, it would seem to have been the families rather than the elite recruits who voiced their resentment at the abrupt end to the private negotiation of exemptions. 'It is not so much those leaving as their families and mistresses who scream in protest', observed the Tuscan director of police, Lagarde, on 8 August 1812; a year later (12 July 1813), he noted that 'The best society, from whose ranks the guards of honour have generally been chosen, is deeply discontented, and many of the guards have still not left'.[8]

For many, service – whether military or civilian – offered the prospect of a good stipend. Officers were in general better paid than their civilian counterparts, although those of modest origins rarely made fortunes. For reasons of prestige, once retired, their presence among the notables was virtually guaranteed; and they then had privileged access to civilian employment. Indeed, from 1811 some posts were reserved for them, arousing an enthusiastic response among the military:

> To have the right to share almost half the posts in civil employ-
> ment is an act of such generosity that what soldier, what officer
> would not give his last drop of blood for the most magnanimous
> sovereign there has ever been? My brother Amédée has asked for
> a tobacco warehouse in the Mont-Blanc or Léman department,

wrote V.-A. de Lannoy, a former officer of the Sardinian army.[9]

The evidence is equally clear that collaboration came early and was widespread at the middling ranks of the civilian administration, if not initially at the highest level. There was never any problem in recruiting the democrats of the 1790s, whose offer of services not only exceeded the supply of posts, but also frightened the moderate leaders. Indeed, where the post-Brumairean settlement was imposed on previous revolutionary agitations – as in the southern Rhineland (Sarre, Mont-Tonnerre), Belgium, the Italian republic, or southern Piedmont – the consistent presence of former democrats in the lower echelons of the administrations and magistracies constituted a powerful lobby against the recruitment of nobles, counteracting the efforts of the prefects. Soon, even in these regions and from the outset in areas without a revolutionary past, competition for posts was brisk, not least because stipends were high (at least for the heads of administrative, financial and judicial services) or offered lucrative possibilities, such as for justices of the peace. Increasingly the main obstacle to service was the practical implications of transfer to another area, costly in terms of income and influence.

It is probable that collaboration was encouraged by the principle – applied with greater or lesser conviction – that all except the top posts should be generally reserved for the local population of annexed or satellite territories. Competition for posts underlay the sometimes vitriolic exchanges about character and talent between native and French administrators. In practice, it was inevitable that the vast majority of positions should have gone to residents rather than newcomers, particularly at the middling and local administrative and fiscal levels and in the magistracy, for reasons of language, local knowledge and connections. There was a marked continuity between former office-holders and the newly appointed, in Naples as much as in Holland or the Hanseatic departments. Stipend, interest and the fresh prestige associated with the post of functionary, all contributed to attract local notables to take office, especially in regions where private fortunes were relatively small and few. It was hardly surprising that the elections to sub-prefectoral and departmental councils should have favoured public officials, lawyers and notaries, as well as increasingly nobles, as these were the persons best known to their peers and clients, even more in the countryside than in the towns. Office thus played a crucial role in the interdependence between public and private interests, which probably grew closer, as networks of relationships closed the means of access to the inner circles.

Ralliement needs to be set in the context of this increasingly favourable climate of collaboration. There were always grand families who ostentatiously refused support or silently withdrew. This was true of the overwhelming majority of Spanish elites. It characterised the hostility of many among the oligarchs of formerly capital cities, like Modena, Venice or Lübeck, or the intransigently Catholic aristocrats of Belgium or Rome. There were noble landowners whose initial tepid collaboration turned to open hostility, like the baron de Gudenau, who accepted nomination as mayor of Villip (Rhin-et-Moselle), but then refused to be renewed or to be presented to Napoleon in 1811, sold his properties and emigrated to Austria.[10]

Nevertheless the Napoleonic wooing of the old nobility was undoubtedly successful. The threat of confiscation of their properties determined many of the aristocratic émigrés to return. The conviction that the example of the few influences the many was not without basis, as slowly the readiness of a Balbo, a Saluzzo or a Cavour in Piedmont, a Boos-Waldeck or a Belderbusch in the Rhineland, to accept nomination or election to office resolved doubts and isolated those who remained intransigent. By 1806 Joseph de Maistre, the ideologist of the Restoration, appealed in despair for assistance to his exiled monarch in Sardinia:

> Sire, I am the head of one of the most numerous families of your former duchy of Savoy, the only family in the country, I think, that has remained wholly in the service of Your Majesty until the last moment, without exceptions or changes.[11]

In the following years, throughout the Empire and in all the satellite states except Spain, the nobility had re-established their presence in both the army and the civil administrations. From their positions of influence, they regrouped to further the interests of their families and friends, like the Florentine Corsini who 'placed' Fabbroni and other Tuscans in imperial service. Their power and prestige were used to counterbalance or isolate surviving democratic voices.

Collaboration cannot be interpreted purely from the viewpoint of personal or family advantage. It always implies reciprocal dependence. Those who rallied to the Napoleonic regime must in turn have been influenced by the values embodied in the modernising administration. Even reluctant auditors like Cesare Balbo carried the imprint of their early experiences through the Restoration. Collaboration implied acceptance, whatever the mental reservations. It is reasonable to conclude that, but for the sudden military débâcle of Napoleon, *ralliement* and collaboration would have continued silently to push an ever larger number, even among the provincial, status-ridden local elites, towards the new ideas of a lay liberalism, while diluting the progressive modernity of the administration itself.

ECONOMIC OPPORTUNITIES

It is in the nature of major political upheavals, such as war, revolution or conquest, to create in the short term artificial conditions that disrupt established economic patterns and sometimes even question deep-rooted social relations. The military campaigns and institutional reorganisation, on the scale imposed or induced by the French, inevitably created new opportunities as well as imposing new burdens. Much has been written about the great fortunes made (and lost) by the army provisioners and bankers in their golden period during the Directory, like Tort de la Sonde in Belgium, the Poissonnier and Lanchère companies in the Rhineland, the Flachat, Laporte and Castelin group, and their successor the Swiss Haller in Italy, or Ouvrard in Paris.[12] Napoleon bitterly resented his dependence on such civilian contractors, who regained importance at every campaign, despite the existence of a ministry for war administration. But the opportunities open to enterprising bankers, businessmen and speculators, as well as to ordinary citizens, extended far beyond the specific and highly capital intensive field of army supplies. The constant changes in frontiers and hence trade routes blurred the distinction between legal and illegal transactions. Smuggling and protection equally offered opportunities for manufacturer and merchant. The impact of war on capital movements in London and Amsterdam made the fortune of Hamburg bankers, or exceptionally enterprising Jewish financiers like the Rothschilds.

The institutional restructuring was not just unprecedented in scale; through the continuity and insistence of the administrative presence and demands, it led to a hitherto unknown degree of penetration of civil society, at the most intimate levels of family and community. By this very fact, it forced the heads of households (identified by the functionaries as the base line of authority) to assume responsibilities in a new manner in order to mediate the growing pressure. But, for identical reasons, it offered novel opportunities. At Castelletto, in southern Piedmont, for example – where the community had traditionally maintained a certain autonomy through the collective exercise of decision-making in a frontier region with poor communications and disputed distant seigneurial authority – the years of French rule operated a process of selection among the heads of household, in which the most enterprising families turned to their profit the increasing fiscal and military demands.[13]

The number, powers and social status of the administrative personnel led to overlaps, and sometimes identification, of public and private interests. Compared to the patrimonial concept of office of the ancien regime, the Napoleonic ethic polemically affirmed the distinction between public and private. But the very procedures and responsibilities laid down for functionaries gave ample opportunities to make killings in the sales of national properties, to procure contracts or sell licences (like Bourrienne in Hamburg), perhaps above all to reinforce family and community ties by judicious recommendations for appointments. Equally, the investment in infrastructures of this modernising administration opened up new peacetime perspectives as lucrative as those of the armies. Rambuteau, as a young prefect of the Alpine Simplon department, was indignant that the local civil engineer continued to give huge contracts for the St Bernard roadworks worth over 1 million francs to a local entrepreneur, when an Italian competitor with considerable experience offered 16 per cent discount.[14] But roads and bridges have always offered particularly fertile terrain for collusion and corruption.

The philosophy of the Napoleonic regime was premised on the separation of the administration from the economy. But insistence on the presence of the state also led to expectations that the government should always be present and ready to give support. Encouragement of entrepreneurship implied a growing demand for concessions or monopolies of production and trade. Alexandre Boury, owner of an iron foundry at Saint Denis, proposed to increase France's metal ore supplies, if he was given a monopoly to exploit the isle of Elba's deposits. The annexation of Rome kindled entrepreneurial ambitions, as French and Italians vied with each other in asking for convents and ancient Roman sites (even Diocletian's baths!), besides subsidies, in order to set up mechanised textile factories to employ the city's idle orphans. In Bavarian Trent, the Pangrazzi family proposed to commercialise mineral water by piping it from the source.[15] Manufacturers in 'old France' rejected proposals of potential competition, whether from established firms across the Rhine or through the establishment of a technical school at Prato.[16] The demand for protection became incessant and was in good part responsible for the Berlin decrees. But the patently unfair discriminations of the blockade and occupation up to the Baltic encouraged manufacturers and traders all across Europe to demand compensatory measures from their own governments or engage in smuggling.

The economic opportunities embedded in the institutional restructuring should not be seen exclusively as always relating directly to personal or family advantage. The possibility also existed of using institutional mechanisms to limit or distort measures that local notables regarded as damaging their interests. Where such measures were considered by the government as vital to the immediate needs of war – as in the extension of the blockade and annexation of Hamburg, despite the destruction of its role as entrepôt and financial centre – opposition was ineffective. Otherwise the responses to unpopular decisions with potentially damaging consequences could make themselves heard at a variety of levels, from formal complaints at the sub-prefectoral or departmental councils to informal lobbying of prefect or Parisian protector. In Piedmont, the local notables successfully carried their complaints against interference with the communal boundaries to the council of state.[17]

Perhaps the most interesting example is that of the cadaster. A rational land tax was essential, not only definitively to settle the continuing complaints within France, but even more in the annexed and satellite territories as the foundation on which to construct the whole complex of fiscal and social reforms of a modernising administration. Initially the method had been to evaluate the land on the basis of estimates of the types and overall quantities of crops produced within the communal territory. This was replaced in 1807 by a far more ambitious, and theoretically neutral plan to measure every single property as well as its usage. In order to ensure equality of taxation and to temper the radical nature of the cadaster, the Revolutionary principle of representation of landowners was maintained: the evaluations between communes within the canton, and between cantons in the sub-prefecture were submitted for discussion between proprietors and officials. These consultative procedures were exploited so effectively in the Rhineland that they distorted the rationality of the official estimates, to the advantage of the larger landowning notables.[18]

Resistance to boundary changes and to the cadaster showed the capacity of landowners to utilise the new institutional structures in defence of their private property. Purchase of the national properties offers the most general and consistent example of their capacity to take advantage of new possibilities.

The sale of national properties offered the most widespread opportunity to obtain a commitment to the new regimes, as the revolutionaries had realised from the outset. In the eyes of the legislators and administrators, such sales served multiple purposes, symbolic as well as material: the confiscation of properties from the Church and émigré nobles represented a deliberate rupture with the past, while their sale provided a crucial resource for state finances, a means of pledging substantial and influential segments of the population against an anti-Revolutionary property settlement, and (for the more egalitarian) an opportunity to create a society of peasant smallholders. Underlying these more immediate aims was the generalised conviction, inherited from the *philosophes* and physiocrats, that private property was intrinsic to liberty and a precondition for increased production. The experiences of the Revolutionary decade seemed to confirm at least the social implications of the sales, given the eagerness of Frenchmen – even in the most Catholic regions – to buy formerly ecclesiastical properties.

Inevitably the same policy was applied wherever a French presence was established. In territories occupied under the Directory, like Belgium and the Rhenish departments, the confiscations and sales were contemporaneous and motivated by the same immediate pressures as in France. The urgent need to absorb the inflationary circulation of paper money and to obtain further credit through the settlement of at least some of the accumulated debts to army provisioners, bankers and local elites explains the hasty alienation of institutional properties, sold without prior division into smaller lots, and hence effectively excluding peasants. The terms of the sales – payment of the greater proportion in paper credits, with extended periods for the settlement of the remainder in cash – encouraged collusion and speculation among the purchasers. But, as in France, demand sufficiently outstripped supply to uphold the prices well above the initial valuations and normally to ensure reasonable market values. The main difference from France was the virtual absence of émigré properties, since the threat of sale persuaded the relatively few great nobles and landowners who had fled to return. In Mont-Tonnerre, for example, even families like that of the future Austrian chancellor Stadion, who had followed the elector of Mainz across the Rhine, returned to save their sequestered estates.[19]

After Brumaire, the sale of national properties formed an intrinsic part of the new administrative measures introduced by the French. Not surprisingly, they were put into practice more systematically than in the Directorial years, since expertise had been accumulated and the end of the throttlehold of the army provisioners ensured substantially greater financial breathing space.

The sources of these properties varied considerably: Crown or domain possessions were a constant element, guild or similar institutional properties were normally not very substantial, émigré estates rarely materialised, except in Spain. But within French-controlled territories, a fundamental distinction, which conditioned the dimensions of the alienable patrimony, was that between Protestant and Catholic countries. In Protestant states, like Holland or many German principalities, there were no monastic properties, as they had already been expropriated centuries earlier, during the Reformation. By contrast, Napoleon's encouragement of the abolition of the prince-bishoprics in the Holy Roman Empire at the Rezes of 1803 gave German princes a unique opportunity to secularise ecclesiastical possessions, sometimes on a scale far greater than in Italy or France: in Bavaria, ecclesiastical property was estimated in 1800 to include 14,000 of a total 30,000 farms, with 47,000 families of a total 116,000; here the Crown was able to amortise its public debt by the sale of monastic lands, and still increase public revenues by perhaps a quarter through the enlargement of its own domain. In general, the French example of confiscating Church lands was widely followed in Germany, more frequently to incorporate them in the domain than to sell them, not just by rulers under French influence – as in Württemberg, Baden, Hessen-Darmstadt and Berg – but even by Prussia. Only Austria refused, as much because of Joseph II's earlier attack on the monastic orders as for ideological reasons.[20]

More than in France, the sales of national properties were carried out in order to reduce or extinguish the public debt. This explains the rapidity with which inventories of the patrimony of the religious orders were drawn up in the annexed territories, compared for example to the leisurely pace of secularisation in parts of Germany, even in a Napoleonic state like Berg, where eleven chapters were still intact in 1812.[21] The acceptance of responsibility by the new rulers for the state's debt towards most private creditors not only corresponded to the conventional respect of property, but also was a necessary and tangible measure to win the support of influential members of the local elites. In this sense, the consolidation of the public debt functioned as a counterpart to the sale of national properties, as it represented a means of committing creditors to the stability of the new order. While institutional creditors lost heavily in the partial conversion of their patrimonies into state bonds, wealthy individuals and families – who had sometimes been penalised by forced loans during a recent military occupation – were salvaged through recognition of their credits, at the same time as they were offered advantageous opportunities to acquire properties.

Absence of such possibilities could have profoundly negative effects on the new regime's credibility: in Holland, Napoleon's reduction of the public debt by two-thirds at the stroke of a pen (like the Directory's declaration of bankruptcy in 1797) was disastrous for the merchant and banking community of Amsterdam and other cities, whose transactions were premised on the honouring of debts. Elsewhere the potential of the national properties as a means of attachment to the new rulers was also severely limited, particularly in the later years, by Napoleon's reservation of substantial portions of the domain as endowments for favoured institutions and persons (even if some of these properties – as in Rhin-et-Moselle – subsequently reached the market for pressing fiscal reasons). In the department of Mont-Tonnerre (formerly part of the Palatinate), 9,400 hectares of a total 32,000 were reserved for the Legion of Honour and the imperial stud farm of Deux-Ponts; in the kingdom of Italy, the incomes guaranteed to the grand feudatories jeopardised the national debt sinking fund; in Poland, 20 per cent of the income of Crown properties was committed to the endowments of twenty-seven marshals and generals.[22]

The opportunities provided by the sale of national properties varied in each region, according to the pre-existing structures of agricultural exploitation, the scale, formalities and period of sale, the availability of capital, and (in exceptional cases, like Spain) the political situation.[23] In the department of Jemappes, for example, farms in the Hainaut region were of medium size (40–60 hectares), whereas around Mons the smallholdings allowed peasant acquisitions. In Tuscany, the properties offered for sale ranged from the classic share-cropping farms near Siena to the large holdings without farms of the Maremma. The methods of sale could be crucial in determining the social composition of the purchasers. In Piedmont, the first and most substantial sale, ordered by the republican General Jourdan in July 1800, encouraged peasant participation by the facility of dividing up properties; while a sale later in the same year was a barely disguised form of forced contribution, imposed on wealthy citizens, who were obliged to pay the entire cost in cash within twelve months. Nine years later, in Tuscany, the overriding concern to extinguish the public debt was expressed in the nomination of a commission composed of the state's major creditors, who rapidly decided to limit competition at the land auctions by reimbursing those with small credits of less than 300 francs. Where capital was lacking, as in most of the provinces of the kingdom of Naples, the sales failed to live up to expectations; by the later years, where there were repeated sales, such was the case even in wealthy states like the kingdom of Italy, given the contemporaneous pressure of fiscal exactions and the poorer quality of the properties on offer. In Spain, there were virtually no purchasers for the lands of the powerful grandee families opposed to the French, whereas there was a high demand for the communal lands that local administrations (in Guipúzcoa, for example) were forced to put up for sale in order to pay the exactions of the occupying armies.

The sales offered to vast strata of the peoples of western (and, to a lesser degree, of central) Europe the chance to acquire properties over a short period of time and usually on an unprecedented scale. Moreover, this occurred after a prolonged period in which access to the land market had been severely restricted by ecclesiastical mortmain, juridical definitions of status and aristocratic inheritance practices. Alienation of ecclesiastical possessions was not new. Indeed, it had become the standard practice of reformist monarchs, often with the agreement of the Papacy; even the most anti-Revolutionary ruler, like the last king of Sardinia, Charles Emanuel IV, had had no scruples about imitating the French in a last desperate effort to pay for his war against them. Probably only the alienations of Peter Leopold of Tuscany, his brother Joseph II of Austria and Charles IV of Spain affected larger areas than those of the Napoleonic years. In some departments as much as 11 per cent (Jemappes) or even 16 per cent (Rhin-et-Moselle) of the cultivated land became national properties; 28,000 hectares were put up for sale in Tuscany, 62,000 in Piedmont, 92,000 in the Rhineland departments.

Hence it is not surprising that the response to this new opportunity should have been so positive. Where detailed studies exist, they show that the purchasers varied in their social composition and bought land

and buildings for very different reasons. Inevitably, given the predominance of explicitly fiscal over social purposes, the sales of national properties everywhere attracted those with capital resources. The presence of Jews among the large purchasers, from Italy to Poland, was not surprising, given their important mercantile activities and the fact that previously they had been forbidden from buying landed property. Monastic buildings were bought or begged by manufacturers to set up workshops. Urban bourgeois bought town houses.

Leading civilian and military functionaries and courtiers were to be found in most regions. A president of the criminal court, a general in command of the department, an inspector of domains, all outsiders to the department, were in a good position to know about worthwhile properties, whose acquisition represented an excellent investment. Where there was a court – in Munich, Turin, Florence, Naples or Madrid – the great and lesser nobles bought some of the largest estates. In Tuscany, the nobility constituted 39 per cent of all purchasers in the Arno department; families like Cavour in Piedmont, Dandolo in Venetia, Lullin de Châteauvieux in Léman (Switzerland) expanded their substantial properties for livestock breeding. Some aristocrats, like Countess Isabelle von Waldbott-Bassenheim in Rhin-et-Moselle, or the Milliet d'Arvillard in Mont-Blanc, were able to buy back their confiscated estates from the new owners.[24] New families, often close to the administration, established their wealth and status through systematic pursuit of such opportunities, accumulating vast patrimonies, like the Bolognese Antonio Aldini or the son of the former steward of the Tuscan grand-ducal estate of Foiano, Ferdinando Redditi, or the Flemish functionary Charles Ghillenghien. In Spain, ministers like Miot de Mélito and the duke of Campo Alegre were particularly prominent, whether to set an example, or to make up for the reluctance of local capitalists, or because of favourable prices.

As in France, the largest and most valuable properties attracted a handful of men, often speculators. In the kingdom of Naples, 154 or 7 per cent of all purchasers were responsible for 65 per cent of all sales. Of the 1866 purchasers in the Rhin-et-Moselle department, the top twenty-four spent 23 per cent of the total capital. They were described as 'proprietor', 'trader', 'notary', 'clerk to the justices', 'wine merchant', 'cloth manufacturer'; a few were Jewish. Though most lived in the capital, Coblenz, some came from cities like Cologne in nearby departments. For the most expensive purchases, these leading capitalists grouped together, as they bought with the deliberate intention of reselling, usually rapidly: 60 per cent of the properties bought by the largest Rhin-et-Moselle purchasers were resold.

Alongside such major figures, who bought national properties as a means of investing capital, sometimes – like Jewish banker-merchants at Leghorn – because of the limited alternatives during the blockade, sometimes as pure speculation, there was always a substantial number of smaller purchasers. There can be no doubt that the numbers of new proprietors increased significantly, as well as of those expanding their holdings. Entry into the land market was facilitated by the relatively lengthy periods of time allowed for payment, as well as the use of the national properties to reimburse state creditors. The social location of these proprietors was as one would expect: rentiers and tenant farmers buying the farms they cultivated, lawyers and others exercising free professions, merchants and traders acquiring country properties, usually near their city of residence, as a form of security for their commercial activities as much as for reasons of prestige. In Piedmont, 'traders' and 'merchants' constituted over 19 per cent of all purchasers and bought 31 per cent of the land, free professionals and employees each numbered over 17 per cent with 19 per cent of the land. In Rhin-et-Moselle merchants and traders were responsible for over 17 per cent of the capital, wine growers another 7 per cent, innkeepers, bakers and millers a further 6 per cent. In Hainaut the liberal and commercial professions bought middling and small properties amounting to 40 per cent of the land; in highly urban areas, like Charleroi, their share rose to 82 per cent.

In all regions a substantial proportion of the purchases were of minute or small plots of land – over 70 per cent in Tuscany, over 50 per cent in Guipúzcoa. This was not necessarily proof of strong peasant participation, but merely of that of local inhabitants, at all social levels, consolidating their properties, as well as buying the land they worked; in Rhin-et-Moselle, 60 per cent of the purchasers bought more than one lot – a clear sign that they were not peasants. Nevertheless, even though the sales, from the Directory onwards, were structurally unlikely to facilitate peasant purchases – given the predominance of explicitly fiscal over social purposes – the very dynamics of so large-scale and accelerated a process of property transfer in some regions boosted peasant ownership. The peasants ranged from wealthy tenants of abbeys to the poorer. In the Mons sub-prefecture of Jemappes, where 35 per cent of the alienated properties were bought by the peasants, twenty-one of them bought over 50 hectares each; religious scruples seem to have held back peasant participation in this department until the Concordat of 1801, after which an evidently poorer stratum bought lots of 1 hectare or less.

The Rhineland was the region where the peasantry most benefited. Their land-hunger was reflected in the massive purchase of properties that were split up and resold on the market by the initial large purchasers. In the Trier sub-prefecture (Sarre) 40 per cent of ecclesiastical properties were resold by 1814; the average size of plots bought by peasants in these resales was 0.88 hectares (and only 0.13 hectares for vineyards), and the number of new peasant and day-labourer owners increased by 95 per cent. In the Rhin-et-Moselle department, about a quarter of the peasant tenants were able to buy their land. The effects of these resales were to continue into the 1830s and 1840s in some regions of Germany. Elsewhere, especially in Italy, the peasantry seem to have obtained little. Even where auctions were aimed to favour them (as in General Jourdan's auction of July 1800 in Piedmont), it was the non-peasant professional and trading classes who were able to buy medium-sized farms.

Nevertheless, whether by choice or necessity, the ideological determination to confiscate ecclesiastical property and encourage private ownership provided unprecedented opportunities in many, perhaps most areas of French-controlled Europe. The wealthy were able to create or increase their landed holdings, and substantial numbers of bourgeois and peasants became proprietors. The sales of national properties were least successful, or even failed, only in regions where capital was scarce and political conditions disturbed: Calabria, Spain and, to a lesser degree, Poland (where the collapse of land prices under the blockade was, to a limited extent, counterbalanced by the important presence of Jews).

Even then, the division of communal lands, as in Léman, or their enforced sale, as in Guipúzcoa, multiplied ownership by the alienation of small plots, but increased the social differentiation within the villages. The most influential families appropriated the best communal land at the expense of the poorer. The result was to increase the gap between owners and landless within the ranks of the peasantry. The process was vividly described in 1816 by the representative of the village of Elgneta (Guipúzcoa):

> As a result the poor and less poor have been expelled from the right to collect ferns and leaves to dung and manure their land. The consequence has been to deprive the worker of his liberty and leave him short of the greater part of the vegetable matter he needs to grow his crops. Thus, those who bought commonlands

have benefited, as they have profited from their natural products, whereas most of their neighbours, greater in number and of lesser wealth, find themselves deprived of manuring their crops with the facility and abundance that they previously enjoyed.[25]

RELIGION

In no area as much as that of religion can one observe the differences between the norms of the administrators and the practices of the administered. It is customary to interpret the religious history of the period in terms of direct conflict: the resistance of faithful Catholics to the dechristianising onslaught of the revolutionaries, and of Rome to Napoleonic aggression. The reality was more complex, not just because the Catholic Church incorporated an infinite variety of institutional situations and social relations, particular to each locality, but even more because the radical institutional restructuring of all organised religions modified profoundly established relationships and repercussed at the most intimate level of community and family.

The authorities were never interested in popular religious life, at least after the initial expectation that the people could be won over to the new revolutionary creed, whose discourse, symbols and rituals owed so much to Catholic practices. Religion – for the revolutionaries and Napoleonic administrators, as for their opponents – was identified with its organisational forms; and expressions of religious faith were interpreted through intellectual or political filters. The revolutionaries were the heirs of the enlightened reformers and progressive clergy in their conviction that external signs of popular religious devotion, such as processions or veneration of relics, were proof of the ignorant people's dependence on intriguing (and usually as ignorant) priests. Intransigent anti-revolutionaries, whether the parish priests of the Vendée, Flanders or Arezzo, or Cardinal Ruffo in Calabria in 1799, manipulated religious devotion for the purposes of political revolt.

In a comparative perspective, it is reasonable to assume as a starting-point that the severity of the language and decrees of the French authorities corresponded to the degree of external visibility of popular religious life. This applied to the entire period and may well have been exacerbated by the religious insensibility of the military in the Napoleonic years, which was to contribute to such disastrous consequences in Spain. Charles Lafolie, a French administrator in the kingdom of Italy, recalled the offence caused by Ramel, the French adjutant-general at Rome in 1806, who galloped with twenty-four dragoons through a canonisation ceremony of some new saints: 'It is a feast-day that greatly attracts the people.'[26] In earlier years, particularly during the Directory, the distinction between the attitude of military and civilian authorities towards religious manifestations was by no means so clear-cut. The closure of chapels and shrines, the removal of crosses, the dismantling of church bells, all formed part of a common conviction that superstitious beliefs could be eradicated by their removal from public view. There was surprise, as much as indignation, at the repeated and sometimes unexpected resistance as, for example, the insistence by a participant at a funeral on the use of a burial cross as a sign of social distinction, 'which he wanted in the manner of all the citizens of the town, that burials should be held according to custom. Such an innovation did not exist even at Mainz. He insisted that dying Catholics should not be buried like Jews, Protestants or dogs'.[27] In some regions, like Flanders, the Swiss Catholic inner cantons (Schwyz, Uri, Unterwalden), the Aretino or Calabria in 1798–9, as later in Spain, resistance (never just for religious reasons) was to lead to revolt. It is difficult to explain why the response was not so violent in other regions, like the Rhineland. It seems likely that where an established practice of regulation of religious life by state authorities already existed – as in Mainz, where the pre-Revolutionary prince was also an archbishop, but also in Lombardy or Venetia – the faithful adapted to interference in their religious practices in a less intransigent manner.

The bitter experience of the religious divide during the Revolutionary years, whether in France or the early occupied territories, made both state and Catholic Church more cautious. The French representatives in such territories were mostly careful in their application of the Revolutionary decrees. In the Rhineland, for example, the days chosen for the Revolutionary public holidays were those of popular religious ones. For both Napoleon and Pius VII the Concordat was essential in order to restore order and authority. But the Concordat abruptly terminated the utopian hopes of democratic clergy, like Grégoire, for the inner renovation of the Church, while also cutting short the painful search for a new political theology of the more perspicacious of the émigré episcopate.

The Napoleonic administrators recognised the utility of a Church firmly subordinated to the state, and the functionality of a register of civil status maintained by the parish priests. But they remained suspicious of the power over the people that they attributed to such priests. Felici, minister of the interior of the Italic kingdom, expressed the official view in a report to Napoleon in 1805:

Although the conduct of the ministers of religion cannot be described as totally negative, it has always been obscure and enterprising. Despite the mystical affectations in which this class of persons tries to cloak itself, in general it must be considered as not attached to the new order of things. Political theology, which has always tended towards independence, indeed towards domination, cannot submit to the idea of even a minimal restriction of ecclesiastical pretensions. The true character and inner nature of this class is revealed by the occasional statement or expression that sometimes escapes the lips of some zealous preacher or missionary.[28]

Given the dismemberment and incorporation of the Papal States in the kingdom of Italy and the French empire, the hostility of a clergy whose temporal loyalties to the Pope coincided with their spiritual dependence is hardly surprising. The French annexation of Rome signified a massive upheaval in the social relations of a city structured around the religious and charitable patronage of cardinals and nobles close to the Curia.

New political frontiers and institutional reforms forced fundamental changes on all religions, not just the Catholic Church. Their effects inevitably repercussed on the comportment of both clerics and laity, as they disturbed credos and practices consolidated within each Church, in defence and opposition to other faiths, in the centuries since the wars of religion. Traditionalism and reform were equally affected by the radical nature of the Napoleonic restructuring of religion.

Above all in Germany, but also in Switzerland and wherever political frontiers had marked out the territory of a state religion in the sixteenth and seventeenth centuries, the abolition of ecclesiastical principalities and free cities and the continuous remodelling of states led to the coexistence for the first time under the same ruler of Catholics and Protestants of differing sects: Catholic Münster became part of Protestant Prussia, Catholics, Lutherans and Calvinists found themselves subject to laws of religious tolerance under French rule on the left bank of the Rhine, in Berg, Westphalia and Holland. Tolerance, as the twentieth century has tragically demonstrated, is a quality that is more easily accepted for others than in one's backyard. In Bavaria, the last abbot of Weltenberg opposed the lifting of the ban on Protestant immigration to this most Catholic of states. In the French Rhineland, where non-Catholics constituted over 40 per cent of the population in the departments of the Sarre and Mont-Tonnerre, there was as little love lost between Calvinists and Lutherans as between both sects and Catholics, and a generalised intolerance of Jews.[29]

The reforms imposed on these religions were aimed at reinforcing the structure of authority within the organisation of the creed in correspondence to the hierarchical representation of civil society. It was not surprising that Napoleon should have preferred Lutheranism to Calvinism given, on the one hand, the former's close identification with the state and, on the other, the democratic participatory practices of the Calvinist communities. Nevertheless, the apparent success of the Concordats (France 1801, Italian republic 1803) in recruiting the clergy as a subsidiary corps of functionaries in the service of the state and the Napoleonic credo in the necessity of rationally structured administrations under identifiable and responsible leaders justified the imposition of parallel organisational reforms on Calvinists, Lutherans and even Jews.

In the Catholic case, the ecclesiastical boundaries (fixed unilaterally by Napoleon in the Organic articles attached to the Concordat) strictly reflected the civilian administration's concern with population and territory: the number of bishops and parish priests was reduced according to the population of departments and cantons. Calvinists, Lutherans and subsequently Jews (1808) were grouped in consistories similarly based on population and administrative boundaries, each under a council of wealthy notables and a pastor or rabbi, with the faithful responsible for the property and good order of the community; on paper, a hierarchical structure grouped these separate organs under a central consistory. Such a module, for the Calvinists and Jews at least, fundamentally contradicted the proud insistence on independence of each community and the egalitarian participation of clerics and faithful which lay at the core of the maintenance of their identity in hostile environments. The Napoleonic reform transmuted existing economic distinctions into formalised social disparities by the identification of the lay leadership with the most wealthy and the assumption that pastors and rabbis played a similar role of control to that of parish priest and bishop.

At the same time, the removal of the cohesive force of minority segregation and the pressure towards assimilation that followed from the Revolutionary decrees of religious toleration weakened the ties on which the religious identity of these non-Catholic communities depended. In the case of the Calvinists, the communities survived by maintaining the autonomous practices of each parish. In the case of the Jews, whose traditionally minded religious leaders had complained of the corrosive effects of the emancipation decreed in 1790–1, the structures created in 1808 re-established authority, but created innumerable tensions, not only between communities, but also internally between rabbis and laity, rich and poor. Outside France, even in Westphalia – the only German state where full emancipation was decreed – the leadership of the enlightened banker Israel Jacobson led to widespread complaints among the Jews because of his authoritarian attempts to utilise the Napoleonic model of centralised control to impose heavy taxes and 'revolutionise the former state of the Jews from the ecclesiastical and lay point of view'.[30]

Uniformity was the order of the day. But popular responses denied the very premisses on which such uniformity was attainable. Two examples can be given, the first revelatory of the reactions of the faithful themselves, the second confirming popular hostility to toleration.

In religions based on an individual relationship to the faith, whose identities depended on deep distrust of other sects as much as on past histories of persecution, uniformity had no sense. Nowhere could this be seen better than in Holland, where Napoleon – impatient with the anarchy of practical tolerance – urged his representative Lebrun to simplify the organisation of the creeds by forcing the small sects to merge into three officially recognised religions. Lebrun, an enlightenment sceptic of the old school, was horrified: 'It is both politic and convenient not to create one single faction, but to leave the Churches separate, to recognise each one's consistorial churches.' He then elaborated on the problems, demonstrating in the process how religious differences were inextricably entwined with social prejudices. The Dutch and French-speaking (Walloon) Calvinists agreed on dogma and discipline. But the Dutch

> only know their own language and customs; they have no contact except with the most middling class of society and no influence on the rest. They do not want to be under the control of the Walloons: so, on their side, all that can be expected is disorder and discord, in which the people will take part. The Walloons are more French, they pride themselves on their more refined education, their better social ties, their more elegant style of life and conversation.

The anabaptists could not unite with the pure Calvinists, not only because of their reciprocal dislike, but also because they turned towards the anabaptists of Germany and the Hanseatic departments. The remonstrants were rejected by the Protestants and in any case were harmless. It would be dangerous to join the Jansenists to the pure Catholics, lest they gain control. The old and new Lutherans 'hate each other cordially'. Finally, 'you would imagine that here at least there would be no problem with the Jews', but the Portuguese (Sephardi) and German (Ashkenazi) communities could not stand each other and an enforced union would make the Portuguese Jews in England break relations with Amsterdam. 'All that can be said about this double type of Jews is that they will always be separated, whatever one does. The Portuguese Jews would feel degraded by a reunion, while the Germans would not be uplifted.'[31]

Whatever the social distinctions between Sephardi and Ashkenazi Jews, the centuries of anathema launched against them by the Churches made all Jews unacceptable to ordinary Christians. It was only through the special pleading of Grégoire and Mirabeau that they had been emancipated in France. The dense, crowded, poor Ashkenazi communities in Alsace and Lorraine aroused a popular antisemitism, which Napoleon shared. Alone among religions, all Jews were subjected by the Emperor for a period of ten years to a series of restrictions on their civil rights and economic activities which were intended to cure them of what was considered their innate vice of usury and accelerate their regeneration (30 May 1806). Uniformity again displayed its limits, as the prefects and elites of the departments with long-established Sephardi communities in south-east France and Italy protested. But quite apart from this official introduction of discrimination, antisemitism at all levels limited the practical effects of emancipation. In most of the Rhenish Confederation states, specific restrictions on Jews were lifted, without the concession of full citizen rights; even in the reforming states of Bavaria and Baden some discrimination was retained. In Westphalia, where emancipation was complete, the head of the police arbitrarily prohibited Jews from freedom of movement without prior authorisation and the payment of a special tax; artisan woollen cloth producers protested at the competition of Jewish pedlars. In Rome, there were popular outcries against Jews opening shops in the central Corso to sell liturgical objects from confiscated churches.[32] Official and popular prejudice combined to defeat the attempt of an enlightened minority to remove by decree age-old, religiously inspired discrimination.

Such radical intervention by the state aroused a variety of responses among both clergy and laity and forced the Catholic Church to reconsider its role. The attack on the monastic orders combined with the unremitting pressure of government control to reinforce the authority of the episcopate. In Bavaria and the kingdoms of Italy and Naples, as much as in the Empire, civil administrators and bishops resumed with greater vigour the efforts of their pre-Revolutionary predecessors to raise the level of instruction and comportment of the priesthood and to contain, if not repress, what were regarded as superstitious practices among the laity. In the kingdom of Italy the Jansenist minister of religion Bovara provided a personal link with the reformist years of Joseph II in his suspicious control of clergy and church. His Neapolitan colleague Ricciardi affirmed categorically about parish priests that 'a few good ones are enough to serve the church, the bad ones are a deadweight, indeed harmful to it'. Mass-priests, a widespread phenomenon in the southern Italian state, who were independent of the bishop's control as they derived their living from endowed masses under the patronage of local notable families, now found themselves in difficulties. In Venice the bureaucratic rationalisation of parishes, with the closure of alternative local places of worship, confraternities and schools, accelerated the insertion of the parish priests within the state under the close supervision of their bishops.[33]

The results were by no means those anticipated by the civilian authorities. Collaboration by bishops and clergy seemed successful in states with an earlier reforming tradition, like the kingdoms of Italy and Naples, the Rhineland and Bavaria, or where Catholics had previously lived in discriminatory conditions as a religious minority, in Utrecht or Swiss Fribourg. Parish priests used their influence to convince the peasants to accept conscription, taught the imperial catechism or celebrated the Emperor's victories or even St Napoleon's feast-day. The bishops, in words of the prefect of the Ourthe, were 'apostles of the state as much as of the Church'.[34] In states without a tradition of religious reform – such as the Papal States or Belgium – clerical collaboration was far less sure: even though the bishops appointed in Belgium from 1803 were all French, many of them identified with the ultramontanism of their clergy. Everywhere the interference of the state, contemporaneous with the compromises and persecution of the Popes, not only forced the episcopate to search for new relations with civil power, but also aroused reservations about the claims of Rome. Missionaries had to be trained, the people had to be 'recovered'. The abduction and imprisonment of Pius VII in 1809 restored to Rome the moral authority of martyrdom. At Fribourg a new generation of priests emerged, better trained in the seminaries than their predecessors, and ultramontane, who were prepared to enter secret associations and then to propagate their principles openly after Napoleon's fall. In Venetia, under Jesuit influence, 'Christian friendships' were formed among the laity. Tempered by the secular onslaught of enlightenment, revolution and Napoleonic control, some among the clergy responded by the affirmation of the superior values of Christianity incorporated in the authority of the Papacy.

An essential element of this renewed reforming drive within the Catholic Church was the attempt to assert a closer control over the laity. Perhaps the deepest fear of the clergy during the 1790s was the withdrawal of the people from the sacraments, the very essence of religion. In France, Grégoire, a convinced revolutionary, was just as concerned as the clergy who had refused to swear the oath to the republic and set up a nationwide network of correspondence to advise and uphold the morale of the constitutional priests. At the other extreme, an anonymous exponent of the non-jurors circulated a pamphlet from London, after the Concordat of 1801, that denounced

> those villages where instead of religion without worship, there is worship without religion. The peasants go to church every Sunday, chant in the choir every morning and evening, but nobody goes near the confessional. . . . Without confession, there is no communion; without sacraments, there is no religion; without religion, there is no morality. That's the chain.[35]

Such a fear was not limited to France. It characterised every Catholic region under French control or influence. At Modena in 1803 the bishop lamented the expulsion of the Jesuits, followed by that of missionaries from the order of St Vincent de Paul in 1796, given 'the evil that subsequently affected the souls of this country, especially in the past few years, when philosophism and incredulity caused such terrible slaughter'.[36]

The Napoleonic years witnessed an intense campaign to win back the people to their religious obligations. Redemptorists, Passionists, Lazarists, as well as the priests newly trained in the reopened seminaries, crisscrossed the western European countryside in repeated missions. Books of devotion, which had proved their reliability by their longevity, were circulated in Germany and along the Rhine, even if some of them encouraged 'popular devotions based on apocryphal and ridiculous legends'. In the diocese of Treviso, a former Jesuit, Luigi Mozzi, led successful popular pilgrimages to sanctuaries.[37] The tone of this organised and controlled evangelical campaign was redolent with echoes of the 'recovery' of the people following the Council of Trent. Popular piety had to be encouraged but guided. Local devotions that smacked of superstition, processions and pilgrimages to pray for the intervention of saints to ensure health and protection for men, animals and crops, were disapproved of, but almost with resignation:

> The people refused to give up frequenting such places, even when the pilgrimages were abolished. There are some striking examples: Monsignor de Saint-Simon banned a chapel called Rehbach, no services are held there anymore; despite this, the people continue to go there to pray for rain.[38]

The diffusion of the Marian cult and of the stations of the cross can be considered as attempts to retain and direct the obstinate persistence of popular religion.

The clergy were caught between their fear of losing the people and the strait-jacket of Napoleonic control: in the kingdom of Italy missions were forbidden after the imprisonment of the Pope. The people, on the other hand, demonstrated a remarkable capacity to find their own routes amidst the crisis of the Church and the dechristianising interference of the state. There can be little doubt that, at least among the French, the experiences of the Revolution and the armies secularised many: the soldier Jacquin's travel notebook is noteworthy in its absence of any references to religion; the soldiers dying in military hospitals at Moscow resolutely refused the sacraments.

This was certainly not the case with the majority of peasant families outside France. Here the laity insisted in their faith in a variety of ways, that ranged from the secret or priestless masses of Flanders to exploitation of new possibilities, such as adoption of the Protestant example of election of priests by parishioners in the Rhineland. The people were not necessarily faithful to their parish priests, but to what they identified with as their religion. This could lead to a regular exorcism, as at Montaigne (Dyle) at the peak of Directorial anticlericalism; to the successful insistence on maintaining the right to elect the priest in a parish in Pamplona diocese; to the insistence of 50,000 faithful at Rome that they had seen a statue of the Virgin in tears in 1798; or to the participation of all classes in the traditional processions in the kingdom of Naples.[39] But popular faith was also expressed in an infinity of adaptations to the new conditions that were separate from and even in opposition to their priests. In the Ourthe, during the worst moments of persecution of the non-jurors, many parishioners distanced themselves from their priests, petitioning the government to reopen their church and liturgical ornaments: 'The undersigned inhabitants have no power to oblige their parish priest to swear the oath, while it is because of his insubordination that they are deprived of all their objects of religion.' In Napoleonic Rome, the churches remained empty when the government ordered a Te Deum. In the Rhineland, where the former bishop-princes had accustomed their subjects to such patriotic rites, a peasant could welcome the reunion with France, as 'now at last we are free; now at last we can hold our services in total liberty, that is in Latin'.[40]

The gap between popular and reformed ecclesiastical practices was certainly greater in areas without previous reforming traditions. Here, as in Piedmont, a patriot priest who played an active administrative role, like the theologian Vigna who was sub-prefect at Alba, lost his reputation among the faithful, as the republican governor-general Jourdan recognised: 'A priest who busies himself with other things besides the duties of his office is regarded as a sort of political monster'.[41] In Spain parish priests increased their influence by their identification of the French with anti-Christ. But for the most part the clergy were conscious of their difficulties in regaining their traditional influence over the people. Missions might prove momentarily successful, through the fervour of the orator, yet this was precisely because they were exceptional and ably staged. But, as a Modenese parish priest reflected: 'True conversion of sinners does not normally occur in a moment. It requires time, reflection and a readiness to stop and consolidate; this means patience, instruction and prayer.'[42] The spontaneous growth of lay initiatives, such as pilgrimages and the Marian cult, were to deepen the differences between the elite and popular representations of religion. Such were the responses to the Revolutionary-Napoleonic regulation of the Church.

SOCIAL PRACTICES

The years of French dominion in Europe constitute too short a period to identify unequivocal shifts in the slow process of change of mentalities – except in France itself, the epicentre of this violent drive towards extension of the social base and enforced administrative modernity. Nevertheless, the impact of this new presence on the multiple forms of sociability that characterised the heterogeneity of space and varieties of cultural identity in Europe merits a discussion, however brief, as it offers yet another spy into the intangible but crucial relationship between the expectations of the French and the comportment of the local elites. Three very different fields – freemasonry, education and charity – provide valuable examples of the limits of the regime's attempts to penetrate existing forms of sociability and superimpose their own.

Sociability was of importance to the French elites for conceptual as much as for practical reasons. D'Alembert, in the *Encyclopédie*, described France as 'a nation primarily characterised by sociability'. Portalis, Napoleon's minister of cults, expressed a conviction, relayed by the *philosophes* and *idéologues*, that 'man's perfection is tied to his sociability'. What was at issue was the relationship between private virtues, collective habits and the progress of civilisation.[43] France's primacy as standard-bearer of civilisation was demonstrated in the superiority of her forms of sociability, as much as in her language, revolutionary values and administrative practices. By sociability was understood the quality of institutions which set public rules for social relationships that transgressed conventional status barriers: for example, academies and learned societies, salons or masonic lodges. Other countries could vaunt their primacy in alternative forms of civilised sociability, such as the English coffee-house or the Italian opera. But the French model, which developed apace in the eighteenth century, was accepted and envied across Europe.

This was the moment of triumph of that distinctively female institution, the Parisian salon, which had played a central role for the *philosophes* in testing and directing opinion by providing an informal setting where aristocrats and writers could meet and converse. In the Directory and Consular years, noted de Gérando's wife, who was of German origin and kindly disposition, Madame Récamier embodied the virtues that the male elite desired: 'The French want only youth, charm, pleasures and vivacity in the sex they so spoil. Madame Récamier is the very embodiment of this sort of person.'[44] Madame de Staël, Marie-Anne de Gérando's friend, was out of fashion as well as out of favour. The unconventionality of the salon as a form of sociability which overrode separation of the sexes perhaps explains the difficulties of its acceptance in countries with rigid social and status barriers, as well as those of gender. Even if the salon spread to German provincial capitals, like Berlin, Dresden, Leipzig or Vienna, it was virtually killed by (false) association with Jacobinism in the anti-Revolutionary reaction of the 1790s. In Berlin, after Frederick II's death, only wealthy, cultured Jewish ladies, like Henrietta Herz and Rachel Levin, succeeded in creating successful salons, precisely because they were Jewish and hence provided a neutral terrain where nobles, intellectuals, Germans, foreigners, Jews and Christians could exchange conversation on what seemed to the young theologian Friedrich Schleiermacher an astonishingly wide range of topics. Such salons were slowly to contribute to what in the nineteenth century would be a typically German form of sociability.[45]

Export of French modes of sociability thus formed an integral part of that process of raising the level of civilisation of other nations. More pragmatically, French administrators were always highly sensitive towards local associative structures and other less formal expressions of sociability as they provided precisely the ambience and occasions of cordial contact and conversation in which outmoded social distinctions or political dislikes could be overcome, new relationships forged or consolidated and elites integrated within the new order. For Napoleon sociability was an essential part of administrative responsibility.

The memoirs of the period about occupied territories, whether of civilians or military, are replete with descriptions of receptions, dinners, balls and social events. Their tone oscillates between indulgence towards the old-fashioned way of life and the conviction that the new French style was successfully winning over the local elites. Duret de Tavel, an officer in Calabria, wrote home in 1808 that:

> Since the arrival of the French, Cosenza has gained considerably in terms of sociability. There are balls and many brilliant social circles where liqueurs and sorbets are offered. . . . Charmed by our manners, the ladies have become very accessible. . . . The voluptuous waltz has taken over from the bizarre dances of this country.[46]

Germans, rather than Italians, required particular attention, presumably because to the French they appeared more distant from practices of civilised behaviour, as well as potentially more hostile. Beugnot, in Düsseldorf, described his troubles to his daughter:

> His Majesty the Emperor and King had ordered me to represent him with dignity. Now what the Germans most enjoy on formal occasions is that they can dance. On the anniversary of the coronation, there was a grand dinner, a great ball and a veritable onslaught of finery. Only one thing was forgotten – the supper! Because here one needs to reverse the proverb 'after the belly, the ball'. Twenty officers dying of hunger at two in the morning, just as many ladies, who eat like officers, and girls with appetites like wolves. For all that, the only expedient my wife could find was a milk soup. . . . For the next ball I've told her in private to kill a stag.

In Cologne, the prefect Ladoucette decided on more total identification with the local people: to celebrate the birth of Napoleon's son (June 1811), he invited the local *Mädchen*, confraternities and farmers to come in their medieval costumes.[47] The purpose of such festive occasions, as spelt out by the prefect of the Bouches du Weser, the Belgian d'Arberg, was to 'to profit from every favourable circumstance to further fusion and little by little work towards the disappearance of that separation between old and new French which differences of customs and habits still maintain in these regions'. He too had held a ball and supper at Bremen for the birth of the king of Rome, to which he had invited the 500 'wealthiest and most worthy of the upper bourgeoisie, a class that includes an interesting part of the population which enjoyed no consideration under the former sovereigns.' Six months later, at his next ball, he felt satisfied with his progress: 'The occasion was remarkable in terms of a certain intimacy and a greater union than at previous balls. . . . One and all of the guests seemed to belong to a single family.'[48] We have no means of knowing whether his guests were of the same opinion.

Such festive occasions provide an excellent example of the determination of the Napoleonic regime to superimpose its own forms of sociability on existing associative structures. Napoleon and his collaborators were always concerned to revive or encourage institutions and associations which attracted and hence involved local notables with the administration. Under the Consulate, two-thirds of the pre-Revolutionary French provincial academies had been reopened, with official subventions and the prefect as honorary president. In Tuscany, where relations with Paris were solidly established among scientists and intellectuals, progressive landowners of the academy of the Georgofili hastened to elect to their ranks the members of the French junta, like de Gérando and Menou, in reciprocity for their interest. If associations were viewed as potentially dangerous and not socially open, they could be suppressed. Napoleon was very angry that at Turin nobles and bourgeois held balls reciprocally excluding the other class: 'this division displeases me and is contrary to the principles of government'. At Florence, the *casino*, or noble circle, exclusively limited to families in the golden book, was closed. Otherwise associations were to be encouraged.

This applied in particular to scientific societies which, out of a common matrix of 'useful' sciences, became increasingly specialised; but artistic, musical and even historical societies were also established in Germany, Switzerland and elsewhere in French-controlled Europe; a great archaeological programme was initiated in Rome.

Political criticism was not tolerated in this most official of regimes, as was soon apparent with the expulsion of Constant from the Tribunate (January 1802), the closure of the *idéologue*-dominated class of moral and political sciences of the Institut (January 1803), the exile from Paris of Madame de Staël (October 1803), and the progressively tighter censorship of the press. This still left ample domains where official patronage of culture and science could be extremely beneficial: Berthollet, organiser of the Société d'Arcueil, hub of the international scientific network during the regime, was able to publish the memoirs of its members through money advanced by Napoleon.[49]

Alongside this policy of casting the official cloak over local social institutions, the regime introduced its own forms of sociability. With military discipline, the Emperor set the example with his Court, copying the ceremonial of the ancien regime and offering banquets distasteful to his frugal eating habits. At a Tuileries recital he displayed more musical discernment than his concert secretary anticipated, as Hector Berlioz later recounted. His sisters, Elisa, Pauline and Caroline held salons, even before their elevation to thrones, frequented by the elites and administrators of Europe. Napoleon was insistent that his family, ministers and marshals follow his example, and even justified his notable generosity towards them as providing the means to uphold their rank. Marbot commented that the grand dignitaries vied with each other in organising social occasions. Between the sumptuous dinners of a Cambacérès or Talleyrand and the masked balls of a Marescalchi, there can be no doubt that the most hostile legitimist families were seduced. 'In the first period of the Empire', recalled Madame de Boigne,

> it was extremely agreeable to be in the company of the opposition. . . . This lasted for three or four years; but then desertions became more frequent, until the marriage with the archduchess [Marie Louise] did the rest. From then on, it was easy to count the women who did not go to Court.[50]

The collapse of the Empire was to revive and exacerbate the divisions.

What was fashion at Paris was law elsewhere. The Courts of Napoleon's family performed the same function at Turin, Florence, Naples, The Hague and Cassel; only in Madrid (which he was twice forced to abandon precipitously) was Joseph unable to attract a broad spectrum of the old aristocracy. Taking the waters – at Spa (Belgium), Aix (Savoy), Baden (Germany), Montecatini (Tuscany),

Barège or Eaux-Bonnes (Pyrenees) – revived again as a form of sociability among functionaries, lawyers, notaries and especially proprietors and rentiers (as well as wounded military), in the wake of the Bonapartes, Talleyrand, marshals and ministers.[51] The ubiquitous presence of often thick clusters of functionaries guaranteed at least an appearance of success to these official forms of sociability.

In social terms, probably the most successful forms of sociability deliberately diffused by the regime were the army and freemasonry. There is no need to elaborate further on the spread of military values discussed on pp. 167–70. It is enough to note that the continuous presence of French troops outside the Empire's frontiers, particularly in peacetime, accentuated the identity of the officers as a group, separate from both civilian administrators and the local elite, and with a distinctive pattern of life. Social contact with local notable families always existed, not least because the officers were frequently lodged in their houses; but it was structured around entertainments, usually described with overtones of galantry, and only filled interludes in an otherwise monotonous routine. Shooting, hunting and riding were the mainstay of Stendhal's description of his life in Brunswick. Griois, commander of the Longone fort on Elba, searched for distractions in visits to hermitages, picnics and weekly balls.[52] The life style and forms of sociability of the officers all derived from the idea of glory, from the uniforms and parades to the heroic gestures and medals. They influenced the society that surrounded them, where civilian administrators wore uniforms and lycées were organised with military attributes. But they remained parallel to, rather than part of civil forms of sociability.

The major exception to this was freemasonry. After the serious persecutions of the Terror in France and the counter-revolutionaries elsewhere, freemasonry had re-emerged, in its different sects, during the Directory. With Napoleon, it was absorbed into the establishment and, like all official organisations, was peremptorily centralised under a single rite, the deist, rationalist obedience of the Grand Orient. Headed by Napoleon's brothers, led by Cambacérès and Lebrun, populated by ministers, generals, prefects and administrators, alongside local notables, freemasonry rapidly expanded in France: by 1814 the Grand Orient controlled 886 lodges and 337 chapters. Not surprisingly, given the hierarchical associative structure of the military, it spread most rapidly in the armies, despite the republican and anticlerical loyalties of many of the veterans: by 1805, there were 132 masonic lodges in the regiments, and the initiated included a quarter of all infantry officers.

French freemasonry followed the routes of the victorious armies, contacting and often absorbing indigenous lodges and creating new ones. Army officers set up some 400 masonic lodges in French-controlled Europe. 'How can one not admire the Great Napoleon who has bound masonic ties ever tighter in establishing his Grand Empire and confederating nations?', proclaimed the lodge of *La Confiance* at Novi in 1810.[53] In Germany, Italy and Switzerland, the local notables joined forces with the French in the new lodges. Only in Bavaria was freemasonry strictly forbidden, following the dangerous experience of the radical sect of 'Illuminati' in the 1780s. In the Rhineland, the number of lodges rose from three to seventeen, with 170 French and 345 local members. In Tuscany, lodges were founded at Leghorn, Siena, Florence and Portoferraio, where the prefects Capelle and Gandolfo swore obedience alongside nobles like Marquis Torrigiani, Jewish merchants from Leghorn like Giuseppe Luzzatti, national property speculators, police commissioners, intellectuals, lawyers and rentiers. Some freemasons withdrew, for reasons of pique or for more serious ideological motivations. Others exploited the very mystery of masonic rites to maintain their old faith or assert their new ones in secret groups within the womb of the official organisation. In terms of the exponents of the regime, freemasonry functioned as an effective form of sociability to win the confidence of the local elites. Indeed, its failure to penetrate certain countries can be taken as an indicator of the limits of acceptance. In annexed Holland, the Grand Orient was able to set up only nine feeble lodges. In the grand-duchy of Warsaw, where freemasonry had been an important social institution before the French arrived, the Catholic clergy identified freemasonry with collaboration. Above all in Portugal and Spain, where the French military introduced freemasonry, the local notables refused to join the French military lodges, even in cities where they set up their own indigenous ones. Such were the difficulties of reconciling the perspectives of the new regime with those of the local establishments, at least in countries where political and religious opposition was able to brand such secular forms of sociability as tainted by the invader.[54]

The French perceived of social institutions as a crucial means of penetration for their ideas. But the very forms of sociability denied the possibility of direct control which their administrative approach assumed. Associations, salons, reading rooms or coffee-shops could be regulated or spied upon. But, as all authoritarian regimes have discovered, society offers the resourceful individual, family or group a constant possibility of withdrawal or escape. The spoken word is ephemeral, the content of social gatherings can lend itself to different readings. Whatever the compression of the private sphere within the embrace of the Napoleonic order, alternative spaces could often be identified in which to assert old values or cultural identities, whether within or outside the officially approved forms of sociability. If administrative sensitivity towards what might be construed as political criticism reduced the printed channels of expression that had proved so effective in the late enlightenment and Revolution, the existence of what were officially recognised as apolitical institutions provided an ambiguous terrain where the views and comportment of the local elites did not necessarily correspond to the expectations of the regime.

On many matters there was a convergence of ideas or practical ends between administrators and administered. Intellectuals like the Tuscan Giovanni Fabbroni or the Swiss Jean de Müller were in close unison with the Napoleonic model of modernity, whatever their mental reservations about national identity. Police repression of petty thieves and vagrants was warmly supported by right-thinking notables. Napoleonic town planning, with its destruction of city walls, wide straight avenues, and bridges, offered major opportunities to local citizens for building speculation and commerce (whatever the reservations about new Napoleonic names of squares and streets). On a more frivolous level, no doubt there was a meeting of minds among those so inclined about the renewed authorisation of gambling in the ample foyers of Italian opera houses.[55]

In other respects, however, it is not difficult to observe divergences. The learned historical associations that were founded in Switzerland or Prussia, like the award of a prize by the Turin intellectual establishment to Alessandro Saluzzo's *History of the Piedmontese militia and the wars of Piedmont from the year 1536 until 1747*, were muted references and hence appeals to the survival of a cultural identity. Language and literary precedents, like history, assumed new importance in intellectual debates in the annexed territories as they could be read as indirect protests against the suffocating administrative imposition of French uniformity. In the heartland of Flemish-speaking Belgium a theatrical piece in Flemish was printed and performed for the first time in the imperial years.[56] Education offered perhaps the most significant terrain for this battle of shadows between opposing perceptions of culture.

The revolutionaries, in the sister republics as much as in France, had shared a conviction of the importance of universal, public free education, which they saw as complementary to the liberty of culture. Hence – in the projects of Condorcet and Talleyrand and the practices of the Directory – primary schooling went hand in hand with the radical revision of secondary education and university instruction in favour of scientific, technical and useful knowledge. With the Consulate, education was explicitly linked to the representation of society as properly pyramidal. In Chaptal's words: 'the different degrees of public education . . . must correspond to the great divisions that can be noted in the social body'.[57] The implication was abandonment of interest and relative neglect of primary education, which was left to the whims of each prefect, and increasingly centralised control of secondary and university instruction, which was to culminate in the creation of the single Imperial University, with subordinate academies across the Empire (1806–8). The effective competition of private Catholic schools, following the Concordat, underlay the concern to impose the control of the lay state; although the choice as grand master of the University of Elisa Bonaparte's protégé, the conservative Catholic Fontanes, left recurrent suspicions that the educational system was less than intransigent in its attitude towards the Church.

Within the annexed and satellite territories, imperial educational policy was contested both within and outside the official institutions. There was no appeal against the closure of famous universities like Siena or Louvain. But where such institutions were renamed and given full official recognition as academies, they could offer greater possibilities than hitherto existed to indigenous intellectuals willing to seize their opportunity. In Turin, the Piedmontese nobles who had founded the Academy of Sciences, like Cesare Saluzzo and Prospero Balbo, supported by professors many of whom had participated in the republican experiences, now attempted to further their projects for educational reform through their control of the academy.

Outside the frontiers of the Empire, primary education retained its importance for influential members of society. Pestalozzi's methods, open to observation at his school in Yverdon, attracted considerable attention and imitation outside the public sector, not only in Switzerland but also in central Europe among both advanced Catholic and liberal educators. In the kingdom of Italy the purpose of education for country boys was at the opposite extreme from Pestalozzi's Rousseauian ideal of developing individual personality, except in the prohibition of corporal punishment: hygiene, religious principles, respect for king, patria and officials and 'above all the gratitude that is due to those who have obtained a free education for them and endeavour to ennoble their spirit', were to reinforce instruction aimed at improving the skills practised by their parents. Nevertheless, despite Napoleon's insistence on uniformity with the French model and the restrictions of wealth and selectivity that characterised a system of secondary education directed towards the technical training of future administrators, free primary education suitable for peasants and artisans was systematically and relatively successfully pursued in the kingdom of Italy, particularly in the poorer rural areas. Above all in Holland, Adriaan van den Ende not only translated the patriots' conviction of the moral duty of primary education into a national system, based on Pestalozzi's philanthropism, but also convinced Louis Bonaparte, anxious to identify with his subjects, of the validity of this Dutch concern and, after annexation, obtained the powerful support of Cuvier for its continuation.[58] The examples of both the Italic kingdom and Holland point to the possibility of local opinion utilising the resources and opportunities provided by the new administrative structures to exploit that space of educational policy abandoned by French policy in order to develop systems of primary education consonant with what were judged to be the needs of the country.

Determination to penetrate and utilise modes of sociability, casting over them the official protection of public approval, thus proved uncertain and sometimes treacherous terrain for the French administrators in their pursuit of social integration. Their concern, which resulted inevitably from their dichotomic analysis of society, was exclusively with the fusion of the elites. This led to a conventionally repressive attitude towards popular forms of sociability. Knives, which in Piedmont as much as Naples, were used to settle private vendettas (as well as on French soldiers looking for women), should be confiscated, were it only possible.[59] Festivities were judged likely to cause public disorder; cabarets, gambling and drink were seen as morally debauching and responsible for outbreaks of violence; popular religious manifestations were disapproved of for analogous reasons. There was nothing new in the French ideology, only in the greater thoroughness of the repressive machinery.

Whether such repression led to changes within popular forms of sociability can be known only after detailed local research. It is possible that the legitimising of the soldier, alongside the weakening of obedience to the Church, led to a diffusion of the beerhouse and tavern and a greater promiscuity, particularly in popular dancing, that was denounced by rural parish priests and urban social observers in the years of the Restoration.[60]

What is certain is that the entire corpus of changes imposed by French rule – with their insistence on individualism, property and highly regulated social relations – accentuated the divide between the respectable and the poor labouring classes. Official legitimising of the respectable reached far deeper into the social structure than during the ancien regime, as much because of the requirements of the administrative machine as through the sales of national properties. The pressures of war and fiscality that marked the later years of the Empire worsened the divide, as they rendered the presence of the poor more visible. It was not fortuitous that administrative measures and local initiatives in the relief of poverty should have assumed a higher profile at precisely this moment.

Reflections on poverty and charity and on how best to organise assistance could vaunt distinguished ancestry. The application of useful science and statistics to the relief of the poor had led to radical initiatives already in the 1780s, particularly in Germany and Holland, along the lines proposed by Rumford (now married to Lavoisier's widow at Auteuil), Voeght and Büsch. Charity provided another instance of a terrain where there was a convergence of preoccupations between regime and local notables, exemplified in the person of de Gérando, senior functionary and philanthropist, who knew or corresponded with the leading figures of European charity. But here too the approaches of administrators and private notables differed fundamentally. For the authorities, relief of poverty demanded a rationalisation of administrative structures and a clear demarcation between the worthy and the unworthy, the former meriting assistance, the latter requiring punishment. The local notables, often inspired by an inner religiosity characteristic of the new century, agreed to serve in the charitable administrations not only for humanitarian motives, but also out of an extreme concern to uphold communal solidarities. Municipal and private poor relief again assumed a central role: the good burghers of Amsterdam and Hamburg extended their welfare system of income supplementation and family support outside the governmental structures, precisely at the peak of the blockade.[61]

In these same years, the failure of the regime to appropriate a space that traditionally formed part of local notable initiative was demonstrated in a minor but revealing episode: the transformation of a private Parisian association to assist poor pregnant mothers – the Society of Maternal Charity – into an Imperial Society under the patronage of Marie Louise. It was decided, at the highest level, that this female voluntary association (so much more controllable than the salons) should be extended across the Empire. Despite the strongest recommendations of the minister of the interior and determined efforts of the prefects, only the wives of top functionaries and a handful of wealthy proprietors and merchants closely tied to the administration could be persuaded to pay their admission fee to this exclusive social club.[62] Charity remained within the sphere of civil society and the Church.

Attitudes towards poverty provide yet one more facet of the elusive, intangible quality of social modes of comportment that resisted the drive of the French administrative modernisers to rationalise and categorise. The representations of poverty by local notables were not antagonistic to those of the government. They reflected an anxiety at the consequences of what they perceived, by the final years, as the daemonic pursuit of an unachievable end: the absolute conquest of Europe by Napoleon in order to render it uniform. It is less evident that the local notables were aware that the very ideology of the regime, by its driving concern for the conditions of social order and stability that would guarantee individual property and person, reinforced the new self-image of a bourgeois society, from which the popular classes were excluded.

RESISTANCE

Armed resistance is always an ultimate choice, in any period, under any regime. It is an irrevocable gesture of defiance against the constituted authorities of a territory, a renunciation of alternative forms of protest. Armed resistance thus represents the negative counterpart to collaboration, although both may share certain values. In Napoleonic Europe, for example, family, military glory and an elitist perception of society were values common to Italian generals in Napoleon's armies, like the Lechi brothers, and to the Spanish commander of the army of Navarre resisting the French invasion, Espoz y Mina; and the conscripted peasants who killed each other on the unending sequence of battlefields undoubtedly held to a common social representation of family and land. Hence it is as important to set armed resistance to Napoleonic rule in the perspective of alternative comportments, as to enquire carefully into the examples of armed resistance, above all of the Spanish people.

The previous chapters have been concerned to discuss responses to the imposition of French rule as forms of adaptation. Even collaboration rarely implied unconditional acceptance, as each individual interpreted the different aspects of so radical a regime through the filter of his pre-existent hierarchy of values. For some, like the Piedmontese Cavour and Saluzzo, expectation of the improvements that would come from the new administration outweighed loyalties to a deposed dynasty; for others, like the Belgian C. A. Ghillenghien, the economic opportunities overcame all scruples. Yet others, like the Tuscan noble F. A. Corsi Salviati, limited their collaboration to areas where they felt a strong commitment, such as charity, while otherwise maintaining a dignified distance.

Collaboration was not always a free choice. In extreme cases, members of leading noble families could be drafted by direct order of the Emperor, like the young Cesare Balbo. Far more frequently, at a modest level, heads of household were obliged to accept local office through the pressure of their peers as an expression of communal solidarity. Senior French administrators always complained (frequently with reason) about the lack of competent personnel in villages and small towns. Seen through the eyes of the wealthy peasant, artisan or petty lawyer, service as mayor or councillor was not just a more time-consuming duty than before, given the implacable activism of the new administration; the extended range of responsibilities, because of their very novelty, placed the office-holder at risk. Custom was affronted, established practices abused, privacy invaded by the removal of cemeteries outside the habitat, the alignment of roads, or the imposition of minimal hygienic precautions; such thankless tasks as making up the lists of the conscriptable, allocation of the new taxes, or even division of communal properties, were destructive of the ties of reciprocal trust on which pacific coexistence within the village depended. When the mayor of the Alpine village of Neydens (Léman) attempted to measure illegally appropriated communal land in 1803, he was threatened by one François Dufour:

> He said to me like a madman, 'What are you measuring there?' I replied, 'I'm measuring the land you usurped from the commune.' He replied, 'And if I took your yard-stick and smashed it over your head, what would you have to say about that?'[63]

Small wonder that collaboration was sometimes unwilling; or that many who filled the French criteria for candidates for office resisted the blandishments of the authorities.

Such withdrawal into the private sphere, or refusal to be involved in public activities, was certainly a reflection of the conditions particular to the later years of the Napoleonic Empire. It could be a sign of opposition, and was usually interpreted in that way by prefects and police commissioners. There was every reason to be cautious, as open signs or even suspicions of opposition could provoke disproportionate reactions. Personal family reasons, which were regularly put forward as excuse, were often true. But prudence characterised the attitude of the local elites, even initially in Spain. As the Seville clergyman Félix José Reinoso recalled in 1816: 'No general, no magistrate, no provincial leader, no guild, no scholar raised the cry of battle. Were they French collaborators? Or did they take more time to think and feared that we were powerless to wage the battle?' The Savoyard Marquis Costa justified silent withdrawal as the only realistic possibility for legitimists, even when Napoleon's final débâcle was close:

> The Savoyards must hold their silence about their discontent and regrets . . . until further order. They must consider their country as no more than a province whose fate has not been decided and whose unhappy inhabitants have done all they could when submitting to force, supplying labour and paying taxes. Those who depart from such a line will put their head on the block and risk confiscation only too easily. Such a risky attitude is to be discouraged, above all for heads of families and great landowners; I doubt that under any circumstances it could lead to esteem and fortune in the future. . . . The only thing to be done now is to hold to an individual neutrality, which nobody has the right to make us quit; and to expect anything and everything from impending events which we are unable to hasten through vain efforts and dangerous steps.[64]

In other cases there was a genuine dislike of the demands and artificiality of the Napoleonic style of socialising, which contrasted so totally with the intense, highly personal religiosity or sentimentality that began to penetrate the more intellectual among the post-Revolutionary elites. Marie-Anne de Rathsamshausen, de Gérando's serious-minded German wife, writing in 1808, expressed the heritage of Rousseau and the young Werther in her private complaints about the obligations of her position: 'Proprieties are the sacred code of narrow spirits and withered hearts . . . I hold to my retreat in so far as proprieties allow it.' As she confessed to the worldly prince-primate Dalberg, she resented her obligations at Court:

> the atmosphere at Court is not for me; life seems to me to pass so quickly that I would like to make better use of it. . . . I feel sorry for those who appear so singularly agitated, even the most sensible

of them, when it is a question of getting to the foremost positions so as to attract a glance, to be in the right place where one can hope for a word from the sovereign or a sign of distinction.[65]

Madame de Gérando was always conscious of the different perspectives that gender imposed, which she accepted with greater resignation than her friend Madame de Staël: 'I don't know what my feeling would be if I were a man, but as a woman my ambition does not go far.' Outside France, for educated young men raised on a diet of literary individualism and military heroism, a sense of cultural identity could arouse contrasting responses. Two examples can be given, both from Italy, indicative of the more general issue of national identity that began to be voiced in many parts of Europe in reaction to French imposition of uniformity.

For the 16-year-old Cesare Balbo and his adolescent comrades from the cream of the Piedmontese aristocracy, the utilisation of the well-used model of the literary society was the only means to vindicate the identity of Italians. The programme of the Accademia dei Concordi, which was proclaimed in the privacy of the Balbo family palace in 1805, was explicit:

It becomes clearer day by day that language is a national tie, a reliable countermark of a people, the only one in Italy, divided and so strangely subjected as she is to so many dominant foreigners. If the different Italian peoples recognise themselves as brothers since Dante, this is because of that blessed harmony that is our language. And to think that now they want to remove even that sign from us![66]

Almost contemporaneously, in 1804, a young officer from Vicenza, Ermolao Federigo, writing home from Boulogne, where the Grande Armée was waiting to invade England, proposed a very different solution to the affirmation of identity:

I never disapprove of those means that can contribute to make Italians into good soldiers. I believe this should be the primary thought of every good Italian. . . . What does it matter whether one is serving the ambition of this or that man? The great aim must be to learn to make war, which is the only skill that can free us. . . . I see matters in this light. I serve my country when I learn to be a soldier, and even if I served the Turk, it wouldn't matter. Our [Italic] Republic will certainly gain a greater reputation and glory from its few soldiers than from all the sessions and laws that the Legislative body can pass. Let us think of being soldiers and when we'll have a hundred thousand bayonets, then we can start talking. In the meantime, let us thank heaven that we have not been deprived of the sole means of one day being free, that is, by being soldiers.[67]

Armed resistance against the French occurred sporadically throughout the Napoleonic years. For Napoleon, such risings were a regular consequence of occupation: 'Be quite clear in your calculations', he wrote to Joseph in 1806, 'that two weeks earlier or later you will have an uprising. It always happens in a conquered country'.[68] His initial underestimate of the Spanish revolt was undoubtedly influenced by such assumptions. Established techniques existed to deal with such episodes: rapid despatch of gendarmerie or other army units to the site of the troubles, exemplary punishment of those identified as responsible, and if necessary temporary transfer of administrative authority to the general in command. Some of his collaborators urged a more humane approach. Lebrun, as governor-general of Liguria, affirmed on the occasion of an insurrection in the Apennine valleys between Parma and Piacenza in 1805 that, once it had been put down, it need be followed only by 'serious disarming of the population (not just a hand-over of good or poor weapons, simply on the word of the parish priests), punishment of some of those responsible and leniency for the rest'; Napoleon promptly gave responsibility for the area to General Junot, who was ordered to burn five or six villages and execute some sixty persons.[69]

The initial revolts under the Directory, in 1798 and above all in 1799, in Belgium, Switzerland and Italy, constituted massive responses against the brutal exploitation of the French occupants, with strongly religious connotations – as in the Vendée – in reaction to the Revolutionary assault on the Church. The rising of the Arezzo peasants in 1799 to the cry of 'Long live the Virgin Mary' was the explosive culmination of popular hostility to the pre-Revolutionary Leopoldine reform movement, and especially its ecclesiastical policies. The Calabrian 'Holy Faith' revolt against the Parthenopean republic was so powerful because it combined popular despair over disastrous economic conditions, land-hunger and religious fanaticism with vendettas between the rural elites. In these early risings – as later in Spain – religion could intensify, legitimise and momentarily gel peasant protest, but it was never adequate by itself as the motor of revolt: Cardinal Ruffo had continually to reform his Sanfedist army, as few peasants were prepared to march beyond their own region.

The counter-revolution of 1799 branded a deep scar in the official memory. The concordats and subordination of the Church were important to Napoleon, as they neutralised an enemy of unknown potential, whose resources were restored to the conventional role of established religion, that of preaching obedience to constituted authority. The less intelligent of the functionaries continued to live with the neurosis that the people, incited by priest and legitimist noble, would seize the first occasion to rise against them. Unlike the police, they failed to realise that urban plotters – 'the gentlemen of next week', as a Turin police commissioner contemptuously described the royalists – neither wished nor were capable of starting up mass peasant risings. Even the 'Jacobin' patriots who were behind the Bologna disturbances of 1802 were incapable of moving outside the city.[70]

As the Napoleonic administration acquired experience in assimilating new territories, armed protest became less frequent. Banditry and disorder continued, primarily in the remoter areas of the European countryside, although the institution of the gendarmerie was more effective than its ancien regime equivalents, at least in times of peace. The front-line of the Empire and its allies was always more liable to disturbance than the interior, because of the ease of communications, supplies and escape routes to foreign territory. The distinction between conventional banditry and armed revolt was always a fine one, as use of arms and smuggling were traditional pastimes wherever there were frontiers; while deserters, particularly from defeated armies, nourished the ranks of those living outside the law. But the distinction was blurred even more by the tendency of exponents of the tougher branches of the administration – the gendarmerie, Customs and *droits réunis* officials – to describe as brigandage any manifestation of collective resistance and disorder. For brigandage permitted the due processes of law to be set aside.

In practice, outbreaks of collective political opposition were rare and local. They usually occurred in coincidence with military campaigns (Parma 1805, Tyrol 1809), when the forces of order were temporarily thinner on the ground; foreign promises, and sometimes practical assistance, encouraged the rebels. Until the final years, such revolts seemed characteristic of Mediterranean Europe, rather than the northern or central areas: differences in terrain, between the mountainous south and great plains of northern-central Europe, played their part; as did the closer presence of the British fleet. But in the final débâcle, revolt moved to the north, with risings of industrial workers in Berg, of the population in Hamburg and the fisherfolk in Holland (1813).

Wherever they occurred, the risings were linked directly to a sudden worsening of economic conditions and taxation. Over the period, conscription seems to have been accepted increasingly with resignation, although it took time before it could acquire in each annexed region the quality of an unavoidable curse: in Holland, only recently annexed and totally lacking a military tradition, conscription sparked off the riots at Scheveningen and other small ports in 1813. Taxation aroused the most generalised resentment everywhere, particularly the administration of the *droits réunis* on alcohol, salt and tobacco, whose officials often behaved brutally. Of the Spanish functionaries of Joseph's government who fled to France in 1814, over 40 per cent were employees of the ministry of finances, compared to 21 per cent police officials.[71] The spread of revolt from the Tyrol in 1809 to the valleys north of Brescia owed as much to the dreaded introduction of a new consumption tax as to the excess production crisis of their iron ore mines: alongside the peasantry, millers, bakers, innkeepers, winesellers and shopkeepers had closed shop in protest against the new tax. In Berg, the revolt of the manufacturing workers in January 1813 was caused by the acute industrial crisis.

Apart from Spain, only two revolts seriously challenged French authority: the endemic war in Calabria and the Tyrol rising. Both were dependent on outside support from a major power. In Calabria, initially the English general operating from Sicily, Sidney Smith, continued to pay the rebel bands, as otherwise they would have dissolved. Favoured by the inhospitable terrain, the brigand bands in Calabria persisted, despite the ferocious tactics of Murat and Manhés, because they were locked into the thick texture of faction and clientist kin and community networks. These bands of notorious fame – like those of Fra Diavolo or Sciabolone – fought the new regime not because they were ardent Bourbon royalists, but because the French were foreigners and representatives of state authority.[72]

The Tyrol revolt was more complex, as well as more worrying for French authority. It consisted of a general rising of the peasantry, initially supported by innkeepers and cattle-dealers, whose livelihood had been seriously threatened by the collapse of the transit trade following French-imposed protection of the Italian market. But the rising was far more than a protest against economic crisis. It was a clarion call to the political and cultural identity of the region, against the centralising measures of Bavaria, to whom this semi-autonomous province had been ceded by a defeated Austria (1805). Without the Austrian propagandist Hormayr and the military support of Archduke John, it is doubtful whether Andreas Hofer could ever have succeeded in rousing his compatriots to the cry of 'God, Emperor and Fatherland'. It was the exemplary counter-revolution, with religious overtones, discrimination against foreigners, Protestants and Jews, and demands for a return to the privileges and liberties of yesteryear. But the Tyrol rising, by its very identification with its own local and ethnic identity, could never act as a focal point for a broader revolt, despite incursions into the Venetian and Lombard valleys. The example of Spain had provided a model for the Tyrolese conspirators; until Napoleon's defeat of Austria, the French feared the Tyrolese example might spread to Berg. In practice, although peasant risings affected two-thirds of the departments in the Italic kingdom, each remained closely tied to the horizons of its local community; there was no sense of common identity or attempt at coordination, least of all with the Tyrolean Austrians.

Armed resistance in Spain was of a different order. The French invasion of Portugal aroused a similar popular reaction, but it was quickly overshadowed by the Spanish revolt and controlled by the occupation of the country by the British army. In Spain too, popular resistance, whether in guerrilla bands or army units, could hardly have continued so long and effectively without the campaigns of Wellington's army. The inability of the French generals, divided by personal rivalries, to destroy the British army decisively was an essential precondition of the Spanish resistance.

Nevertheless, the Spanish war was a war of the people, from the immediate risings of 2 May 1808 in Madrid, immortalised by Goya, to Suchet's final withdrawal from Catalonia in February 1814. In this, it differed from the Russian resistance in 1812, which developed essentially in the wake of the military campaign against the Grande Armée already in retreat. Hence the uniqueness of the Spanish revolt requires explanation.

Spanish historiography has long interpreted this dramatic episode in the country's history as a nationalist war; for conservative writers, it is usually also regarded as a Catholic crusade for throne and altar. Unquestionably it was a war of independence (as it is described in Spain), in the sense that it was directed against a foreign invader, as had been the Catalan and Basque resistance to the French Convention's invasion in 1794. It is also beyond doubt that the representatives of the constitutional structure that emerged from the anti-French resistance, in particular the Cortes of Cadiz, saw themselves as spokesmen for the Spanish nation. But the evidence of this prolonged struggle – from the popular seizure of the initiative in 1808 to the composition and character of the 'war by bands' – argues against any identity of view between the guerrillas and people of the different regions of Spain and either the constitutionalists or the Church. Regional particularism, always so powerful in the Spanish monarchy, was stronger in 1808 than it had been under Charles IV, although it would be historically anachronistic to ascribe to the popular resistance in Catalonia or elsewhere in Spain a political nationalism that was to develop only later in the nineteenth century. As for the Church, although individual clerics were among the guerrillas and there were strong religious overtones in many episodes of this ferocious war, both episcopate and secular clergy preached obedience to Joseph's government.

The seizure of the initiative by the people, after Murat's heavy suppression of the 'May the Second' tumult, occurred because of the total loss of credibility of all groups of the ruling classes. The weakness of the enlightenment reforms in Spain, the discredit thrown on the political class by the public-faction fighting around the rival figures of Charles IV, his heir Ferdinand and the Queen's favourite Godoy, and the economic crisis and financial bankruptcy caused by the interruption of trade with the American colonies and the French war had already created a dangerous situation of loss of credibility when Napoleon deposed the Bourbon dynasty in 1808. Unlike France in 1789, however, there was no Third Estate or other social group able to profit from this vacuum, because of the weakness of the Spanish middle classes and passivity of the established organs of government. Murat's appeal to 'gentry, landowners, merchants and manufacturers' to use their influence in defence of social order proved as illusory as the conviction of Joseph's Spanish advisers that the local elites could exert their traditional influence. Popular pressure was responsible for the creation of the eighteen provincial juntas (May–June 1808) which assumed the responsibilities of government. But the fear of revolution facilitated the dominance of conservative notables within these bodies and even more in the central junta (September 1808).

The very fact of the war facilitated the affirmation of counter-revolutionaries within the central junta and then the extraordinary Cortes of Cadiz (September 1810): one-third of the deputies at the Cortes were ecclesiastics, one-fifth were lawyers and nearly as many functionaries. It is hardly surprising that the liberal deputies – like their French predecessors in 1790–1 – compromised over radical social measures, such as the abolition of feudalism, or were forced to concede in the constitution – in exchange for acceptance of individual liberty and representation – the recognition of Catholicism as the sole religion of the Spanish nation. There is an ideological parallelism running through the reforms and administrative modernisation proposed by Joseph's government and by his constitutional opponents. But just as popular threats isolated the French collaborators or *afrancesados*, cutting through the normal ties of family and friendship, so the constitutional liberals were always on the defensive, caught between the constant demonstration of the loss of social control and the rhetoric of the counter-revolutionary exponents of a regression to absolute monarchy and spiritual discipline.

The war operated in highly localised contexts, in which the main concern of the guerrillas was to harass and drive out the invaders. Initially, entire populations rose to defend their provinces, as in Galicia, the Asturias and Catalonia. The ties between the armed bands and local patterns of land distribution or seasonal migration remain unknown, but they must have existed, given the scale of guerrilla warfare, and would have reinforced provincial identity. Then, the very method of constituting a 'war by bands' accentuated local identity, at the same time as it diluted the calls to patriotism. The central junta offered a full pardon to all smugglers who joined the bands. As the considerable number of mountain peasants and fishermen who habitually practised contraband were joined by soldiers from the former Spanish armies, Spanish deserters from the French armies, peasants and outlaws of all types, the blurring of the distinction between collective resistance and brigandage upheld by the French became ever more realistic. Indiscipline, desertions, and highly personal motivations were intrinsic to the war by bands, whose presence was often far from welcome to local villagers. General Noguès, in command of the Catalonian city of Gerona, noted how the artisans were 'too often pillaged and ill-treated both by our troops and Pyrenean irregulars and by their guerrillas'.[73] Despite the growth in scale, organization and discipline of some guerrilla forces between 1809 and 1812 – especially those of Espoz y Mina, who commanded an army of 13,000 by 1813 and administered Navarre as effectively as Soult ruled Andalusia – the armed bands continued to contribute their elements of ferocity and fanaticism to this cruel war.[74]

National historiographies have always done less than justice to the experience of the French conquest of Europe. Later developments –

the struggles for national independence, the formation of new nation-states – provided historians with a teleological interpretation that saw the nation-state as an inevitable culmination. In such a context, French occupation could be seen at best only as a negative interlude, at worst as an insult to the nation. But it is misleading to write of a national identity in a political sense where a nation-state had not yet emerged. The Polish gentry and intellectuals certainly asserted their right to restore a recently lost national independence; the Dutch and Swiss retained their national identity. Napoleon played on the hopes of the former and kept a wary eye on the latter. In Portugal, the double insult of French invasion and the proposition to incorporate the country – yet again – in the Spanish state confirmed an apparent tie between this small, proud people and its exiled monarchy; here, as in Spain, religious fanaticism reinforced monarchical counter-revolution. In Spain, Napoleon's affront to national pride led to national resistance, although those in revolt expressed themselves – in accord with the history of the Spanish monarchy – most immediately in the form of many nationalisms, Asturian, Catalan, Galician, Valencian and so on, and only at a more distant and traditional level by identification with the legitimate king of Spain.

Far more problematic are the territories which were only later to become nation-states. The nationalism of the Belgians (even of the Flemish speakers) was not aroused by French rule, but by the enforced incorporation into Holland in 1815. Patriotism, in a generically national sense, certainly emerged among some young intellectuals in Italy and Germany as a response to the increasingly rigid uniformisation imposed by Napoleon, as much as by his final military campaigns. The rapidity with which it acquired its new connotation can be gauged by comparing it to Madame de Gérando's reflections on what was a patriot in the years of the Consulate. Classical culture and modern philanthropy combined to limit the reproductive power of patriotism to its dimensions of a local identity:

> Love of one's country should not be represented as an abstract and unnatural sentiment; but it is limited, like all human faculties, and cannot dilate over too large a space. . . . The Frenchman and the German possess the vanity of their race rather than a patriotic passion. Because 20 or 30 million individuals need to be rallied around the tie that unites them to their compatriots, the tie itself so loosens that, in place of a patriotic enthusiasm, all that is felt is a sort of general benevolence. . . . A deep attachment to one's native land nowadays exists above all in small states, and even

more in the free cities which rule themselves, where everybody is interested in the prosperity, conservation of the monuments and public security of the city where he was born and will die.[75]

The Italians, with rare exceptions like some Piedmontese and Roman aristocrats, were ready to adapt and take advantage of the French presence, even if they never accepted Gallic pretensions to a superior civilisation. In Germany, idealist philosophy and romanticism provided props for the construction of a reactionary alternative theory of civilisation – that of the German community, based on Herder's theory of language and the Grimm brothers' image of the *Volkstum*. It was an intellectual construct, which circulated in German universities. The French were aware of the hostility among some intellectuals and, as always, suspected plots among the student secret societies. For Bignon, writing in 1812, 'a feeling for the ideal of so-called German independence, this Germanic purity which wants its own philosophy, its own literature, its own political existence, is a commonplace to be found in all contemporary writings'. But for the experienced Alsatian diplomat Reinhard nationalism in Germany was no danger: 'In Germany there is no reason to fear any event similar to those of Spain because there exist neither ideas nor interests that can act uniformly on a great mass of persons'.[76] He might have added a few years later, with his knowledge of the Prussia that Stein, Hardenberg and Gneisenau had renovated, that for such German leaders the Spanish example was also a warning against the dangers of appealing to the people except under carefully controlled conditions. The significance of this was to emerge after the end of the French conquest of Europe.

6 Epilogue: the heritage

In France . . . everything had been moving towards democracy already for a long time. Anyone who refuses to be taken in by external appearances, who has a clear idea of the state of moral impotence into which the clergy had fallen, the poverty and degradation of the nobility, the wealth and enlightenment of the Third Estate, the remarkable division of landed property that already existed and the large number of mediocre fortunes, who recalls the theories professed at the time, the principles tacitly but almost universally admitted; such a person, I say, who has assembled these different aspects into a single point of view, cannot fail to conclude that France – for all its nobility, state religion, laws and aristocratic usages – was, all considered, already then the most truly democratic nation of Europe; and that Frenchmen at the end of the eighteenth century, in terms of their social status, civil constitution, ideas and habits, were far in advance even of those peoples who today move most visibly towards democracy.

(Alexis de Tocqueville, *Etat social et politique de la France avant et depuis 1789*, 1836)

Civilisation as progress is an ideology with a very distinguished ancestry, from ancient Rome to the Spanish conquest of South America and China. Cultural imperialism as a means of justifying conquest and integration was not new and, expressed in terms of an ethnocentric mission, was to play an ever more explicit role in the imperialism of the later nineteenth and twentieth centuries. The civilising claims that accompanied the Directorial conquest and Napoleonic attempt at integration of Europe may appear easy to dismiss as little more than legitimising the imposition of uniform administrative rule on the cultural diversity that characterised groups and peoples in Europe.[1] But in at least two respects such claims are of importance because of their immediate and continuing influence.

On the one hand, it was not just the French administrators and their intellectual allies who were confident that they had elaborated scientific methods that allowed them to understand and govern the mechanisms of society. Such convictions were to remain unquestioned after the military collapse of the Napoleonic regime: statistics, utilitarian principles, administrative science, and a professional bureaucracy were typical aspects of the development of the nineteenth-century state, supported by a burgeoning social science that demanded an active presence of the state, irrespective of its constitutional base.[2]

On the other hand, in the decades that followed Waterloo, at least until the revolutions of 1848, the experience of French rule reinforced the sense of French civilisation among the educated elites of Europe, whether by acceptance or by refusal. In part, this reflected the personal experiences of an entire generation of men, who had participated directly in the Napoleonic administration or armies and had frequented the Parisian salons; for many, it was the formative experience of their early life, which they were to carry through to 1848 and beyond. For others, like the young Leopardi, the underlying parameter of civil progress remained the France that had emerged from the Revolution, where the salons, academies, circles and societies imposed rules and judgements, providing that stimulus of honours and public recognition which he searched for in vain in Italy; it was France that Leopardi had in mind when he contrasted the 'customs' – expression of the common culture of civil nations – with the 'usages' or inherited habits of backward societies like Rome, where public commitment was lacking and life turned around the promenade, public spectacles and the Church. 'Italians have no customs; they have usages, just like all civil peoples who are not nations.'[3]

Certainly France's cultural claims were now strongly contested – by a Giuseppe Mazzini or a Friedrich Karl von Savigny, for example – in the name of national individuality. But this very antagonism reflected the depth of penetration of Napoleonic rule. The radical political and administrative rupture with the past, the attempt to create and consolidate new loyalties in place of traditional passive ties of authority, deference and local identity, the even more ambitious aspiration to forge out of the heterogeneity of the European past a new identity on the model of Napoleonic France inevitably provoked resistance, less at the immediately political level than among the deeper social relationships of each society. In reaction to the Napoleonic experience old solidarities, tempered by centuries of exercise – such as language, community or popular religion – were reinforced; new solidarities emerged, like the discovery and construction of national individuality. The Napoleonic conquest of Europe, because of the determination and relative effectiveness of its administrative class, backed up by armies, acted as a liberating force, albeit often in ways unintended by its exponents. Its repercussions were felt far beyond Europe, as in Brazil, where it could be argued that the achievement of independence and national integration was an indirect consequence of Junot's invasion of Portugal.[4] In the European scale of its ambitions, it bequeathed a heritage that cut across national frontiers and imposed an unusual, perhaps unprecedented unity on political behaviour within the different European states during the Restoration. Until 1848 or even 1870, and indirectly until much later, the impact of these years conditioned the aspirations and practices of the opponents as much as of the friends of the Revolution and Napoleonic modernity. The complexity of this heritage can be illustrated by a brief discussion of three themes – nationalism, liberalism and administrative modernisation.

Nationalism, which was to become so dominant a theme of European politics by 1848, is considered in modern historiography as a consequence of the French Revolution. Unquestionably the Revolutionary wars stimulated a popular loyalty in France, as Napoleonic imperialism aroused a reaction among peoples resentful of the weight and exactions of the French presence. It is necessary, however, to distinguish between these two very different responses. In France, a nation-state was forged, as much by the legitimising of the leading role of the state as by military patriotism; the survival of a strong 'spirit of locality' (to employ the language of the July monarchy) was compatible with, and in times of extreme necessity subordinate to, identification with France; there was no longer a principled antagonism between local and national loyalties. Elsewhere, nationalism could be invoked as a means of arousing enthusiasm against the French invader: in Britain, Spain or Russia, it achieved a notable popular response; in a state like Prussia, uncertainties about peasant reactions persuaded even a farsighted leader like Hardenberg to proceed cautiously.

Military defeat, not nationalism, was the cause of the sudden collapse of the Napoleonic empire. The elites everywhere were immediately concerned – like the French administrators – to ensure the maintenance of order through a peaceful handover of authority. In so far as popular loyalty manifested itself, it was towards a dynasty rather than a nation – Victor Emanuel I in Piedmont, Ferdinand IV in Naples, the Elector William of Hesse-Cassel in the rump of Napoleonic Westphalia. Legitimism, or restoration of the dynasty, was an obvious and effective rallying cry at the moment of the anti-French reaction. More significant was the response in regions without a 'native' dynasty – in Lombardy, Genoa, the Belgian provinces, even the Swiss cantons. Here the elites sought in vain to retain or restore their regional identities, even fomenting popular demonstrations, as in the Ligurian valleys; or, as in the former Rhineland departments, remained loyal to France. Whatever the assumptions of some literary-minded patriots, nationalism could not function as a rallying-cry, simply because it was devoid of significance to the mass of the people and appeared as a dangerous abstraction to most of the elites in territories without experience of a nation-state – and even within such states.

Nationalism was to be constructed as a powerful ideology in the subsequent decades, when the experience of the French occupation became part of the armoury of the political struggle to attain independence. For Mazzini or von Savigny, those years gave birth to the emergence of an awareness of an innate national identity. For the Belgian patriots in 1830, as for the Lombards, whether liberal or conservative, some of whom had made careers in the Napoleonic administration, a political sense of national identity only developed against the foreign rulers imposed by the Congress of Vienna, whether the Dutch King William I or the Austrian Emperor Francis. Nowhere did nationalism as a political ideology replace the pre-existing loyalties to community and region or integrate state with nation. Only after the creation of such nation-states, from Greece and Belgium to the ethnic states of the Austrian empire, was nationalism to be constructed, in opposition to what were considered as the disaggregative forces of local identities, by the transference within national boundaries of the same techniques of administrative uniformity, linguistic imposition and pressure for social integration that had characterised the European experience of the Napoleonic regime. Like the imperial administrators, the politicians and bureaucrats of these new states were to meet with social adaptations and resistance that made the building of an integrated nation a prolonged process.

Liberalism was more directly related to the Napoleonic experience. In its political connotations of constitutionalism, widened liberty and economic liberalism, as voiced by Benjamin Constant and

Jean-Baptiste Say, it expressed a reaction against the authoritarian centralism and economic dirigisme of the Napoleonic state. The reaction was strongest in France, to the point that to foreigners, Restoration France appeared as the country of liberty, possibly even more so than Britain before the electoral reform of 1832, with its system of representation extended to local government, formal equality of civil rights, limitation of state intervention and affirmation of landed notables. Constitutions, as the mechanism to reconcile liberty with monarchical order, were invested with the force of a symbolic value for the liberals of Restoration Europe, from Cadiz, Palermo and Lisbon to Brussels, Vienna and Berlin. Economic liberalism or *laissez-faire*, by which was understood an end to state interference over international trade and the maintenance of entrepreneurial freedom, was enthusiastically promoted by Britain and theorised by Continental economists like Jean-Baptiste Say, Frédéric Bastiat and Friedrich von Hermann.

In reality, liberalism rapidly lost its distinctive quality as opposition to the Napoleonic experience. Liberalism as the practice of government derived from the same matrix as Napoleonic administration, with the single and practically restricted exception of elected representation as a check on arbitrary rule. Like the Napoleonic functionaries, liberals were convinced that they embodied social and economic progress, were favourable to science and technology, and proclaimed rational, utilitarian principles as the basis of a superior and neutral administration. The continuity between the Napoleonic experience and liberalism was accentuated by the strong defence of former imperial administrators against the legitimist claims of some Restoration monarchies, as well as by their leading role in statistical propositions to resolve social problems. In terms of economic theory, the political economy of Say, however influential in France, was contested in Italy by the philosophy of statistics of Melchiorre Gioia and in Germany by Friedrich List's analysis of the comparative advantages of protection. In economic practice, the flooding of the Continental markets with British manufactures led many governments to revalue the lessons of the Continental blockade and conserve protective Customs barriers. Above all, the political liberalism of the Restoration bore an indelible imprint from the Napoleonic years in its identification with the propertied bourgeoisie and its insensitivity towards the labouring classes.

Liberalism, whose popularity in 1815 was based on the progressives' opposition to Napoleonic despotism (in contrast to the reactionary and religious opposition of a Joseph de Maistre), was ambivalent in its attitude towards administrative modernisation. Like the enlightenment *philosophes*, the liberals were seduced by the apparent application of their ideas by the prince, but diffident towards the dangers of the concentration of power. A state guided by utilitarian principles was seen as necessary for the moral elevation of the labouring classes as much as for national identity; while despotism, it was hoped, could be avoided by representation restricted to the notables.

In fact, the Napoleonic experience of administrative modernisation was to serve as a model as much for the opponents of French domination as for their supporters. Very few rulers attempted to abolish the Napoleonic reforms, and those who did – like the Sardinian King Victor Emanuel – were soon forced to abandon such utopian reaction. In most states or regions that had experienced French dominion, the Restoration monarchs retained the structures, if not the names, of the Napoleonic administrative, fiscal or juridical reforms: an excellent example is the completion of the French cadaster in the former Rhineland departments by the king of Prussia and in Tuscany by the grand-duke. The unprecedented restructuring of the organisation of the state and social system by Prussia, as the price of its survival after Jena, was conceived by Stein and Hardenberg through critical observation of the French model. The Austrian civil code of 1811 and administrative centralisation, which were to be applied to the Lombard-Venetian kingdom after 1815, owed as much to Napoleon as to Joseph II. The administrative unification of the kingdoms of Naples and Sicily in 1816 would have been inconceivable without the French decade at Naples. Even in Britain utilitarians like Jeremy Bentham urged their government to acquire statistical information as the basis for a more interventionist policy. In some states, like Bavaria, Baden and Württemberg, the collapse of the Napoleonic Empire was without any negative effect on the process of administrative modernisation, which accelerated between 1809 and 1819 under the leadership of Montgelas, Reitzenstein, Brauer and Friedrich of Württemberg, and proved more successful than Prussia in forging a unified state identity.[5]

Centralised administrative modernisation has become the characteristic of the nation-state. The Napoleonic model, with its expectations that the pace of national integration could be forced through the administrative grid, underlay the practices of the governments of many of the European states that survived the collapse of the Napoleonic Empire and most of those that achieved independence subsequently in the nineteenth century. The social limits of such a bureaucratic shortcut to national integration in the Napoleonic period have been explored in the earlier chapters. A final general remark on this fundamental question of the relationship between state and society may not appear out of place.

National integration, in the Napoleonic experience, required the subordination and ultimate disappearance of what were in effect two different oppositions, even if they were not normally distinguished – loyalty towards what were formerly separate political territories, and defence of the privileges and autonomy of specific social groups and communities. In territories where there was a strong identification between state and dynasty, where the addition of new territories was marginal to the pre-existing core of population, with a thick texture of relationships between state and society – as in the south German states, Piedmont or France itself – uniformising administrative reform and the formation of a sizeable professional bureaucracy that identified with the state could subordinate the privileges and independence of such social groups as the aristocracy or guilds. In states with a substantial agglomeration of territories – like Prussia or Austria after 1815 – resistance to imposed administrative change was strengthened and facilitated by the ability of the local elites (whether the east Prussian landed magnates, the Rhineland bourgeoisie or the Lombard aristocratic nobles) to defend their privileges in terms of the traditional social relations and loyalties of their region. It was the strength of these regional elites and their capacity of resistance that conditioned the attitude of modernising administrations towards maintaining tight control over local government or granting elective forms of representation; and it was such attitudes in turn that contributed to the contemporary reputation of administratively minded governments as 'liberal' or 'reactionary'. In Lombardy, the Austrian administration alienated the landowners who retained a fundamental role as opinion leaders. In Baden, to a Restoration liberal like Ludwig Winter, administrative reform could be hailed in pure enlightenment terms as the triumph of civilisation over the traditional forces of obscurity:

> The struggle between the institutions of the Middle Ages and the needs of our epoch is over, the inalienable rights of state power have reverted to their original source . . . the obstacles to progress towards constitutional liberty have been removed.[6]

Whatever the political connotation of a government, its practices of administrative modernisation – as under Napoleon – reinforced the social position of the propertied classes and bureaucracy and their separateness from the people. Even though the consequences of the post-Napoleonic industrial revolution were the prime cause of the class tensions and conflict that were to characterise the nineteenth century, the pressure for the integration of elites that was an intrinsic part of the Napoleonic philosophy of administration widened the social gap between the propertied and property-less. This was the final and most profound heritage of the Napoleonic experience. Alexis de Tocqueville foresaw the danger:

> The French Revolution, which abolished all privileges and destroyed all exclusive rights, has still let one survive – that of property.
>
> Landowners should be under no illusions about the strength of their situation, nor should they imagine that the right of property is an insurmountable bulwark because it has not yet been overcome. . . .
>
> Soon, without any doubt, the struggle of political parties will be between those who own and those who do not own. The great battlefield will be property . . .[7]

Appendix: chronology 1789–1821

FRANCE	EUROPE OUTSIDE FRANCE	BATTLES
1789 May 5 Opening of the Estates-General July 9 National Constituent Assembly July 14 Taking of the Bastille August 4 Feudal privileges relinquished August 26 Declaration of the Rights of Man November 2 Property of the clergy put at the disposal of the nation **1790** May 15–22 Discussion on the right of peace and war July 12 Civil constitution of the clergy **1791** January 3 Clergy obligated to take oath to the civil constitution May 7–15 Debate on the colonies and the rights of coloured men May 14/May 22 Two 'Le Chapelier' laws outlawing coalitions June 20–1 Flight of the royal family, and their arrest at Varennes		

August 4 First volunteer
battalions raised

August 5 'Declaration of Peace
to the World' by the
Constituent Assembly

October 1 Legislative assembly

December 12/January 2
Robespierre's speeches against
war

1792 April 20 War declared on the
'king of Bohemia and
Hungary'

May 5 New raising of national
volunteers

July 11 The Assembly declares
the country in danger

August 10 Taking of the Tuileries
and fall of the throne

August 11 Establishment of
universal suffrage

September 20 End of the
Legislative assembly
Convention

September 21 Abolition of the
throne

September 25 The republic is
declared 'one and indivisible'

November 19 France pledges
'fraternity and aid' to all
peoples

August 27 Declaration of Pillnitz
by the European Powers
against the French Revolution

July 25 'Brunswick Manifesto'
threatening Paris with
retaliations

September 24 French occupation
of Savoy

November 6 French occupation
of the Austrian Low Countries
(Belgium)

September 20 Valmy

November 6 Jemappes

FRANCE	EUROPE OUTSIDE FRANCE	BATTLES
	November 27 Annexation of Savoy to France	
1793 January 21 Execution of Louis XVI	January 23 Second partition of Poland between Prussia and Russia	
February 1 France declares war on Britain and Holland. Start of the first coalition	January 31 Annexation of Nice to France	
February 21 'Amalgam' of the volunteers and regulars		
February 24 300,000 men raised		
March 7 The Convention declares war on the king of Spain		
March 11 Start of the revolt in the Vendée		March 18 Defeat of Neerwinden
April 11 Forced circulation of the *assignat*		
April 26 Beginnings of Chappe's optic telegraph		
April 27 Surrender of Toulon to the British		
July 13 Assassination of Marat	July 23 Mainz evacuated by French troops	
October 5 Adoption of the republican calendar		September 6–8 Hondschoote
October 10 The government is declared revolutionary until		October 16 Wattignies

the advent of peace		
October 16 Execution of Marie Antoinette		
December 19 Toulon retaken by Bonaparte		December 26 Geisburg
1794	July 8 The French occupy Brussels	June 26 Fleurus
July 27–30 (Thermidor 9–12) Arrest and execution of Robespierre and his followers	July 19 Insurrection in Geneva in favour of France	
	November 4 Maastricht capitulates	
	November 8 The French occupy Nijmegen	
1795	January 3 Third partition of Poland between Prussia, Russia and Austria	
	January 20 The French occupy Amsterdam	
	January 23 The Dutch fleet is captured at the Helder	
	April 5 Peace of Basel between France and Prussia	
	May 16 Treaty of alliance between France and Holland	July 21 Quibéron
August 22 Constitution adopted by the Convention	October 1 Annexation of Belgium to France	
October 26 Bonaparte becomes general at the head of the home army		

FRANCE	EUROPE OUTSIDE FRANCE	BATTLES
1796 March 2 Bonaparte named general at the head of the army of Italy March 9 Marriage of Napoleon Bonaparte and Josephine de Beauharnais		
	April 28 Franco-Sardinian armistice of Cherasco	April 12 Montenotte April 13 Millesimo April 15 Dego April 21 Mondovì May 10 Lodi
	May 20 Bonaparte gives his troops half their pay in cash May 23 Anti-French rising in the region of Pavia June 12 French troops invade the Legations June 23 Pope Pius VI signs the armistice at Bologna	June 4 Altenkirchen
		July 9 Ettlingen August 5 Castiglione August 23 Defeat of Bernadotte at Neumarkt August 24 Defeat of Moreau at Amberg September 8 Bassano
	October 16 Proclamation at Bologna of the Cispadane Republic	

November 15–17 Arcole

January 14 Rivoli

1797

December 15 The French fleet departs for Ireland

February 2 Fall of Mantua
February 19 Treaty of Tolentino with the Pope
March French offensive towards the Tyrol
April 17 Anti-French rising at Verona
April 18 Leoben peace preliminaries
April 20 Moreau crosses the Rhine
June Creation of the Cisalpine republic

September 4 Anti-royalist *coup d'état*
September 30 Official state bankruptcy

October 17 Peace of Campoformio
November 28 Congress of Rastadt

December 25 Bonaparte elected to the Institut

1798

January Revolt of the Vaudois (Switzerland)
January 11 Berthier marches on Rome

FRANCE	EUROPE OUTSIDE FRANCE	BATTLES
	January 22 *Coup d'état* in Holland	
	January–April Annexation of Mulhouse, Bienne and Geneva to France	
	February 11 Berthier enters Rome	
	February 15 Roman republic	
	April Helvetic republic. Batavian republic	
	May 19 The French fleet leaves Toulon for Egypt	
	July 7 The French land at Alexandria	July 21 Pyramids
	summer–autumn Anti-French revolt in central Switzerland and Nidwald	
		August 1–2 Naval defeat of Abukir (on the Nile)
September 5 Jourdan-Delbrel law on conscription		
	October 12 Start of the 'Peasants' war' in Belgium	
	October 21 Anti-French rising in Cairo	
November 23 Land tax law		
November 24 Creation of tax on doors and windows		

1799

January 23 Championnet enters Naples
January 26 Parthenopean republic

February 15 El-Arich
March 25 Defeat of Jourdan at Stokach

March 7 Taking of Jaffa
March 19 Siege of Saint-Jean d'Acre
April 10 Pius VI taken to France
April 28 Assassination of the French representatives at Rastadt
April 29 Suvarov in Milan
May 17 Bonaparte lifts the siege of Saint-Jean d'Acre

April 5 Defeat of Schérer at Magnano

July 25 Abukir

August 23 Bonaparte leaves Egypt
August 27 British landing at the Helder

September 25–7 Zürich

October 16 Bonaparte arrives in Paris
November 9–10 (Brumaire 18–19) *Coup d'état.* Bonaparte provisional consul with Sieyès and Roger Ducos
December 15 Proclamation of the Constitution

FRANCE	EUROPE OUTSIDE FRANCE	BATTLES
December 22 Inauguration of the council of state		
December 27 Inauguration of the Senate		
1800 January 1 Inauguration of the Tribunate and the Legislative body		
February 13 Creation of the Bank of France		
February 17 Institution of the prefects		
	May–June France regains Piedmont and Lombardy	June 14 Marengo
	September Conquest of Malta by the British	
	October 1 Spain cedes Louisiana to France	
		December 2 Hohenlinden
December 24 Attempt on Bonaparte's life		
1801	February 9 Peace of Lunéville: Austria relinquishes northern and central Italy. Annexation of the left bank of the Rhine to France	
	March 21 Treaty of Aranjuez: Etruria to the Bourbons of Parma; Naples cedes the island of Elba to France. Creation of the Republic of Lucca	March 21 Canope

April 18 Concordat

April 2 The British bombard Copenhagen
April 24 Act of Malmaison: failure of French mediation in Switzerland
June–September The French army in Egypt capitulates to the British
July Revolt of Santo Domingo
August 24 Franco-Bavarian treaty
December 24–6 Napoleon president of the Cisalpine republic
January *Consulta* of Lyons. Italian republic
February French expedition to Santo Domingo
March 25 Peace of Amiens

May 29 French–Swiss alliance

1802

April 3 Organic articles of the Concordat
May 1 Creation of the *lycées*
May 19 Institution of the Legion of Honour
August 2 Plebiscite to name Napoleon Bonaparte consul for life
August 4 (16 Thermidor Year X) Constitution of Year X

FRANCE	EUROPE OUTSIDE FRANCE	BATTLES
1803	September 11 Annexation of Piedmont to France	
	September Secession of the Valais	
	October The French occupy Parma	
	February 19 Act of mediation and creation of the Swiss Confederation	
	February 25 Rezes of Regensburg: abolition of the ecclesiastical principalities of the Germanic Holy Roman Empire	
	May 3 Sale of Louisiana to the United States	
	May 12–16 Rupture with Britain	
	October Spanish treaty of neutrality	
1804 February 15 Order for the arrest of Moreau		
March 21 Execution of the duke of Enghien		
May 18 Napoleon Bonaparte proclaimed Emperor of the French		
May 19 Naming of eighteen marshals of the Empire		

July 20 Napoleon reaches
  Boulogne to prepare for the
  landing in Britain
August 11 Francis II takes the
  title of emperor of Austria
September Napoleon at Mainz.
  Alliance between France and
  the princes of southern
  Germany

March 19 Napoleon king of Italy
March Creation of the Grand
  Pensionary, Schimmelpenninck
March–June Creation of the
  principalities of Piombino,
  Lucca and Guastalla for Elisa
  Baciocchi
May 18 Coronation of Napoleon
  at Milan
June Annexation of Genoa to the
  Empire
August Rupture with Austria and
  Prussia
September 10 Austria attacks
  Bavaria

December 2 Coronation of
  Napoleon

1805

October 15–20 Ulm
October 21 Defeat of Trafalgar
December 2 Austerlitz

FRANCE	EUROPE OUTSIDE FRANCE	BATTLES
	December 15 Treaty of Schönbrunn: Hanover passes over to Prussia	
	December 26 Treaty of Presburg: Austria cedes Venetia, Istria and Dalmatia to the kingdom of Italy, and the Tyrol to Bavaria	
1806	February 14 Masséna enters Naples	
	March 15 Duchy of Berg and Cleves given to Murat	
	March 30 Principality of Neuchâtel created for Berthier. Joseph Bonaparte king of Naples	
April 4 Imperial catechism	April Orders in the British Council on the naval blockade	
May 10 Founding of the Imperial University	May 3 Louis Bonaparte king of Holland	
	May 16 British Order in Council declaring the coast of Elba under blockade	
	June 10 Decree to make the kingdom of Italy a reserved market	
	July 12 to August 1 Creation of the Confederation of the	

October 14 Jena and Auerstädt

February 8 Eylau
June 14 Friedland

Rhine. End of the Holy
Roman Empire. Murat grand-
duke of Berg.
Summer Revolt in Calabria
October 27 Napoleon enters
Berlin
November Revolt in Prussian
Poland at the approach of the
French
November 18 French occupation
of Hamburg
November 21 Berlin decree:
French Continental blockade

1807

July 7 Tilsit treaty
July 22 Creation of the grand-
duchy of Warsaw
July Napoleon gives eastern
Frisia and Emden to Holland
August 18 Jerome king of
Westphalia
September The British bombard
Copenhagen
October–November Napoleon's
journey to northern Italy
autumn Reinforcement of British
blockade measures
October Stein chancellor of
Prussia

August 19 Suppression of the
Tribunate
September 16 Creation of the
Audit Office

FRANCE	EUROPE OUTSIDE FRANCE	BATTLES
	October 27 Franco-Spanish convention of Fontainebleau	
	October 30 French–Swedish alliance	
	October–December Decrees of Fontainebleau and Milan enforcing the Continental blockade	
	November The British seize Heligoland	
	November 30 Junot enters Lisbon	
	December Installation of the Braganças in Brazil. United States Embargo Act on exports. Annexation of Tuscany to the Empire	
	February War between Russia and Sweden	
1808		
March 1 Creation of the imperial nobility	March 16-17 'Motin d'Aranjuez'	
	March–April The kingdom of Italy gives Dalmatia to France in exchange for the Marches	
	April Occupation of the Papal States	
	April–May Bayonne meeting	
	May 2 General revolt in Spain	
	May Annexation of Parma and	

Piacenza to the Empire
June 4 Joseph Bonaparte king of Spain
June 15 Murat king of Naples
June 20 Joseph enters Madrid

July 19–22 Defeat of Dupont at Baylen
August 30 Defeat of Junot at Cintra

August The British land in Portugal
September 27 Erfurt meeting between Napoleon and Tsar Alexander
October Second British landing in Galicia
November–December Counter-offensive by Napoleon in Spain
December 4 Madrid capitulates to Napoleon

1809

February 20–1 Saragossa
April 22 Eckmühl

April–May Austrian invasion of Bavaria, the Tyrol and Saxony

May 21–2 Essling
July 6 Wagram
July 27–8 Talavera

July 6 Arrest of Pius VII

August–September British expedition on Walcheren and Flessingen
October 14 Treaty of Schönbrunn: Austria cedes Galicia to the grand-duchy of

FRANCE	EUROPE OUTSIDE FRANCE	BATTLES
	Warsaw. The kingdom of Italy gives France Istria in exchange for the southern Tyrol	November 29 Ocana
December 15 Divorce of Napoleon and Josephine	December Creation of the Illyrian provinces. Revolt of Mexico, Venezuela and New Grenada, Chile and the Rio de la Plata	
1810	January 6 French–Swedish alliance	
	January–April Soult's expedition to Andalusia. Suchet pacifies Aragon and Catalonia. Creation of military governments in Spain	
	February 17 Annexation of Rome to the Empire	
	April–May Napoleon visits Belgium	
April 2 Marriage of Napoleon and Marie Louise	July 9 Annexation of Holland to the Empire	
	July Annexation of the Valais to the Empire	
	July 5, September 12 Decrees of Trianon and Saint-Cloud: protective Customs duties for France	

	August 21 Bernadotte elected heir to the throne of Sweden	
	September Meeting of the Spanish Legislative assembly at Cadiz	
	October 10, 18 A tighter Continental system is introduced	
	December 31 Rupture of the French–Russian alliance. Annexation of Oldenburg to the Empire	
1811	January 22 Creation of the Hanseatic departments	
	January French–Italian occupation of the Ticino (Switzerland)	
	March The British conquer the Dalmatian islands	March 12 Naval defeat of Lissa
		May 5 Defeat of Masséna at Fuentes de Oñoro
		May 16 Defeat of Soult at La Albuera
	March 20 Birth of the king of Rome	
	June 9 Baptism of the king of Rome	
1812	October Napoleon visits Holland	
	January 'Liberal' revolution at Palermo. French occupation of Swedish Pomerania	January 19 Defeat of Soult at Ciudad Rodrigo
	March 4 Franco–Prussian alliance	
	March Constitution of Cadiz	

FRANCE	EUROPE OUTSIDE FRANCE	BATTLES
	April 5–9 Russian–Swedish alliance	
	May Russian campaign	
	June Anglo-American war.	
	Napoleon refuses to recognise the restoration of the kingdom of Poland	
	June 24 Napoleon crosses the Niemen	
		July 22 Defeat of Marmont at the Arapiles
		September 7 Borodino
	September 14 Napoleon enters Moscow	
	October 18 Napoleon decides to leave Moscow	
October 23 *Coup d'état* by General Malet		November 27 Berezina
	December 5 Napoleon leaves the retreating army	
1813 January 25 Concordat of Fontainebleau	January The Russians occupy the grand-duchy of Warsaw	
	March 17 Prussia declares war on France	
	March Revolt of northern Germany	
	April 14 Metternich breaks the alliance with France and offers to mediate	
	May The French evacuate Madrid	May 2 Lützen

May 20 Bantzen
June 21 Defeat of Joseph at
    Vitoria

June 4 Pleiswitz armistice
July Evacuation of northern and
    central Spain
August 5–10 Congress of Prague
August 12 Austria declares war
    on France
September–October Second
    German campaign. Austrian
    invasion of southern Germany,
    Switzerland, the Tyrol,
    Venetia and Illyria. The
    French retreat behind the
    Rhine. Suchet retreats from
    Aragon and Catalonia

October 16–19 Defeat of Leipzig
October 30 Hanau

November 6 Lebrun leaves
    Holland
November 16 Holland is lost to
    France
December 11 Treaty of Valençay
    restoring Ferdinand VII as
    king of Spain
December 30 The Austrians
    occupy Switzerland. The
    Confederation declares its
    neutrality

FRANCE	EUROPE OUTSIDE FRANCE	BATTLES
1814		
	January Restoration of the Geneva republic. France loses the left bank of the Rhine. The Papal States are returned to the Pope	January 29 Brienne
	January 17 Murat's defection: campaign in central Italy	
	January 25 Fall of Lerida, last French stronghold	
	March 30–1 Surrender of Paris	March 13 Rheims
	end of April Ferdinand arrives in Spain. White terror	
	spring Return of the prince of Orange. Kingdom of the Netherlands including Holland and Belgium	
	spring–summer Re-establishment of Austrian influence in all of Italy and southern Germany	
April 2 The Senate declares the deposition of Napoleon	June 30 Treaty of Paris	
April 6 Abdication of Napoleon	November 1 Opening of the Congress of Vienna	
May 4 Napoleon lands on the island of Elba		
1815		
	February 25 Napoleon's escape from the island of Elba	
March 1 Napoleon lands on the Golfe-Juan	March 30 Murat's proclamation at Rimini	
March 20 Napoleon in Paris	April Creation of the Lombard-Venetian kingdom	
April 22 The Additional Act		

May 30 Defeat of Murat at
    Tolentino
June 16 Ligny
June 18 Defeat of Waterloo

June The Swiss Confederation
    occupies Geneva
June 7 Victor Emmanuel king of
    Sardinia takes control of
    Genoa
October 13 Murat executed by
    firing squad
November 20 Treaty of Paris:
    Savoy restored to Victor
    Emanuel. Creation of the
    German Confederation. The
    Rhineland is ceded to the king
    of Prussia. Creation of the
    kingdom of Poland

June 22 Abdication of Napoleon

November 16 Napoleon arrives
    at St Helena

1821 May 5 Death of Napoleon

Notes

Preface

1 H. Berlioz, 'Les concerts des Tuileries sous l'Empire', *Revue et Gazette Musicale de Paris*, 34, 1837, pp. 379–80; P. P. de Ségur, *De 1800 à 1812. Un aide de camp de Napoléon*, Paris, 1894–5, vol. 1, p. 395; W. Friedländer, 'Napoleon as "roi thaumaturge" ', *Journal of the Warburg and Courtauld Institutes*, 4, 1940–1, p. 141 n. 1; G. Pascoli, 'Romagna' (1892).

1 The Revolutionary-Napoleonic ideals of conquest

1 Quoted in C. Capra, 'Il Settecento', in D. Sella and C. Capra, *Il Ducato di Milano dal 1535 al 1796*, Turin, 1984, p. 411.
2 N. Broc, *La Géographie des philosophes. Géographie et voyageurs français au XVIIIe siècle*, Lille, 1972, pp. 182–204.
3 D. Roche, *Le Siècle des lumières en province. Académies et académiciens provinciaux, 1680–1789*, Paris – La Haye, 1978, I, p. 322.
4 First published 1775, with six editions by 1788.
5 *Catalogue des livres, la plupart précieux, de la bibliothèque du feu M. Duquesnoy*, Paris, 1808, in S. Woolf, 'Les bases sociales du Consulat. Un mémoire d'Adrien Duquesnoy', *Revue d'Histoire Moderne et Contemporaine*, 31, 1984, pp. 605–6.
6 Woolf, 'Les bases sociales', p. 605.
7 J.-C. Perrot, *L'Age d'or de la statistique régionale française (an IV – 1804)*, Paris, 1977; S. Woolf, 'Towards the history of the origins of statistics: France, 1789–1815', in J.-C. Perrot and S. Woolf, *State and Statistics in France 1789–1815*, Chur – London – Paris – New York, 1984; M.-N. Bourguet, *Déchiffrer la France. La statistique départementale à l'époque napoléonienne*, Paris, 1988.
8 *Recueil des mémoires sur les établissements de l'humanité*, nos 1–38, Paris, ans VII–XII.
9 C.-F. Volney, *Questions de statistique à l'usage des voyageurs*, Paris, an III (*Oeuvres complètes*, Paris, 1864, pp. 748–52), quoted in F. Sofia, 'La

statistica come scienza politica e dell'amministrazione', in *L'Amministrazione nella storia moderna*, Milan, 1985, I, p. 580, and cf. pp. 628–9 n. 8, 607–9.
10 Woolf, 'Origins of statistics', pp. 106–8.
11 J. Godechot, *La Grande Nation. L'expansion révolutionnaire de la France dans le monde de 1789 à 1799*, Paris, 1983 (second edition), p. 64.
12 Godechot, *Grande Nation*, p. 16.
13 *Recueil des lettres circulaires, instructions, programmes, discours et autres actes publics du ministère de l'Intérieur* (16 vols, Paris, an VII – 1816), vol. 3 (an X), 21 floréal an VII, p. 38.
14 *Correspondance de l'Empereur Napoléon Ier* (28 vols, Paris, 1857–69), vol. 21 (1867), no. 16,824, 23 August 1810.
15 L. de Lanzac de Labourie, *Paris sous Napoléon*, Paris, t. 8, 1913, p. 234.
16 Archives Nationales, Paris, F² 1,367 to 1,377[12].
17 Godechot, *Grande Nation*, pp. 75–6.
18 M. Dunan, *Napoléon et l'Allemagne. Le système continental et les débuts du royaume de Bavière 1806–1810*, Paris, 1942, p. 273.
19 A. Dansette, *Napoléon, pensées politiques et sociales*, Paris, 1969, p. 398, quoted in F. Bluche, *Le Bonapartisme. Aux origines de la droite autoritaire (1800–1850)*, Paris, 1980, p. 16.
20 O. Connelly, *Napoleon's Satellite Kingdoms*, New York, 1965, pp. 333–5, ascribes the change in policy also to Napoleon's new belief that he could father an heir, following the birth of an illegitimate son to Countess Walewska (4 May 1810).

2 The tools of conquest

1 *Exposé de la situation de l'Empire, présenté au Corps législatif dans sa séance du 25 février 1813 par Son Excellence M. le comte de Montalivet, ministre de l'Intérieur*, Paris, 1813; *Atlas administratif de l'Empire français rédigé par ordre de S. E. M. le Duc de Feltre, ministre de la Guerre. Au Dépôt Général de la Guerre*, 1812 (partially republished, with explanatory notes, by F. de Dainville and J. Tulard, Geneva – Paris, 1973).
2 Cited in M. Dunan, *Napoléon et l'Allemagne. Le système continental et les débuts du royaume de Bavière 1806–1810*, Paris, 1942, p. 311.
3 *Correspondance de l'Empereur Napoléon Ier* (28 vols, Paris, 1857–69), vol. 22 (1867), no. 18,042, 17 August 1811.
4 Marbot, *Mémoires du général baron de Marbot* (2 vols, Paris, 1983), vol. 1, p. 296.
5 S. Woolf, *The Poor in Western Europe in the Eighteenth and Nineteenth Centuries*, London, 1986, pp. 102–3.
6 Ch. Schmidt, *Le Grand-Duché de Berg (1806–1813). Etude sur la domination française en Allemagne sous Napoléon Ier*, Paris, 1905, p. 409.
7 M. Dunan, 'Napoléon et le système continental en 1810', *Revue d'Histoire Diplomatique*, January–April 1946, p. 1.
8 Schmidt, *Grand-Duché de Berg*, p. 287 n.
9 P. Verhaegen, *La Belgique sous la domination française* (5 vols, Bruxelles, 1923–9), vol. 4 (1929), p. 14.
10 Of the 930 members appointed to the Legislative body between 1800 and 1813, 88 were Italians, 55 Belgians and Luxembourgeois, 26 Dutch, 23

Germans, 4 Swiss and 7 Savoyards. Of the 121 new members of the Senate nominated between Year IV and 1813, there were 18 Italians, 4 Belgians, 3 Germans and 6 Dutch. J.-L. Halperin, 'Corps Législatif' and 'Sénat', in J. Tulard (ed.), *Dictionnaire Napoléon*, Paris, 1987.

11 Lebrun insisted, as governor-general of the Ligurian departments, that as 'sole repository' of the Emperor's authority, all ministers – especially the police – had to correspond with him, not directly with officials in the departments: *Opinions, rapports et choix d'écrits politiques de Charles François Lebrun, duc de Plaisance*, Paris, 1829, p. 106 n. 1. Tournon, prefect of Rome, expressed enormous relief when the Roman Consulta was wound up at the end of 1810, because of its interference in his relations with ministers at Paris: J. Moulard, *Le Comte Camille de Tournon. 2. Préfet de Rome 1809–1814*, Paris, 1929, p. 101.

12 J. Bourdon, 'L'Administration militaire sous Napoléon 1er', *Revue des Etudes Napoléoniennes*, 1917; F. Monnier, 'Intendance des armées' and 'Inspection aux revues', *Dictionnaire Napoléon*, cit.

13 *Correspondance*, vol. 14 (1863), no. 12,178, 26 March 1807.

14 *Correspondance*, vol. 17 (1865), no. 13,900, 16 May 1808.

15 Marbot, *Mémoires*, vol. 2, p. 185.

16 *Correspondance*, vol. 17 (1865), no. 13,923, 18 June 1808.

17 G. Six, *Les Généraux de la Révolution et de l'Empire*, Paris, 1948, p. 301; the careers of individual generals are taken from G. Six, *Dictionnaire biographique des généraux et amiraux de la Révolution et de l'Empire (1792–1814)*, Paris, 1934.

18 J. Courvoisier, *Le Maréchal Berthier et sa principauté de Neuchâtel (1806–1814)*, Neuchâtel, 1959, p. 34.

19 E. Las Cases, *Mémorial de Sainte-Hélène*, cited in *Dictionnaire Napoléon*, p. 136.

20 Six, *Les Généraux*, pp. 298–301.

21 *Correspondance*, vol. 12 (1863), no. 9951, 9 March 1806, cited in Courvoisier, *Le Maréchal Berthier*, pp. 30–1.

22 Marbot, *Mémoires*, vol. 2, pp. 45–7, 81–3, 103, 149–50.

23 All figures relating to the diplomatic corps come from Ch. Prettre, 'Le Consulat et le premier Empire', in *Les Affaires Etrangères et le Corps Diplomatique Français*, 2 vols, Paris, 1984, and A. E. Whitcomb, *Napoleon's Diplomatic Service*, Durham, 1979.

24 Ch. Prettre, 'Le Consulat et le premier Empire', vol. 1, p. 418.

25 F. R. de Chateaubriand, *Mémoires d'Outre-Tombe*, Paris, 1964, pp. 94, 716.

26 Prettre, 'Le Consulat', p. 373.

27 Prettre, 'Le Consulat', p. 472.

28 Prettre, 'Le Consulat', p. 461.

29 Details of careers have been assembled from a variety of sources, primarily *Dictionnaire biographique des Français*; R. Bargeton, P. Bougard, B. Le Clère and P.-F. Pinaud, *Les Préfets du 11 ventôse an VIII au 4 septembre 1870*, Paris, 1981; Schmidt, *Grand-Duché de Berg*; Courvoisier, *Le Maréchal Berthier*; *Dictionnaire Napoléon*; Six, *Dictionnaire biographique des généraux*.

30 J. Rambaud, *Naples sous Joseph Bonaparte 1806–1808*, Paris, 1911, p. 276.

31 M. Dunan, *Napoléon et l'Allemagne. Le système continental et les débuts du royaume de l'Allemagne 1806–1810*, Paris, 1942, pp. 395–6.

32 Ch. Durand, 'L'Emploi des conseillers d'état et des maîtres de requête en dehors du Conseil', *Annales de la Faculté de Droit, Université d'Aix*, n. 5, 45, 1952, pp. 5–142.

33 A. E. Whitcomb, 'Napoleon's prefects', *American Historical Review*, 79, 1974, pp. 1,089–118. All figures relating to the entire prefectoral corps come from this article. Those for the annexed departments have been elaborated by myself from Bargeton *et al.*, *Les Préfets*, from which I have drawn most biographical details.

34 One Italian department, Tanaro, was suppressed in 1805, so that the annexed departments numbered 43 of the total 130 in 1812.

35 The figures have been calculated on the basis of all appointments of prefects (excluding those who never took office). Hence some prefects are counted more than once, for a total 112 tenures of office (by 98 men).

36 Other examples are: A. de Sauzay (b. 1745), prefect of Mont-Blanc 1800–2, J. Bexon d'Ormschwiller (b. 1738), prefect of Sarre 1800–3, F. M. J. de Viry (b. 1736), prefect of Lys 1800–4, or F. Becaus-Ferrand (b. 1726), prefect of Meuse-Inférieure 1800–2.

37 Isnard was sent to the kingdom of Italy, Thoron-Montirat and Pommard to Naples, and Le Couteux and Doäzen to Italy in 1806–7 to report on trading prospects, Bardel to Spain and Portugal in 1807, Camille Périer to Germany in 1807–8, Héron de Villefosse to Berg and various German states in 1807–9 to examine the metal mines, Mottet de Gérando to the Frankfurt and Leipzig fairs in 1810.

3 The practices of conquest: administrative integration

1 *Recueil des lettres circulaires, instructions, programmes, discours et autres actes publics du ministère de l'Intérieur* (16 vols, Paris, an VII – 1816), vol. 3, 16 ventôse an IX (7 March 1801).

2 J. Courvoisier, *Le Maréchal Berthier et sa principauté de Neuchâtel (1806–1814)*, Neuchâtel, 1959, p. 149.

3 M.-N. Bourguet, *Déchiffrer la France. La statistique départementale à l'époque napoléonienne*, Paris, 1988.

4 C. J. Bonnin, *Principes d'administration publique*, Paris, 1812 (third edition), vol. 1, p. 167, quoted in F. Sofia, *Una Scienza per l'amministrazione. Statistica e pubblici apparati tra età rivoluzionaria e restaurazione*, Rome, 1988, vol. 1, pp. 104, 247.

5 J. M. de Gérando, *Programme du cours de droit public positif et administratif, à la faculté de droit de Paris, pour l'année 1819–1820*, Paris, 1819, pp. 25–6, quoted in Sofia, *Una Scienza*, pp. 110–11.

6 Ch. Schmidt, *Le Grand-Duché de Berg (1806–1813). Etude sur la domination française en Allemagne sous Napoléon Ier*, Paris, 1905, p. 484.

7 Schmidt, *Grand-Duché de Berg*, pp. 310–13; Archives Nationales, Paris, F[14] 1,058, 1,094.

8 A. de Plancy, *Souvenirs*, Paris, 1904, p. 29.

9 Bibliographies of the statistical memoirs are in: J. C. Perrot, *L'Age d'or de la statistique régionale française (an IV – 1804)*, Paris, 1977, pp. 71–235,

and Bourguet, *Déchiffrer la France*, pp. 373–7. Piedmont merited only a memoir covering all six departments, on its annexation in 1802.

10 S. Schama, *Patriots and Liberators. Revolution in the Netherlands 1780–1813*, London – New York, 1977, p. 618.

11 Archivo de la Corona de Aragón, Barcelona, Guerra de la Independencia, Hacienda, Caixa 1, 'Mémoire statistique, historique et administratif présentant le tableau de l'administration du département des Bouches de l'Ebre avant la guerre, les changemens qu'elle a éprouvés depuis la guerre et sa situation au 1 janvier 1813'.

12 C. F. Lebrun, *Opinions, rapports et choix d'écrits politiques de Charles François Lebrun, duc de Plaisance*, Paris, 1829, p. 102, n. 1: 'Smuggling would not stop me, as I would place thirty brigades in the Alps which would be enough to check the counterband of tobacco. Salt smuggling cannot be stopped' (Napoleon to Lebrun, 11 prairial year XIII).

13 M. G. Broers, 'The restoration of order in Napoleonic Piedmont, 1797–1814', unpublished D.Phil. thesis, Oxford, 1986, pp. 310–19 (quotation p. 319).

14 W. C. Quigley, 'The public administration of the first kingdom of Italy 1805–1814', unpublished Ph.D. thesis, Harvard, 1938, p. 906.

15 Schama, *Patriots*, p. 621.

16 S. Woolf, 'Towards the history of the origins of statistics: France, 1789–1915', in J.-C. Perrot and S. Woolf, *State and Statistics in France 1789–1815*, Chur – London – Paris – New York, 1984, p. 115.

17 Schmidt, *Grand-Duché de Berg*, p. 485.

18 P. E. A. du Casse (ed.), *Mémoires et correspondance politique et militaire du roi Joseph*, vol. 2, Paris, 1855, p. 84.

19 Schama, *Patriots*, p. 458.

20 L. Antonielli, *I Prefetti dell'Italia napoleonica. Repubblica e Regno d'Italia*, Bologna, 1983, pp. 71–2, 99–101, 266, 307–9.

21 Broers, 'Restoration of order', p. 175.

22 Schmidt, *Grand-Duché de Berg*, pp. 241–2; J. A. Davis, 'Naples during the French "decennio". A problem unresolved?', in *Villes et territoires pendant la période napoléonienne (France et Italie)*, Rome, 1987, p. 342.

23 N. P. Desvernois, *Mémoires*, Paris, 1898, pp. 420–1.

24 Stendhal, *Oeuvres intimes*, vol. 2, Paris, 1982, p. 507.

25 S. J. Woolf, 'Les bases sociales du Consulat. Un mémoire d'Adrien Duquesnoy', *Revue d'Histoire Moderne et Contemporaine*, 31, 1984, p. 610.

26 M. Molé, *Souvenirs d'un témoin de la Révolution et de l'Empire (1791–1803)*, Geneva, 1943, p. 371.

27 Antonielli, *Prefetti*, pp. 236–7.

28 Woolf, 'Les bases sociales', p. 601.

29 Molé, *Souvenirs*, p. 376.

30 J. Vidalenc, 'Les "départements hanséatiques" et l'administration napoléonienne', *Francia*, 1, 1973, p. 427. The ideal and the practice did not necessarily coincide: the Roman Consulta, whose task was to introduce the new regime by 1 January 1810, survived until the end of 1810. But its presence was resented by the prefect Tournon as interfering with the proper hierarchical lines of authority: J. Moulard, *Le Comte Camille de Tournon*, vol. 2, Rome, 1929, p. 101; C. Nardi, *Napoleone e Roma. La*

politica della Consulta Romana, Rome, 1989.

31 Antonielli, *Prefetti*, 53–7; Sofia, *Una Scienza*, 163–71.
32 Schama, *Patriots*, pp. 363–9, 380, 458, 544–5.
33 J. Rambaud, *Naples sous Joseph Bonaparte 1806–1808*, Paris, 1911, p. 312.
34 *Correspondance de l'Empereur Napoléon Ier* (28 vols, Paris, 1857–69), vol. 16 (1864), no. 13,315, 31 October 1807; M. Dunan, *Napoléon et l'Allemagne. Le système continental et les débuts du royaume d'Allemagne 1806–1810*, Paris, 1942, p. 109.
35 *Correspondance*, vol. 16 (1864), no. 13,357, 13 November 1807.
36 Schmidt, *Grand-Duché de Berg*, pp. 220–4.
37 Schmidt, *Grand-Duché de Berg*, p. 215. Lafolie, who served as a functionary in the kingdom of Italy from 1805 to 1814, was convinced that the imposition of the French codes without adaptation was a failure, as the Italian judges interpreted their application: C. Lafolie, *Mémoires sur la cour du prince Eugène et sur le royaume d'Italie*, Paris, 1824, p. 63.
38 L. Bergeron and G. Chaussinand-Nogaret, *Les 'masses de granit'. Cent mille notables du Premier Empire*, Paris, 1979, have analysed the lists of the *grands notables*; see also the dictionary of departmental notables, edited by L. Bergeron and G. Chaussinand-Nogaret, *Grands Notables du Premier Empire*, Paris, 1978–, 17 volumes published by 1988.
39 Fouché's enquiry was in April 1809, that of Savary in 1811. But only relatively few replies by the prefects were sent, such as Archives Nationales, Paris, F^7 3,670 (Doire), F^7 3,682 (Marengo), F^7 3,685 (Pô).
40 Antonielli, *Prefetti*, p. 448, n. 18.
41 Casse, *Mémoires . . . du roi Joseph*, vol. 2, pp. 86–7.
42 Broers, 'Restoration of order', p. 381.
43 Quigley, 'Public administration', pp. 328–33, 703.
44 F. Bodmann, *Annuaire statistique du départment du Mont-Tonnerre pour l'an 1808*, Mayence, n.d.; *Annuaire du département du Léman pour l'année 1811*, Geneva and Paris, 1811; *Almanach du départment de l'Escaut pour l'année 1811*, Gand, n.d.; *Calendario politico-statistico del dipartimento dell'Arno*, Florence, n.d.
45 C. Capra, 'Il Settecento', in D. Sella and C. Capra, *Il Ducato di Milano dal 1535 al 1796*, Turin, 1984, p. 413; H. Kiesel and P. Münch, *Gesellschaft und Literatur im 18 Jahrhundert*, Munich, 1977, p. 90.
46 Antonielli, *Prefetti*, p. 361, n. 53.
47 Antonielli, *Prefetti*, pp. 302–3.
48 Schmidt, *Grand-Duché de Berg*, p. 142, n. 2.
49 Broers, 'Restoration of order', p. 380.
50 S. J. Woolf, 'Frontiere entro la frontiera: il Piemonte sotto il governo napoleonico', in C. Ossola, C. Raffestin and M. Ricciardi (eds), *La Frontiera da stato a nazione. Il caso Piemonte*, Rome, 1987.
51 C. Zaghi (ed.), *I Carteggi di Francesco Melzi d'Eril duca di Lodi* (9 vols, Milan, 1958–66), vol. 4, p. 418, quoted in Antonielli, *Prefetti*, p. 182.
52 Antonielli, *Prefetti*, p. 83.
53 K. G. Farber, 'Die Rheinländer unter Napoleon', *Francia*, 1 (1973), p. 385.
54 M. Ardit Lucas, *Rivolución liberal y rivuelta campesina. Un ensayo sobre la disintegración del régimen feudal en el País Valenciano (1793–1840)*,

Barcelona, 1977, pp. 202–7; L.-G. Suchet, *Mémoires* . . . *sur ses campagnes en Espagne*, Paris, 1828, vol. 2, pp. 283–301.
55 Schmidt, *Grand-Duché de Berg*, p. 145.
56 H. C. F. Barthélemy, *Souvenirs d'un ancien préfet 1787–1848*, Paris, 1885, p. 76.
57 Archives Nationales, Paris, AF IV. 1710B (December 1807), cited in Quigley, 'Public administration', pp. 978–85.
58 Schama, *Patriots*, p. 529.
59 Antonielli, *Prefetti*, p. 168.
60 A. Beugnot (ed.), *Mémoires du comte Beugnot (1783–1815)*, Paris, 1866, vol. 1, p. 321.
61 H. Berding, *Napoleonische Herrschafts- und Gesellschaftspolitik im Königreich Westfalen 1807–1813*, Göttingen, 1973, p. 117, n. 12.
62 Lebrun, *Opinions* . . . *de* . . . *Lebrun*, p. 101, n. 1.
63 Zaghi, *I Carteggi di Francesco Melzi*, vol. 3, pp. 241–2.
64 Rambaud, *Naples sous Joseph*, p. 98; Casse, *Mémoires* . . . *du roi Joseph*, vol. 2, p. 89.
65 Dunan, *Napoléon et l'Allemagne*, p. 121.
66 Archivo de la Corona de Aragón, Barcelona, Guerra de la Independencia, Hacienda, Caixa 1, 'Mémoire statistique', ch. 5.
67 Marbot, *Mémoires du général baron de Marbot* (2 vols, Paris, 1983), vol. 2, pp. 264–8.
68 Rambaud, *Naples sous Joseph*, p. 313, n. 5.
69 Schmidt, *Grand-Duché de Berg*, p. 485.
70 Casse, *Mémoires* . . . *du roi Joseph*, vol. 2, p. 87.
71 Lebrun, *Opinions* . . . *de* . . . *Lebrun*, p. 105.
72 P. Vilar, 'Quelques aspects de l'occupation et de la résistance en Espagne en 1794 et au temps de Napoléon', in *Occupants occupés 1792–1815*, Brussels, 1969, pp. 250–1.
73 Rambaud, *Naples sous Joseph*, p. 218.
74 Schama, *Patriots*, p. 700, n. 198.
75 Rambaud, *Naples sous Joseph*, p. 376.
76 Schmidt, *Grand-Duché de Berg*, p. 100; Stendhal, *Oeuvres intimes*, p. 487.
77 Antonielli, *Prefetti*, p. 284.
78 Schmidt, *Grand-Duché de Berg*, p. 284.
79 Rambaud, *Naples sous Joseph*, p. 96; Barthélemy, *Souvenirs*, pp. 27–8; D. A. P. Thiébault, *Mémoires*, Paris, 1962, p. 277.
80 Schama, *Patriots*, p. 399; Casse, *Mémoires* . . . *du roi Joseph*, vol. 2, p. 86.
81 Schmidt, *Grand-Duché de Berg*, p. 236.
82 Schmidt, *Grand-Duché de Berg*, pp. 192–5.
83 Barthélemy, *Souvenirs*, p. 76; Antonielli, *Prefetti*, p. 168.
84 Courvoisier, *Maréchal Berthier*, p. 122; Ardit Lucas, *Rivolución liberal*, p. 207.
85 Schama, *Patriots*, p. 456.
86 F. R. Chateaubriand, *Mémoires d'Outre-Tombe*, Paris, 1964, pp. 710–13; Antonielli, *Prefetti*, p. 393, n. 40; P. Verhaegen, *La Belgique sous la domination française* (5 vols, Bruxelles, 1923–9), vol. 4 (1929), pp. 43–6.
87 Dunan, *Napoléon et l'Allemagne*, p. 100.

88 *Correspondance*, vol. 16 (1864), no. 13,361, 15 November 1807.
89 Schmidt, *Grand-Duché de Berg*, p. 485; cf. S. Woolf, 'French civilization and ethnicity in the Napoleonic empire', *Past and Present*, 124, 1989, pp. 96–106.
90 Schmidt, *Grand-Duché de Berg*, p. 206.
91 Berding, *Napoleonische Herrschaftspolitik*, p. 54.
92 *Mémoires et correspondance du roi Jérôme et de la reine Catherine* (6 vols, Paris, 1861–5), vol. 3, p. 116, 17 December 1807, cited in Berding, *Napoleonische Herrschaftspolitik*, p. 28.
93 *Correspondance*, vol. 21 (1867), no. 16,894, 11 November 1810.
94 Berding, *Napoleonische Herrschaftspolitik*, pp. 46–8, 127–8, and passim.
95 Antonielli, *Prefetti*, p. 475.
96 Suchet, *Mémoires*, vol. 1, pp. 276–318.

4 The practices of conquest: exploitation

1 Prefect of Dordogne to C. A. Costaz, 7 October 1812, in S. Woolf, 'Contribution à l'histoire des origines de la statistique: France, 1789–1815', in *La Statistique en France à l'époque napoléonienne*, Brussels, 1981, p. 123.
2 L. Bergeron, *Banquiers, négociants et manufacturiers parisiens. Du Directoire à l'Empire*, Lille – Paris, 1975, vol. 2, p. 796, n. 1.
3 J.-A.-C. Chaptal, *Essai sur le perfectionnement des arts chimiques en France*, Paris, Year VIII (1800), quoted in Dunan, *Napoléon et l'Allemagne. Le système continental et les débuts du Royaume de Bavière 1806–1810*, Paris, 1942, p. 323.
4 J. B. Harrison, 'The Continental system in Italy as revealed by American commerce', Ph.D. thesis, Wisconsin, 1937, p. 41.
5 S. Schama, *Patriots, and Liberators. Revolution in the Netherlands 1780–1813*, London – New York, 1977, p. 687, n. 101.
6 Dunan, *Napoléon et l'Allemagne*, p. 311.
7 E. Olivé y Serret, 'Pirates i comerciants. Les relacions d'un corsari francès amb comerciants catalans (1807–1811)', *Ricerques*, 17 (1985).
8 J.-A.-C. Chaptal, *Mes souvenirs sur Napoléon*, Paris, 1893, p. 275.
9 G. Ellis, *Napoleon's Continental Blockade. The case of Alsace*, Oxford, 1981, pp. 118–19.
10 Ellis, *Napoleon's Continental Blockade*, pp. 136, n. 70, 288–9.
11 Ellis, *Napoleon's Continental Blockade*, pp. 285–6.
12 S. Chassagne, 'Aspects des phénomènes d'industrialisation et de désindustrialisation dans les campagnes françaises au XIXe siècle', *Revue du Nord*, 63, 1981; L. Bergeron, 'Remarques sur les conditions du développement industriel en Europe occidentale à l'époque napoléonienne', *Francia*, 1, 1973, p. 552, n. 31; Bergeron, *Banquiers*, vol. 2, ch. 9.
13 Bergeron, *Banquiers*, vol. 2, p. 758.
14 Ellis, *Napoleon's Continental Blockade*, p. 116 and n. 24.
15 Bergeron, *Banquiers*, vol. 2, p. 770.
16 Bergeron, *Banquiers*, vol. 2, ch. 9; M. Lévy-Leboyer, *Les Banques européennes et l'industrialisation internationale dans la première moitié du XIXe siècle*, Paris, 1964, p. 55; B. Mitchell, *European Historical Statistics*, London, 1975, p. 427; P. Butel, 'Crise et mutation de l'activité économi-

que à Bordeaux sous le Consulat et l'Empire', *Revue d'Histoire Moderne et Contemporaine*, 17, 1970, pp. 540–58.

17 Ellis, *Napoleon's Continental Blockade*, p. 143.

18 Dunan, *Napoléon et l'Allemagne*, pp. 326–39.

19 Ch. Schmidt, *Le Grand-Duché de Berg (1806–1813). Etude sur la domination française en Allemagne sous Napoléon Ier*, Paris, 1905, pp. 385, 492–7.

20 Dunan, *Napoléon et l'Allemagne*, p. 356.

21 M. Brunet, *Le Roussillon. Une société contre l'Etat 1780–1820*, Toulouse, 1986, p. 104.

22 G. Assereto, 'La fine dell'antico regime: la dominazione napoleonica a Prato', in E. Fasano Guarini (ed.), *Prato storia di una città. 2. Un microcosmo in movimento (1494–1815)*, Prato – Florence, 1986, pp. 802–3.

23 Harrison, 'Continental system', p. 104.

24 Harrison, 'Continental system', p. 184.

25 Schmidt, *Grand-Duché de Berg*, p. 344 and n.

26 S. Marzagalli, *Amburgo nell'età napoleonica: una città mercantile di fronte ai problemi del blocco e dell'occupazione*, tesi di laurea, Milan University, Faculty of Letters, 1987–8, pp. 177–8.

27 Schmidt, *Grand-Duché de Berg*, p. 497.

28 R. Dufraisse, 'La contrebande dans les départements réunis de la rive gauche du Rhin à l'époque napoléonienne', *Francia*, 1, 1973, p. 515; Brunet, *Le Roussillon*, p. 326; Marzagalli, *Amburgo*, pp. 166–70.

29 Marzagalli, *Amburgo*, pp. 180–1; Brunet, *Le Roussillon*, pp. 166–7.

30 Marzagalli, *Amburgo*, p. 161; Dufraisse, 'La contrebande', pp. 528–9; Harrison, 'Continental system', p. 85.

31 C. Schmidt, 'Sismondi et le blocus continental', *Revue Historique*, 115, 1914, pp. 89–91.

32 S. Woolf, 'L'impact de l'occupation française sur l'économie italienne', *Revue Economique*, 40, 1989, p. 1,115.

33 Bergeron, *Banquiers*, vol. 2, p. 652.

34 Marzagalli, *Amburgo*, p. 168.

35 A. Corvisier, *L'Armée française de la fin du XVIIe siècle au ministère de Choiseul: le soldat*, Paris, 1964; S. F. Scott, *The Response of the Royal Army to the French Revolution: the role and development of the line army 1787–93*, Oxford, 1978.

36 Scott, *The Response*, pp. 106, 155, 177; J. A. Lynn, *The Bayonets of the Republic. Motivation and Tactics in the Army of Revolutionary France, 1791–94*, Urbana – Chicago, 1984, p. 72.

37 *Discours prononcé par Daru, orateur du Tribunat, sur la conscription militaire. Séance du 28 floréal an 10. Corps législatif*, pp. 39–40, quoted in I. Woloch, 'Napoleonic conscription: state power and civil society', *Past and Present*, 111 (1986), p. 105, and *passim* for an excellent summary of conscription procedures.

38 R. Darquenne, *La Conscription dans le département de Jemappes (1798–1813)*, Mons, 1970, pp. 184–5.

39 The most thorough study of Hargenvilliers' tables is that of Darquenne, *La Conscription*, pp. 184–5, especially tables 8 and 11.

40 A. Forrest, 'Conscription and crime in rural France during the Directory

and Consulate', in G. Lewis and C. Lucas (eds), *Beyond the Terror: Essays in French Regional and Social History*, Cambridge, 1983; Forrest, 'Le recrutement, les désertions et l'Etat napoléonien', paper delivered at the Convegno Internazionale sull'Armata Napoleonica, Portoferraio, Elba, 17–20 September 1986.

41 A. de Caumont, duc de la Force, *L'Architrésorier Lebrun, gouverneur de la Hollande 1810–1813*, Paris, 1907, p. 204; D. van Hogendorp, *Mémoires*, The Hague, 1887, p. 278.

42 *Correspondance de l'Empereur Napoléon Ier* (28 vols, Paris, 1857–69), vol. 12 (1863), no. 10,009, 23 March 1806.

43 J. A. Davis, 'The Neapolitan army during the *decennio francese*', *Rivista Italiana di Studi Napoleonici*, 25, 1988, pp. 174–5.

44 O. Connelly, *Napoleon's Satellite Kingdoms*, New York, 1965, pp. 165–7; Schmidt, *Grand-Duché de Berg*, pp. 58–9; J. Corvoisier, *Le Maréchal Berthier et sa principauté de Neuchâtel (1806–1814)*, Neuchâtel, 1959, pp. 282–4; van Hogendorp, *Mémoires*, pp. 181–3, 219.

45 Noguès, *Mémoires du général Noguès (1777–1853) sur les guerres de l'Empire*, Paris, 1922, p. 218.

46 F.-J. Jacquin, *Carnet de route d'un grognard de la Révolution et de l'Empire*, Paris, 1960, pp. 54–5.

47 Archivo de la Corona de Aragón, Barcelona, Guerra de la Independencia, Hacienda, Caixa 1, 'Mémoire statistique . . . 1 janvier 1813'.

48 M. Molé, *Souvenirs d'un témoin de la Révolution et de l'Empire (1791–1803)*, Geneva, 1943, p. 144.

49 J.-P. Bertaud, 'Napoleon's officers', *Past and Present*, 112, 1986, p. 94.

50 P. Crouzet, *Discours sur l'honneur prononcé à la distribution des prix du Prytanée militaire français, le 14 août 1806*, Paris, 1806.

51 Crouzet, *Discours sur l'honneur*, pp. 4, 11.

52 Courvoisier, *Maréchal Berthier*, p. 282.

53 Quoted in J. Tulard, *Le Mythe de Napoléon*, Paris, 1971, p. 37.

54 Jacquin, *Carnet de route*.

55 Noguès, *Mémoires*, pp. 215–16.

56 Noguès, *Mémoires*, p. 225; Jacquin, *Carnet de route*, pp. 73–5.

57 G. Six, *Dictionnaire biographique des généraux et amiraux français de la Révolution et de l'Empire (1792–1814)*, Paris, 1934; Darquenne, *La Conscription*, tables 8 and 11; W. Barberis, *Le Armi del principe. La tradizione militare sabauda*, Turin, 1988, p. 251.

58 C. F. Lebrun, *Opinions, rapports et choix d'écrits politiques de Charles François Lebrun, duc de Plaisance*, Paris, 1829, p. 105 and n.

59 Dunan, *Napoléon et l'Allemagne*, p. 395.

60 Darquenne, *La Conscription*, pp. 107–8, 176, 186, table 21; J. Garnier, 'Campagne de Russie (1812)', in *Dictionnaire Napoléon*, pp. 355–8. The figures quoted for the Grande Armée in its invasion of Russia vary according to the geographical point of assembly where their numbers were estimated.

61 J. Gabillard, 'Le financement des guerres napoléoniennes et la conjoncture du premier Empire', *Revue Economique*, 4, 1953, pp. 548–72.

62 P. E. A. du Casse (ed.), *Mémoires et correspondance politique et militaire du roi Joseph*, vol. 2, Paris, 1855, pp. 81–3, 105–6; Davis, 'The

Neapolitan army', pp. 165–6; H. Berding, *Napoleonische Herrschafts- und Gesellschaftspolitik im Königreich Westfalen 1807–1813*, Göttingen, 1973, pp. 25–6, 28–9; Connelly, *Napoleon's Satellite Kingdoms*, p. 143.

63 B. Abrahamsson, *Military Professionalization and Political Power*, Stockholm, 1971; S. Andreski, *Military Organization and Society*, London, 1968.

64 H. C. F. Barthélemy, *Souvenirs d'un ancien préfet 1787–1848*, Paris, 1885, pp. 83–92.

65 L. Bergeron and G. Chaussinand-Nogaret, *Les 'Masses de granit'. Cent mille notables du Premier Empire*, Paris, 1979; R. Forster, 'The French Revolution and the "new" elite, 1800–1880', in J. Pelensky (ed.), *The American and European Revolutions Reconsidered, 1776–1848*, Iowa, 1980.

66 L. Bergeron, *L'Épisode napoléonienne. Aspects intérieurs 1799–1815*, Paris, 1972, p. 140; L. Bergeron, 'La place des gens d'affaires dans les listes de notables du premier Empire, d'après les exemples du Piémont et de la Ligurie', *Annuario dell'Istituto Storico Italiano per l'Età Moderna e Contemporanea*, 23–4, 1971–2, pp. 316–17; C. Capra, 'Nobili, notabili, élites: dal modello francese al caso italiano', *Quaderni Storici*, 37, 1978, p. 30.

67 J. Tulard, *Napoléon et la noblesse d'Empire*, Paris, 1986, p. 40.

68 Tulard, *Napoléon et la noblesse*, pp. 33–50. Officers of the Legion received 1,000 francs, and ordinary Legionaries 250 francs, when the income of a small farm above the subsistence level might be 500 francs: Bergeron and Chaussinand-Nogaret, '*Masses de granit*', p. 51.

69 Woloch, 'Napoleonic conscription', pp. 231–46, 314–15, 320, 336–7.

70 Bertaud, 'Napoleon's officers'; Berding, *Napoleonische Herrschaftspolitik*, pp. 66, 151; Woloch, 'Napoleonic conscription', p. 261 n. 51.

71 P. H. Earl Stanhope, *Notes of Conversations with the Duke of Wellington, 1831–1851*, London, 1888, p. 81, quoted in M. Howard, *War in European History*, Oxford, 1976, p. 82.

72 van Hogendorp, *Mémoires*, pp. 198–9.

73 Tulard, *Napoléon et la noblesse*, p. 89.

74 Tulard, *Napoléon et la noblesse*, p. 26 n. 8; Bertaud, 'Napoleon's officers', pp. 109–11.

75 J. Tulard, 'Problèmes sociaux de la France napoléonienne', *Revue d'Histoire Moderne et Contemporaine*, 17, 1970, p. 656.

76 Tulard, *Napoléon et la noblesse*, pp. 148–50.

77 S. Woolf, *The Poor in Western Europe in the Eighteenth and Nineteenth Centuries*, London, 1986, pp. 91, 138; S. Woolf, 'The Société de Charité Maternelle', in C. Jones and J. Barry (eds), *Medicine and Charity Before the Welfare State*; Tulard, *Napoléon et la noblesse*, pp. 157–9.

78 Tulard, *Napoléon et la noblesse*; J. Zieseniss, 'Noblesse d'Empire', in *Dictionnaire Napoléon*, pp. 1,243–50; Capra, 'Nobili, notabili', pp. 30–2.

79 6 May 1808, quoted in Zieseniss, 'Noblesse d'Empire', p. 1249.

80 van Hogendorp, *Mémoires*, pp. 198–9.

81 Fain, *Mémoires*, Paris, 1908, pp. 92, 95, quoted in Berding, *Napoleonische Herrschaft*, pp. 65–6, 133 n. 38; see also the tables in Berding, pp. 48–51; and H. Berding, 'Les dotations impériales dans

le royaume de Westphalie', *Revue de l'Institut Napoléon*, 192, 1976, pp. 91–101.

82 Tulard, *Napoléon et la noblesse*, pp. 111–13.

5 Responses to conquest

1 For a fuller discussion of the relationship between the stages of civilisation and the structures of society, see S. Woolf, 'French civilization and ethnicity in the Napoleonic Empire', *Past and Present*, 124, 1989, pp. 96–106.

2 P. E. A. du Casse (ed.), *Mémoires et correspondance politique et militaire du roi Joseph*, vol. 2, Paris, 1855, p. 89.

3 M. Artola Gallego, *Los Afrancesados*, Madrid, 1976, p. 65.

4 W. Barberis, *Le Armi del Principe. Le tradizione militare sabauda*, Turin, 1988, p. 243; R. Pilati, *La Nunziatella. L'organizzazione di un'accademia militare 1787–1987*, Naples, 1987, pp. 74–99; R. Pasta, *Scienza politica e rivoluzione. L'opera di Giovanni Fabbroni (1752–1822) intellettuale e funzionario in servizio dei Lorena*, Florence, 1989, pp. 535–79.

5 S. Schama, *Patriots and Liberators. Revolution in the Netherlands 1780–1813*, London – New York, 1977, pp. 497–513, 618–20; Schama, 'Schools and politics in the Netherlands, 1796-1814', *Historical Journal*, 13, 1970, pp. 589–610.

6 C. Durand, *Les Auditeurs au Conseil d'Etat de 1803 à 1814*, Aix, 1958, p. 77 n. 45.

7 J. Nicolas, 'Le ralliement des notables à l'Empire dans le département du Mont-Blanc', *Revue d'Histoire Moderne et Contemporaine*, 19, 1972, p. 122 n. 4.

8 J. P. Filippini, 'Ralliement et opposition des notables toscans à l'Empire français', *Annuario dell'Istituto Storico Italiano per l'Età Moderna e Contemporanea*, 23–4, 1971–2, p. 347 n. 49.

9 Nicolas, 'Le ralliement', p. 107 n. 2.

10 R. Dufraisse, 'Les notables de la rive gauche du Rhin à l'époque napoléonienne', *Revue d'Histoire Moderne et Contemporaine*, 17, 1970, p. 773.

11 Nicolas, 'Le ralliement', p. 126.

12 J. Godechot, *La Grande Nation. L'expansion révolutionnaire de la France dans le monde de 1789 à 1799*, Paris, 1983 (second edition), pp. 443–6; L. Bergeron, *Banquiers, négociants et manufacturiers parisiens. Du directoire à l'Empire*, Lille – Paris, 1975, vol. 1, pp. 395–427.

13 L. Carle, *L'Identité cachée. Paysans propriétaires dans l'Alta Langa aux XVIIe – XIXe siècles*, Paris, 1989.

14 *Mémoires du comte de Rambuteau*, Paris, 1905, pp. 110–11.

15 I. Tognarini, 'Siderurgia e "guerra marittima": iniziative e insuccessi di uno dei "meilleurs mécaniciens de France" all'isola d'Elba (1803–1810)', in I. Tognarini (ed.), *La Toscana nell'età rivoluzionaria e napoleonica*, Naples, 1985, pp. 307–20; Archives Nationales, Paris, F^{12}1612; R. Taiani, 'L'Acqua e la sua anima: il contributo della scienza chimica allo sfruttamento delle fonti di acqua minerale nella prima metà del XIX secolo', in course of publication in *Nuncius*, 2, 1991.

16 See above, pp. 147, 149.

17 S. Woolf, 'Frontiere entro la frontiera: il Piemonte sotto il governo napoleonico', in C. Ossola, C. Raffestin and M. Ricciardi (eds), *La*

Frontiera da stato a nazione. Il caso Piemonte, Rome, 1987, pp. 171–81.
18 M. Samland, 'La riforma francese della contribuzione fondiaria ed i suoi effetti in Toscana e nei paesi del Reno', EUI unpublished paper, 1989.
19 Dufraisse, 'Les notables', p. 756.
20 *Les Dix commandements du bourgeois et du paysan* (1800), in M. Dunan, *Napoléon et l'Allemagne. Le système continental et les débuts du royaume de Bavière 1806–1810*, Paris, 1942, pp. 112–13.
21 Ch. Schmidt, *Le Grand-Duché de Berg (1806–1813). Etude sur la domination française en Allemagne sous Napoléon Ier*, Paris, 1905, p. 314.
22 W. Schieder and A. Kube, *Säkularisation und Mediatisierung. Die Veräusserung der Nationalgüter im Rhein-Mosel-Department 1803–1813*, Boppard am Rhein, 1987, pp. 34–5; R. Dufraisse, 'Diskussion', in E. Weis and E. Müller-Luckner (eds), *Reformen im rheinbündischen Deutschland*, Munich, 1984, pp. 47–8; W. C. Quigley, 'The public administration of the first kingdom of Italy 1805–1814', unpublished Ph.D. thesis, Harvard, 1938, pp. 386–7; M. Senkowska-Gluck, 'La propriété foncière en Pologne (1789–1815)', *Annales Historiques de la Révolution Française*, 53, 1981, pp. 524–5.
23 Details of the following discussion are to be found in : I. Delatte, *La Vente des biens nationaux dans le département de Jemappes*, Brussels, 1938; P. Notario, *La Vendita dei beni nazionali in Piemonte nel periodo napoleonico (1800–1814)*, Milan, 1980; F. Mineccia, 'La vendita dei beni nazionali in Toscana (1808–1814): i Dipartimenti dell'Ombrone e del Mediterraneo', in I. Tognarini (ed.), *La Toscana nell'età rivoluzionaria*; P. Villani, *La Vendita dei beni dello Stato nel Regno di Napoli (1806–1815)*, Milan, 1964; R. Zangheri, *La Proprietà terriera e le origini del Risorgimento nel Bolognese*. I. *1789–1804*, Bologna, 1961; M. Müller, *Säkularisation und Grundbesitz. Zur Sozialgeschichte des Saar-Mosel-Raumes 1794–1813*, Boppard, 1980; Schieder and Kube, *Säkularisation*; C. Dipper, 'Vente des biens nationaux et développement du capitalisme en Allemagne', *La Révolution française et le développement du capitalisme*, *Revue du Nord*, Hors-Série, Collection Histoire, N° 5, 1989; A. Otaegui Arizmendi, 'Guerra y crisis de la hacienda local: las ventas de biens comunales en Guipúzcoa, 1793–1814', doctoral thesis, Universidad Autónoma de Barcelona, 1988; *Desamortización y hacienda publica*, Madrid, 1986.
24 Schieder and Kube, *Säkularisation*, p. 93; J. Nicolas, 'Le ralliement des notables au régime impérial dans le département du Mont-Blanc', *Revue d'Histoire Moderne et Contemporaine*, 19, 1972, p. 119.
25 Otaegui Arizmendi, 'Guerra y crisis', pp. 381–2.
26 C. Lafolie, *Mémoires sur la cour du prince Eugène et sur le royaume d'Italie*, Paris, 1824, pp. 129–30.
27 H. G. Molitor, 'La vie religieuse populaire en Rhénanie française, 1794–1815', in B. Plongeron (ed.), *Pratiques religieuses dans l'Europe révolutionnaire: mentalités et spiritualités, 1770–1820*, Turnhout, 1989, p. 64.
28 L. Antonielli, *I Prefetti dell'Italia napoleonica. Repubblica e Regno d'Italia*, Bologna, 1983, pp. 492–3.
29 Molitor, 'Vie religieuse', pp. 59–61.
30 H. Berding, 'L'émancipation des juifs dans la Conféderation du Rhin',

Revue de l'Institut Napoléon, 139, 1982, p. 60.
31 C. F. Lebrun, *Opinions, rapports et choix d'écrits politiques de Charles François Lebrun, duc de Plaisance*, Paris, 1829, pp. 138–41 n. (13 and 28 November 1811).
32 Berding, 'L'émancipation', pp. 53, 58–60; J. Moulard, *Le Comte Camille de Tournon*. 2. *Préfet de Rome 1809–1814*, pp. 97–9.
33 E. Robertazzi delle Donne, 'Potere politico e clero parrochiale nel Regno di Napoli durante il governo dei Napoleonidi', *Ricerche di Storia Sociale e Religiosa*, 13, 1978, p. 162; G. De Rosa, 'Rapport', in *Pratiques religieuses*, pp. 55–6; A. Gambasin, 'Parrochia veneta: evoluzione strutturale dalle riforme napoleoniche al neogiuseppismo asburgico', *La Società religiosa nell'età moderna*, Naples, 1973, pp. 269–305; F. Python, 'De quelques effets de la Révolution dans le diocèse de Lausanne (1798–1818)', in *Pratiques religieuses*, pp. 147–53.
34 J. Godechot, *Les Institutions de la France sous la Révolution et l'Empire*, Paris, 1968, p. 720.
35 B. Plongeron, *Conscience religieuse en Révolution*, Paris, 1969, p. 171.
36 G. Orlandi, *Le Campagne modenesi fra rivoluzione e restaurazione (1790–1815)*, Modena, 1967, pp. 317–18.
37 R. Schneider, 'Dévotions et vie spirituelle dans les paroisses de Moselle selon une enquête de 1807', in *Pratiques religieuses*, pp. 631–2; O. Chadwick, *The Popes and European Revolution*, Oxford, 1981, p. 524.
38 Schneider, 'Dévotions', p. 629.
39 Plongeron, *Conscience religieuse*, p. 159; De Rosa, 'Rapport', pp. 35–6, 50.
40 A. Minke, 'La vie religieuse dans le département de l'Ourthe de 1797 à 1802', in *Pratiques religieuses*, p. 72; Molitor, 'Vie religieuse', p. 66.
41 M. G. Broers, 'The Restoration of order in Napoleonic Piedmont 1797–1814', unpublished D.Phil. thesis, Oxford, 1986, p. 202.
42 Orlandi, *Campagne modenesi*, p. 323 n. 131.
43 M. Agulhon, 'Introduction. La sociabilité est-elle objet d'histoire?', in E. François (ed.), *Sociabilité et société bourgeoise en France, en Allemagne et en Suisse (1750–1850)*, Paris, 1986, pp. 14 n. 3, 20. Similar concerns were expressed in Germany in these same years by Friedrich Schleiermacher, *Versuch einer Theorie des geselligen Betragens* (1799).
44 *Lettres de la baronne De Gérando née de Rathsamshausen suivies de fragments d'un journal écrit par elle de 1800 à 1804*, Paris, 1881, pp. 185–6.
45 R. Vierhaus, 'Jüdische Salons in Berlin und Wien zu Beginn des 19. Jahrhunderts', in François (ed.), *Sociabilité et société bourgeoise*, pp. 95–102.
46 J. Rambaud, *Naples sous Joseph Bonaparte 1806–1808*, Paris, 1911, pp. 526–7.
47 Schmidt, *Grand-Duché de Berg*, p. 425; K. G.Faber, 'Die Rheinländer unter Napoleon', *Francia*, 1, 1973, pp. 377.
48 J. Vidalenc, 'Les "départements hanséatiques" et l'administration napoléonienne', *Francia*, 1, 1973, pp. 422–3.
49 J. P. Chaline, 'Sociétés savantes et académies de province en France dans la première moitié du XIXᵉ siècle', in François (ed.), *Sociabilité et société bourgeoise*, p. 171; M. Tabarrini, *Degli studi e delle vicende della Reale*

Accademia dei Georgofili nel primo secolo di sua esistenza, Florence, 1856; M. Tacel, 'L'agitation royaliste à Turin de 1805 à 1808', *Revue de l'Institut Napoléon*, 52, 1954, pp. 94–5; Filippini, 'Ralliement', p. 346; U. Im Hof, 'Vereinswesen und Geselligkeit in der Schweiz, 1750–1850', in François (ed.), *Sociabilité et société bourgeoise*, p. 59; C. Nardi, *Napoleone e Roma*; M. Crosland, *The Society of Arcueil. A View of French Science at the Time of Napoleon I*, Cambridge, Mass., 1967, pp. 277–8.

50 H. Berlioz, 'Les concerts des Tuileries sous l'Empire', *Revue et Gazette Musicale de Paris*, 34, 1837, pp. 379–80; Marbot, *Mémoires du général baron de Marbot* (2 vols, Paris, 1983), vol. 2, pp. 29–30; J. P. Aron, *Le Mangeur du XIXe siècle*, Paris, 1973, pp. 29–31, 40–1; *Récits d'une tante. Mémoires de la comtesse de Boigne, née d'Osmond*, Paris, 1921, vol. 3, pp. 209–10.

51 P. Gerbord, 'Une forme de sociabilité bourgeoise: le loisir thermale en France, en Belgique, et en Allemagne (1800–1850)', in François (ed.), *Sociabilité et société bourgeoise*, pp. 106–7.

52 Stendhal, *Oeuvres intimes*, vol. 1, Paris, 1981, pp. 473–510; *Mémoires du général Griois 1792–1822*, vol. 1, Paris, 1909, pp. 141–2.

53 J. L. Quoy-Bodin, 'Une religion laïque: la franc-maçonnerie dans les armées (1793–1808)', in François (ed.), *Sociabilité et société bourgeoise*, p. 421.

54 F. Collaveri, *La Franc-Maçonnerie des Bonaparte*, Paris, 1982; J. L. Quoy-Bodin, *L'Armée et la Franc-Maçonnerie: au déclin de la monarchie, sous la Révolution et l'Empire*, Paris, 1987; Dufraisse, 'Les notables', pp. 771–2; F. Bertini, 'La massoneria in Toscana dall'età dei lumi alla restaurazione', in Z. Ciuffoletti (ed.), *Le Origini della massoneria in Toscana (1730–1890)*, Foggia, 1989; J. A. Ferrer Benimeli, 'La masonería bonapartista en España', in *Les Espagnols et Napoléon*, Aix-en-Provence, 1984, pp. 335–86. For the opposition to Napoleon within freemasonry: J. M. Roberts, *The Mythology of the Secret Societies*, London, 1972, ch. 8.

55 J. Rosselli, *The Opera Industry in Italy from Cimarosa to Verdi*, Cambridge, 1984, p. 28.

56 I wish to thank Paul Lambrechts for this information.

57 J. A. Chaptal, *Rapport et projet de loi sur l'instruction publique*, Paris, an IX (1801), p. 24.

58 Barberis, *Le Armi del Principe*, pp. 256–73; E. Brambilla, 'L'Istruzione pubblica nella Repubblica Cisalpina al Regno Italico', *Quaderni Storici*, 23 (1973), pp. 520–1; S. Schama, 'Schools and politics'.

59 Broers, 'Restoration of order', p. 299; Rambaud, *Naples sous Joseph*, p. 95.

60 F. Mineccia, 'La montagna pistoiese e le migrazioni stagionali: tradizioni e mutamento tra età leopoldina e restaurazione', in I. Tognarini (ed.), *Il Territorio pistoiese e i Lorena tra 700 e 800: viabilità e bonifiche*, Naples, 1990, p. 242 n. 153. For the 'moral statistics' of the Restoration years, which were to crystallise in the representation of the urban poor as 'dangerous classes', L. Chevalier, *Classes laborieuses et classes dangereuses à Paris pendant la première moitié du XIX siècle*, Paris, 1958.

61 S. Woolf, *The Poor in Western Europe in the Eighteenth and Nineteenth*

Centuries, London, 1986, pp. 23, 128–45; S. Marzagalli, *Amburgo nell'età Napoleonica: una città mercantile di fronte ai problemi del blocco e dell'occupazione*, tesi di laurea, Milan University, Faculty of Letters, 1987–8 pp. 52–9; M. Lindemann, 'Unterschichten und Sozialpolitik in Hamburg, 1799–1814', in A. Herzig, D. Langewiesche and A. Sywottek (eds), *Arbeiter in Hamburg. Unterschichten, Arbeiter und Arbeiterbewegung seit dem ausgehenden 18. Jahrhundert*, Hamburg, 1973, pp. 61–70.

62 S. Woolf, 'The Société de Charité Maternelle', in C. Jones and J. Barry (eds), *Medicine and Charity Before the Welfare State*, London, 1991.

63 P. Guichonnet, 'Biens communaux et partages révolutionnaires dans l'ancien département du Léman', *Etudes Rurales*, 36, 1969, p. 28 n. 3.

64 F. J. Reinoso, *Examen de los delitos de infidelidad a la patria imputados a los españoles sometidos bajo la dominación francesa*, quoted in J. Fontana, *La Crisis del Antiguo Régimen*, Barcelona, 1979, p. 103; Nicolas, 'Le ralliement', p. 120.

65 *Lettres de la baronne De Gérando*, pp. 199, 224–5, 403.

66 Barberis, *Le Armi del Principe*, p. 252.

67 S. Woolf, *A History of Italy 1700–1860*, London, 1979, p. 205.

68 *Correspondance de l'Empereur Napoléon Ier* (28 vols, Paris, 1857–69), vol. 12 (1863), no. 9,911, 2 March 1806.

69 Lebrun, *Opinions . . . de . . . Lebrun*, pp. 111 n. 2, 144 n. 1; *Correspondance*, vol. 11 (1863), no. 9,678, 19 January 1806; vol. 12, no. 9,744, 4 February 1806.

70 Tacel, 'L'agitation royaliste', p. 102; Antonielli, *Prefetti*, pp. 103–55.

71 G. Dufour, 'Pourquoi les Espagnols prirent-ils les armes contre Napoléon?', in *Les Espagnols et Napoléon*, p. 321.

72 Rambaud, *Naples sous Joseph*, pp. 89–125; A. Mozzillo, *Cronache della Calabria in guerra (1806–1811)*, Naples, 1972; G. Cingari, *Brigantaggio, proprietari e contadini nel Sud 1799–1900*, Reggio Calabria, 1976.

73 Noguès, *Mémoires du général Noguès (1977–1853) sur les guerres de l'Empire*, Paris, 1922, p. 249.

74 Excellent analyses of the Spanish war can be found in: J. R. Aymes, *La Guerra de la Independencia en España (1808–1814)*, Madrid, 1974; L. Roura i Aulinas, 'La crisis del Antiguo Régimen. Del "panico" de Floridablanca a la guerra de la Independencia', in A. Dominguez Ortiz (ed.), *Historia de España. 9. La Transición del Antiguo al Nuevo Régimen (1789–1874)*, Barcelona, 1988, pp. 91–136.

75 *Lettres de la baronne De Gérando*, pp. 420–1.

76 Schmidt, *Grand-Duché de Berg*, pp. 447–8.

6 Epilogue: the heritage

1 S. Woolf, 'French civilisation and ethnicity in the Napoleonic Empire', *Past and Present*, 124, 1989, pp. 96–106; L. Febvre, *Civilisation: le mot et l'idée*, Paris, 1930; J. B. Bury, *The Idea of Progress*, London, 1920; I. Sachs, 'Selvaggio/barbaro/civilizzato', in *Enciclopedia*, vol. 12, Turin, 1981; A. Pagden, *The Fall of Natural Man: the American Indian and the Origins of Comparative Ethnology*, Cambridge, 1982; W. T. Rowe, 'Education and empire in southwest China: Ch'en Hung-mou in Yunnan,

1733–38', unpublished paper to the Conference on Education and Society in Late Imperial China, Montecito, California, 8–14 June, 1989.

2 S. Woolf, 'Statistics and the modern state', *Comparative Studies in Society and History*, 31, 1989.

3 P. Boutry, 'Società urbana e sociabilità delle élites nella Roma della Restaurazione: prime considerazioni', in M. Malatesta (ed.), *Sociabilità nobiliare, sociabilità borghese*, Reggio Emilia, 1989, p. 59.

4 E. da Cunha, *A Marjem da história*, Porto, 1926, pp. 218–19.

5 P. Nolte, *Staatsbildung als Gesellschaftsreform. Politische Reformen in Preussen und den süddeutschen Staaten 1800–1820*, Frankfurt, 1990. This important work has unfortunately appeared too late for me to take it into adequate account.

6 Nolte, *Staatsbildung*, p. 206.

7 A. de Tocqueville, 'De la classe moyenne et du peuple', in *Oeuvres complètes*. T. 3. *Ecrits et discours politiques*, Paris, 1985, p. 740.

Bibliography

This bibliography is highly selective and lists only those works that I have found directly useful or that I believe could be of value to the reader who wishes to pursue further the history of individual countries or themes discussed in the preceding pages. Virtually all the works cited in the notes are included. I have divided the bibliography into publications by contemporaries relating to France, general works and individual countries.

CONTEMPORARY PUBLICATIONS

Almanach du départment de l'Escaut pour l'année 1811, Gand, n.d.
Annuaire du département du Léman pour l'année 1811, Geneva – Paris, 1811.
Barthélemy, H. C. F. de, *Souvenirs d'un ancien préfet 1787–1848*, Paris, 1885.
Beugnot, A. (ed.), *Mémoires du comte Beugnot (1783–1815)*, Paris, 1866, 2 vols.
Bodmann, F., *Annuaire statistique du départment du Mont-Tonnerre pour l'an 1808*, Mayence, n.d.
Boigne, comtesse de, *Récits d'une tante. Mémoires de la comtesse de Boigne, née d'Osmond*, 4 vols, Paris, 1907.
Bonnin, C. J., *Principes d'administration publique*, Paris, 1812.
Calendario politico-statistico del dipartimento dell'Arno per l'anno 1813, Florence, n.d.
Chabrol de Volvic, G. J. G., 'Essai sur les moeurs des habitans modernes de l'Egypte', in *Description de l'Egypte*, 2:2. *Etat Moderne*, Paris, 1822.
Chaptal, J. A., *Rapport et projet de loi sur l'instruction publique*, Paris, an IX (1801).
—— *Mes Souvenirs sur Napoléon*, Paris, 1893.
Chateaubriand, F. R. de, *Mémoires d'Outre-Tombe*, 4 vols, Paris, 1964.
Combier, A. (ed.), *Mémoires du général Radet*, St Cloud, 1892.
Constant de Rebecque, B., *De l'Esprit de conquête*, Lausanne, 1980.
Crouzet, P., *Discours sur l'honneur prononcé à la distribution des prix du Prytanée militaire français, le 14 août 1806*, Paris, 1806.
Dainville, F. de and Tulard, J., *Atlas administratif de l'Empire français rédigé par ordre de S.E. M. le duc de Feltre, ministre de la Guerre. Au Dépôt Général de la Guerre, 1812*, Geneva – Paris, 1973.
Dansette, A., *Napoléon, pensées politiques et sociales*, Paris, 1969.

De Gérando, J. M., *Programme du cours de droit public positif et administratif, à la faculté de droit de Paris, pour l'année 1819–1820*, Paris, 1819.

De Gérando, Mme, *Lettres de la baronne De Gérando née de Rathsamshausen suivies de fragments d'un journal écrit par elle de 1800 à 1804*, Paris, 1881.

Desvernois, N. P., *Mémoires du général baron Desvernois*, Paris, 1898.

Exposé de la situation de l'Empire, présenté au Corps Législatif dans sa séance du 25 février 1813 par Son Excellence M.le comte de Montalivet, ministre de l'Intérieur, Paris, 1813.

Fain, baron, *Mémoires*, Paris, 1908.

Fairon, E. and Heuse, H., *Lettres de grognards*, Courville, 1936.

Griois, général, *Mémoires du général Griois 1792–1822*, 2 vols, Paris, 1909.

Jacquin, F.-J., *Carnet de route d'un grognard de la Révolution et de l'Empire*, Paris, 1960.

Lafolie, C., *Mémoires sur la cour du prince Eugène et sur le royaume d'Italie*, Paris, 1824.

Las Cases, E. de, *Mémorial de Sainte-Hélène*, 2 vols, Paris, 1951.

Lebrun, Ch. F., *Opinions, rapports et choix d'écrits politiques de Charles François Lebrun, duc de Plaisance*, Paris, 1829.

Marbot, J.-B.-A.-M., *Mémoires du général baron de Marbot*, 2 vols, Paris, 1983.

Miot de Melito, *Mémoires du comte Miot de Melito*, 3 vols, Paris, 1873.

Molé, M., *Souvenirs d'un témoin de la Révolution et de l'Empire (1791–1803)*, Geneva, 1943.

Napoléon, *Correspondance de l'Empereur Napoléon Ier*, 32 vols, Paris, 1858–69.

Noguès, A., *Mémoires du général Noguès (1777–1853) sur les guerres de l'Empire*, Paris, 1922.

Plancy, A. de, *Souvenirs du comte de Plancy (1798–1816)*, Paris, 1904.

Rambuteau, *Mémoires du comte de Rambuteau*, Paris, 1905.

Recueil des lettres circulaires, instructions, programmes, discours et autres actes publics du ministère de l'Intérieur, 16 vols, Paris, an VII – 1816.

Ségur, P.-P., comte de, *De 1800 à 1812. Un aide de camp de Napoléon. Mémoires du général de Ségur*, 3 vols, Paris, 1894–5.

Senfft von Pilsach, F. C. L., Graf, *Mémoires du comte de Senfft ancien ministre de Saxe. Empire. Organisation politique de la Suisse 1806–1813*, Leipzig, 1863.

Stanhope, P. H. Earl, *Notes of conversations with the Duke of Wellington, 1831–1851*, London, 1888.

Stendhal, *Oeuvres intimes. 1. Journal*, Paris, 1981.

Thiébault, D. A. P., *Mémoires*, 2 vols, Paris, 1962.

GENERAL WORKS

Bargeton, R., Bougard, P., Le Clère, B. and Pinaud, P.-F., *Les Préfets du 11 ventôse an VIII au 4 septembre 1870*, Paris, 1981.

Bercé, Y. M. (ed.), *La Fin de l'Europe napoléonienne, 1814. La vacance du pouvoir*, Paris, 1990.

Centro Studi Napoleonici e di Storia dell'Elba, *Studi napoleonici. Atti del primo e secondo Congresso internazionale 3–7 maggio 1962/3–6 maggio*

1965, Firenze, 1969.

Chadwick, O., *The Popes and European Revolution*, Oxford, 1981.

Collaveri, F., *La Franc-maçonnerie des Bonaparte*, Paris, 1982.

Connelly, O., *Napoleon's Satellite Kingdoms*, New York, 1965.

Crawley, C. W. (ed.), *New Cambridge Modern History*. 9. *War and Peace in an Age of Upheaval, 1733–1830*, Cambridge, 1965.

Crouzet, F., *L'Economie britannique et le blocus continental, 1806–1813*, 2 vols, Paris, 1958.

—— 'Wars, blockade and economic change in Europe, 1792–1815', *Journal of Economic History*, 24, 1964.

—— 'Bilan de l'économie britannique pendant les guerres de la Révolution et de l'Empire', *Revue Historique*, 234, 1965.

Dictionnaire de biographie française.

Dunan, M., 'Napoléon et le Système Continental en 1810', *Revue d'Histoire Diplomatique*, January–April 1946.

François, E. (ed.), *Sociabilité et société bourgeoise en France, en Allemagne et en Suisse (1750–1850)*, Paris, 1986.

Furet, F. and Ozouf, M. (eds), *Dictionnaire critique de la Révolution française*, Paris, 1988.

Godechot, J., *L'Amérique et l'Europe à l'époque napoléonienne*, Paris, 1967.

Martin, A. and Walter, G., *Catalogue de l'histoire de la Révolution française*, 6 vols, Paris, 1936–43.

Napoléon et l'Europe, Paris – Brussels, 1961.

Occupants occupés 1792–1815, Brussels, 1969.

Les Pays sous domination française, 1799–1814, Paris, 1967.

Plongeron, B. (ed.), *Pratiques religieuses dans l'Europe révolutionnaire: mentalités et spiritualités, 1770–1820*, Turnhout, 1989.

Popkin, J. D., 'The book trades in western Europe during the revolutionary era', *Papers of the Bibliographical Society of America*, 78, 1984.

Roberts, J. M., *The Mythology of the Secret Societies*, London, 1972.

Sofia, F., 'La statistica come scienza politica e dell'amministrazione', in *L'Amministrazione nella storia moderna*, Milan, 1985.

Tarle, E. V., *Napoléon*, Paris, 1937.

Tulard, J., *Bibliographie critique des mémoires sur le Consulat et l'Empire*, Geneva, 1971.

—— *Le Mythe de Napoléon*, Paris, 1971.

—— (ed.), *Dictionnaire Napoléon*, Paris, 1987.

Villat, L., *La Révolution et l'Empire*, Paris, 1936.

Woolf, S., 'French civilization and ethnicity in the Napoleonic Empire', *Past and Present*, 124, 1989.

—— 'Statistics and the modern state', *Comparative Studies in Society and History*, 31, 1989.

FRANCE

Les Affaires étrangères et le corps diplomatique français, 2 vols, Paris, 1984.

Aron, J. P., *Le Mangeur du XIXe siècle*, Paris, 1973.

Bastid, P., *Siéyès et sa pensée*, Paris, 1970.

La Bataille, l'armée, la gloire. Actes du colloque de Clermont-Ferrand, 1983, Clermont-Ferrand, 1985.

Bergeron, L., *L'Episode napoléonien. Aspects intérieurs 1799–1815*, Paris, 1972.

—— 'Remarques sur les conditions du développement industriel en Europe occidentale à l'époque napoléonienne', *Francia*, 1, 1973.

—— *Banquiers, négociants et manufacturiers parisiens. Du Directoire à l'Empire*, 2 vols, Paris, 1975.

Bergeron, L. and Chaussinand-Nogaret, G., *Les 'Masses de granit'. Cent mille notables du Premier Empire*, Paris, 1979.

—— *Grands notables du Premier Empire*, 17 vols (1988), Paris, 1978–.

Berlioz, H., 'Les concerts des Tuileries sous l'Empire', *Revue et Gazette Musicale de Paris*, 34, 1837.

Bertaud, J.-P., 'La "petite guerre" des honneurs sous Napoléon', *L'Histoire*, 66, 1984.

—— 'Napoleon's officers', *Past and Present*, 112, 1986.

Bertho, J., *Naissance et théologie d'une théologie de guerre chez les évêques de Napoléon*, Paris, 1975.

Bluche, F., *Le Bonapartisme: aux origines de la droite autoritaire (1800–1850)*, Paris, 1980.

Bourdon, J., 'L'administration militaire sous Napoléon 1er', *Revue des Etudes Napoléoniennes*, 1917.

Bourguet, M.-N., 'Désordre public, ordre populaire à l'époque napoléonienne', in *Mouvements populaires et conscience sociale*, Paris, 1985.

—— *Déchiffrer la France. La statistique départementale à l'époque napoléonienne*, Paris, 1988.

Broc, N., *La Géographie des philosophes. Géographie et voyageurs français au XVIIIe siècle*, Lille, 1972.

Brunet, M., *Le Roussillon. Une société contre l'Etat 1780–1820*, Toulouse, 1986.

Butel, P., 'Crise et mutation de l'activité économique à Bordeaux sous le Consulat et l'Empire', *Revue d'Histoire Moderne et Contemporaine*, 17, 1970.

—— 'Le port de Bordeaux sous le régime des licences, 1808–1815', *Revue d'Histoire Moderne et Contemporaine*, 19, 1972.

Charles-Roux, F., *Bonaparte, gouverneur d'Egypte*, Paris, 1936.

Chassagne, S., 'Aspects des phénomènes d'industrialisation et de désindustrialisation dans les campagnes françaises au XIXe siècle', *Revue du Nord*, 63, 1981.

Chevalier, L., *Classes laborieuses et classes dangereuses à Paris pendant la première moitié du XIX siècle*, Paris, 1958.

Chisick, Harvey, *The Limits of Reform in the Enlightenment: Attitudes towards the Education of the Lower Classes in Eighteenth-Century France*, Princeton, NJ, 1981.

Church, C., *Revolution and Red Tape: The French Ministerial Bureaucracy, 1770–1850*, Oxford, 1981.

Corvisier, A., *L'Armée française de la fin du XVIIe siècle au ministère de Choiseul: le soldat*, Paris, 1964.

Crosland, M., *The Society of Arcueil. A View of French Science at the Time of Napoleon I*, Cambridge, Mass., 1967.

Delpech, F., 'Les juifs en France et dans l'Empire et la genèse du Grand Sanhédrin', in *Le Grand Sanhédrin de Napoléon*, Toulouse, 1979.

Dufraisse, R., 'Blocus et système continental. La politique économique de Napoléon', *Revue de l'Institut Napoléon*, 99, 1966.

Durand, C., *Les Auditeurs au Conseil d'Etat de 1803 à 1814*, Aix-en-Provence, 1958.

Durand, Ch., 'Le régime juridique de l'expropriation pour utilité publique sous le Consulat et le premier Empire', *Annales de la Faculté de Droit d'Aix*, 41, 1948.

—— 'L'emploi des conseillers d'état et des maîtres de requête en dehors du Conseil', *Annales de la Faculté de Droit d'Aix*, 45, 1952.

—— 'L'exercice de la fonction législative de 1800 à 1814', *Annales de la Faculté de Droit d'Aix*, 48, 1955.

—— 'Le pouvoir napoléonien et ses légitimités', *Annales de la Faculté de Droit d'Aix*, 58, 1972.

Ellis, G., *Napoleon's Continental Blockade. The Case of Alsace*, Oxford, 1981.

Forrest, A., 'Conscription and crime in rural France during the Directory and Consulate', in G. Lewis and C. Lucas (eds), *Beyond the Terror: Essays in French Regional and Social History*, Cambridge, 1983.

—— 'Le recrutement, les désertions et l'Etat napoléonien', paper delivered at the Convegno Internazionale sull'Armata Napoleonica, Portoferraio, Elba, 17–20 September 1986.

Forster, R., 'The French Revolution and the "new" elite, 1800–1880', in J. Pelensky (ed.), *The American and European Revolutions Reconsidered, 1776–1848*, Iowa City, 1980.

'La France à l'époque napoléonienne', *Revue d'Histoire Moderne et Contemporaine*, 17, 1970.

Friedlaender, W., 'Napoleon as "Roi Thaumaturge"', *Journal of the Warburg and Courtauld Institutes*, 4, 1940–1.

Gabillard, J., 'Le financement des guerres napoléoniennes et la conjoncture du premier Empire', *Revue Economique*, 4, 1953.

Godechot, J., *Les Institutions de la France sous la Révolution et l'Empire*, Paris, 1969.

—— *La Grande nation. L'expansion révolutionnaire de la France dans le monde de 1789 à 1799*, Paris, 1983.

—— 'Les variations de la politique française à l'égard des pays occupés', in *Occupants occupés 1792–1815*, Bruxelles, 1969.

Gusdorf, G., *Les Sciences humaines et la pensée occidentale. 8. La Conscience révolutionnaire. Les idéologues*, Paris, 1978.

Huart, S. d', 'Daru et le projet impérial de code militaire', *Revue de l'Institut Napoléon*, 88, 1963.

James, E., 'Napoléon et la pensée économique de son temps', *Revue de l'Institut Napoléon*, 100, 1966.

Langlois, C., 'Le plébiscite de l'an VIII ou le coup d'état du 18 pluviôse an VIII', *Annales Historiques de la Révolution Française*, 24, 1972.

Lanzac de Labourie, L. de, *Paris sous Napoléon*, Paris, 8 vols, 1905–13.

Latreille, A., *L'Ere napoléonienne*, Paris, 1974.

Lefebvre, G., *Napoléon*, Paris, 1965.

Lévy-Leboyer, M., *Les Banques européennes et l'industrialisation internationale dans la première moitié du XIXe siècle*, Paris, 1964.

L'Huillier, F., *Recherches sur l'Alsace napoléonienne de brumaire à l'inva-*

sion (1799–1813), Strasburg, 1945.

Lynn, J. A., *The Bayonets of the Republic. Motivation and Tactics in the Army of Revolutionary France, 1791–94*, Urbana – Chicago, 1984.

Marion, M., *Histoire financière de la France depuis 1715*, 6 vols, Paris, 1927–31.

—— *Le Brigandage pendant la Révolution*, Paris, 1934.

Masson, F., *Le Département des Affaires Etrangères pendant la Révolution, 1787–1804*, Paris, 1877.

Morvan, J., *Le Soldat impérial*, 2 vols, Paris, 1904.

Ozouf, M., 'De thermidor à brumaire: Le discours de la Révolution sur elle-même', *Revue Historique*, 243, 1970.

—— *L'Ecole de la France. Essais sur la Révolution, l'utopie et l'enseignement*, Paris, 1984.

Perrot, J.-C., *L'Age d'or de la statistique régionale française (an IV – 1804)*, Paris, 1977.

Perrot, J.-C. and Woolf, S., *State and Statistics in France 1789–1815*, Chur – London – Paris – New York, 1984.

Plongeron, B., *Conscience religieuse en révolution. Regards sur l'historiographie religieuse de la Révolution française*, Paris, 1969.

Ponteil, F., *Napoléon I et l'organisation autoritaire de la France*, Paris, 1965.

Poulot, D., 'Les musées à la gloire de l'Empire: notes pour une recherche', *Gazette des Beaux-Arts*, 1981.

Quoy-Bodin, J. L., *L'Armée et la franc-maçonnerie: au déclin de la monarchie, sous la Révolution et l'Empire*, Paris, 1987.

—— 'Une religion laïque: la franc-maçonnerie dans les armées (1793–1808)', in E. François (ed.), *Sociabilité et société bourgeoise en France, en Allemagne et en Suisse (1750–1850)*, Paris, 1986.

Regaldo, M., *Un Milieu intellectuel: la Décade philosophique (1974–1807)*, 5 vols, Lille, 1976.

Roche, D., *Le Siècle des lumières en province. Académies et académiciens provinciaux, 1680–1789*, 2 vols, Paris – La Haye, 1978.

Schmidt, C., 'Jean-Baptiste Say et le blocus continental', *Revue d'Histoire des Doctrines Economiques et Sociales*, 4, 1911.

Scott, S. F., *The Response of the Royal Army to the French Revolution: the Role and Development of the Line Army 1787–93*, Oxford, 1978.

Shinn, J., *L'Ecole Polytechnique, 1794–1914. Savoir scientifique et pouvoir social*, Paris, 1980.

Six, G., *Dictionnaire biographique des généraux et amiraux français de la Révolution et de l'Empire (1792–1814)*, Paris, 1934.

—— *Les Généraux de la Révolution et de l'Empire*, Paris, 1948.

La Statistique en France à l'époque napoléonienne, Brussels, 1981.

Tocqueville. Alexis de, *Etat social et politique de la France avant et depuis 1789*, 1836.

Tulard, J., 'Problèmes sociaux de la France napoléonienne', *Revue d'Histoire Moderne et Contemporaine*, 17, 1970.

—— *Le Grand Empire, 1804–1815*, Paris, 1982.

—— *Napoléon et la noblesse d'Empire*, Paris, 1986.

Welch, C. B., *Liberty and Utility. The French Idéologues and the Transformation of Liberalism*, New York, 1984.

Whitcomb, A. E., 'Napoleon's prefects', *American Historical Review*, 79, 1974.
—— *Napoleon's Diplomatic Service*, Durham, N. C., 1979.
Woloch, I., 'Napoleonic conscription: state power and civil society', *Past and Present*, 111, 1986.
Woolf, S., 'Les bases sociales du Consulat. Un mémoire d'Adrien Duquesnoy', *Revue d'Histoire Moderne et Contemporaine*, 31, 1984.
Ymbert, J.-G., *Moeurs françaises. Moeurs administratives*, 2 vols, Paris, 1825.
Zieseniss, J., 'Noblesse d'Empire', in J. Tulard (ed.), *Dictionnaire Napoléon*, Paris, 1987.

BELGIUM

Darquenne, R., *La Conscription dans le département de Jemappes (1799–1813)*, Mons, 1970.
Delatte, I., *La Vente des biens nationaux dans le département de Jemappes*, Brussels, 1938.
Devleeshouwer, R., 'Le Cas de Belgique', in *Occupants occupés 1792–1815*, Brussels, 1969.
François, L., 'Politikie integratie of exclusie? Belgische notabelen tussen 1785 en 1835', *Revue Belge d'Histoire Contemporaine*, 1–2, 1977.
Lanzac de Laborie, L. de, *La Domination française en Belgique: Directoire, Consulat, Empire, 1795–1814*, 2 vols, Paris, 1895.
Minke, A., 'La vie religieuse dans le département de l'Ourthe de 1797 à 1802', in B. Plongeron (ed.), *Pratiques religieuses dans l'Europe révolutionnaire: mentalités et spiritualités, 1770–1820*, Turnhout, 1989.
Verhaegen, P., *La Belgique sous la domination française 1792–1814*, 5 vols, Brussels, 1923–9.

GERMANY

Berding, H., *Napoleonische Herrschafts- und Gesellschaftspolitik im Königreich Westfalen 1807–1813*, Göttingen, 1973.
—— 'Les dotations impériales dans le royaume de Westphalie', *Revue de l'Institut Napoléon*, 132, 1976.
—— 'L'émancipation des juifs dans la Conféderation du Rhin', *Revue de l'Institut Napoléon*, 139, 1982.
—— 'Le royaume de Westphalie, état-modèle', *Francia*, 10, 1982.
Blanning, T. C. W., *The French Revolution in Germany: Occupation and Resistance in the Rhineland 1792–1802*, Oxford, 1983.
Bonaparte, Jerome, *Mémoires et correspondance du roi Jérôme et de la reine Catherine*, 6 vols, Paris, 1861–5.
Bruguière, M., 'Remarques sur les rapports financiers entre la France et l'Allemagne du Nord à l'époque napoléonienne: Hambourg et "le parti de la paix" ', *Francia*, 1, 1973.
Brunschwig, H., *La Crise de l'état prussien à la fin du XVIIIe siècle et la genèse de la mentalité romantique*, Paris, 1947.
Demel, W., *Der bayerische Staatsabsolutismus, 1806/08–1817*, Munich, 1983.
Deutsches Historisches Institut in Paris, *Francia. Forschungen zur westeuropäische Geschichte*, 1, 1973.

Diefendorff, J. M., *Business and Politics in the Rhineland, 1789–1834*, Princeton, NJ, 1980.

Dipper, C., 'Vente des biens nationaux et développement du capitalisme en Allemagne', *Revue du Nord*, Hors-Série, Collection Histoire, 5, 1989.

Dreyfus, F. G., 'Bilan économique des Allemagnes en 1815', *Revue d'Histoire Economique et Sociale*, 43, 1965.

Dufraisse, R., 'Les notables de la rive gauche du Rhin à l'époque napoléonienne', *Revue d'Histoire Moderne et Contemporaine*, 17, 1970.

—— 'La contrebande dans les départements réunis de la rive gauche du Rhin à l'époque napoléonienne', *Francia*, 1, 1973.

—— 'L'influence de la politique économique napoléonienne sur l'économie des états du Rheinbund', in E. Weis (ed.), *Reformen im rheinbündischen Deutschland*, Munich, 1984.

Dunan, M., *Napoléon et l'Allemagne. Le système continental et les débuts du royaume de Bavière 1806–1810*, Paris, 1942.

Faber, K. G.,'Die Rheinländer und Napoleon', *Francia*, 1, 1973.

Grab, W., 'La réaction de la population de Rhénanie face à l'occupation par les armées révolutionnaires françaises 1792–1799', in *Occupants occupés 1792–1815*, Brussels, 1969.

Klueting, H., 'Die Folgen der Säkularisation. Zur Diskussion der wirtschaftlichen und sozialen Auswirkungen der Vermögenssäkularisation in Deutschland', in H. Berding and H.P. Ullmann (eds), *Deutschland zwischen Revolution und Restauration*, Königstein/Ts., 1981.

Lesage, C., *Napoléon 1er, créancier de la Prusse (1807–1814)*, Paris, 1924.

Lindemann, M., 'Unterschichten und Sozialpolitik in Hamburg, 1799–1814', in A. Herzig, D. Langewiesche and A. Sywottek (eds), *Arbeiter in Hamburg. Unterschichten, Arbeiter und Arbeiterbewegung seit dem ausgehenden 18. Jahrhundert*, Hamburg, 1973.

Marzagalli, S., *Amburgo nell'età napoleonica: una città mercantile di fronte ai problemi del blocco e dell'occupazione*, tesi di laurea, Università Statale di Milano, 1987–8.

Molitor, H. G., 'La vie religieuse populaire en Rhénanie française, 1794–1815', in B. Plongeron (ed.), *Pratiques religieuses dans l'Europe révolutionnaire: mentalités et spiritualités, 1770–1820*, Turnhout, 1989.

Müller, M., *Säkularisation und Grundbesitz. Zur Sozialgeschichte des Saar-Mosel-Raumes 1794–1813*, Boppard am Rhein, 1980.

Nolte, P., *Staatsbildung als Gesellschaftsreform. Politische Reformen in Preussen und den süddeutschen Staaten 1800–1820*, Frankfurt, 1990.

Patemann, R., 'Die Beziehungen Bremens zu Frankreich bis zum Ende der französischen Herrschaft 1813', *Francia*, 1, 1973.

Schieder, W. and Kube, A., *Säkularisation und Mediatisierung. Die Veräusserung der Nationalgüter im Rhein-Mosel-Department 1803–1813*, Boppard am Rhein, 1987.

Schmidt, C., *Le Grand-duché de Berg (1806–1813). Etude sur la domination française en Allemagne sous Napoléon Ier*, Paris, 1905.

Schneider, R., 'Dévotions et vie spirituelle dans les paroisses de Moselle selon une enquête de 1807', in B. Plongeron (ed.), *Pratiques religieuses dans l'Europe révolutionnaire: mentalités et spiritualités, 1770–1820*, Turnhout, 1989.

Vidalenc, J., 'Les notables des départements hanséatiques', *Revue d'Histoire*

Moderne et Contemporaine, 17, 1970.
—— 'Les "départements hanséatiques" et l'administration napoléonienne', *Francia*, 1, 1973.
Vierhaus, R., 'Jüdische Salons in Berlin und Wien zu Beginn des 19. Jahrhunderts', in E. François (ed.), *Sociabilité et société bourgeoise en France, en Allemagne et en Suisse (1750–1850)*, Paris, 1986.
Weis, E. and Müller-Luckner, E. (eds), *Reformen im rheinbündischen Deutschland*, Munich, 1984.

HOLLAND

Alphonse, baron d', *Eenige hoofdstukken uit het 'Aperçu sur la Hollande, présenté à S.E.le ministre de l'Intérieur par M. d'Alphonse'*, The Hague, 1900.
Bonaparte, Louis, *Documents historiques et réflexions sur le gouvernement de la Hollande*, 3 vols, Brussels, 1820.
Caumont, A. de la Force, *L'Architrésorier Lebrun, gouverneur de la Hollande 1810–1813*, Paris, 1907.
Duboscq, A., *Louis Bonaparte en Hollande, d'après ses lettres*, Paris, 1911.
Hogendorp, D. van, *Mémoires du général Dirk van Hogendorp*, The Hague, 1887.
Kossman, E. H., 'The crisis of the Dutch state, 1780–1813: nationalism, federalism, unitarism', in J. S. Bromley and E. H. Kossman, *Britain and the Netherlands*, vol. 4, The Hague, 1971.
Schama, S., 'Schools and politics in the Netherlands, 1796–1814', *Historical Journal*, 13, 1970.
—— The exigencies of war and the politics of taxation in the Netherlands 1795–1810', in J. M. Winter (ed.), *War and Economic Development*, Cambridge, 1975.
—— *Patriots and Liberators. Revolution in the Netherlands 1780–1813*, New York – London, 1977.

ILLYRIA

Pivec-Stelé, M., *La Vie économique des provinces illyriennes (1809–1813)*, Paris, 1930.
Senkowska-Gluck, M., 'Illyrie sous la domination illyrienne 1809–1813', *Acta Poloniae Historica*, 41, 1980.

ITALY

Antonielli, L., 'Alcuni aspetti dell'apparato amministrativo periferico nella Repubblica e nel Regno d'Italia', *Quaderni Storici*, 37, 1978.
—— *I Prefetti dell'Italia napoleonica. Repubblica e Regno d'Italia*, Bologna, 1983.
Assereto, G., 'I gruppi dirigenti liguri tra la fine del vecchio regime e l'annessione all'impero napoleonico', *Quaderni Storici*, 37, 1978.
—— 'La fine dell'antico regime: la dominazione napoleonica a Prato', in E. Fasano Guarini (ed.), *Prato storia di una città. 2. Un microcosmo in movimento (1494–1815)*, Prato-Florence, 1986.

Barberis, W., *Le Armi del principe. La tradizione militare sabauda*, Turin, 1988.

Bergeron, L., 'La place des gens d'affaires dans les listes de notables du premier Empire, d'après les exemples du Piémont et de la Ligurie', *Annuario dell'Istituto Storico Italiano per l'Età Moderna e Contemporanea*, 23–4, 1971–2.

Bertini, F., 'La massoneria in Toscana dall'età dei Lumi alla restaurazione', in Z. Ciuffoletti (ed.), *Le Origini della massoneria in Toscana (1730–1890)*, Foggia, 1989.

Bertoli, B. and Tramontin, S. (eds), *La Visita pastorale di Ludovico Flangini nella diocesi di Venezia (1803)*, Rome, 1969.

Bollati, G., *L'Italiano. Il carattere nazionale come storia e come invenzione*, Turin, 1983.

Borel, J., *Gênes sous Napoléon 1er*, Paris, 1929.

Boutry, P., 'Società urbana e sociabilità delle élites nella Roma della Restaurazione: prime considerazioni', in M. Malatesta (ed.), *Sociabilità nobiliare, sociabilità borghese*, Reggio Emilia, 1989.

Boyer, F., 'La famille de Cavour et le régime napoléonien', *Revue Historique*, 185, 1939.

Brambilla, E., 'L'istruzione pubblica dalla Repubblica Cisalpina al Regno Italico', *Quaderni Storici*, 23, 1973.

Broers, M. G., 'The restoration of order in Napoleonic Piedmont, 1797–1814', unpublished D.Phil. thesis, Oxford, 1986.

Caldora, U., *Calabria napoleonica, 1806–1815*, Naples, 1960.

Capra, C., 'Nobili, notabili, élites: dal modello francese al caso italiano', *Quaderni Storici*, 37, 1979.

—— 'Il Settecento', in D. Sella and C. Capra, *Il Ducato di Milano dal 1535 al 1796*, Turin, 1984.

Carle, L., *L'Identité cachée. Paysans propriétaires dans l'Alta Langa aux XVIIe – XIXe siècles*, Paris, 1989.

Cingari, G., *Brigantaggio, proprietari e contadini nel Sud 1799–1900*, Reggio Calabria, 1976.

'Colloquio internazionale sulla storia dell'Italia giacobina e napoleonica', *Annuario dell'Istituto Storico Italiano per l'Età Moderna e Contemporanea*, 23–4, 1971–2.

Davico, R., 'Prix et conjoncture: la période napoléonienne en Piémont', *Revue Historique*, 503, 1972.

—— *Peuple et notables (1750–1816). Essais sur l'ancien régime et la Révolution en Piémont*, Paris, 1981.

Davis, J. A., 'Naples during the French "decennio". A problem unresolved?', in *Villes et territoires pendant la période napoléonienne (France et Italie)*, Rome, 1987.

—— 'The Neapolitan army during the *decennio francese*', *Rivista Italiana di Studi Napoleonici*, 25, 1988.

Della Peruta, F., *Esercito e società nell'Italia napoleonica. Dalla Cisalpina al Regno d'Italia*, Milan, 1988.

Du Casse, P. E. A. (ed.), *Mémoires et correspondance politique et militaire du roi Joseph*, 10 vols, Paris, 1853–4.

Filippini, J. P., 'Ralliement et opposition des notables toscans à l'Empire français', *Annuario dell'Istituto Storico Italiano per l'Età Moderna e*

Contemporanea, 23–4, 1971–2.

Gambasin, A., 'Parrocchia veneta: evoluzione strutturale dalle riforme napoleoniche al neogiuseppismo asburgico', *La Società religiosa nell'età moderna*, Naples, 1973.

Harrison, J. B., 'The continental system in Italy as revealed by American commerce', unpublished Ph.D. thesis, University of Wisconsin, 1937.

Madelin, L., *La Rome de Napoléon*, Paris, 1906.

Marmottan, P., *Le Royaume d'Etrurie (1801–1807)*, Paris, 1896.

—— *Le Général Menou en Toscane*, Paris, 1903.

Mineccia, F., 'La vendita dei beni nazionali in Toscana (1808–1814): i dipartimenti dell'Ombrone e del Mediterraneo', in I. Tognarini (ed.), *La Toscana nell'età rivoluzionaria e napoleonica*, Naples, 1985.

Montagna, L., *Il Dominio francese in Parma (1791–1814)*, 1906.

Mori, G., 'Clero e istituzioni religiose nel distretto napoleonico delle Alpi Apuane', *Studi Parmensi*, 24, 1979.

Moulard, J., *Le Comte Camille de Tournon*, 3 vols, Paris, 1929–1933.

Mozzillo, A., *Cronache della Calabria in guerra (1806–1811)*, Naples, 1972.

Nardi, C., *Napoleone e Roma. La politica della Consulta Romana*, Rome, 1989.

Nicolas, J., 'Le ralliement des notables au régime impérial dans le département du Mont-Blanc', *Revue d'Histoire Moderne et Contemporaine*, 19, 1972.

'Notabili e funzionari nell'Italia napoleonica', *Quaderni Storici*, 37, 1978.

Notario, P., *La Vendita dei beni nazionali in Piemonte nel periodo napoleonico (1800–1814)*, Milan, 1980.

Orlandi, G., *Le Campagne modenesi fra rivoluzione e restaurazione (1790–1815)*, Modena, 1967.

Outram, D., 'Education and politics in Piedmont, 1796–1814', *Historical Journal*, 19, 1976.

Paci, R., *L'Ascesa della borghesia nella Legazione di Urbino dalle riforme alla restaurazione*, Milan, 1966.

Passerin d'Entrèves, E., *La Giovinezza di Cesare Balbo*, Florence, 1940.

—— 'Dal Piemonte pre-rivoluzionario al Piemonte costituzionale', *Bollettino Storico-Bibliografico Subalpino*, 57, 1959.

Pasta, R., *Scienza politica e rivoluzione. L'opera di Giovanni Fabbroni (1752–1822) intellettuale e funzionario in servizio dei Lorena*, Florence, 1989.

Pilati, R., *La Nunziatella. L'organizzazione di un'accademia militare 1787–1987*, Naples, 1987.

Quarantotti, G., *Trieste e l'Istria nell'età napoleonica*, Florence, 1954.

Quigley, W. C., 'The public administration of the first kingdom of Italy 1805–1814', unpublished Ph.D. thesis, Harvard, Mass., 1938.

Rambaud, J., 'L'église de Naples sous la domination française', *Revue d'Histoire Ecclésiastique*, 9, 1908.

—— *Naples sous Joseph Bonaparte 1806–1808*, Paris, 1911.

Robertazzi delle Donne, E., 'Potere politico e clero parrocchiale nel Regno di Napoli durante il governo dei Napoleonidi', *Ricerche di Storia Sociale e Religiosa*, 13, 1978.

Saitta, A., 'Appunti per una ricerca sui notabili', *Critica Storica*, 9, 1972.

Savarese, G., *Tra Rivoluzioni e reazioni. Ricordi di Giuseppe Zurlo*

(1759–1828), Turin, 1941.

Scirocco, A., 'I corpi rappresentativi nel Mezzogiorno dal "decennio" alla restaurazione: il personale dei consigli provinciali', *Quaderni Storici*, 37, 1978.

Sofia, F., *Una Scienza per l'amministrazione. Statistica e pubblici apparati tra età rivoluzionaria e restaurazione*, Rome, 1988.

Tacel, M., 'L'agitation royaliste à Turin de 1805 à 1808', *Revue de l'Institut Napoléon*, 52, 1954.

Tarle, E. V., *La Vita economica dell'Italia nell'età napoleonica*, Turin, 1950.

Tognarini, I. (ed.), *La Toscana nell'età rivoluzionaria e napoleonica*, Naples, 1985.

—— (ed.), *Il Territorio pistoiese e i Lorena tra 700 e 800: viabilità e bonifiche*, Naples, 1990.

Ungari, P., *Storia del diritto di famiglia in Italia (1796–1942)*, Bologna, 1974.

Vaccarino, G., 'Annessionismo e autonomia nel Piemonte giacobino dopo Marengo', *Studi in memoria di Gioele Solari*, Turin, 1954.

Villani, P., *Italia napoleonica*, Naples, 1978.

Villes et territoire pendant la période napoléonienne (France et Italie), Rome, 1987.

Woolf, S., *A History of Italy 1700–1860*, London, 1979.

—— *The Poor in Western Europe in the Eighteenth and Nineteenth Centuries*, London – New York, 1986.

—— 'Frontiere entro la frontiera: il Piemonte sotto il governo napoleonico', in C. Ossola, C. Raffestin and M. Ricciardi (eds), *La Frontiera da stato a nazione. Il caso Piemonte*, Rome, 1987.

—— 'L'impact de l'occupation française sur l'économie italienne', *Revue Economique*, 40, 1989.

—— 'The Société de Charité Maternelle', in C. Jones and J. Barry (eds), *Medicine and Charity Before the Welfare State*, London, 1991.

Zaghi, C. (ed.), *I Carteggi di Francesco Melzi d'Eril duca di Lodi*, 9 vols, Milan, 1958–66.

—— *Potere chiesa e società. Studi e ricerche sull'Italia giacobina e napoleonica*, Naples, 1984.

—— *L'Italia di Napoleone dalla Cisalpina al Regno*, Turin, 1986.

Zangheri, R., *La Proprietà terriera e le origini del Risorgimento nel Bolognese. I. 1789–1804*, Bologna, 1961.

POLAND

Bielecki, R., 'L'effort militaire polonais 1806–1815', *Revue de l'Institut Napoléon*, 132, 1976.

Grochulska, B., 'L'économie polonaise et le renversement de la conjoncture (1805–1815)', *Revue d'Histoire Moderne et Contemporaine*, 17, 1970.

Jedlicki, J., 'Bilan social du duché de Varsovie', *Acta Poloniae Historica*, 14, 1966.

Senkowska-Gluck, M., 'Pouvoir et société en Illyrie napoléonienne', *Revue de l'Institut Napoléon*, 113, 1980.

—— 'La propriété foncière en Pologne (1789–1815)', *Annales Historiques de la Révolution Française*, 53, 1981.

PORTUGAL

Neto, V. (ed.), *A Revolução francesa e a península ibérica*, Revista de *Historia das Ideas*, 10, Coimbra, 1988.

'A Revolução francesa e a península ibérica', *Revista Portuguesa de Historia*, 23, 1987.

SPAIN

Ardit Lucas, M., *Rivolución liberal y rivuelta campesina. Un ensayo sobre la disintegración del régimen feudal en el País Valenciano (1793–1840)*, Barcelona, 1977.

Artola-Gallego, M., *Los Afrancesados*, Madrid, 1953.

Aymes, J.R., *La Guerra de la independencia en España (1808-1814)*, Madrid, 1974.

Canales, E., 'Patriotismo y deserción durante la guerra de la independencia en Cataluña', *Revista Portuguesa de Historia*, 23, 1987.

Delgado Ribas, J. M., 'Catalunya y el sistema de libre comercio (1778–1818). Una reflexión sobre las raices del reformismo borbónico', unpublished Ph.D. thesis, Universitat de Barcelona, 1981.

Desamortización y hacienda publica, Madrid, 1986.

Esdaile, C., *The Spanish Army in the Peninsular War*, Manchester, 1988.

Les Espagnols et Napoléon. Actes du colloque international d'Aix-en-Provence 13, 14, 15 octobre 1983, Aix – Marseille, 1984.

Ferrer Benimeli, J. A., 'La masonería bonapartista en España', in *Les Espagnols et Napoléon. Actes du colloque international d'Aix-en-Provence 13, 14, 15 octobre 1983*, Aix – Marseille, 1984.

Fontana, J., *La Crisis del Antiguo Régimen*, Barcelona, 1979.

—— *La Quiebra de la monarquía absoluta 1814–1820*, Barcelona, 1987.

—— *La Fi de l'Antic Règim i la industrialització (1787–1868). 5. Història de Catalunya*, Barcelona, 1988.

Fontana, J. and Garrabou, R., *Guerra y hacienda. La hacienda del gobierno central en los años de la guerra de la independencia (1808–1814)*, Alicante, 1986.

Fugier, A., *Napoléon et l'Espagne*, 2 vols, Paris, 1930.

'La guerra del Francès, 1808–1814', *L'Avenç*, 113, 1988.

La Invasió napoleónica. Economia, cultura i societat, Bellaterra, 1981.

La Parra López, E., *El Primer liberalismo español y la Iglesia. Las Cortes de Cadiz*, Alicante, 1985.

Mercader Riba, J., *José Bonaparte, rey de España, 1808–1813. Historia externa del reinado*, Madrid, 1971.

—— *José Bonaparte, rey de España (1808–1813). Estructura del estado español bonapartista*, Madrid, 1983.

Moliner Prada, A., 'Estructura, funcionamiento y terminología de las Juntas supremas provinciales en la guerra contra Napoleon: Los casos de Mallorca, Catalunya, Asturias y León', unpublished Ph.D. thesis, Universitat Autònoma de Barcelona, 1981.

Olivé y Serret, E., 'Pirates i comerciants. Les relacions d'un corsari francès amb comerciants catalans (1807–1811)', *Ricerques*, 17, 1985.

Otaegui Arizmendi, A., 'Guerra y crisis de la hacienda local: las ventas de biens comunales en Guipúzcoa, 1793–1814', unpublished Ph.D. thesis,

Universidad Autónoma de Barcelona, 1988.

Roura i Aulinas, L., 'La crisis del Antiguo Régimen. Del "panico" de Floridablanca a la guerra de la independencia', in A. Dominguez Ortiz (ed.), *Historia de España*. 9. *La Transición del Antiguo al Nuevo Régimen (1789–1874)*, Barcelona, 1988.

Suchet, L.-G., duc d'Albufera, *Mémoires du maréchal Suchet, duc d'Albufera sur ses campagnes en Espagne depuis 1808 jusqu'en 1814*, 2 vols, Paris, 1828.

Vilar, P., 'Quelques aspects de l'occupation et de la résistance en Espagne en 1794 et au temps de Napoléon', in *Occupants occupés 1792–1815*, Brussels, 1969.

SWITZERLAND

Bandelier, A., *Porrentruy, sous-préfecture du Haut-Rhin. Un arrondissement communal sous le Consulat et l'Empire, 1800–1814*, Neuchâtel, 1980.

—— 'Les collèges des pays réunis à la France dans l'Université impériale: monopole napoléonien ou concurrence ecclésiastique?', in *Cinq siècles de relations franco-suisses. Hommage à Louis-Edouard Roulet*, Neuchâtel, 1984.

Courvoisier, J., *Le Maréchal Berthier et sa principauté de Neuchâtel (1806–1814)*, Neuchâtel, 1959.

Dictionnaire historique et biographique de la Suisse, 7 vols, 1921–33.

Fankhauser, A., 'Die Exekutive der Helvetischen Republik 1798–1803', *Studien und Quellen. Etudes et Sources. Studi e Fonti*, 12, 1986.

Guichonnet, P., 'Biens communaux et partages révolutionnaires dans l'ancien département du Léman', *Etudes Rurales*, 36, 1969.

Im Hof, U., 'Vereinswesen und Geselligkeit in der Schweiz, 1750–1850', in E. François (ed.), *Sociabilité et société bourgeoise en France, en Allemagne et en Suisse (1750–1850)*, Paris, 1986.

Python, F., 'De quelques effets de la Révolution dans le diocèse de Lausanne (1798–1818)', in B. Plongeron (ed.), *Pratiques religieuses dans l'Europe révolutionnaire: mentalités et spiritualités, 1770–1820*, Turnhout, 1989.

Schmidt, C., 'Sismondi et le blocus continental', *Revue Historique*, 115, 1914.

Suratteau, J., 'Occupation, occupants et occupés en Suisse de 1792 à 1814', in *Occupants Occupés 1792–1815*, Brussels, 1969.

Name index

Subject index

academy 61, 77; military 44, 166–7, 191, 216, 218, 229, 239
administration: financial 95; local 39, 42, 48, 103–4, 106, 112, 114–15, 119, 123, 195; military 61, 89–90, 114, 132, 165, 236; science of 87, 125, 239
administrative centralisation 33, 38, 46, 53–4, 89, 97, 100, 103, 117, 126, 132, 189, 210, 233, 242–3; integration 83–132, 184–7, 217, 238, 243–4; personnel 33, 37, 42, 44, 74–82, 87, 95, 132, 136, 197; system viii, 13, 33, 37, 39, 44, 52, 73–4, 81–2, 103, 112, 116–24, 131, 133–4, 152, 155–6, 161–2, 216, 227, 235, 240, 243
administrators viii, 4–5, 38, 44–5, 52, 69–74, 85, 109, 117, 119, 124, 127–8, 159, 174, 177, 185, 219–21, 227, 235, 239–42; -general 49, 51, 62, 70, 73, 149
afrancesados 190, 235
amalgame 109–10, 117, 166, 218
ambassadors 48, 65–8
ancien regime 12, 49, 63, 66, 83, 102, 104–5, 125, 134, 157, 175, 178, 181, 197, 219, 225, 231
annexation, annexed territories 15, 17–18, 40, 43–4, 46–51, 72–5, 80, 98, 103, 111–12, 142, 147, 149, 153–4, 175, 180–2, 188–9, 192, 194, 198, 201, 208, 223, 232
aristocracy 5, 8, 9, 43–4, 50, 63, 66, 75, 77, 78, 93, 95, 99, 109–11, 113–14, 126, 129–30, 148, 162,

166–7, 175, 177–82, 189–91, 193–6, 199–200, 202–3, 208, 216, 219–20, 227, 229, 231, 237–8, 244
army vii, 10, 11, 18, 29, 45, 54, 69–70, 150, 156–7, 159, 165–74, 177, 193, 214, 220–1, 226–7, 235, 240; inspectors 49, 55–6; of Italy 9, 18, 58–9, 62; officers 54, 157–8, 165–6, 168–70, 173–4, 177–8, 182, 192–4, 217–18, 220–1, 229; paymasters 55–8, 123; suppliers 18, 45, 55, 173, 196, 199–200; uniforms 54, 165, 168, 178, 220; *see also* conscription; desertion; Imperial Guard
artillery 55–6, 123, 166, 170, 191
artisans 2, 7, 157, 188, 211, 224, 227, 236
assemblies, representative 96–7, 157
assembly: Constituent 13, 37, 128, 157, 174; Convention 14–15, 45, 69, 80, 234; Legislative 13, 19–70, 97; legislative body 43–4, 179, 230; Senate 43–4, 71, 78, 176, 179, 181, 189; Tribunate 43, 79, 176, 219
associations 213, 218–19, 222, 226
auditors 44, 64, 66, 72–4, 76, 81, 88, 100, 115, 166, 192, 196

banditry, bandits 90–1, 149, 164, 235–6
Bank of France 138
banks, bankers 7, 150–1, 153, 196–7, 201, 204, 210
blockade, *see* Continental blockade